LUFTWAFFE EFFICIENCY & PROMOTION REPORTS

Also by the Author

The Camp Men: The SS Officers Who Ran the Nazi Concentration Camp System
The Cruel Hunters: SS-Sonderkommando Dirlewanger, Hitler's Most Notorious Anti-partisan Unit
The Field Men: The SS Officers Who Led the Einsatzkommandos - the Nazi Mobile Killing Units
The Ghetto Men: The SS Destruction of the Jewish Warsaw Ghetto, April-May 1943
Quiet Flows the Rhine: German General Officer Casualties of World War II

LUFTWAFFE EFFICIENCY & PROMOTION REPORTS

for the Knight's Cross Winners

Volume Two

French L. MacLean

Schiffer Military History
Atglen, PA

Acknowledgements

As with my previous works, I could not have written this book without significant help, both actual pen to paper and moral support. These unsung heroes, over the years, included the following family, friends, colleagues and acquaintances: my wife Olga; my father Mac; my mother Julie; my brother Dave; my grandmothers Marie and Grace; Aunt Carroll and Uncle Dave; Hank Adams; Bob Biondi; Marv Decker; Lou DiMarco; Marianne Driscoll; Mike Dykes; John Fede; Georgia Garrett; Andre Huesken; Bruno Kahl; Sir John Keegan; Hans-Georg Lemm; Mike Mahan; Steve McAuliffe; Montgomery C. Meigs; Detlev Niemann; Jack Pattison; Terry Patton; George Peterson; Scott Pritchett; Jakob Schmitt; Dave Shutt; Tim Smith; Manfred Sommer; Martin Steglich; Tom Veve; Jodie White; Alan Windsor; Hans Winzer; John Womack; Brook and Paymon of Advanced Photo Inc.; the hundreds of Soldiers, Non-Commissioned Officers and Officers, who put up with a lieutenant/captain/major/lieutenant colonel/colonel, whom they knew obviously marched to the beat of a different drummer; countless document collectors, who graciously donated exhibits in this book; our dogs Max and Benji.

Badge photography and book design by Robert Biondi.

Library of Congress Catalog Number: 2007921527.

Printed in China.
ISBN: 978-0-7643-2658-5

Published by Schiffer Publishing Ltd.
4880 Lower Valley Road
Atglen, PA 19310
Phone: (610) 593-1777
FAX: (610) 593-2002
E-mail: Info@schifferbooks.com.
Visit our web site at: www.schifferbooks.com
Please write for a free catalog.
This book may be purchased from the publisher.
Please include $3.95 postage.
Try your bookstore first.

In Europe, Schiffer books are distributed by:
Bushwood Books
6 Marksbury Ave.
Kew Gardens, Surrey TW9 4JF
England
Phone: 44 (0)20 8392-8585
FAX: 44 (0)20 8392-9876
E-mail: info@bushwoodbooks.co.uk
www.bushwoodbooks.co.uk
Free postage in the UK. Europe: air mail at cost.
Try your bookstore first.

INTRODUCTION

Introduction

The initial intent of this project was to produce a single volume devoted to about 75 *Luftwaffe* Knight's Cross winners. Due to the extremely positive response of several sources for these efficiency reports and requests for promotion documents – around which the book is built – over 110 actually became available, with the author and editor feeling that including these additional reports would greatly enhance the reader's understanding of the subject. However, this led to a second challenge, pointed out by the layout and binding experts – a single volume this large would not hold up well (e.g. the binding might fall apart) due to the hundreds of pages of illustrations. We apologize if this expansion causes you to have to acquire a larger bookshelf.

Organization

Volume 2 is organized in the same manner as the first volume. Volume 1 began, in part, with a description of several awards, many of which were won by the officers described in this series. Part 1 of Volume 2 presents an overview of several additional awards frequently mentioned in the efficiency reports and requests for promotion. Part 2 of Volume 2 presents – in alphabetical order beginning with Knight's Cross winners whose last name began with M or after – some 60 *Luftwaffe* Knight's Cross winners, whose efficiency reports and promotion recommendations appear in the book. Each description contains a biography, as well as the most important piece – a translation of key segments of the narrative of the report. Many of the biographies also show a photograph of the report and often a photograph of the individual. Part 3 of Volume 2 presents a shortened biography – also in alphabetical order – of each of the men who signed the reports, so the reader can put this information into context, and to assist autograph collectors in identification. Part 4 of Volume 2 is a glossary of German words and definitions associated with efficiency reports to assist historians and collectors, as well as a bibliography.

German Awards and Decorations

Luftwaffe Qualification Badges

Prior to the outbreak of World War II, the *Luftwaffe* created several qualification badges designed to recognize the specific qualifications of *Luftwaffe* airmen. Rather than combat awards, they were earned upon completion of specialized training. A soldier could earn more than one type of qualification award; photographs of the period, however, generally show that only one qualification badge was worn at any one time.

Pilot's Badge

On August 12, 1935, Hermann Göring instituted the *Luftwaffe* Pilot's Badge. Requirements for the badge centered on qualifying for the military pilot's license. The recipient could be a commissioned officer, a non-commissioned officer or even a relatively junior enlisted man.[1] While we do not know how many Pilot's Badges were awarded from 1935 to 1945, the number must have been significant. On many of the award documents for the badge, there is an annotation in the lower left corner with a number and the year in which that badge was awarded. In one example, the number shown was 159 993/44, possibly indicating that 159,993 had already been awarded!

Pilot's Badge – awarded to military personnel qualifying for the military pilot's license. This example is an early-war model of heavy silver and nickel alloy, produced by the firm of F.W. Assmann in Lüdenscheid.

Observer's Badge – awarded upon completion of two months of qualifying service, or after conducting five operational flights as an observer, bombardier or navigator. This example is an early-war model of heavy silver and nickel alloy, produced by the firm of Paul Meybauer in Berlin.

Observer's Badge

The *Luftwaffe* introduced the Observer's Badge on March 26, 1936; it was intended to recognize airmen, who served in the position of observer, navigator or bombardier. Qualification occurred after two months of qualifying service – which during wartime could be compressed to completion of five operational flights. If the airman was wounded in one of these five flights, award of the badge could occur immediately.[2]

Combined Air Gunner, Radio Operator and Flight Engineer Badge – awarded to air gunners, radio operators and flight engineers, who successfully completed two months training or had participated in a minimum of five operational flights. This example is an early-war model of heavy silver and nickel alloy, produced by the firm of C.E. Juncker in Berlin.

Combined Air Gunner, Radio Operator and Flight Engineer Badge

On March 26, 1936, *Luftwaffe* regulations promulgated the award of the Combined Air Gunner, Radio Operator and Flight Engineer Badge. The badges were intended to be awarded to air gunners, radio operators and on-board flight engineers/mechanics. Like the Observer's Badge, qualification for this award occurred after two months of qualifying service – which during wartime could be compressed to completion of five operational flights. Again, if the airman was wounded in one of these five flights, award of the badge could occur immediately.[3]

Air Gunner's and Flight Engineer's Badge

On June 22, 1942, the *Luftwaffe* instituted a very similar award to the Combined Air Gunner, Radio Operator and Flight Engineer Badge – the Air Gunner's and Flight Engineer's

Air Gunner's and Flight Engineer's Badge – awarded to air gunners, aircrew meteorologists and flight engineers, who successfully completed two months training or had participated in a minimum of five operational flights. This example is an early-war model of heavy silver and nickel alloy, produced by the firm of Imme & Sohn in Berlin.

Verleihungsurkunde

Ich verleihe dem

Obergefreiten

H e i n z A eng e n v o o r t

das Abzeichen für

Flugzeugführer

Berlin, den 8.April 1944

**Der Reichsminister der Luftfahrt
und Oberbefehlshaber der Luftwaffe**

J. A.:

Der Chef des Luftwaffenpersonalamts

Nr. 159 993 /44

Generaloberst

Award Document for the Pilot's Badge – to an enlisted man, with a stamped signature of the head of the *Luftwaffe* Personnel Office, Colonel General Bruno Loerzer

Verleihungsurkunde

Ich verleihe dem

Leutnant

Peter Dolberg

das Abzeichen für

Beobachter

Berlin, den 28. Juli 1941

Der Reichsminister der Luftfahrt und Oberbefehlshaber der Luftwaffe

I. A.

Der Chef des Luftwaffenpersonalamts

Nr. 82 470/41 H

General der Flieger

Award Document for the Observer's Badge – to a second lieutenant, with a stamped signature of the head of the *Luftwaffe* Personnel Office, Lieutenant General Gustav Kastner-Kirdorf.

Badge. The badge was identical in every respect except that the lightning bolts (representative of the radio operator) were omitted. In addition to air gunners and flight engineers, aircrew meteorologists were eligible for the award. Qualification for this award occurred after two months of qualifying service – which could be compressed to completion of five operational flights. Again, if the airman was wounded in one of these five flights, award of the badge could occur immediately.[4]

Parachutist's Badge – awarded to all *Luftwaffe* personnel, who successfully completed six parachute jumps. This example is an early-war model of heavy silver and nickel alloy, produced by the firm of C.E. Juncker in Berlin.

Parachutist's Badge

On November 5, 1936, the *Luftwaffe* instituted the Parachutist's Badge for all officers, non-commissioned officers and enlisted men who successfully completed six parachute jumps at the Parachute Training School at Stendal. During the war, due to logistical limitations, training for parachute qualification was delegated to paratrooper regimental headquarters' training courses. On May 2, 1944, award for the badge was extended to those soldiers who made a single combat jump, although by this stage of the war, those operations were few and far between.[5]

Wound Badges

The Wound Badge originated in World War I. On September 1, 1939, the day that war commenced in Europe with the German invasion of Poland. Adolf Hitler – who had been wounded several times as in infantryman on the Western Front in the Great War – reinstituted the award.

The Wound Badge came in three classes. The badge in black was awarded for one or two cumulative wounds. When a soldier's cumulative total reached three or four, he would receive the badge in silver. Once a soldier accumulated five wounds, he received the badge in gold.

If a wound was severe and caused the loss of an eye or a single limb, the soldier received the badge in silver, even if that wound was his first. For soldiers who were totally disabled – the loss of both eyes, more than one limb – or in the case of death, the gold badge was awarded.

When a soldier was wounded, the chain of command made an appropriate entry in his service record, and either the unit or medical staff at a hospital issued a certificate and appropriate badge to the soldier. Only the highest single badge was worn at one time on the uniform.[6]

Wound Badge in Black

Wound Badge in Silver

Wound Badge in Gold

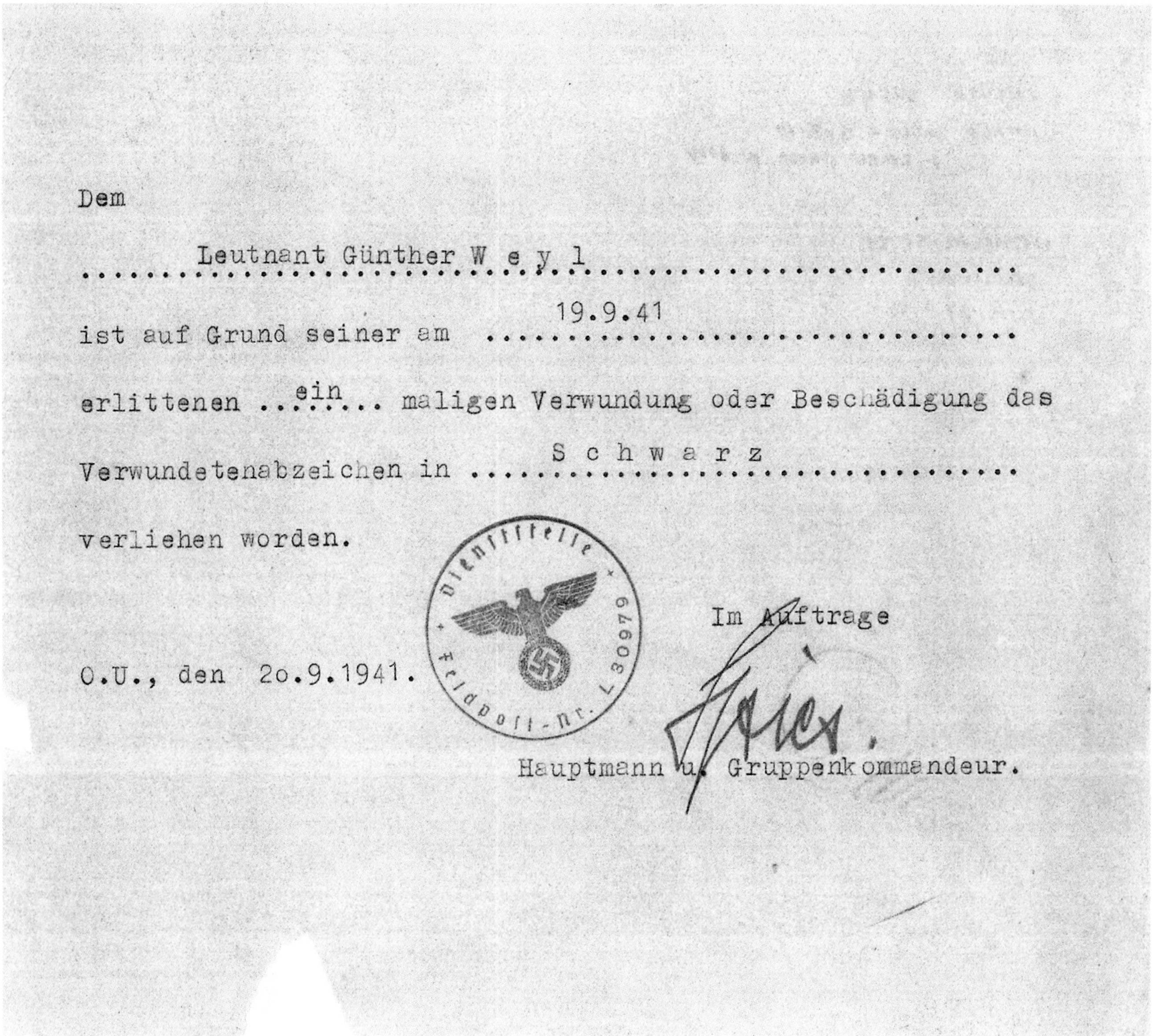

Dem

Leutnant Günther W e y l

ist auf Grund seiner am 19.9.41

erlittenen ..ein.. maligen Verwundung oder Beschädigung das

Verwundetenabzeichen in S c h w a r z

verliehen worden.

O.U., den 2o.9.1941.

Im Auftrage

Spies

Hauptmann u. Gruppenkommandeur.

Award Document for Wound Badge in Black – to German Cross in Gold winner, Second Lieutenant Günther Weyl, for a single wound received on September 19, 1941. Signed by Knight's Cross with Oak Leaves winner, Captain Wilhelm Spies, in the 26th Destroyer Wing.

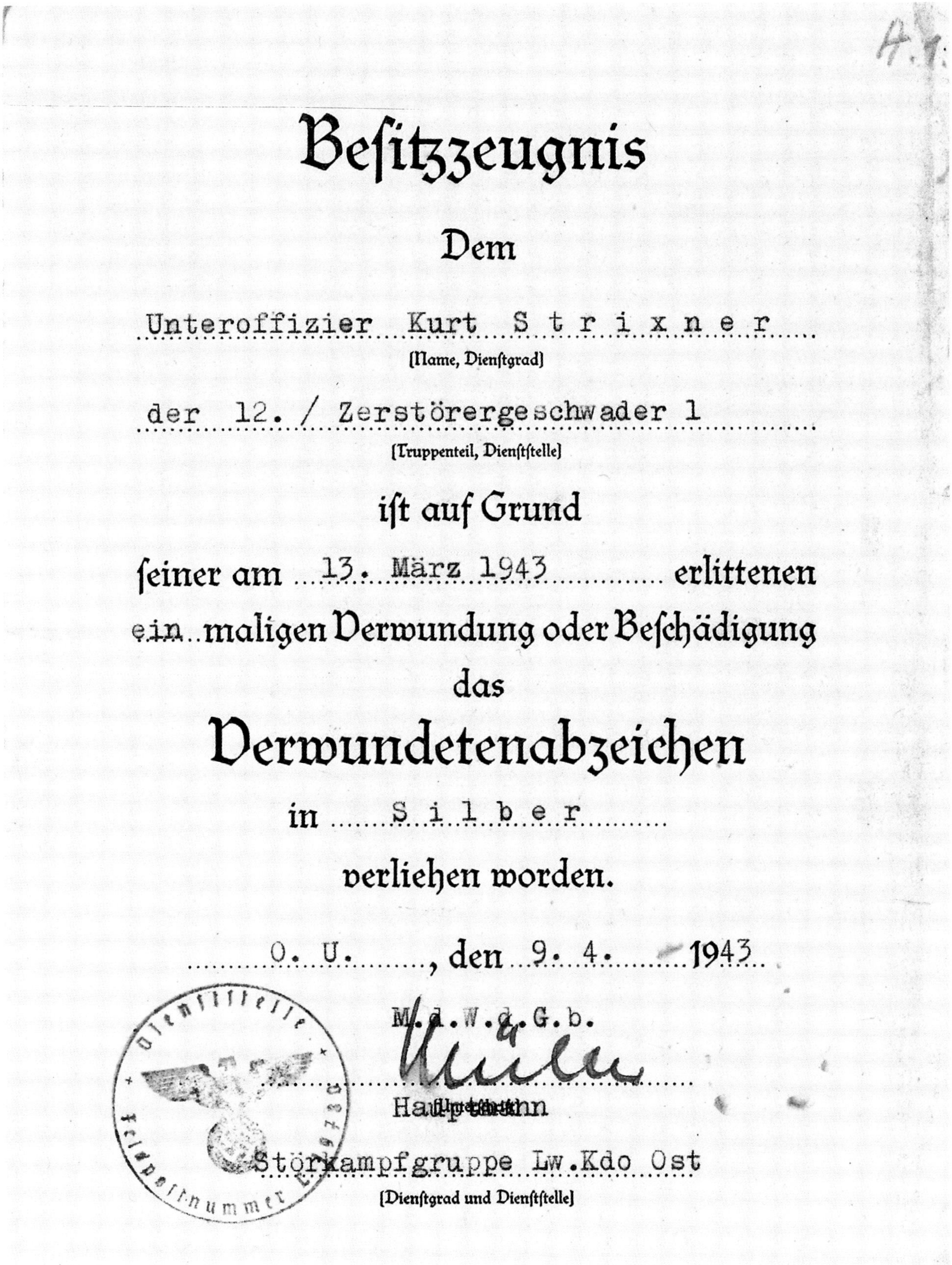

Besitzzeugnis

Dem

Unteroffizier Kurt S t r i x n e r
(Name, Dienstgrad)

der 12. / Zerstörergeschwader 1
(Truppenteil, Dienststelle)

ist auf Grund

seiner am 13. März 1943 erlittenen

ein maligen Verwundung oder Beschädigung

das

Verwundetenabzeichen

in S i l b e r

verliehen worden.

O. U., den 9. 4. 1943

M.d.W.d.G.b.

Hauptmann

Störkampfgruppe Lw.Kdo Ost
(Dienstgrad und Dienststelle)

Award Document for Wound Badge in Silver – to an enlisted man for a single wound that probably resulted in the loss of an eye or limb in the 1st Destroyer Wing.

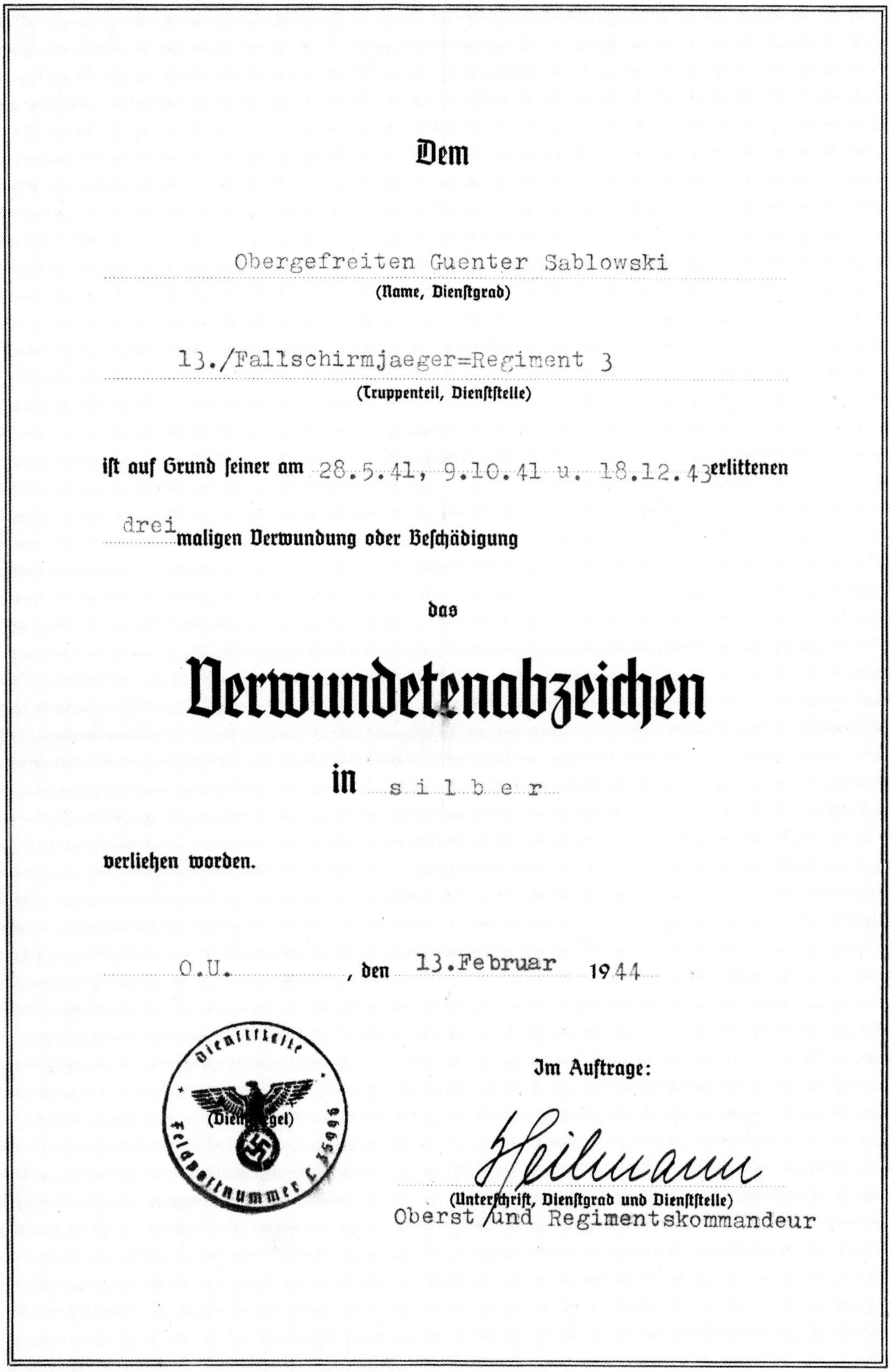

Dem

Obergefreiten Guenter Sablowski

(Name, Dienstgrad)

13./Fallschirmjaeger=Regiment 3

(Truppenteil, Dienststelle)

ist auf Grund seiner am 28.5.41, 9.10.41 u. 18.12.43 erlittenen

drei maligen Verwundung oder Beschädigung

das

Verwundetenabzeichen

in silber

verliehen worden.

O.U., den 13.Februar 1944

Im Auftrage:

Heilmann

(Unterschrift, Dienstgrad und Dienststelle)

Oberst und Regimentskommandeur

Award Document for Wound Badge in Silver – to an enlisted man for a cumulative total of three wounds, on May 28, 1941 (in Crete), October 9, 1941 (in Russia), and December 18, 1943 (in Russia). Signed by Knight's Cross with Oak Leaves and Swords winner, Colonel Ludwig Heilmann, 3rd Paratroop Regiment.

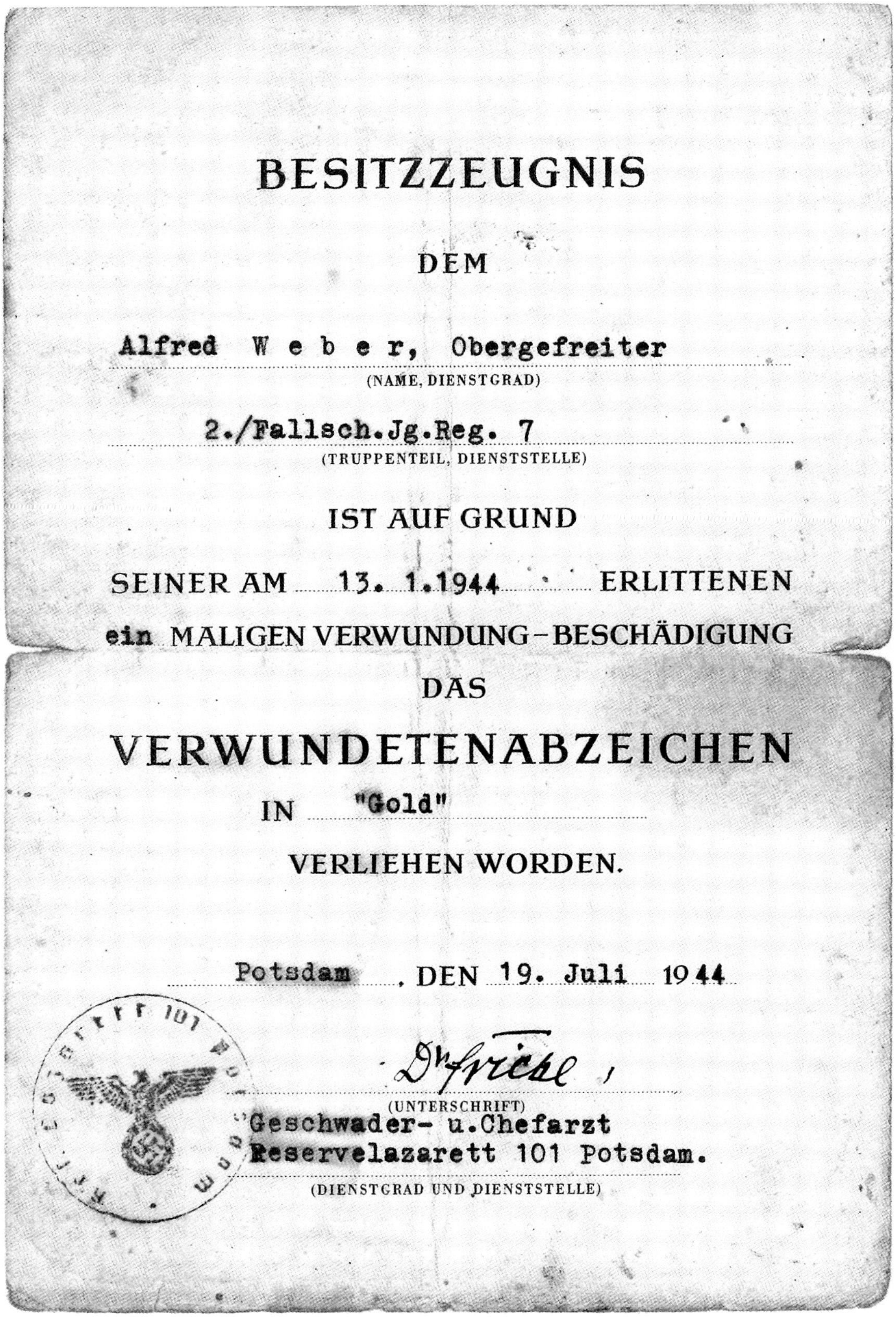

BESITZZEUGNIS

DEM

Alfred W e b e r, Obergefreiter

(NAME, DIENSTGRAD)

2./Fallsch.Jg.Reg. 7

(TRUPPENTEIL, DIENSTSTELLE)

IST AUF GRUND

SEINER AM 13. 1.1944 ERLITTENEN

ein MALIGEN VERWUNDUNG-BESCHÄDIGUNG

DAS

VERWUNDETENABZEICHEN

IN "Gold"

VERLIEHEN WORDEN.

Potsdam, DEN 19. Juli 1944

Dr. Fricke,

(UNTERSCHRIFT)

Geschwader- u.Chefarzt
Reservelazarett 101 Potsdam.

(DIENSTGRAD UND DIENSTSTELLE)

Award Document for Wound Badge in Gold – to an enlisted man, in the 7th Paratroop Regiment, for one wound that occurred on January 13, 1944, which later in July resulted in his death, complete blindness or amputation of two limbs. Signed by a doctor in Potsdam.

CONTENTS

Biographies in Volume 2

Walter Matoni
Fighter Pilot

"Mentally, interested and versatile."

Major Walter Matoni was born on June 27, 1917 at Duisburg in North-Rhine Westphalia. Prior to joining the *Luftwaffe*, he had been a student and had passed the *Abitur* – the pre-requisite test to enter a university. Matoni was posted as a corporal to the 9th Squadron, 27th Fighter Wing (*Jagdgeschwader 27*) in the summer of 1940. He accumulated four victories with this unit, including his first, a RAF Hurricane fighter over Turnbridge Wells, England, on September 30, 1940 during the Battle of Britain. Matoni received the Iron Cross 2nd Class on September 12, 1940, the Iron Cross 1st Class on November 11, 1940 and the Operational Flying Clasp for Fighters in Gold on May 15, 1941. He was promoted to technical sergeant on October 1, 1940. In July 1941, Matoni, operating over Russia, claimed three further victories to raise his victory total to four.

On July 12, 1941, Major Bernhard Woldenga, Commodore, 27th Fighter Wing, wrote a short efficiency report on Technical Sergeant Matoni. At this point in his career, Matoni had flown 136 combat missions, of which 7 were fighter-bomber missions and 19 were ground attacks. Matoni still had only one aerial victory to his credit. Woldenga wrote:[1]

> Physically very well talented; mentally, interested and versatile. His military accomplishments are good and skillful, not enough practice. A very good fighter pilot.

On August 17, 1941, Matoni transferred to the 5th Squadron, 26th Fighter Wing "Schlageter" (*Jagdgeschwader 26 "Schlageter"*), based on the Channel Front. He was transferred to the 7th Squadron on September 21. He was badly wounded in aerial combat – the first in a string of aerial mishaps during the war – resulting in a lengthy convalescence and then transferred on October 20, 1942 to *Jagdgruppe Ost* for a tour as an instructor as part of his recovery program. He served with the unit until February 13, 1943 and was then assigned to the 2nd Group, 26th Fighter Wing "Schlageter," based in France, as a second lieutenant. He shot down an RAF Spitfire fighter on June 17, 1943 to record his fifth victory. On August 31, First Lieutenant Matoni's Focke-Wulf Fw 190A-5 was hit by return fire from USAAF B-17 Flying Fortresses, which were on a mission to attack the airfields at Amiens, France, and he was wounded. He made a forced landing at Montdidier. Matoni was back in action in December, claiming a RAF Spitfire fighter shot down near Boulogne, France on December 21 as his 8th kill. In an action against American B-26 Marauder twin-engine bombers on January 14, 1944, Matoni shot down a RAF Spitfire fighter escorting the bombers. On February 24, 1944, he shot down an unescorted B-24 Liberator (from the 2nd Bomb Division, 8th Air Force, returning from a mission against Gotha and Eisenach) near Frankfurt for his 13th – and *Jagdgeschwader 26's* 2000th – victory.

Matoni was appointed the 5th Squadron Commander on February 25, 1944. On March 6, 1944, during the first USAAF full-scale daylight raid on Berlin, Matoni shot down a B-17G of the 381st Bomber Group near Jülich.[2] He won the *Luftwaffe* Honor Goblet on March 31, 1944 and the German Cross in Gold on May 10 for 20 victories.[3] By June, Matoni had been promoted to captain and on August 15, 1944 was appointed the 1st Group Commander, 11th Fighter Wing (*Jagdgeschwader 11*). He was then appointed Commander, 1st Group, 2nd Fighter Wing "Richthofen" (*Jagdgeschwader 2 "Richthofen"*) on September 24. On December 5, 1944, Matoni was injured in a take-off crash, at Merzhausen, so seriously that he was unable to undertake any further combat flying. Walter Matoni was awarded the Knight's Cross of the Iron Cross on January 2, 1945 and was appointed commander of the 2nd Group, 2nd Fighter Wing "Richthofen" in January 1945, fulfilling the role in a non-flying capacity. He held this position until February 28, 1945, when he entered a fighter pilot's rest-home at Bad Wiessee, Bavaria, where he ended the war.

Walter Matoni was credited with 34 victories in over 400 combat missions, a sortie-to-victory ratio of 11.76 to 1; 34 of his victories occurred over the Western Front and included 14 four-engine bombers. Not a pilot who routinely scored multiple kills on a single day, Matoni's deadliest days of the war were on March 8, 1944, when he destroyed two B-17 Flying Fortresses in ten minutes, and on April 12, 1944, when he shot down two B-24 Liberators – from the 2nd Bomb Division, 8th Air Force attacks on Zwickau and Aschersleben – in 23 minutes.[4] Walter Matoni died on June 26, 1988 at Frankfurt. He is buried at the *Friedhof Eschersheim* (Gewann Freiliegend [Frl.], Grave 957).

Feststellung der ausserdienstlichen Eignung erfolgt durch den Truppenteil.

Formblatt 1

Luftflotte: 2
Waffengattung: Fliegertruppe
Flugzeugführer
Truppenteil: III./Jagdgeschwader 27
9. Staffel

Heimat-Luftgau: I,Königsberg/Pr.
W.B.K.: Königsberg Pr.

(wird von L.P. ausgefüllt)

Name: Matoni
Vorname: Walter
Dienstgrad: Feldwebel

Geburtstag: 27.6.1917
Geburtsort: Duisburg a. Rh.
Beruf: Schüler
Abiturient: ja/~~nein~~

Militärischer Werdegang:

Aktive Dienstzeit in der neuen Wehrmacht: vom 19.10.36 bis
bzw. Kurzausbildung)
Weitere Dienstverpflichtung auf 3 = 4 1/2 = 12 u.mehr Jahre: 12 Jahre verpflichtet
Bei ehem. Soldaten, Dienstgrad bei Eintritt in die neue Wehrmacht:.

Friedensübungen: ./.

Dienstzeit während des mobilen Verhältnisses: 1.9.1939

Beförderungen: 1.10.37 zum Gefreiten
1.10.38 zum Obergefreiten
1. 3.39 zum Unteroffizier
1.10.40 zum Feldwebel

Tag der Ernennung zum R.O.A. ./. bzw. K.O.A. 1.7.194

Hat nicht an einem Kriegsoffizier - Nachwuchslehrgang
von ./. bis ./. teilgenomme

Efficiency Report for Technical Sergeant Walter Matoni (front side) – dated July 12, 1941, on blank paper, with typed comments.

Zur Beförderung zum Offizier vorgeschlagen: ./.

Bewährung vor dem Feinde: 136 Feindflüge,
7 Jagdbombenangriffe
19 Tiefangriffe
1 Abschuss: Hurricane am 30.9.1940

Auszeichnungen: E.K.II am 12.9.1940
E.K. I am 11.11.1940
Frontflugspange in Gold am 15.5.41

Bestrafungen: Keine

Kurze Beurteilung: Körperlich sehr gut veranlagt, geistig interessiert und vielseitig. Militärische Leistungen gut und gewandt, etwas wenig Praxis.
Sehr guter Jagdflieger.

Uk.-Stellung während des Krieges:
von ./. bis ./.

Kurze Angabe des Grundes ./.

Im Felde, den 12.7.1941
(Ort und Datum)

Jagdgeschwader 27 Stab

Woldenga
Major u. Geschwaderkommodore
(Unterschrift)

Efficiency Report for Technical Sergeant Walter Matoni (back side) – signed by Major Bernhard Woldenga, Commodore, 27th Fighter Wing.

Wilhelm Mayer

Fighter Pilot

"He shows talent for quick comprehension and great mental flexibility."

Second Lieutenant Wilhelm Mayer was born on December 5, 1917 at Fürth in Bavaria. He was posted to the 2nd Squadron, Supplemental Group, 26th Fighter Wing "Schlageter" (*Jagdgeschwader 26 "Schlageter"*) on August 1, 1941, following completion of his basic flying training. On January 9, 1942, Staff Sergeant Mayer transferred to the 6th Squadron, 2nd Group of the 26th Fighter Wing. He flew his first combat missions in support of "Operation *Donnerkeil*" (Thunderbolt), the *Luftwaffe's* aerial protection of the German Navy's battle cruisers *Scharnhorst* and *Gneisenau* and heavy cruiser *Prinz Eugen* as they made their English Channel dash from Brest, France to Wilhelmshaven, Germany on February 12, 1942. On July 17, 1942, his Focke-Wulf Fw 190A-2 had engine problems, which forced Sergeant Mayer to belly-land in Abbeville-Drucat, France. He also participated in the aerial action over the Allied amphibious landings at Dieppe, France on August 19, 1942 without result. Mayer started slowly and had only four unconfirmed claims before he was able to record his first confirmed victory, a RAF Spitfire fighter shot down over the Somme Estuary on March 14, 1943. On July 30, 1943, Technical Sergeant Mayer was shot down by return fire from B-17 Flying Fortresses (flying an 8th Air Force mission against Kassel) near Apeldoorn, the Netherlands, and suffered slight injuries in the successful crash-landing of his Focke-Wulf Fw 190A-5 at Netterden. He recorded his fifth confirmed victory – a B-17 Flying Fortress – on September 3, 1943.

Mayer transferred to the 7th Squadron on September 15, 1943 and by the end of 1943, he had recorded nine victories, the last another B-17. On February 18, 1944, the squadron was ordered to scramble from Grevillers, France to intercept a British formation of fifteen RAF De Haviland Mosquito twin-engine bombers, escorted by eight Typhoon fighters, on the attack on the Amiens' prison to aid the escape of the French Resistance members held there. Mayer shot the tail off a Mosquito, most likely flown by the officer commanding the mission, Group Captain Charles Pickard, for his 13th aerial victory.[5] Mayer received the *Luftwaffe* Honor Goblet on March 31, 1944, and on April 16, 1944 he was awarded the German Cross in Gold for 15 aerial victories. On April 5, 1944, Mayer was transferred to Fighter Group West (*Jagdgruppe West*) to undertake instructing duties and remained with this unit until July 23, 1944. He returned to the 26th Fighter Wing on July 24, 1944 and was assigned to the 5th Squadron. During the Allied airborne landings at Arnhem, "Operation Market Garden," Mayer shot down two USAAF P-51 Mustang fighters over Nijmegen on September 19, 1944, in a span of two minutes. He recorded his last victories, two RAF Spitfire fighters shot down near Kirchhellen, Germany, on November 19, 1944, again in a span of just two minutes.

On October 9, 1944, Major and acting commander of the 2nd Group, Anton Hackl, submitted a special efficiency report on Mayer, requesting promotion to commissioned officer, based on bravery in the face of the enemy. Hackl wrote:[6]

> Mental dispositions are good. With diverse interests, he shows talent for quick comprehension and great mental flexibility. Particularly in battle, harshness and endurance mark him. Mature appearance, can bear burdens. Developed and open character with self-reliant attitude. Due to his long period of service, he is well formed as a soldier, shows good military knowledge and accomplishments and is capable of handling every situation. As an experienced and successful fighter pilot, he attained the following aerial victories during 121 combat missions against the enemy:
>
> | | |
> |---|---|
> | 17 | one-engine fighters |
> | 2 | two-engine aircraft |
> | 5 | four-engine bombers |
> | 1 | four-engine bomber (shot out of formation) |
>
> Since April 16, 1944, Mayer wears the German Cross in Gold and has been employed as flight leader. He has often temporarily led the squadron in the air and is capable to do this in the future. After promotion to officer and further guidance, in a short time he could also lead a squadron on the ground. Mayer possesses his own initiative and is able to improvise. He is a positive National Socialist and capable to pass on his wealth of thought to others.

Lieutenant Colonel, and Commodore, *Jagdgeschwader 26 "Schlageter,"* Josef "Pips" Priller, signed the report the following day, but added no separate subjective comments of his own.

The following month and a half were uneventful, but on January 4, 1945, a formation of Focke-Wulf Fw 190s took off from Nordhorn, Germany and, while the airplanes were still forming up, RAF Spitfires bounced them. In the ensuing combat, he was shot down and killed in his Fw 190D-9 over Lohnerbruch, Germany, near the Dutch border. Wilhelm Mayer was posthumously awarded the Knight's Cross of the Iron Cross on March 12, 1945.

Wilhelm Mayer was credited with 27 victories achieved in 124 missions, a sortie-to-victory ratio of 4.59 to 1. Included in his total were 6 four-engine bombers and a Mosquito. Additionally, compared to his confirmed total, he had a relatively high number of unconfirmed kills at 12.[7] Wilhelm Mayer is buried in the military section of the *Neuer Friedhof* in Lingen, Germany (Grave 31).

Mayer's report follows. Someone stamped "*Ritterkreuz-Träger*" at the top of the report, probably in the *Luftwaffe* Personnel Headquarters, and clearly after March 12, 1945, the date of the posthumous award. Someone also noted in blue pencil a cross on the form, presumably a death annotation. Finally, someone noted that on December 12, 1944 Mayer was promoted to second lieutenant.

West

Ritterkreuz-Träger

Vorschlag

1.12.44/12.44

zur Beförderung zum Kriegsoffizier wegen besonderer Tapferkeit vor dem Feinde.

Zur Beförderung zum Leutnant (Kr.) wird vorgeschlagen:

Fhj.-Oberfeldwebel (Kr.) M a y e r , Wilhelm, geb. am 5.12.1917,

W.B.K.: Nürnberg, II./JAGDGESCHW."SCHLAGETER" Nr.26 - 5.Staffel -

Heimatanschrift: Nürnberg - W , Wenzelstrasse 7, kv.

Sämtliche geforderten Voraussetzungen sind erfüllt.

Ausserdienstliche Eignung festgestellt durch II./Jagdgeschwader "Schlageter" Nr.26.

Offz.Nachw.Lehrgang: Nein. Letzte Beförderung: 1.5.44 zum Ofw.

Gefechtsstand, den 10. Oktober 1944.

Priller

Oberstleutnant und Geschwaderkommodore.

Request for Promotion to Officer for Officer Candidate Wilhelm Mayer (front side) – dated October 10, 1944, on blank paper, with typed comments. Signed by Lieutenant Colonel Josef "Pips" Priller, Commodore, 26th Fighter Wing. Pencil annotation indicates that Mayer was promoted to second lieutenant on December 1, 1944.

II./JAGDGESCHWADER "SCHLAGETER" Nr.26   Gefechtsstand, den 9.10.1944.

Beurteilung.

Geistige Anlagen sind gut. Vielseitig interessiert, zeigt er schnelle Auffassungsgabe und grosse geistige Beweglichkeit. Härte und Ausdauer zeichnen ihn besonders im Kampf aus. Gefestigte Erscheinung, belastbar.

Reifer und offener Charakter von selbstbewusster Haltung.

Auf Grund langer Dienstzeit ist er soldatisch geformt, zeigt gute militärische Kenntnisse und Leistungen und ist jeder Lage gewachsen. Als erfahrener und erfolgreicher Jagdflieger erzielte er in 121 Feindflügen folgende Abschusserfolge:

17 1-mot. Jäger,
2 2-mot. Flugzeuge,
5 4-mot. Kampfflugzeuge,
1 4-mot. Kampfflugzeug als Herausschuss.

M. trägt seit dem 16.4.44 das Deutsche Kreuz in Gold und ist als Schwarmführer eingesetzt. Des öfteren führte er fliegerisch die Staffel, wozu er auch weiterhin jederzeit in der Lage wäre. Nach Beförderung zum Offizier und weiterer Anleitung würde er in Kürze auch e[illegible]e Staffel am Boden führen können. M. besitzt Eigeninitiative und kann improvisieren. Er ist positiver Nationalsozialist und in der Lage, sein Gedankengut anderen zu vermitteln.

[illegible]
Major und Gruppenkommandeur
m.d.F.b.

Request for Promotion to Officer for Officer Candidate Wilhelm Mayer (back side) – signed by Major Anton Hackl, acting group commander, 2nd Group.

Maximilian Mayerl

Fighter Pilot

"He brought back the old enthusiastic spirit of the entire squadron."

Captain Maximilian Mayerl was born on May 28, 1918 at Aigen in the Steiermark region of Austria. He entered the *Luftwaffe* on November 1, 1937 and after pilot training was assigned in July 1939 to the 2nd Squadron, 20th Fighter Wing (*Jagdgeschwader 20*, which in July 1940 became the 8th Squadron, 51st Fighter Wing [*Jagdgeschwader 51*]). He flew in Poland and during the French campaign, where on June 8, 1940 he recorded his first aerial victory – a Blenheim bomber – over Alléry, France. Mayerl recorded over 100 combat missions over England. On July 19, 1940, he downed a Spitfire six miles south of Dover. On August 8, 1940, he shot down another Spitfire over Dover, while on August 18, 1940, he shot down a third Spitfire south of London. In-between, on August 13, 1940, Sergeant Mayerl's Messerschmitt Me 109E-1 was damaged in aerial combat, and he was forced to make a belly-landing at Calais-Marck, sustaining 80% damage to the plane. Promoted to second lieutenant on December 1, 1940, he transferred to the Eastern Front in July 1941 and by the end of the year had amassed 15 aerial victories. He scored his 20th kill on February 17, 1942, when he dispatched an I-61 fighter twelve miles northeast of Rzev. In May and June of 1942, Mayerl specialized in flying ground-attack and fighter-bomber missions; he was awarded the *Luftwaffe* Honor Goblet on June 29. On August 7, 1942, he took command of the 9th Squadron; he shot down a LaGG-3 for his 30th victory on September 11, 1942 east of Rzev. By the end of October, Mayerl had reached his 34th kill and on November 27, 1942, he received the German Cross in Gold. Mayerl continued his achievements in 1943, being promoted to first lieutenant on January 1 and scoring his 40th victory on February 24.

On May 5, 1943, Mayerl's chain of command submitted an efficiency report on him. Major Karl-Heinz Schnell, 3rd Group Commander, wrote:[8]

> First Lieutenant Mayerl is of slender, strong physique; he makes a good appearance. His mental degree, in comparison to the average officer, is relatively high. He is a wartime officer and was promoted to Second Lieutenant on December 1, 1940 and to First Lieutenant on January 1, 1943. From August 10, 1942, he has been a squadron leader. Since August 1, 1939, First Lieutenant Mayerl has belonged to the 3rd Group, JG 51 as fighter pilot. On a steady basis in more than 500 combat missions, he has accomplished excellent results as a fighter pilot, particularly later as a squadron leader. To date, he has succeeded in gaining a total of 46 kills, four of which in the air battle against England and 42 in Russia. On the ground, First Lieutenant Mayerl always leads his squadron without criticism. Of particular mention are his untiring willingness for combat, the good and responsible leadership of his squadron on the ground as well as in the air and also his expressed talent for improvisation during the most difficult situations. Since August 10, 1942, First Lieutenant Mayerl has been engaged as a squadron leader, and the group recommends his preferential promotion to Captain.

Two days later, Lieutenant Colonel Karl-Gottfried Nordmann, the wing commodore, added his own comments:

> First Lieutenant Mayerl is one of the oldest pilots of the 3rd Group, *Jagdgeschwader "Mölders."* He attained his personal success due to his exemplary steady willingness for combat, his healthy courage and his steadfastness. After his promotion to officer, he developed in an excellent way as a group leader in the air and he demonstrates vivid interest in troop service. Any capabilities lacking at the beginning can be corrected. Due to the type of missions, the squadron had to disperse and required a high degree of leadership from First Lieutenant Mayerl. Due to his flexibility and talent for improvisation, he showed that he was up to these demands. The circumstances under which First Lieutenant Mayerl took over the leadership of the 9th Squadron is of particular mention. In the difficult fighting around Rshev [Rzev], the [former] squadron commander and all the officers of the squadron were killed over a short period of time. First Lieutenant Mayerl was called back from leave and tasked with the leadership of this squadron. Within the shortest time, he brought back the old enthusiastic spirit of the entire squadron and the pilots' willingness for combat through his personal example and his optimistic ways. Without reservation, the wing recommends First Lieutenant Mayerl for preferential promotion to Captain.

The same day that Nordmann wrote his remarks (May 7, 1943), Mayerl was wounded by ground fire in his Focke-Wulf Fw 190A-5 and would remain out of action until the end of June. However, on July 6, 1943, he scored his 47th through 50th kills in the Orel-Kursk region. By July 16, he reached his 60th and on August 10, 1943 achieved his 71st. But he fell ill on August 27, 1943 and remained in a hospital for seven months. During this period, on November 22, 1943 First Lieutenant Maximilian Mayerl received the Knight's Cross of the Iron Cross, having attained 76 aerial victories. He relinquished command of the squadron on December 8, 1943. In early 1944, Mayerl transferred to Supplemental Group East (*Ergänzungsgruppe Ost*) – an operational training unit; on September 1, 1944, he assumed command of Supplemental Group North (*Ergänzungsgruppe Nord*), another operational training unit, which was later designated the 1st Group, 1st Supplemental Fighter Wing (*Ergänzungsjagdgeschwader 1*). He survived the war.

Maximilian Mayerl recorded 76 aerial victories (of which four were in the West) in 647 combat missions, a sortie-to-victory ratio of 8.51 to 1. He also flew 42 ground-attack and fighter-bomber missions.[9]

III./ Jagdgeschwader Mölders   O.U., den 5. Mai 1943.

Beurteilung für Oblt.(Kr.O.) Maximilian Mayerl.

Oblt. Mayerl ist von schlanker, kräftiger Gestalt; in seinem Äußeren von guter Erscheinung. Sein geistiges Niveau ist gemessen am Durchschnittsoffizier verhältnismäßig hoch. Er ist Kriegsoffizier, wurde am 1.12.1940 zum Leutnant und am 1.1.1943 zum Oberleutnant befördert. Seit dem 10.8.1942 führt er eine Staffel. Oblt. Mayerl gehört seit dem 1.8.1939 als Jagdflugzeugführer der III./ J.G. 51 an. In über 500 Feindeinsätzen hat er gleichbleibend ausgesprochen gute Leistungen als Jagdflieger besonders später als Verbandsführer gezeigt. Er erzielte bisher insgesamt 46 Abschüsse, davon vier im Luftkrieg gegen England und 42 in Rußland. Auf dem Boden führte Oblt. Mayerl seine Staffel stets ohne Beanstandungen. Besonders hervorzuheben sind seine unermüdliche Einsatzfreudigkeit, die gute, verantwortungsfreudige Führung seiner Staffel sowohl am Boden als auch in der Luft und sein ausgesprochenes Improvisationsvermögen gerade auch währnnd schwierigeren Situationen.

Da Oblt. Mayerl seit dem 10.8.42 als Staffelführer eingesetzt ist, schlägt die Gruppe bezugnehmend auf die Verfügung des R.d.L.u. Ob.d.L., L.P., Az. 21, Nr. 71489/42 (2, I D) v. 22.12.42 ihn zur außerplanmäßigen Beförderung zum H a u p t m a n n vor.

Schnell

Major und Gruppenkommandeur.

Efficiency Report for First Lieutenant Maximilian Mayerl (front side) – dated May 5, 1943, on blank paper, with typed comments. Signed by Major Karl-Heinz Schnell, 3rd Group Commander, 51st Fighter Wing.

Jagdgeschwader Mölders den 7.Mai 1943.

Stellungnahme des Geschwaderkommodore.

Oblt. M a y e r l ist mit der älteste Flugzeugführer der III./J.G.Mölders.

Seine eigenen Erfolge erzielte er mit vorbildlicher gleichbleibender Einsatzfreude, gesundem Draufgängertum und Durchstehvermögen. Nach seiner Beförderung zum Offizier entwickelte er sich als Verbandsführer in der Luft hervorragend und zeigte reges Interesse in truppendienstlicher Hinsicht. Anfänglich bestehende Lücken konnte er hierdurch schließen.

Eine durch die Art des Einsatzes erforderliche längere Abzweigung der Staffel des Oblt.Mayerl forderte von ihm hohe Führereigenschaften. Diesen Erfordernissen zeigte er sich durch scene Wendigkeit und sein Improvisationsvermögen gewachsen.

Besondere Erwähnung verdienen die Umstände, unter welchen Oblt.Mayerl die Führung der 9.Staffel übernahm. In den schweren Kämpfen bei Rshew waren in kürzester Folge der Staffelkapitän und sämtliche Offiziere der Staffel gefallen. Oblt.Mayerl wurde aus dem Urlaub zurückgerufen und mit der Führung dieser Staffel beauftragt. Binnen kürzester Zeit verstand er es die Niedergeschlagenheit der Flugzeugführer durch sein persönliches Beispiel und seine optimistische Art in die alte Frische und Einsatzfreude zu verwandeln und damit wieder den alten schwungvollen Geist in die ganze Staffel zu bringen.

Das Geschwader schlägt Oblt.Mayerl unter Zugrundelegung der Verfügung R.d.L.u.Ob.d.L., LP. Nr. 71 489/42 v. 22.12.42 uneingeschränkt zur bevorzugten Beförderung zum H a u p t m a n n (Kr.O.) vor.

Nordmann

Oberstleutnant u. Geschwaderkommodore.

Efficiency Report for First Lieutenant Maximilian Mayerl (back side) – signed by Lieutenant Colonel Karl-Gottfried Nordmann, Commodore, 51st Fighter Wing.

Julius Meimberg

Fighter Pilot

"Very passionate, outstanding fighter pilot."

Major Julius Meimberg was born in Münster, Westphalia, on January 11, 1917. Nicknamed "Jule," he was promoted to second lieutenant on August 1, 1939 and, after receiving flight training at Schleissheim, he was assigned on December 11, 1939 to the 4th Squadron, 2nd Fighter Wing "Richthofen" (*Jagdgeschwader 2 "Richthofen"*) at Zerbst. He scored his first aerial victory – a Hurricane over Tournai, France – flying a Messerschmitt Me 109E on May 19, 1940, while flying escort for He 111 bombers. This was only eight days after Meimberg cracked up his Messerschmitt Me 109E on landing at Hamminkeln. Meimberg then shot down a Curtiss fighter over Epernay, France on June 3, 1940. During the Battle of Britain, Meimberg shot down: a Spitfire on September 4, two Spitfires on September 6, a Hurricane on October 10, a Hurricane on November 7 and a Spitfire on November 28. His last victory of the year was a Blenheim bomber over the English Channel on November 29. Meimberg was named the Commander, 3rd Squadron, 2nd Fighter Wing on April 15, 1941. On July 24, 1941, flying a Messerschmitt Me 109E-7, he shot down three British bombers (two Hampdens and a Wellington), but crash-landed and was seriously wounded. He did not return to combat until May 3, 1942. During the intervening time, he received the *Luftwaffe* Honor Goblet on July 30, 1941 and was promoted to first lieutenant on October 1, 1941.

On July 11, 1942, he reached his 20th victory, and on August 1, 1942 assumed command of the 11th Squadron – the specialized high-altitude squadron equipped with Messerschmitt Me 109G-1s with pressurized cockpits and nitrous-oxide injection into the supercharger to boost power at higher altitudes. He shot down two Spitfires over Dieppe on August 19, 1942 during the attempted Allied amphibious landing. Meimberg was rewarded with the German Cross in Gold on October 29, 1942 and led his unit to North Africa in November, but only after he made an emergency belly-landing at Mannhein-Sandhofen before departing Germany, which seriously damaged his Messerschmitt Me 109G-1. On December 4, flying in a Messerschmitt Me 109G-1, he shot down three Bisley bombers in ten minutes over Mateur, Tunisia, and shot down three Spitfires a day later. The following day, he downed a Spitfire south of Tebourba.

On January 14, 1943, Lieutenant Colonel and the commodore of the 53rd Fighter Wing "Ace of Spades" (*Jagdgeschwader 53 "Pikas"*) Günther von Maltzahn submitted a request for a preferred promotion for First Lieutenant Meimberg. Von Maltzahn wrote:[10]

> Very passionate, outstanding fighter pilot with 30 aerial victories. From May 17, 1941, he was engaged as squadron commander and has fulfilled this position in an excellent manner. He understands how to sweep along his squadron and to lead them to successes of the highest order.

The adjutant of the Air Commander Tunisia (*Fliegerführer Tunis*), Colonel Benno Kosch, added: "Second the judgment."

The acting commander of the 2nd Air Corps, Brigadier General Martin Harlinghausen, added: "favorably forwarded."

On February 1, 1943, Meimberg shot down a B-17 Flying Fortress over Pont-du-Fahs, but he was also shot down in the encounter. He parachuted to safety but was seriously wounded in the attempt. He would remain out of combat for six months with serious burns to his hands, in a hospital at Munich-Oberföhring. Meimberg would be assigned to the staff of *Jagdgeschwader 53 "Pikas"* in Italy from August to December (and would shoot down a P-51 Mustang over Cassino on December 13), but returned to a hospital in Vienna (he was operated on in February) until April 20, 1944, when he assumed command of the 2nd Group, *Jagdgeschwader 53 "Pikas"* in Eschborn. On May 12, 1944, Meimberg was shot down again north of Eschborn after combat with P-51s. He successfully bailed out of his Messerschmitt Me 109G-6 and would lead his unit in Normandy (including shooting down two P-47 Thunderbolts in eleven minutes over Caen on July 5, 1944) and in the skies over Germany. The commander of the 7th Fighter Division, Colonel Karl Hentschel, presented the Knight's Cross of the Iron Cross to Captain Julius Meimberg on October 24, 1944 at Malmsheim near Stuttgart. On December 26, 1944, he shot down three P-47 Thunderbolts, reaching his 50th aerial victory, but once again had to bail out of his Messerschmitt Me 109G-14. His last two victories came on April 10, 1945, a P-47 over Crailsheim and on April 17, 1945, when he dispatched a French Air Force Spitfire over Biberach. After this last victory, Meimberg's Messerschmitt Me 109G-14 was struck by ground fire, as he was conducting a ground-attack against an American column on the Nürnberg *Autobahn*, and crashed – but again he survived by bailing out first. He disbanded the 2nd Group at Waal on April 27, 1945.

Julius Meimberg flew over 250 combat missions and shot down 53 enemy aircraft, all in the West. His total included 2 four-engine bombers.[11]

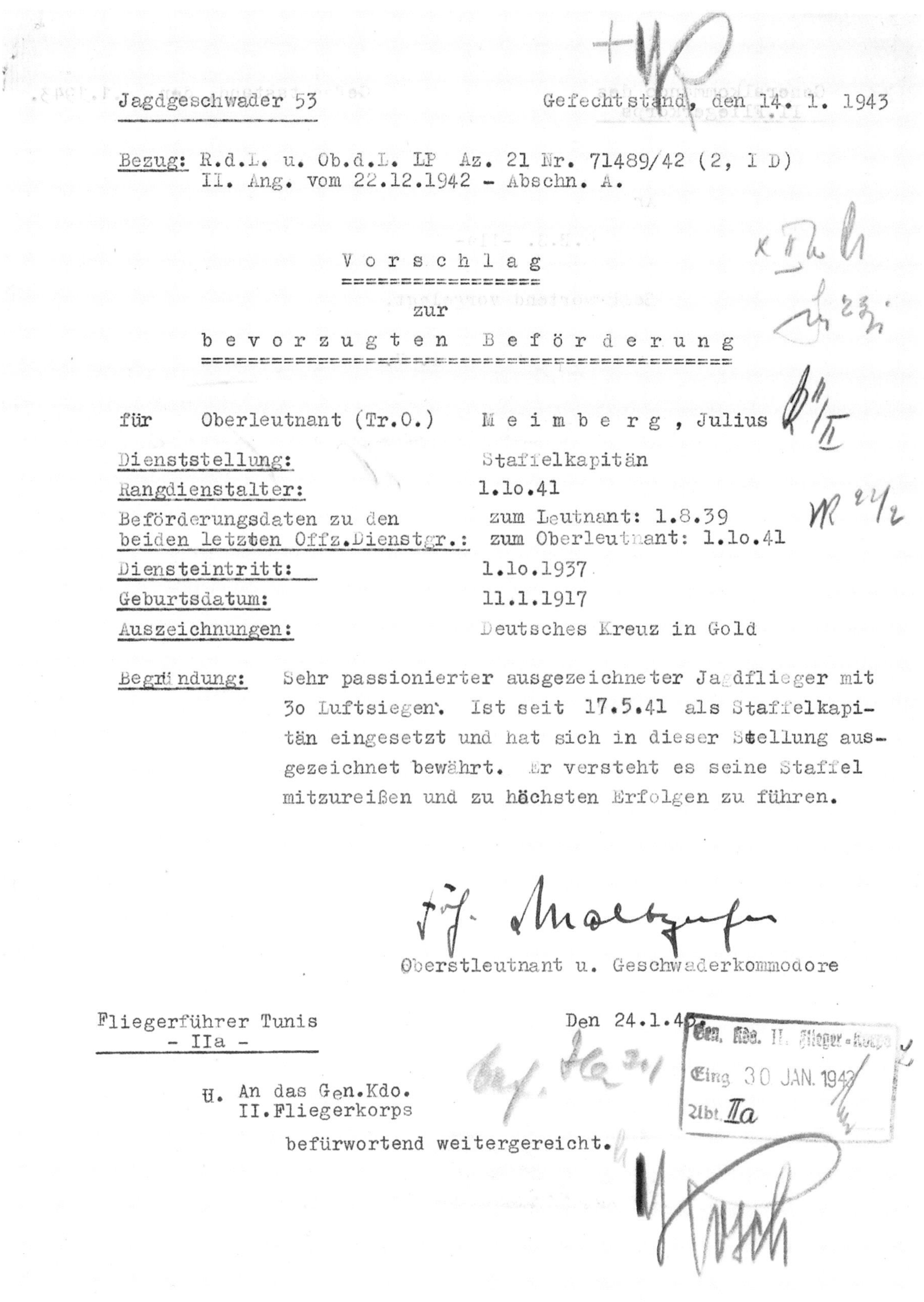

Jagdgeschwader 53 Gefechtstand, den 14. 1. 1943

Bezug: R.d.L. u. Ob.d.L. LP Az. 21 Nr. 71489/42 (2, I D)
II. Ang. vom 22.12.1942 - Abschn. A.

V o r s c h l a g
zur
b e v o r z u g t e n B e f ö r d e r u n g

für Oberleutnant (Tr.O.) M e i m b e r g , Julius

Dienststellung: Staffelkapitän

Rangdienstalter: 1.1o.41

Beförderungsdaten zu den beiden letzten Offz.Dienstgr.: zum Leutnant: 1.8.39 zum Oberleutnant: 1.1o.41

Diensteintritt: 1.1o.1937

Geburtsdatum: 11.1.1917

Auszeichnungen: Deutsches Kreuz in Gold

Begründung: Sehr passionierter ausgezeichneter Jagdflieger mit 3o Luftsiegen. Ist seit 17.5.41 als Staffelkapitän eingesetzt und hat sich in dieser Stellung ausgezeichnet bewährt. Er versteht es seine Staffel mitzureißen und zu höchsten Erfolgen zu führen.

Oberstleutnant u. Geschwaderkommodore

Fliegerführer Tunis
- IIa -

Den 24.1.43

U. An das Gen.Kdo.
II.Fliegerkorps

befürwortend weitergereicht.

Gen. Kdo. II. Flieger-Korps
Eing. 30 JAN. 1943
Abt. IIa

Request for Preferred Promotion for First Lieutenant Julius Meimberg (front side) – dated January 14, 1943, on blank paper, with typed comments. Signed by Lieutenant Colonel Günther von Maltzahn, Commodore, 53rd Fighter Wing, and Colonel Benno Kosch, adjutant, Air Commander Tunis.

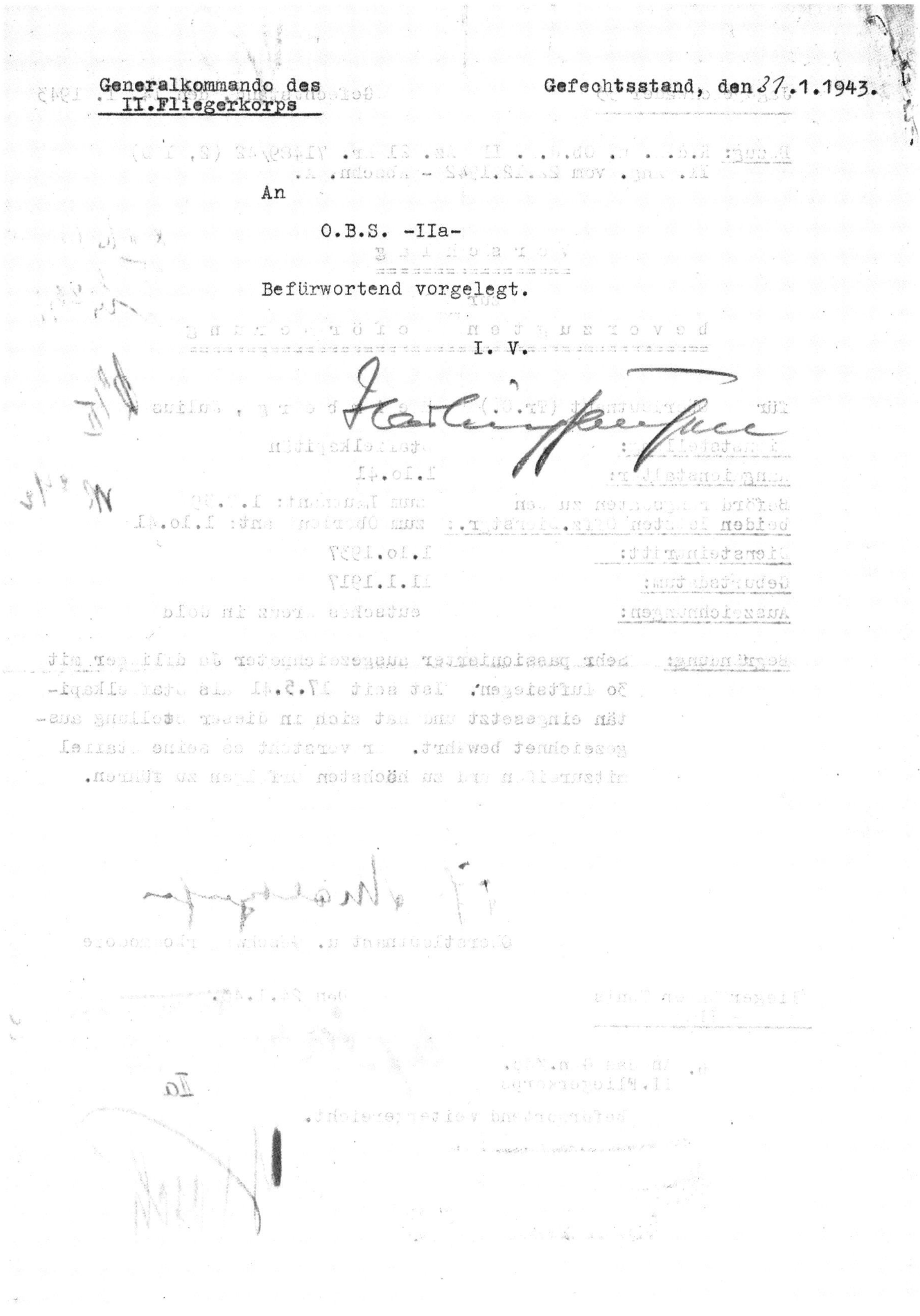

Generalkommando des
II.Fliegerkorps

Gefechtsstand, den 31.1.1943.

An

O.B.S. -IIa-

Befürwortend vorgelegt.

I. V.

Request for Preferred Promotion for First Lieutenant Julius Meimberg (back side) – Signed by Brigadier General Martin Harlinghausen, Air Commander Tunis.

Joachim Meissner

Fallschirmjäger

"'Lieutenant Meissner' will be a valuable addition for the Luftwaffe."

Captain Joachim Meissner was born in Freystadt, Lower Silesia on October 15, 1911. He served in the *Reichswehr* from 1929 to 1934 as an enlisted man, when he then joined the Foreign Section (Southeast Europe) in the *Reich* Sports Office. On August 26, 1939, he was mobilized with the 8th Engineer Battalion, but transferred to the *Luftwaffe* and joined the 1st Paratroop Regiment (*Fallschirmjäger-Regiment 1*) on January 1, 1940. Meissner then joined the secret Test Detachment Friedrichshafen, earmarked for the upcoming glider assault on the Belgian fortress of Eben Emael.

On January 30, 1940, Captain Walter Koch, the commander of Test Detachment Friedrichshafen (the code name for the special paratroop engineer assault detachment), submitted a recommendation for promotion to second lieutenant for Technical Sergeant Meissner. In addition to basic information concerning Meissner's place of birth, religion and military service, Koch added:[12]

> "Lieutenant Meissner" will be a valuable addition for the *Luftwaffe*.

Meissner certainly was a valuable addition. He was promoted to second lieutenant (Reserve) on March 20, 1940. Early on the morning of May 10, 1940, as the second in command of Assault Group Iron (*Eisen*), Meissner watched as the Belgians blew up the bridge at Canne over the Albert Canal before his group, that was tasked to capture it intact, could land. He then observed the commander of his group, Second Lieutenant Martin Schächter, getting seriously wounded shortly after landing. Meissner then took command of the group. At about 6:10 a.m., the heavy machinegun section landed 550 yards too far to the west and suffered 14 killed and 8 wounded. After landing, the 8th Squad destroyed enemy machinegun-positions on the high ground with hand grenades, while the 3rd Squad took the valley and the trench-system on the northern hill. They also blew up three houses and the entrance to a bunker

Adolf Hitler with three key paratroopers, who captured the fortress of Eben Emael. Second Lieutenant Joachim Meissner is next to Hitler with First Lieutenant Witzig (center) and Captain Koch (right).

at the bridge, and captured the crew of the two bunkers there. The squad then moved into the village and captured 25 men and 1 officer. At 10:30 a.m., the first Belgian counterattack against Meissner's group failed, when the Belgians were bombed by the *Luftwaffe*; however, as radio communication with the 8th Air Corps was insufficient, some bombs fell on the German positions.

The crew of the Belgian bunker on the high ground overlooking Canne surrendered around noon. The Belgians then launched organized counterattacks from the west and southwest at 3:00 p.m. and 6:00 p.m., but these were stopped by combined artillery and air support. Meissner then sent paratroopers from the 8th Squad to swim east across the Albert Canal to lead reinforcements from the German Army's 151st Infantry Regiment and 51st Engineer Battalion forward. The Belgians began their own artillery preparation about 8:00 p.m. for a planned attack just after midnight. At 11:30 p.m., the German reinforcements finally arrived and helped repel the Belgian attack. The following morning, Meissner led the remaining elements of Assault Group Iron to the eastern side of the canal; the group had suffered 22 dead, 26 wounded and 1 missing in action. In return, they had inflicted 150 killed, 50 wounded on the enemy and had taken 190 prisoners.

Adolf Hitler personally awarded Second Lieutenant Joachim Meissner the Knight's Cross of the Iron Cross on May 15, 1940. The following day, Meissner received a promotion to first lieutenant (Reserve). In August he joined the 2nd Paratroop Regiment (*Fallschirmjäger-Regiment 2*). He participated in the German airborne invasion of Crete, jumping east of Rethymnon. He became the Ordnance Officer for the 2nd Paratroop Regiment on December 6, 1941 and held this position until July 10, 1942, fighting in Russia. He was promoted to captain on September 30, 1942. On April 1, 1943, Meissner assumed command of the 6th Company, 2nd Paratroop Regiment. On April 16, 1944, Captain Meissner became the acting commander of the 3rd Battalion, 14th Paratroop Regiment (*Fallschirmjäger-Regiment 14*), part of the 5th Paratroop Division (*5. Fallschirmjäger-Division*). Joachim Meissner was killed in action on July 25, 1944 at St. Jean-de-Daye near St. Lô, France, probably during the massive 2,000-bomber Allied carpet bombing that day that destroyed almost the entire 14th Paratroop Regiment and set the stage for the American breakout of Normandy. He is buried at a German Military Cemetery at Marigny, France (Section 4, Row 40, Grave 1552).[13]

Geheim! 4

Versuchsabteilung Friedrichshafen. #5/40 g.

Hildesheim, den 30. Januar 1940.
Fliegerhorst.

Betr.: Vorschlag zur Beförderung zum Leutnant d.R.

Auf dem Dienstweg

Flieg-Div. 7

an

R. d. L. u. Ob. d. L. (L.P.)

Berlin.

Zur Beförderung zum Leutnant d.R. wird in Vorschlag gebracht:

Feldwebel M e i ß n e r , Joachim ,

geb. am 15.10.1911 zu Freystadt Krs. Glogau. Konfession: gottgl.

Verwendet als : Zugführer.

Diensteintritt am 1.10.1929. Vom 31.3.1934 bis 25.8.1939 unterbrochen,

Wiedereintritt am 26.8.1939.

Ernennung zum Res.-Offz.-Anw. am: 21.2.1938.

Der Feldwebel Meißner ist ledig und hat keine Kinder.

Wehrbezirkskommando des Wohnorts: W.Bez. Kdo. X Charlottenburg.

Bestrafungen nach Diensteintritt: keine
Bestrafungen vor Diensteintritt: keine

Zum Offz. gewählt am: 28 Januar 1940.

Beruf vor Diensteintritt: Referent in der Auslandsabteilung des Reichsportführers für Südosteuropa (Balkan.)

Stand und Beruf des Vaters: Bauer

Mutter geborene: Berndt

Anschrift der Eltern: Großwandriß b/Liegnitz - Schlesien.

Bildungsgang: Volksschule, Realgymnasium bis zur mittleren Reife.

Mil. Werdegang: Bef. zum Oberschützen am 1.10.1931, zum Gefr. am 1.10.1933, zum Uffz.-Anw. am 1.11.1933, zum R.O.A. am 21.2.1938, zum Uffz. am 14.4.1938, zum Feldwebel am 1.9.1939.

Der „Leutnant Meißner" wäre ein wertvoller Zuwachs für die Luftwaffe.

Koch,

Hauptmann u. Abt.-Führer.

Request for Promotion to Lieutenant for Technical Sergeant Joachim Meissner (one side only) – dated January 30, 1940, on blank paper with types and hand-written comments. Signed by Captain Walter Koch, Commander, Test Detachment Friedrichshafen.

Hans Hermann Merker

Bomber Pilot

"Well liked by comrades and superiors."

Captain Hans Hermann Merker was born in Bremerhaven on November 23, 1921. The son of a university professor, Merker joined the *Luftwaffe* on November 15, 1939, just before his eighteenth birthday. The following year, he attended a series of military schools, including flight school at Wiener-Neustadt. On March 9, 1941, the chain of command at the 4th Bomber Pilot School (*Grosse Kampffliegerschule 4*) at Thorn submitted a special efficiency report requesting that Merker be promoted to second lieutenant. A lieutenant colonel, the head of the school's 1st Training Group, wrote the following evaluation:[14]

> Straight-forward, quiet and modest human being. Open, decent character. Well liked by comrades and superiors. Physically, he is strong and quite good. Good athlete. His service accomplishments are satisfactory. During instruction, he could be more open. In outside service matters and at the front, he still must become stronger. He strives to expand his knowledge and to constantly better himself. His behavior vis-à-vis his superiors is without criticism. Leadership talent is definitely present. Promises to become a good officer.

Colonel Heinrich Seywald, the school's commander, added: "Agreed!"

Finally, Colonel Alfred Bülowius, the Higher Commander of Bomber and Stuka Pilot Schools, wrote simply: "Noted."

Second Lieutenant Merker received the *Luftwaffe* Honor Goblet on May 25, 1942 and the German Cross in Gold on October 3, 1942, while on the staff of the 1st Group, 3rd Bomber Wing "Blitz" (*Kampfgeschwader 3 "Blitz"*). On June 9, 1944, First Lieutenant Merker received the Knight's Cross of the Iron Cross after flying 323 combat missions, during which he was credited with destroying 48 tanks and 20 enemy aircraft on the ground. Merker transferred to the 3rd Squadron, 7th Night Fighter Wing (*Nachtjagdgeschwader 7*) and later assumed command of the 4th Squadron (Replacements). The unit was finally reorganized as the 2nd Night Fighter Wing (*Nachtjagdgeschwader 2*). Captain Merker assumed his final duty as Commander, 3rd Group, 2nd Night Fighter Wing on April 11, 1945 and led this unit until May 8, 1945. Throughout the war he flew 360 combat missions. Hans Hermann Merker died on January 23, 1988 in St. Märgen/Schwarzwald in Baden-Württemberg. He is buried there at the *Stadtfriedhof* (Section 1, Row 7, Grave 3).[15]

Große Kampffliegerschule 4
Ausbildungsgruppe I
(Truppenteil)
Br.B.Nr.

Thorn, den 9. März 1941
(Ort und Datum)

Betr. : Vorschlag zur Beförderung zum Leutnant.

Auf dem Dienstwege!

an den R.d.L. und Ob.d.L. (L.P.)
Berlin.

Zur Beförderung zum Leutnant wird in Vorschlag gebracht:
Familienname: M e r k e r Vorname: Hans Hermann
geb. am : 23.11.1921 zu Bremerhafen Konfession : evgl.
Dienstgrad: Oberfähnrich verwendet als Flugzeugführer.-Schüler
Diensteintritt am : 15.11.1939 verh./ledig : ledig
Ernennung zum Oberfähnrich : 1.2.1941 Kinder: keine
Offz. Anwärter wann: 1.4.194o
Wehrbez. Kdo des Wohnortes: Gießen
Bestrafung vor Diensteintritt: keine
Bestrafung nach Diensteintritt: keine
Zum Offizier gewählt : 9.3.1941
Beruf vor Diensteintritt: Schüler
Stand und Beruf des Vaters: Universitäts Professor
Mutter geborene: Schüler
Anschrift der Eltern bezw. des Vormundes: Ernst Merker, Giessen/Lahn
Schiffenberg-Weg 17

Bildungsgang: Erziehung im Elternhause
1928 - 1932 Grundschule Giessen
1932 - 1939 Oberschule
Reifezeugnis im Nov. 1939 erhalten

Milt.Werdegang:

15.11.1939	Flg, 2/Fl.Ausb.Regt.51 Königsberg/Pr., eingetreten
2.12.1939	vereidigt
8. 1.194o	Fl.Ausb.Regt.31 - Schüko - versetzt
1. 4. "	Fhj. ernannt
1. 4. "	Fhj. Gefr. befördert
1. 6. "	Fhj. Uffz. befördert
21. 8. "	Flgz.F.Sch. C 8 Wiener- Neustadt versetzt
1. 9. "	Fähnrich befördert
1.12. "	Bl.Fl.Sch.W.-Aspern versetzt
3o.12. "	Blindflugschein 2 Kr. erhalten
15. 1. "	Gr.K.Flg.Sch.4- Ausb-Gr.I- versetzt
1. 2. "	Oberfähnrich befördert

Request for Promotion to Officer for Officer Candidate Hans Hermann Merker (front side) – dated March 9, 1941, on blank paper, with typed comments.

Begründung.

Beurteilung : Gradliniger, stàller und bescheidener Mensch. Offener, anständiger Charakter. Bei Kameraden und Vorgesetzten beliebt. Körperlich ist er kräftig und recht gut. Guter Sportler. Seine dienstlichen Leistungen sind zufriedenstellend. Im Unterricht kann er noch mehr aus sich herausgehen. Im Außendienst und vor der Front muß er noch fester werden. Ist aber bemüht seine Kenntnisse zu erweitern und sich laufend zu bessern. Sein Benehmen Vorgesetzten gegenüber ist einwandfrei. Führereigenschaften sind durchaus vorhanden. Verspricht ein guter Offizier zu werden.

Oberstleutnant und Kommandeur
Ausbildungsgruppe I

Einverstanden !
Thorn, den 11. März 1941

Oberst und Kommandeur.

Höherer Kommandeur der Kampf- und Sturzkampffliegerschulen

Prag, den 17.3.1941

Gesehen.

Oberst und Kommandeur

Request for Promotion to Officer for Officer Candidate Hans Hermann Merker (back side) – signed by Colonel Heinrich Seywald, 4th Bomber School Commander, and by Colonel Alfred Bülowius, Higher Commander of Bomber and Stuka Pilot Schools.

Heinz Meyer

Fallschirmjäger

"He succeeded in such devastating blows to the Americans at Monte Castre that he was recommended for the Oak Leaves to the Knight's Cross of the Iron Cross for this outstanding success."

Major Heinz Meyer was born on April 9, 1916 in Magdeburg. He entered the *Luftwaffe* on November 2, 1937, joining the 14th Company, General Göring Regiment. He transferred to the 4th Company, 1st Paratroop Regiment (*Fallschirmjäger-Regiment 1*), where he then became an officer candidate. Technical Sergeant Meyer jumped into Holland with the 2nd Battalion at Moerdijk, seizing the key railroad bridge over the Maas River and winning the Iron Cross 2nd Class. Meyer then took part in the airborne reinforcement of General Dietl's mountain troops in northern Norway at Narvik.[16] He then became a platoon leader in the 11th Company, 3rd Paratroop Regiment (*Fallschirmjäger-Regiment 3*), when he was promoted to second lieutenant (Reserve) on August 1, 1940. Meyer jumped into Prison Valley at Crete on May 20, 1941 during the German airborne invasion of the island. He received the Iron Cross 1st Class a month later for his actions on Crete. From October 1, 1941 to November 20, 1941, the unit fought along the Newa River east of Leningrad, Russia. In early 1942, Meyer transferred to the 3rd Battalion, 4th Paratroop Regiment (*Fallschirmjäger-Regiment 4*); he became the acting commander of the regiment's 11th Company. On July 1, 1942, Meyer became a first lieutenant (Reserve). He again deployed to Russia from November 5, 1942 to March 28, 1943 with the German 9th Army near Rzev, winning the German Cross in Gold on June 21, 1943.

Meyer and his company then jumped into Sicily in July 1943 as part of the attempt to stop the Allied invasion of the island. South of Catania, defending at the Bottaceto Ditch, Meyer's unit held out until August before being forced to withdraw to the Italian mainland. He was promoted to captain (Reserve) on November 1, 1943. Meyer then took part in the battles at Cassino, defending Hill 593, being wounded in the intense fighting. He became the acting commander of the 3rd Battalion, 4th Paratroop Regiment on February 20, 1944. On March 15, 460 Allied bombers dropped 1,000 tons of bombs on the Italian town of Cassino and its German defenders and followed the aerial attack with an 8-hour artillery barrage in which 890 guns fired 195,696 rounds. The bombardment did not dislodge the *Fallschirmjäger*, and after 96 hours of heavy ground combat – centered on the Continental Hotel – a combined New Zealand, Indian and American armored thrust along the "Cavendish Road" attempted to turn the northern flank of the German positions through the mountains and seize the Albaneta Farm. In their way stood the 4th Paratroop Regiment. The 35-armored-vehicle attack bogged down in the midst of accurate German anti-tank fire and judicious use of anti-tank mines; German sources claim 29 vehicles were destroyed or damaged, while other sources put the losses at 22. In any case, the attack failed; Meyer was awarded the Knight's Cross of the Iron Cross on April 8, 1944.

Meyer became the acting commander of the 3rd Battalion, 15th Paratroop Regiment (*Fallschirmjäger-Regiment 15*) on May 17, 1944. Part of the 5th Paratroop Division (*5. Fallschirmjäger-Division*), the unit fought in France against the Allied advance.

In September 1944, Captain Heinz Meyer's chain of command submitted him for a preferential promotion to major. Lieutenant Colonel Kurt Gröschke, Meyer's regimental commander, wrote the following justification:[17]

Reason for consideration:

Since May 17, 1944, Captain Meyer has led the 3rd Battalion, 15th Paratroop Regiment.

Just as in his prior service positions, he has again proven his outstanding leadership qualities. Within a very short time, Captain Meyer formed a highly valuable battle group out of the battalion, which had only been established shortly before the invasion, and with this unit – under his unsparing personal engagement – he succeeded in such devastating blows to the Americans at Monte Castre that he was recommended for the Oak Leaves to the Knight's Cross of the Iron Cross for this outstanding success.

With an extra-ordinary talent for improvisation, Captain Meyer has no trouble in reaching a set goal. Excelling in numerous missions, like Russia 1941, Russia 1942/43, Sicily and Southern Italy, Captain Meyer was awarded the German Cross in Gold on June 16, 1943 and the Knight's Cross of the Iron Cross on April 8, 1944.

Captain Meyer has stood up to the most difficult tasks.

An excellent officer and outstanding troop commander, he is far ahead of other officers of his service grade as to his concept of duty, maturity and know-how.

There was no comment made by a division commander. However, Lieutenant General Eugen Meindl, the 2nd Paratroop Corps Commander, wrote, "Agreed."

Meyer was promoted to major (Reserve) on October 21, 1944. Major Heinz Meyer received the Oak Leaves to the Knight's Cross on November 18, 1944 for his actions on the Western Front. He ended the war in the Harz Mountains and was captured on May 8, 1945. Heinz Meyer died on September 22, 1987 in Viersen.[18]

V o r s c h l a g

zur

b e v o r z u g t e n B e f ö r d e r u n g.

gem. R.d.L.u.Ob.d.L.LP Nr. 71489/42 (2TD) II. Ang.v.22.12.42

RDA 2 1.5.44

für Hauptmann (Kr.O.)	M e y e r	Heinz
Dienststellung:	Btl. Führer III./Fallschirm - Jäger Rgt. 15	
Rangdienstalter:	ohne	
Beförderungsdaten:	1. 8. 194o	Leutnant (Kr.O.)
	1. 7. 1942	Oberleutnant (Kr.O.)
	1. 11. 1943	Hauptmann (Kr.O.)
Geb. Dat.:	9. 4. 1916	
Auszeichnungen:	EK II, EK I	Juni 194o
	Erdkampfabzeichen der Luftwaffe	2o. 9. 1942
	Ärmelband Kreta	2o. 5. 1943
	Deutsche Kreuz in Gold	16. 6. 1943
	Ritterkreuz zum Eisernen Kreuz 1939	8. 4. 1944

B e g r ü n d u n g:

Hptm. Meyer führt seit dem 17. 5. 1944 das III./ Fallschirm - Jäger Rgt. 15.
Wie in früheren Dienststellungen hat er auch hier wieder seine überragenden Führereigenschaften unter Beweis gestellt. Aus dem kurz vor der Invasion aufgestellten Btl. hat Hptm. Meyer in kurzer Zeit eine hochwertige Kampfgemeinschaft geformt, mit der er unter rücksichtslosem Einsatz seiner Person dem Amerikaner bei Monte Castre so vernichtende Schläge zufügte, daß er für diese weit überragenden Erfolge zum Eichenlaub des Ritterkreuzes zum

Request for Preferred Promotion for Captain Heinz Meyer (front side) – dated September 9, 1944.

Eisernen Kreuz in Vorschlag gebracht wurde.
Hptm. Meyer kennt bei hervorragendem Improvisitationsvermögen keine Schwierigkeiten bis zur Erringung eines gesteckten Zieles.
In zahlreichen Einsätzen, wie Rußland 1941, Rußland 1942/43, Sizilien und Süditalien hervorragend bewährt, wurde Hptm. Meyer am 16. 6. 1943 mit dem Deutschen Kreuz in Gold und am 8. 4. 1944 mit dem Ritterkreuz des Eisernen Kreuzes ausgezeichnet.
Hptm. Meyer war jeder noch so schwierigen Aufgabe gewachsen.
Ein ausgezeichneter Offizier und hervorragender Truppenführer ist er anderen Offizieren seines Dienstgrades an Pflichtauffassung, Reife und Können weit voraus.

Gröschke

Oberstleutnant und Rgt. Kommandeur

Der Kommandierende General
II.Fallschirmkorps

K.St.Qu., 9.9.44

Meindl

General der Fallschirmtruppe

Request for Preferred Promotion for Captain Heinz Meyer (back side) – signed by Lieutenant Colonel Kurt Gröschke, Commander, 15th Paratroop Regiment, and by Lieutenant General Eugen Meindl, Commander, 2nd Paratroop Corps.

Werner Milch

Fallschirmjäger

"Distinguished himself through extraordinary courage and relentless personal engagement."

Major Werner Milch was born in Wilhelmshaven on November 15, 1903. He spent a few weeks in the German Army in 1924 but then left the service. He returned to the Army in a reserve status in 1937, with the 3rd Artillery Regiment. In 1939 he was mobilized on active duty with the 603rd Artillery Regiment as a reserve second lieutenant. Fighting with the unit in the French campaign, he won the Iron Cross 2nd Class on May 16, 1940. Milch fought on the northern sector of the Eastern Front in 1941 and was wounded in action in July. Promoted on October 31, 1941 to first lieutenant (Reserve) and transferring to the *Luftwaffe* in December – where he joined the 5th Battery, 1st Paratroop Artillery Regiment (*Fallschirm-Artillerie-Regiment 1*) – Milch won the Iron Cross 1st Class on February 18, 1942. He would serve in Russia from January 4 to April 13, before transferring home and then to Africa, where he served from August 11 to November 11, 1942. As a battery commander with the 1st *Luftwaffe Jäger* Brigade in Africa, Milch distinguished himself in Africa Corps attacks on August 30 and 31, and in defensive fighting four days later at Bab el Qatarra.

On December 22, 1942, Brigadier General Ramcke sent a letter to the 11th Air Corps, supporting a preferential promotion to captain for First Lieutenant Werner Milch. The letter, signed by Colonel Hans von Fichte for Ramcke, said:[19]

> First Lieutenant Werner Milch first served as a platoon officer, then as an acting battery commander of a 75mm battery in the 1st *Luftwaffe Jäger* Brigade of *Panzer* Army Africa.
>
> During the attack of August 30 to August 31st and the heavy defensive battles during the night of September 3 to 4, 1942 in Dair Alinda east of the desert fort Bab el Qatarra, First Lieutenant Milch particularly distinguished himself through personal courageous engagement. With his section of 105mm light howitzers, he supported the attack of the battle group in an outstanding and effective manner, and on the night of September 3 to 4, with the engagement of his weapons in the front battle line, he stopped the counter-attack by the enemy, whereby under his leadership several enemy tanks and several crew and ammunition transport vehicles were destroyed on the battlefield. With that, the enemy counter-attack against the front of Battle Group Hübner was beaten in a bloody manner. Also here, First Lieutenant Milch distinguished himself through extraordinary courage and relentless personal engagement.
>
> In addition to these examples of personal courage, First Lieutenant Milch has distinguished himself as a thoughtful battery commander who knows how to lead his battery well in the most difficult situations and is always a shining example for his men.
>
> Therefore, I recommend that First Lieutenant Milch be preferentially promoted to captain due to his courage in the face of the enemy.

On January 23, 1943, Milch was promoted to captain (Reserve) and became the battery commander of the 4th Battery, 2nd Paratroop Artillery Regiment (*Fallschirm-Artillerie-Regiment 2*). He returned to the Eastern Front in mid-November 1943, where on December 22, 1943 he became the acting commander of the 2nd Detachment (Battalion) of the artillery regiment until March 20, 1944. Milch then returned to France and took acting command of the newly formed 2nd Paratroop Heavy Mortar Battalion (*Fallschirm-Granatwerfer-Bataillon 2*) of the 2nd Paratroop Division (*2. Fallschirmjäger-Division*) on March 21. On April 15, 1944, Milch received the German Cross in Gold for his actions the previous winter in Russia. Serving on the invasion front in France, Milch commanded the battalion until August 6, when he was transferred to command the Paratroop Heavy Mortar Demonstration and Test Battalion in the vicinity of Nancy, France. During the fight for the crossing sites over the Moselle River near Flavigny, he personally led an assault group in an attempt to eliminate the U.S. bridgehead, an act for which he would be awarded the Knight's Cross of the Iron Cross on January 1, 1945. Promoted to major (Reserve) on January 1, 1945, his unit joined the 7th Paratroop Division (*7. Fallschirmjäger-Division*), ending the war near his hometown of Wilhelmshaven. Werner Milch, who was the brother of *Luftwaffe* Field Marshal Erhard Milch, died November 17, 1984 in Hemer/North-Rhine Westphalia. He is buried there at the *Waldfriedhof* (Section D, Field 21, Grave 176-180).[20]

Abschrift.

Generalmajor Ramcke

Berlin, den 22.12.1942.

An das

Gen.-Kdo.XI.Flg.-Korps

- Abt. II a -

Der Oberleutnant Werner M i l c h gehörte zunächst als Zug-Offizier, dann als Battr.-Führer einer der Lw.-Jägerbrigade 1 von der Panzerarmee Afrika zugewiesenen 7,5-cm-Battr. an.

Bei dem Angriff am 3o.8.-31.8. und bei den schweren Abwehrkämpfen in der Nacht vom 3.-4.9.42 im Deir Alinda ostwärts des Wüstenforts Bab el Qatarra hat Oblt. Milch sich durch persönlichen schneidigen Einsatz besonders ausgezeichnet. Mit seinem Zug 1o,5 cm-Leichtgeschütze hat er den Angriff der Kampfgruppe hervorragend und wirksam unterstützt und in der Nacht vom 3.-4.9. den feindlichen Gegenangriff durch Einsatz seiner Geschütze in vorderster Kampflinie abgeschlagen, wobei unter seiner Leitung mehrere Feindpanzer und mehrere Mannschafts- und Munitionstransportwagen im Vorfeld abgeschossen wurden. Dadurch wurde der feindliche Gegenangriff vor der Front der Kampfgruppe Hübner blutig abgeschlagen. Auch hierbei zeichnete sich Oblt. Milch durch besonderen Schneid und rücksichtslosen Einsatz seiner Person aus.

Neben diesen persönlichen Tapferkeitsbeweisen hat sich Oblt. Milch als umsichtiger Battr.-Führer erwiesen, der seine Batterie auch in schwierigen Lagen gut zu führen wußte und er seinen Leuten immer ein leuchtendes Vorbild ist.

Ich schlage daher vor, den Oberleutnant Milch wegen Tapferkeit vor dem Feinde vorzeitig zum Hauptmann zu befördern.

Oblt.Milch ist dieser bevorzugten Beförderung besonders würdig.

gez. R a m c k e

F. d. R. d. A. 5.1.43

O b e r s t

Request for Preferred Promotion for First Lieutenant Werner Milch (one page only) – dated December 22, 1942, on blank paper, with typed comments. Signed by Colonel Hans von Fichte.

Helmut Missner

Fighter Pilot

"Ability to quickly comprehend."

Master Sergeant Helmut Missner was born May 19, 1921 in Stuttgart-Zuffenhausen, Württemberg. A varnisher/painter by trade, he entered the *Luftwaffe* on November 7, 1938 at age 17. He was promoted to Private First Class on October 1, 1939, to Corporal on October 1, 1940 and to Staff Sergeant on June 1, 1941, after being previously designated as a potential commissioned officer. In the summer of 1942, Missner was assigned to the 1st Group, 54th Fighter Wing "Green Heart" (*Jagdgeschwader 54 "Grünherz"*) and began his climb to a final total of 82 aerial victories – all on the Eastern Front. On July 17, 1943 he shot down a Russian aircraft, the 5,000th overall victory of *Jagdgeschwader 54*. By September 4, 1943, his total stood at 33 kills; he received the *Luftwaffe* Honor Goblet on September 13, 1943 for this achievement. A recipient of both the Iron Cross 2nd and 1st Class, Missner was awarded the German Cross in Gold on January 10, 1944. He was promoted to Master Sergeant on April 4, 1944. Recommended for the Knight's Cross on July 1, 1944 and previously wounded, Missner was transferred from the 3rd Squadron, 54th Fighter Wing "Green Heart" to the 1st Squadron, Supplemental Fighter Group East (*Ergänzungs-Jagd-Gruppe Ost*) to be an instructor in mid-July, shortly after this efficiency report was written.

The following efficiency report was written by Second Lieutenant and 3rd Squadron Commander, *Jagdgeschwader 54*, Otto Kittel on July 5, 1944. The front side lists biographical information as well as dates of promotion. The reverse of the report discusses awards received and conduct in the face of the enemy, which states, "Operations in the East as a fighter pilot (81 kills)." It also mentions that Missner served 4 days of mild arrest; unfortunately it does not provide further details. In his short assessment, Kittel noted:[21]

> Mentally very alert, ability to quickly comprehend, physically strong. Calm, thoughtful, decent and honest character. Very accommodating; a good comrade. A capable leader with good military composure and knowledge.

On September 12, 1944 Helmut Missner – now age 23 – died in an accidental crash of his Focke-Wulf Fw 190A-8 near Sagan, Germany (now Zagán, Poland). The perceived cause of the crash was reported to be altitude sickness brought on by oxygen mask failure at his cruising height of 21,325 feet. On October 10, 1944, he was posthumously awarded the Knight's Cross of the Iron Cross.[22] Helmut Missner recorded 82 aerial victories. His name is listed as among the 5,000 fallen German soldiers lying in a communal grave at Poznan-Milostowo, Poland, although the exact location of his remains is unknown.

Formblatt 1

Luftflotte : 1

Waffengatung *) : Fliegertruppe

Truppenteil : I./ Jagdgeschwader 54
3. Staffel

Heimat-Luftgau : VII

W. B. K. : Esslingen

(Wird von L. P. ausgefüllt)

Name : M i s s n e r

Vorname : Helmut

Dienstgrad : Oberfeldwebel

Ariernachweis erbracht.

Geburtstag : 19. Mai 1921

Geburtsort : Zuffenhausen

Beruf : Angelernter Lackierer

Abiturient ~~ja~~ — nein **)

Ständiger Aufenthalt vor der Einberufung: Miedelsbach Krs. Weilingen, Freiburgerstr. 66

Militärischer Werdegang :

Aktive Dienstzeit in der neuen Wermacht : von 7.11.1938 bis 7.5.1943

(bzw. Kurzausbildung :

Weitere Dienstverpflichtung auf 3 = 4 1/2 = 12 u. mehr Jahre 4 1/2 Jahre

Bei ehem. Soldaten, Dienstgrad bei Eintritt in die neue Wehrmacht : -/-

Friedensübungen : -/-

Dienstzeit wahrend des mobilen Verhältnisses : 1.9.1939 bis jetzt

Beförderungen :
1.10.1939 zum Gefreiten 1.6.41 Uffz.
1.10.194o zum Obergefreiten 1.5.43 Feldwebel
1. 9.194o zum Uffz.-Anw. ernannt 1.4.44 Oberfeldwebel

Tag der Ernennung zum R. O. A. .... bzw. O. A. ....

Hat — nicht — mit Erfolg — ohne Erfolg —**) an einen Kriegsoffizier-Nachwuchslehrgang

von .... bis .... teilgenommen.

*) Unter Waffengattung ist die Spezialausbildung mit anzugeben (Fliegertruppe — Fliegzeugführer, Beobachter, Fallschirmtruppe — sprigendes Personal, Bodenpersonal / / Flakartillerie — schwere Flak, leichte Flak, Scheinwerfer / Luftnachrichtentruppe — Funker, Fernsprecher.

*) Nichtzutreffendes ist zu streichen.

Efficiency Report for Master Sergeant Helmut Missner (front side) – dated July 5, 1944, on pre-printed form from the Peter Kaiser firm in Düsseldorf, with typed comments.

Zur Beförderung zum Offizier vorgeschlagen am: 5. Juli 1944

Bewährung vor dem Feinde : Einsatz im Osten als Jagdflugzeugführer
(81 Abschüsse)

Auszeichnungen : E.K. 2, E.K. 1, Frontflugspange in Gold, Verwundetenabzeichen in Schwarz, Ehrenpokal für besondere Leistungen im Luftkrieg, Deutsches Kreuz in Gold, am 1.7.1944 zum Ritterkreuz des Eisernen Kreuzes eingereicht.

Bestrafungen : 4 Tage gelinden Arrest

Kurze Beurteilung : Geistig sehr rege, von schneller Auffassungsgabe, körperlich kräftig.
Ruhiger besonnener, anständiger und ehrlicher Charakter.
Sehr zuvorkommend und kameradschaftlich.
Guter Vorgesetzter mit guten militärischen Auftreten und Kenntnissen.

Uk-Stellung während des Krieges :

von — bis —

Kurze Angabe des Grundes :

Befehlsstelle, den 5.Juli 1944
(Ort und Datum)

Kittel
(Unterschrift)
Leutnant und Staffelkapitän.

Bestell-Nr P 5

Nr. 398 — Peter KAISER, Wehrmachtformularverlag. — Düsseldorf, Sternstr., 63a. Tel. 384.38. — Brüssel, rue Mont.-aux-Herbes Potagères, 12. Tél. 17.21.80 - 18.09.51. — Paris, rue Taitbout, 3. Tél. Prov. 7830. — Den Haag, Bezuidenhout, 17. Tel. 17129

Efficiency Report for Master Sergeant Helmut Missner (back side) – signed by Second Lieutenant Otto Kittel, Commander, 3rd Squadron, 54th Fighter Wing.

Friedrich-Karl Müller

Fighter Pilot

"Possesses a lot of youthful élan and can be very enthusiastic."

Lieutenant Colonel Friedrich-Karl "Tutti" Müller was born on December 25, 1916 at Berlin-Lichterfelde, Brandenburg. He entered the *Luftwaffe* on October 17, 1936 and was promoted to second lieutenant on December 1, 1938. At the outbreak of World War II, Müller was serving with the 8th Squadron, 53rd Fighter Wing "Ace of Spades" (*Jagdgeschwader 53 "Pikas"*). Starting quickly, by the end of the French Campaign, Second Lieutenant Müller had accumulated eight victories, including his first – a French Curtiss Hawk 75 fighter – northwest of Amiens, France on May 27, 1940. In a foreshadowing of things to come, this included downing three French Morane-Saulnier MS 406 fighters in ten minutes on June 10, 1940. Müller flew in the Battle of Britain with the staff squadron of the 53rd Fighter Wing, adding two RAF Spitfires – on September 5 and 6 – to his tally during the aerial battles over England. Müller was promoted to first lieutenant on September 1, 1940. His Messerschmitt Me 109E-4 crashed into the sea on September 15, 1940, but Müller was rescued safely. The 53rd Fighter Wing then transferred east for the invasion of the Balkans and Russia, and scores began to climb. On July 30, 1941, Müller shot down an I-17 fighter, his 17th victory and the 200th enemy aircraft that the 3rd Group had scored in the Russian campaign. On September 9, 1941, he recorded his 20th aerial victory, a Russian I-16 fighter. On November 1, 1941, Müller became the 1st Squadron Commander. In the spring of 1942, he led the unit to the Mediterranean theater. Operating from bases in Sicily, Müller claimed three RAF Hurricane fighters shot down over Malta to record his 22nd through 24th victories. In May 1942, the unit relocated back to Russia. In August 1942, Müller claimed 25 victories, including five enemy aircraft shot down on August 12. He shot down a further 35 enemy aircraft from September 1st to 19th, including 6 Il-2 Sturmovik ground-attack aircraft dispatched on September 9 and 5 enemy aircraft destroyed on September 17. Müller downed a further 7 enemy planes on September 18. Flying out of the Pitomnik airfield – just west of Stalingrad – on September 19, he claimed his 100th and 101st kills and was awarded the Knight's Cross of the Iron Cross later that day. Four days later, on September 23, he became the 126th recipient of the Oak Leaves to the Knight's Cross.[23]

On October 15, 1942, Müller's chain of command submitted him for a preferential promotion to captain. Lieutenant Colonel and wing commodore Günther von Maltzahn wrote:[24]

> Open, straight character with vivid, temperamental nature. Possesses a lot of youthful élan and can be very enthusiastic. Due to his uninterrupted operations since the beginning of the war on all fronts, he possesses considerable experience in tactical engagement and air combat, and as most successful fighter pilot of the wing, he was awarded the Oak Leaves to the Knight's Cross of the Iron Cross at the end of September 1942. He has accumulated 100 aerial victories, of which 3 were over England and 3 in the Mediterranean theater. As the most successful fighter pilot of the wing and accomplished squadron commander, he should be given the command of a group and, therefore, he is deemed deserving for preferential promotion to Captain.

On November 8, 1942, Captain Müller assumed command of the 1st Group, 53rd Fighter Wing and led the unit to Tunisia. In the period from November 25, 1942 to April 30, 1943, Müller claimed 12 more victories to raise his score to 115. However, he narrowly escaped injury on January 25, 1943, when his Messerschmitt Me 109G-2 overturned on landing at Bizerte, Tunisia. In early May, suffering nervous and physical exhaustion, he embarked on a long leave from the front, but returned to duty on February 12, 1944 (shortly after receiving the *Luftwaffe* Honor Goblet on December 13, and the German Cross in Gold on February 7), as a major and commander of the 4th Group, 3rd Fighter Wing "Udet" (*Jagdgeschwader 3 "Udet"*), operating in the skies over Germany. He claimed three USAAF four-engine bombers shot down on March 8, 1944 to record his 120th through 122nd victories. On March 24, 1944, Major Müller was appointed Commander of the 3rd Fighter Wing "Udet." Müller led by example: on April 11, he shot down two B-17 Flying Fortresses in four minutes; on April 13, he destroyed two B-17s in five minutes; on April 18, he shot down two B-17s in six minutes; and on April 22, he dispatched two B-24 Liberators – from the 2nd Bomb Division, 8th Air Force – in under one minute.

But, like so many of his comrades in the air, his luck did not hold forever. "Tutti" Müller was killed in a landing accident at Salzwedel, Saxony-Anhalt, on May 29, 1944, when his Messerschmitt Me 109G-6 suddenly stalled at a height of fifty feet. He was posthumously promoted to the grade of lieutenant colonel.

"Tutti" Müller was credited with 140 victories in over 600 combat missions, a sortie-to-victory ratio of about 4.28 to 1. He recorded 53 victories in the skies over the Western Front, including 23 four-engine bombers.[25]

Jagdgeschwader 53 Gefechtstand, den 15. 10. 1942

V o r s c h l a g

zur

b e v o r z u g t e n B e f ö r d e r u n g

für Oberleutnant (Tr.O.) M ü l l e r , Friedrich-Karl

Dienststellung: Staffelkapitän

R.D.A.: 1.9.1940

Beförderungsdaten zu den beiden letzten Offz.-Dienstgraden: Lt. : 1.12.1938 Oblt. : 1.9.1940

Diensteintritt: 17.10.1936

Geburtsdatum: 25.12.1916

Auszeichnung: Eichenlaub zum Ritterkreuz des Eisernen Kreuzes

Begründung und kurze Beurteilung:

Offener, gerader Charakter mit frischem, temperamentvollem Wesen. Besitzt viel jugendlichen Schwung und ist sehr begeisterungsfähig.

Durch seinen ununterbrochenen Einsatz seit Kriegsbeginn an allen Fronten verfügt er über umfangreiche Erfahrungen im taktischen Einsatz und Luftkampf und wurde als erfolgreichster Jagdflieger des Geschwaders Ende September 1942 mit dem Eichenlaub zum Ritterkreuz des Eisernen Kreuzes ausgezeichnet. Er hat insgesamt 100 Luftsiege errungen, davon 3 über England und 3 im Mittelmeerraum.

Oblt. Müller soll als erfolgreichster Jagdflieger des Geschwaders und bewährter Staffelkapitän mit der Führung einer Gruppe beauftragt werden und wird deshalb für würdig befunden, bevorzugt zum Hauptmann befördert zu werden.

Oberstleutnant und Geschwaderkommodore

Mit Pers. Ver. Nr. 539/A bev. zum Hauptm. befördert R.D.A. 24.10.42 (2)

Request for Preferred Promotion for First Lieutenant Friedrich-Karl Müller (one page only) – dated October 15, 1942, on blank paper, with typed comments. Signed by Lieutenant Colonel Günther von Maltzahn, Commodore, 53rd Fighter Wing.

Horst Müller

Bomber Pilot

"Sometimes his temperament appears to be boisterous and blustery."

Captain Horst Müller was born in Berlin on February 23, 1916. He flew 8 combat missions in the 1940 French campaign and 42 missions against England. He received the Iron Cross 2nd Class on May 19, 1940 and the Iron Cross 1st Class on June 3, 1940. He received the *Luftwaffe* Honor Goblet on October 20, 1940 and was wounded in action on November 3, 1940. Müller, a member of the 76th Bomber Wing (*Kampfgeschwader 76*), flew numerous missions, including 8 during the French campaign, 42 over England and 60 in Russia. On December 12, 1942, the acting commander of the 2nd Group, 76th Bomber Wing, submitted an efficiency report on Second Lieutenant Horst Müller. Captain Volprecht Riedesel zu Eisenach, a later Knight's Cross with Oak Leaves winner, wrote in part:[26]

> Second Lieutenant Müller is an officer who is well talented mentally and physically. He is open and decent and unburdened in his expression of opinion. In contact with superiors and comrades, he is modest and always friendly and polite. He is very temperamental and vivid. Sometimes his temperament appears to be boisterous and blustery. As to social behavior, Müller is well educated and skillful. He is well liked by his superiors, comrades and subordinates due to his friendly manner. He is a very good comrade. As to his character, Müller is fundamentally decent and sincere. He possesses very good flying and military education. During missions, he must be called a definite daredevil who attacks his target with ease and without remorse. He remains well thought-out and cautious. His dash has resulted in particularly good successes. He fills his position as a group technical officer very well. In general, he is goal-oriented and patient. However, he tends to start too many things at the same time so that he gets lost in detail. He possesses diligence and skill, which will come in well in each service grade according to his position.
>
> All in all, he is an officer very capable for further development and very promising. Second Lieutenant Müller has proven himself during 8 missions in France, 42 in England and 60 in the Russian campaign; he was wounded on November 3, 1940 and awarded the Iron Cross 2nd Class on May 19, 1940 and the Iron Cross 1st Class on June 3, 1940. On October 20, 1940 he was awarded the *Luftwaffe* Honor Goblet. In his philosophy and conduct in life, Müller is well rooted in National Socialism. Müller appears to be fully suitable for promotion to the next-higher service rank.

He won the German Cross in Gold on March 19, 1942. First Lieutenant Horst Müller won the Knight's Cross of the Iron Cross as a pilot in the 2nd Group, 76th Bomber Wing on May 3, 1942.[27] Horst Müller was killed in action over Sicily on July 13, 1943. The location of his remains is unknown.[28]

II./Kampfgeschwader 76 (Dienststelle, Truppenteil) Gefechtsstand, den 12.2. 19 42

Feldpostnummer L 07 697
Luftgaupostamt Königsberg

Beurteilungsnotiz

über den Leutnant (Tr.O.) Flugzeugführer und techn. Offizier
(Dienstgrad, Dienststellung)

Vor- und Zuname Horst Müller geboren: 23.2.1916

verheiratet / ledig / verwitwet / geschieden (Zutreffendes unterstreichen)

Jetzige Verwendung: (z. B. Staffelkapitän seit . .) Flugzeugführer u. techn.Offz. seit 20.6.41

Eignungsbeurteilung: umseitig

Wie wird jetzige Stelle ausgefüllt? sehr gut

Geeignet zur Beförderung zum nächsthöheren Dienstgrad? ja

Erworbene Lw.-Scheine: E.L.F. II K

Strafen: keine

Verwendungsvorschläge: besondere Eignung, weitere Verwendung)

Gruppen-T.O.

[signature] (Unterschrift)

Hauptmann u.m.d.F.d.Gr.b.
(Dienstgrad und Dienststellung)

Lager-Nr. 3310 Heß, Braunschweig-München

Wenden!

Efficiency Report for Second Lieutenant Horst Müller (front side) – dated February 12, 1942, on pre-printed form from the Hess firm in Braunschweig, with typed comments. Signed at the bottom by Captain Volprecht Riedesel zu Eisenach, acting commander of the 2nd Group, 76th Bomber Wing. Form has a place for a photo, but one was never affixed.

Zusätze zur Beurteilungsnotiz:
(Nur bei Vorlage an höhere Dienststelle)

Leutnant Müller ist ein geistig und körperlich gut veranlagter Offizier. Er ist offen und ehrlich und unbeschwert in seiner Meinungsäusserung. Im Umgang mit Vorgesetzten und Kameraden bescheiden und immer freundlich und höflich. Er ist sehr temperamentvoll und lebhaft. Sein Temperament lässt ihn manchmal rauh und polternd erscheinen.

Gesellschaftlich ist M. wohlerzogen und geschickt. Er ist bei Vorgesetzten, Kameraden und Untergebenen auf Grund seines freundlichen Wesens beliebt. Er ist ein sehr guter Kamerad.

Charakterlich ist Müller grundanständig und aufrichtig.

Er verfügt über eine sehr gute fliegerische und militärische Vorbildung. Einsatzmässig ist er als ein ausgesprochener Draufgänger zu bezeichnen, der sein gestecktes Ziel unbeschwert und ohne Hemmungen angreift. Er bleibt hierbei überlegt und vorsichtig. Sein Draufgängertum hat ihm besonders gute Erfolge eingebracht. Seine Stelle als Gruppen T.O. füllt er sehr gut aus. Im allgemeinen ist er zielstrebig und beharrlich. Er neigt jedoch dazu viel Sachen zugleich anzufangen, um sich dann zu verzetteln. Er verfügt über Anstelligkeit und Geschick, die ihn jeder, seinem Dienstgrad entsprechenden Stellung, gerecht werden lassen wird.

Im Ganzen ein sehr entwicklungsfähiger und viel versprechender Offizier.

Leutnant Müller hat sich in 8 Frankreich-, 42 England- und 60 Russlandeinsätzen bewährt; er wurde am 3.11.1940 verwundet, am 19.5.1940 mit dem Eisernen Kreuz II. Klasse und am 3.6.1940 mit dem Eisernen Kreuz I. Klasse ausgezeichnet. Am 20.10.1940 wurde ihm der "Ehrenbecher für besondere Leistungen im Luftkrieg" verliehen.

M. steht in seiner Einstellung und Lebensführung voll auf dem Boden des Nationalsozialismus.

M. erscheint zur Beförderung zum nächsthöheren Dienstgrad voll geeignet.

Hauptmann u.m.d.F.d.Gr.b.

Nichts hinzuzufügen: Gefechtsstand, den 11.Januar 1943

Hauptmann u. Gruppenkommandeur.

Efficiency Report for Second Lieutenant Horst Müller (back side) – signed twice by Captain Volprecht Riedesel zu Eisenach.

Dr. Maximilian Otte

Stuka Pilot

"In difficult situations, he has demonstrated a high degree of courage and decisiveness."

Major Dr. Maximilian Otte was born September 3, 1910 in Rawitsch/Posen. Otte studied in Bonn, Kiel and Munich and received his law degree. He then joined the German Navy in April 1935, but six months later transferred to the *Luftwaffe*. Commencing in August 1937, he attended various flight schools and then served from July 1, 1939 to February 2, 1940 with the 2nd Group, 1st Destroyer Wing (*Zerstörergeschwader 1*). After a brief stay with the 101st Fighter Group (*Jagdgruppe 101*) during the French campaign, Dr. Otte was assigned to the staff of the 77th Fighter Wing (*Jagdgeschwader 77*), where he won the Iron Cross 2nd Class on June 8, 1940.

On July 17, 1940, the Commodore, 77th Fighter Wing, Lieutenant Colonel Eitel-Friedrich Roediger von Manteuffel submitted the following recommendation concerning Dr. Maximilian Otte, which read in part:[29]

> The enclosed documents are being presented with the request for renewed examination of an adjusted date of rank for First Lieutenant Dr. Maximilian Otte. During the campaign in France, First Lieutenant Dr. Otte was repeatedly detailed by the Wing as liaison officer to the Infantry and excelled due to his particular readiness for combat, his risk taking and exemplary attitude. In difficult situations, he has demonstrated a high degree of courage and decisiveness and has proven to be a very diligent front-line officer.

The acting chief of staff of the 3rd Air District (*Luftgau III*), a Lieutenant Colonel, added: "presented in agreement."

One week later, Otte reported to the 1st Stuka School to begin dive-bomber training. He then joined the 9th Squadron, 2nd Stuka Wing "Immelmann" (*Sturzkampfgeschwader 2 "Immelmann"*) in the Balkans where he flew his first Stuka combat missions, winning the Iron Cross 1st Class on May 1, 1941. Maximilian Otte received the *Luftwaffe* Honor Goblet on January 5, 1942 and the German Cross in Gold on February 4, 1942. He received the Knight's Cross of the Iron Cross on April 5, 1942 as a first lieutenant and pilot in the 9th Squadron, 2nd Stuka Wing "Immelmann," after flying 350 combat missions. Otte assumed command of the 2nd Group, 2nd Stuka Wing "Immelmann" on September 10, 1943. Major Otte became the 433rd recipient of the Oak Leaves to the Knight's Cross on March 24, 1944 as Commander, 2nd Group, 2nd Ground-Attack Wing "Immelmann," after flying his 1,000th combat mission. He was killed in action on May 5, 1944 over Koschniza, Romania, when his Junkers Ju 87 was shot down.[30] Post-war sources credit Otte with flying 1,179 combat missions and state that Otte was shot down four times.[31]

Geheim

Jagdgeschwader 77 Gefechtsstand, 17.7.4o.

Br.B.Nr. 1146/4o geh.

Betr.: Festsetzung des Rangdienstalters Oblt. Dr. O t t e .

19. JUL 1940

54 289/40 g

An

Luftgaukommando III

B e r l i n .

Anliegende Unterlagen werden mit der Bitte um nochmalige Nachprüfung des Rangdienstalters des Oblt. Maximilian Dr. O t t e vorgelegt.

Während des Feldzuges in Frankreich wurde Oblt. Dr. Otte vom Geschwader wiederholt als Verbindungsoffizier zur Infanterie kommandiert und hat sich durch besondere Einsatzfreudigkeit, durch Draufgängertum und vorbildliche Haltung ausgezeichnet. In schwierigen Lagen hat er in hohem Maße Mut und Entschlossenheit gezeigt und sich als ein sehr tüchtiger Frontoffizier erwiesen.

Manteuffel

15401

Request for Renewed Examination of an Adjusted Date of Rank for First Lieutenant Dr. Maximilian Otte (front side) – dated July 17, 1940, on blank paper, with typed comments. Signed by Lieutenant Colonel Eitel-Friedrich Roediger von Manteuffel, Commodore, 77th Fighter Wing. Stamp in red shows the request reached the air district headquarters on July 19.

Geheim!

Luftgaukommando III
Abtlg.IIa (1)Nr.54 289/40 geh.

Berlin-Dahlem den 22.7.40
Hausapp.1280

Reichsluftfahrtministerium
Kurierstelle
24. JUL 1940

R.P.
25. JULI 1940
Nr. 15350/40

Reichsluftfahrtministerium
-LP-
Berlin

befürwortend vorgelegt.

Für das Luftgaukommando
Der Chef des Stabes
I.A.
Reisch
Oberstleutnant

Request for Renewed Examination of an Adjusted Date of Rank for First Lieutenant Dr. Maximilian Otte (back side) – signed by Lieutenant Colonel Reisch, acting for the chief of staff of the 3rd Air District. Red stamp shows that the request reached the *Luftwaffe* Personnel Office on July 25.

Karl-August Paulsen

Bomber Pilot

"He is an officer who, by reason of his great sense of justice, will always be a good superior."

Captain Karl-August Paulsen was born on January 23, 1915 in Stolk, Schleswig-Holstein. He joined the 4th Group, 30th Bomber Wing (*Kampfgeschwader 30*) and was promoted to first lieutenant on January 1, 1942.

On March 5, 1942, the commander of the 4th Group, 30th Bomber Wing, Major Martin Schumann, wrote the following in an efficiency report on First Lieutenant Paulsen:[32]

> **Evaluation of Suitability:** First Lieutenant Paulsen is a slender, neat officer, who is very talented athletically and mentally. He is very calm, retiring, decent, trustworthy and correct. Good understanding of service. He attacks his tasks with great diligence. (Somewhat touchy, with a tendency in this case to being stubborn.) [This sentence was a hand-written addition in ink.] Excellent flyer. He is up to all situations. Due to his experience and his calmness, he makes a very good teacher, who is able to pass on his knowledge to his students. His military know-how is also without criticism. He is an officer who, by reason of his great sense of justice, will always be a good superior. As a subordinate, he is very strict and accommodating. His social manners are immaculate. He is very well liked in his circle of comrades.
>
> **How is the current position being fulfilled?** Very well
>
> **Suitable for promotion to next-higher service grade?** n/a
>
> **Earned Air Force certificates:** *Luftwaffe* Advanced Pilot's Certificate, Instrument flight training certificate
>
> **Punishments:** see evaluation notice [Not attached to the report]
>
> **Recommended suitability for:** (particular aptitude, other uses) Technical officer of a group, later squadron commander.[33]

First Lieutenant Paulsen won the *Luftwaffe* Honor Goblet on January 25, 1943. He received the German Cross in Gold on August 31, 1943. Karl-August Paulsen won the Knight's Cross of the Iron Cross on February 29, 1944 as the Commander, 9th Squadron, 30th Bomber Wing.[34]

IV./Kampfgeschwader 3o
(Dienststelle,Truppenteil)
Feldpost- Nr. L 4o 186
Luftgaupostamt Paris

O.U.,den 5. März 1942

Beurteilungsnotiz

über den Oberleutnant u. Flugzeugführer
(Dienstgrad,Dienststellung)

Vor- und Zuname: Karl August Paulsen geb.: 23.1.1915

Rangdienstalter: 1.1.1942 Dienstalterliste: ......

Verheiratet,ledig,verwitwet,geschieden (Zutreffendes unterstreichen)

Jetzige Verwendung : (z.B.Staffelkapitän seit...) Flugzeugführer

Eignungsbeurteilung: Oberleutnant Paulsen ist ein schlanker, gutaussehender Offizier, der sportlich und geistig sehr gut veranlagt ist. Er ist sehr ruhig und zurückhaltend, anständig, ehrlich, aufrichtig. Gute Dienstauffassung. Er geht an seine Aufgaben mit großem Pflichtbewußtsein heran. Etwas empfindlich, neigt in diesem Falle zur [illegible].

Fliegerisch ausgezeichnet. Er ist allen Lagen gewachsen. Durch seine gute Erfahrung und seine Ruhe stellt er einen sehr guten Lehrer dar, der seine Kenntnisse gut seinen Schülern weitergeben kann.

Sein militärisches Können ist ebenfalls ohne Tadel. Er ist ein Offizier, der auf Grund seines großen Gerechtigkeitssinnes stets ein guter Vorgesetzter sein wird. Als Untergebener ist er sehr stramm und zuvorkommend.

Die gesellschaftlichen Umgangsformen sind einwandfrei. Im Kameradenkreise ist er sehr beliebt.

Wie wird jetzige Stelle ausgefüllt ? sehr gut

Geeignet zur Beförderung zum nächsthöheren Dienstgrad? ---

Erworbene Lw. - Scheine : ELF, Blindfluglehrschein

Strafen : siehe Beurteilungsnotiz

Verwendungsvorschläge : (besondere Eignung,weitere Verwendung)
Technischer Offizier einer Gruppe, später Staffelkapitän.

Durch Offizier geschrieben.

(Unterschrift)

Major und Kommandeur.
(Dienstgrad und Dienststellung)

Efficiency Report for First Lieutenant Karl-August Paulsen (one page only) – dated March 5, 1942, on locally-produced pre-printed form, with typed and one hand-written comment. Photo attached to report. Signed by Major Martin Schumann, Commander, 4th Group, 30th Bomber Wing.

Viktor Petermann

Fighter Pilot

"Of particular note are his cold-bloodedness, dare-devil nature and eagerness for action."

First Lieutenant Viktor Petermann was born on May 26, 1916 at Weipert in the Kaaden region of the Sudetenland. Petermann joined the *Luftwaffe* on July 30, 1939 and was posted to the 53rd Aviation Training Regiment, based at Straubing in East Prussia. On April 1, 1941, Petermann transferred to the 3rd Fighter Training School, based at Märkisch. A few weeks later, he was transferred to Fighter Group Drontheim (*Jagdgruppe Drontheim*) for operational training. In October 1941, he transferred to 2nd Squadron, Supplementary Group, 52nd Fighter Wing (*Ergänzungsgruppe, Jagdgeschwader 52*), the operational training group for the wing. Later, on the staff of the 52nd Fighter Wing, he experienced an accident during takeoff on June 4, 1942. Petermann flew 22 combat missions before claiming his first victory on July 1, 1942, when he shot down a Russian LaGG-3 fighter near Wolokonovka. He followed that with a MiG-1 the following day, as Petermann began to fly as the wingman to the wing commander, Major Herbert Ihlefeld. On August 15, during aerial combat, Petermann rammed a Polikarpov I-153 biplane fighter, but managed to continue flying his damaged aircraft 60 miles before belly-landing back at his base at Mineralyje Wody. Three days later, Petermann overshot a landing and crashed at the same location.

By the end of 1942, Petermann had six victories to his credit. He made a forced landing on January 19, 1943. Early March 1943 found Technical Sergeant Petermann serving with the 5th Squadron, 52nd Fighter Wing. He recorded 18 victories in May, including his 30th victory on May 4 and his 40th victory on May 27. On June 6, he was part of a ground-attack mission that sank one Russian gunboat and forced a second to run aground. That afternoon, Petermann flew a mission over the northern front of the Kuban bridgehead in support of army troops. In aerial combat with Russian aircraft, his Messerschmitt Me 109G-4 was hit in the oil cooler and he made a second belly-land, this one behind Russian lines near Petrowskaja. He successfully evaded capture and returned to his unit three days later. Admitted to the hospital due to exposure, dehydration and exhaustion, he was released on July 20. He had been promoted to second lieutenant on July 1 and had received the German Cross in Gold on July 16.

On June 26, 1943, the acting wing commander wrote a special report on Petermann, detailing his recent accomplishments and recommending him for promotion to be a commissioned officer:[35]

> Technical Sergeant Petermann is a typical fighter pilot. Of particular note are his cold-bloodedness, daredevil nature and eagerness for action. Not even in the most difficult situations does he lose his well-liked humor. Up to now, in hard air battles against a greater-numbered superior enemy, he succeeded in scoring 46 victories. No less noteworthy was his success in numerous ground-attacks due to lots of courage and élan, particularly during the winter defensive battles of 1942/43 and the defensive battles at the Kuban bridgehead.
>
> On June 6th, he was shot down southwest of Petrowskaja and had to make an emergency landing in Russian territory in the swamps. Due to his cold-blooded behavior and initiative, after three days he was able to

fight back to the main line of defense and was rescued by German soldiers. During that time, he joined the Russian columns which marched forward during the night. Bunker lines, machinegun positions, rivers, swamps and bogs were no deterrent for him. Machinegun shots and hand grenades also could not hinder him, and he reached his squadron again on June 9, 1943.

Mentally, Technical Sergeant Petermann is above average with a mature character and healthy philosophy on life. He possesses excellent leadership qualities. Due to his outstanding courage before the enemy and his far above-average mental capabilities and character, I second the promotion to officer in any case.

Petermann claimed his 50th victory on July 26. He received the *Luftwaffe* Honor Goblet on September 9, 1943. On September 10, 1943, Petermann was transferred to the 6th Squadron. His most successful day in the war in the air occurred on September 25, when he shot down a Russian Yak-1 fighter and three Il-2 Sturmoviks in just 23 minutes, raising his total to 59.

On October 1, Petermann participated in the escort of forty Heinkel He 111 twin-engine bombers. On the return journey, his Messerschmitt Me 109G-6 mistakenly received a direct hit from German ground fire, and he received severe wounds to his left arm and wrist and his left foot. With his engine on fire, he decided to bail out, but found his parachute had also been damaged. He managed to belly-land in no-man's land between the front lines, where he was rescued by German troops. However, the wounds to his left arm were so severe that amputation was necessary. Additionally, he lost the fourth toe of his left foot. While recovering in the hospital, Viktor Petermann was awarded the Knight's Cross of the Iron Cross on February 29, 1944 for 60 victories.

From May 15, 1944, he served in a staff role with the *Luftwaffe* Air Ministry in Berlin, but his heart belonged at the front. He persisted with the authorities to allow him to return to flying duties. On July 22 he was posted to the Staff Squadron, of the 3rd Group, 52nd Fighter Wing, and began flying a Me 109 on September 24 with an artificial left arm. Petermann transferred to the 10th Squadron on January 7, 1945 and claimed four victories during March. On March 30, 1945, he transferred to the 7th Fighter Wing (*Jagdgeschwader 7*) and began training on the Messerschmitt Me 262 jet fighter, but returned to the 10th Squadron at Schweidnitz on April 11. Promoted to first lieutenant on May 1, he flew his last mission of the war on May 5. On May 8, American troops captured him at Deutsch Brod in Czechoslovakia (now Havlícev, Czech Republic). They handed him over to the Russians the following day, but he was released from Soviet captivity after three months on July 26, 1945, due to the severity of his previous wounds. After the war, he became a farm laborer in the former East Germany; he later worked as an engineer and technical adviser to the largest producer of farm machinery in East Germany. On retirement, Viktor Petermann lived in Freiburg, Saxony, before passing away there on May 19, 2001. He is buried in the Freiburg *Zentralfriedhof* (Main Section 1 U 3, Row 1, Grave 8).

Victor Petermann was credited with 64 missions in 550 missions, a sortie-to-victory ratio of 8.59 to 1.[36] All his victories were recorded over the Eastern Front.[37]

Stellungnahme der Zwischendienststellen

Jagdgeschwader 52 Im Felde, den 26.6.1943

Fw. P e t e r m a n n ist der Typ eines Jagdfliegers. Kaltblütigkeit, Draufgängertum und Einsatzfreudigkeit zeichnen ihn ganz besonders aus. In schwierigsten Situationen verliert er nicht seinen beliebten Humor. Bis heute konnte er in harten Luftkämpfen mit zahlenmäßig weit überlegenen Gegnern 46 bezeugte Abschüsse erzielen. Nicht minder waren seine Erfolge bei den zahlreichen mit Mut und Schneid geflogenen Tiefangriffen, vor allem während der Winterabwehrschlacht 1942/43 und den Abwehrkämpfen am Kubanbrückenkopf.

Am 6. Juni SW Petrowskaja selbst abgeschossen, mußte er auf russischem Gebiet im Moor notlanden. Nur seiner Kaltblütigkeit und Initiative ist es zu verdanken, daß er sich nach 3 Tagen bis zur HKL durchschlagen konnte und von deutschen Soldaten herausgeholt wurde. Dabei schloß er sich des Nachts vormarschierenden russ. Kolonnen an. Bunkerlinien, M.G.-Stellungen, Flüsse, Sumpf und Moor waren für ihn keine Hindernisse. Auch M.G.-Schüsse und Handgranaten konnten es nicht verhindern, daß P. am 9.6.43 wieder zu seiner Staffel zurückkehrte.

Fw. Petermann ist geistig überdurchschnittlich veranlagt mit ausgereiftem Charakter und gesunder Lebensauffassung. Er besitzt ausgesprochene Führereigenschaften.

Auf Grund seiner hervorragenden Tapferkeit vor dem Feinde und den weit über dem Durchschnitt stehenden geistigen Anlagen und Charaktereigenschaften befürworte ich in jedem Falle die Beförderung zum Offizier.

Major u. stellv. Geschwaderkommodore

Request for Promotion to Officer for Technical Sergeant Viktor Petermann (one page only) – dated June 26, 1943, on blank paper with typed comments. Signed by the acting commodore, 52nd Fighter Wing.

Karl Peters

Bomber Pilot

"Great mental flexibility."

Captain Karl Peters was born January 2, 1914 in Frankfurt/ Main, Hesse. He won the Iron Cross 2nd Class on November 24, 1939 and the Iron Cross 1st Class on September 25, 1940. On April 10, 1941, during the German invasion of Greece, his Messerschmitt Me 110 with the 7th Squadron, 2nd Demonstration Wing (*Lehrgeschwader 2*) crash-landed in Yugoslavia, killing his gunner. Peters received the *Luftwaffe* Honor Goblet on April 20, 1942 as a second lieutenant and pilot and the Operational Flying Clasp for Bombers in Gold on June 5, 1942. He assumed command of the 8th Squadron, 3rd Group (Bombers) of the 1st Demonstration Wing (*Lehrgeschwader 1*) on November 20, 1943. Peters received the German Cross in Gold on February 5, 1944 as a first lieutenant in the 3rd Group, *Lehrgeschwader 1*, which flew Junkers Ju 88s. He served as Commander, 2nd Group (Bombers), *Lehrgeschwader 1* from July 1, 1944 to May 8, 1945.

On January 18, 1945, the chain of command of *Lehrgeschwader 1* completed an officer efficiency report on Karl Peters. Colonel and Wing Commodore Hans Helbig wrote the bulk of the report, with Brigadier General Karl-Eduard Wilke, acting commander of the 2nd Fighter Corps, adding his comments at the end. The report said:[38]

> **Short Evaluation** (Personal values, National Socialist attitude, accomplishments before the enemy, service accomplishments, mental and physical attributes and suitability, infantry experience, when and how obtained)**:** Captain Peters is a mature, experienced person. His mental facilities are far above the average. He is well educated both in military as well as general matters. His service accomplishments mirror his high personal values. During the time since July 1, 1944 he has led his group with clarity and at the same time combined his personal experience with great mental flexibility, a myriad of ideas and sober experience. He has accomplished that his group always presents a clear well-rooted picture which has gained great successes in combat. His purposeful severity with which he enthusiastically leads his troops and all the ground personnel leads to sweeping and firm control.
>
> Within the officer corps he is a recognized leader by his superiors and men under his command and he is a very well-liked comrade. He is enthusiastic in his National Socialist philosophy and understands how to educate the men under his command in this subject.
>
> **Strong Traits:** High personal values with demonstrated self-initiative, exemplary combat willingness, highly developed ability as a flyer.
>
> **Summary Assessment:** Average
> (Above Average, Average, Below Average)
>
> **How well is the current position being fulfilled:** Well fulfilled.
> (Use only: Very well fulfilled, well fulfilled, fulfilled, not fulfilled)
>
> **Suitable for promotion to the next higher service grade:** Not possible as he has too few years of officer service.
>
> **Suitable as:** Initially, Group Commander of a Ju 88 unit; later as the Commander of a Supplemental Group.
>
> **Known to the person submitting this review:** since August 1943.
>
> **Subordinated to the person submitting this review:** since August 1943.

Brigadier General Wilke commented that he agreed with the attached report and supported naming Captain Karl Peters as the group commander of 2nd Group, *Lehrgeschwader 1*.

Captain Karl Peters, who had flown missions over the Mediterranean in Italy in 1944 and on the Western Front in 1944-1945, received the Knight's Cross of the Iron Cross on April 1, 1945 as the commander of the 2nd Group.[39] He survived the war, but died in an auto accident at Montabaur/ Westerwald on December 12, 1954.

Lehrgeschwader 1 , den 18. Januar 1945
Dienststelle, nicht Feldpostnummer

Kriegs-Beurteilung zum 18. Januar 1945
für Offz. ausschl. San.-, Vet.-Offz.
über den

Hauptmann (Kr.) — 1.4.44 — Karl — Peters
Dienstgrad ¹) — R. D. A. (Ordn. Nr.) und Dienstalterliste — Vorname — Name

2.1.1914 — ~~verheiratet, ledig, verwitwet, geschieden~~ — kv
geboren am — (Zutreffendes unterstreichen) — Wehrdiensttauglichkeit ²) (kv, gv Feld, gv H., tropentgl., tropenuntgl.)

Schlosser
Zivilberuf (falls vorhanden)

Gruppenkommandeur m.d.W.d.G.b. — Langendiebach / Hanau Main
jetzige Verwendung seit 4.7.44 — Friedensdienststelle und W. B. K. ³)

Ernennung zum Gruppenkommandeur
Anlaß der Vorlage ⁴)

Deutsche Auszeichnungen des jetzigen Krieges mit Verleihungsdaten und Angabe, ob und zu welchen Auszeichnungen vorgeschlagen: EK 2 am 24.11.39, EK 1 am 25.9.40, Frontfl. Spange in Gold am 5.6.42, Ehrenpokal am 20.4.42, Dt. Kreuz in Gold am 5.2.44
172 Kampfeinsätze (215 Frontflüge) – 15 Kampfeinsätze seit 1.7.44

¹) Genaue Angabe, ob Tr.-Offz., Erg.-Offz., Offz. z. D., Res.-Offz., Kr.-Offz., z.V.-Offz. – ²) In zweifelhaften Fällen neu festzustellen. – ³) Dienststelle, welche Friedensgebührnisse zahlt und zuständiges Wehrbezirkskommando. – ⁴) z. B.: Versetzung zur III./K. G 2, terminmäßige Vorlage zum 1. 5. 43.

Kurze Beurteilung (Persönlichkeitswert, nationalsozialistische Haltung, Bewährung vor dem Feinde, dienstliche Leistungen, geistige und körperliche Anlagen und Eignung, infanteristische Erfahrungen, wann und wo erworben): Hptm. Peters ist eine reife, lebenserfahrene Persönlichkeit. Seine geistigen Anlagen liegen weit über dem Durchschni
Er hat eine gute militärische wie Allgemeinbildung.
Seine dienstlichen Leistungen entsprechen seinem hohen Persönlichkeitswert. Er hat in der Zeit seit dem 1.7.44 seine Gruppe klar ausgerichtet und verband dabei persönliche Erfahrung mit großer geistiger Beweglichkeit, Ideenreichtum und nüchterner Erfahrung. Er hat so erreicht, daß sein Verband trotz schwerer abwehrbedingter Verluste stets ein klares gefestigtes Bild abgibt und dabei im Einsatz gute Erfolge erringt. Hervorzuheben ist seine sinnvolle zweckmäßige Härte, womit er seine Besatzungen und das gesamte Bodenpersonal schwungvoll führt und sicher in der Hand hat.
Dem Offizierkorps ist er ein von Vorgesetzten und Untergebenen anerkannter Führer und sehr beliebter Kamerad.
Er ist durchdrungen von der nationalsozialistischen Weltanschauung und versteht es, seine Untergebenen in diesem Sinne zu erziehen.
Schwache Seiten:
Starke Seiten: Hoher Persönlichkeitswert mit ausgeprägter Eigeninitiative, beispielgebende Einsatzfreude, hohes fliegerisches Können.

Zusammenfassendes Urteil: (über Durchschnitt, Durchschnitt, unter Durchschnitt): Durchschnitt

Wie wird jetzige Stelle ausgefüllt? (Es sind nur die Ausdrücke „sehr gut ausgefüllt", „gut ausgefüllt", „ausgefüllt", nicht ausgefüllt" zu verwenden) Gut ausgefüllt.

Geeignet zur Beförderung zum nächsthöheren Dienstgrad? Steht noch nicht heran, da noch zu wenig Offz.-Dienstjahre.

Lager-Nr. 1278 Heß, Braunschweig-München-Berlin 05 43

Efficiency Report for Captain Karl Peters (front side) – dated January 18, 1945, on pre-printed form from the Hess firm in Braunschweig, with typed comments.

Eignung

für welche nächsthöhere Verwendung [5])? Vorerst weiterhin Kommandeur Ju 88 -Einsatzgruppe.

für welche besondere oder anderweitige Verwendung [6])? Später Kdr. einer Erg.-Gruppe

Vorschlag für Verwendung in nächster Zeit [7])?

Sprachkenntnisse (keine Schulkenntnisse)

a) abgelegte Prüfungen: ------

(z. B.: Dolmetscherprüfung 1. 10. 42)

b) Beherrschung der Sprache:

(z. B.: durch Aufenthalt im Ausland)

Eröffnung zu welchen Punkten, wann, wie (mündlich oder schriftlich) und durch wen? -------

---

Strafen sind mit vollem Straftenor sowie Vermerk über Vollstreckung abschriftlich als Anlage der Kriegsbeurteilung beizuheften.

Dem Beurteilenden **bekannt seit** / **unterstellt seit**) August 1943.

Ausbildung

a) erworbene Scheine: ELF Bl II

(L. F., E. L. F., L. B. usw.)

b) Sonderausbildung:

(z. B. Bild-Offz., Techn. Offz., Meß-Offz., Funk-Drahtnachr.-Offz., W. K. S.)

Helbig
Unterschrift

Oberst und Geschwaderkommodore
Dienstgrad und Dienststellung

Beitrag des Chefs des Generalstabes der vorgesetzten Kommandobehörde (nur bei Genst.-Offz. in Stabsstellungen und zur Dienstleistung zum Generalstab kommandierten Offizieren):

Zusätze vorgesetzter Dienststellen:

Der Kommandierende General des II. Jagdkorps — 25. Januar 1945.

Ich schließe mich vorstehender Beurteilung an und befürworte die Ernennung des Hptm. (Kr.O.) Karl P e t e r s zum Kommandeur der II./L.G.1.

I.V.
Wilke
G e n e r a l m a j o r.

[5]) Gilt für alle Offz., für Truppen-Offz. hinsichtlich Eignung zur Führung des nächsthöheren Verbandes, für Genst.-Offz. hinsichtlich Eignung zum Chef oder Ia, Ic der Luftfl., Flieger-Korps, Flak-Korps, Fl.-Div., Flak-Div., zur Versetzung in den Genst., zur Kommandierung in den Genst.

[6]) z. B.: Höherer Adjutant, Erzieher, Lehrer auf Spezialgebieten, auf Grund von Sprachkenntnissen im Attachédienst; für Genst.-Offz. hinsichtlich Eignung für Verwendung im Quartiermeisterdienst, im Ic-Dienst, im Transportwesen, als Lehrer für Genst.-Lehrgang (Taktik bzw. Qu.-Dienst); besondere Anlagen für Kriegsgeschichte, Wehrwirtschaft.

[7]) z. B.: „noch halbjährige Belassung in bisheriger Stelle" oder „alsbaldige Verwendung als Geschw.-Kommodore".

Efficiency Report for Captain Karl Peters (back side) – signed by Colonel and Commodore, 1st Demonstration Wing, Hans Helbig, and Brigadier General Karl-Eduard Wilke, acting commander of the 2nd Fighter Corps.

Hubert Pölz

Stuka Pilot

"Takes remarks of a general nature too personal."

Captain Hubert Pölz was born in Leonstein, Austria on January 24, 1917. After attending various flight schools, Pölz was assigned to the 6th Squadron, 2nd Stuka Wing "Immelmann" (*Sturzkampfgeschwader 2 "Immelmann"*) in January 1941. He won the Iron Cross 2nd Class and was promoted to second lieutenant on April 12, 1941. The first two years of his combat career were spent in the Mediterranean, where he flew numerous missions against Malta, British forces in North Africa and American forces in Tunisia. On June 24, 1941, he scored a direct hit on the British destroyer *HMS Auckland* north of Tobruk. Pölz's Junkers Ju 87 was hit during the attack and he was forced to make an emergency landing of the burning aircraft. He won the Iron Cross 1st Class on July 16, 1941.

On March 1, 1942, Pölz assumed command of the 6th Squadron, 3rd Stuka Wing (*Sturzkampfgeschwader 3*). Pölz sank a 10,000-ton transport south of Crete on June 14, 1942 (he received the *Luftwaffe* Honor Goblet the following day); he received the German Cross in Gold on October 2, 1942. On April 3, 1943, he was shot down and wounded by American fighters and spent until July 18, 1943 in a hospital.[40] Pölz then transferred to the Russian Front, where he assumed command of the 7th Squadron, 3rd Stuka Wing. His first combat on the Eastern Front was near Orel during the latter stages of the Battle of Kursk. He received the Operational Flying Clasp for Bombers in Gold with Pendant on August 17, 1943 and was promoted to first lieutenant on October 1, 1943. Five days later, Pölz, with eight Stukas from his squadron, sank the Soviet Black Sea Fleet destroyers *Khar'kov*, *Besposhchadnyy* and *Sposobnyy* 100 miles off the Caucasus coast (Pölz is believed to have scored the killing hit on the *Khar'kov*). Hubert Pölz won the Knight's Cross of the Iron Cross on February 5, 1944 as Commander, 7th Squadron, 3rd Ground-Attack Wing (*Schlachtgeschwader 3*), having flown 672 combat missions.

On March 3, 1944, the chain of command in the 3rd Ground-Attack Wing submitted an efficiency report on Hubert Pölz. The acting commander, 3rd Group, Captain Fritz Eyer, wrote:[41]

> **Short Evaluation** (Personal values, National Socialist attitude, accomplishments before the enemy, service accomplishments, mental and physical attributes and suitability, infantry experience, when and how obtained)**:** A personality, which is steeped in fanatic Nationalism, a particularly well-expressed social attitude are what characterize Pölz as an officer and leader who stands far above the crowd. Accommodating in his behavior, truthful and decent in his attitude make him well liked everywhere. Mentally of diverse interests, well read, he understands how to motivate his people in word and deed and to sweep them along. Strict, yet just and caring superior.
>
> **Strong traits:** Passionate pilot. Good unit and troop leader.
>
> **Weak traits:** Takes remarks of a general nature too personal.
>
> **Summarized evaluation:** above average
> (Above Average, Average, Below Average)
>
> **How is the current position being fulfilled:** very well fulfilled.
> (Use only: Very well fulfilled, well fulfilled, fulfilled, not fulfilled)
>
> **Suitable for promotion to next higher service grade?** Yes - Captain
>
> **Suitable:**
> **For which next higher position?** Exchange from the front to the homeland.
>
> **For which particular or other position?** Group commander.
>
> **Known to the person writing this review:** since February 5, 1941.
>
> **Subordinated to the person writing this review:** since January 25, 1944.

Eyer then continued with his hand-written narrative in a block marked "Contribution of the Chief of the General Staff of the higher command:"

> A very capable pilot and squadron leader with energizing eagerness for battle and fresh, yet deliberate daring. Has excelled particularly against the enemy. Knight's Cross winner. A titled landowner, Pölz is deeply rooted in National Socialism. Personal initiative and talent for improvisation are present.

The wing commodore, Lieutenant Colonel Kurt Kuhlmey added: "In agreement with the recommendation and evaluation."

Pölz became the 661st recipient of the Oak Leaves to the Knight's Cross on November 25, 1944 after flying his 1,000th combat mission. On the same day, he was promoted to captain and named as the acting commander of the 1st Group, 151st Ground-Attack Wing (*Schlachtgeschwader 151*). Hubert Pölz drowned in Spain, while on vacation, on January 7, 2002. During the war, Pölz's experiences bordered on the unbelievable: he was shot down four times and wounded three times. He flew 1,055 combat missions, shot down 11 enemy aircraft, sank two destroyers and destroyed 76 tanks.[42]

III./Schlachtgeschwader 3 — Gefechtsstand, den 3.3. 1944

Dienststelle, nicht Feldpostnummer

Kriegs-Beurteilung zum .... 19 ....

für Offz. ausschl. San.-, Vet.-Offz.

über den

Oblt. (Kr.O.)	1.9.41 (D)	Hubert	Pölz
Dienstgrad [1]	R. D. A. (Ordn. Nr.) und Dienstalterliste	Vorname	Name

25.1.1917 — geboren am

verheiratet, <u>ledig</u>, verwitwet, geschieden (Zutreffendes unterstreichen)

kv. — Wehrdiensttauglichkeit [2] (kv, gv Feld, gv H., tropentgl., tropenuntgl.)

Techniker — Zivilberuf (falls vorhanden)

Staffelkapitän seit 28.9.43 — jetzige Verwendung seit

Fl.H.Kdtr.Wertheim/Main, Linz/Donau — Friedensdienststelle und W. B. K. [3]

Bevorzugte Beförderung zum nächsthöheren Dienstgrad mit Wirkung vom 1.4.1944 — Anlaß der Vorlage [4]

Deutsche Auszeichnungen des jetzigen Krieges mit Verleihungsdaten und Angabe, ob und zu welchen Auszeichnungen vorgeschlagen: 12.4.41 E.K.II, 16.7.41 E.K.I, 10.6.42 Ehrenpokal, 7.8.43 Deutsches Kreuz in Gold, 17.8.43 Frontfl.Sp.i.Gold mit Anhänger 20.2.44 Ritterkreuz des Eisernen Kreuzes.

[1] Genaue Angabe, ob Tr.-Offz., Erg.-Offz., Offz. z. D., Res.-Offz., Kr.-Offz., z.V.-Offz.
[2] In zweifelhaften Fällen neu festzustellen.
[3] Dienststelle, welche Friedensgebührnisse zahlt und zuständiges Wehrbezirkskommando.
[4] z. B : Versetzung zur III./K. G. 2, terminmäßige Vorlage zum 1. 5. 43.

Kurze Beurteilung:
(Persönlichkeitswert, nationalsozialistische Haltung, Bewährung vor dem Feinde, dienstliche Leistungen, geistige und körperliche Anlagen und Eignung, infanteristische Erfahrungen, wann und wo erworben)

[illegible]

Starke Seiten:

Vollkommener Flugzeugführer. Guter Menschen- und Truppenführer.

Schwache Seiten:

Nimmt Beanstandungen allgemeiner Art zu persönlich.

Zusammenfassendes Urteil:
(über Durchschnitt, Durchschnitt, unter Durchschnitt)

Über Durchschnitt

Wie wird die jetzige Stelle ausgefüllt?
(Es sind nur die Ausdrücke „sehr gut ausgefüllt", „gut ausgefüllt", „ausgefüllt", „nicht ausgefüllt" zu verwenden)

Sehr gut ausgefüllt.

Geeignet zur Beförderung zum nächsthöheren Dienstgrad?

Ja. Hauptmann.

Lager-Nr. 1278 Heß, Braunschweig-München-Berlin 07 43

Efficiency Report for First Lieutenant Hubert Pölz (front side) – dated March 3, 1944, on pre-printed form from the Hess firm in Braunschweig, with typed and hand-written comments.

Eignung
für welche nächsthöhere Verwendung [5])?
für welche besondere oder anderweitige Verwendung [6])?
Vorschlag für Verwendung in nächster Zeit [7])?

[illegible handwriting]

Sprachkenntnisse (keine Schulkenntnisse)
a) abgelegte Prüfungen:
(z. B.: Dolmetscherprüfung 1. 10. 42)
b) Beherrschung der Sprache:
(z. B.: durch Aufenthalt im Ausland)

Keine

Eröffnung zu welchen Punkten, wann, wie (mündlich oder schriftlich) und durch wen?

Keine

Strafen
sind mit vollem Straftenor sowie Vermerk über Vollstreckung abschriftlich als Anlage der Kriegsbeurteilung beizuheften.

Keine

Dem Beurteilenden **bekannt seit** 5. II. 1941
unterstellt seit 25. I. 1944

Ausbildung
a) erworbene Scheine: L. F.
(L. F., E. L. F., L. B. usw.)
b) Sonderausbildung:
(z. B. Bild.-Offz., Techn. Offz., Meß-Offz., Funk-Drahtnachr.-Offz., W. K. S.)

[signature] .... Unterschrift

Hauptmann u. Gruppenkommandeur. m.d.W.d.G.b. .... Dienstgrad und Dienststellung

Beitrag des Chefs des Generalstabes der vorgesetzten Kommandobehörde:
(nur bei Genst.-Offz. in Stabsstellungen und zur Dienstleistung zum Generalstab kommandierten Offizieren)

[illegible handwriting]

Zusätze vorgesetzter Dienststellen:

Mit Vorschlag und Beurteilung einverstanden.

[signature]

Oberstleutnant und Geschwaderkommodore.

[5]) Gilt für alle Offz., für Truppen-Offz. hinsichtlich Eignung zur Führung des nächsthöheren Verbandes, für Genst.-Offz. hinsichtlich Eignung zum Chef oder Ia, Ic der Luftfl., Flieger-Korps, Flak-Korps, Fl.-Div., Flak-Div., zur Versetzung in den Genst., zur Kommandierung in den Genst.

[6]) z. B.: Höherer Adjutant, Erzieher, Lehrer auf Spezialgebieten, auf Grund von Sprachkenntnissen im Attachédienst; für Genst.-Offz. hinsichtlich Eignung für Verwendung im Quartiermeisterdienst, im Ic-Dienst, im Transportwesen, als Lehrer für Genst.-Lehrgang (Taktik bzw. Qu.-Dienst); besondere Anlagen für Kriegsgeschichte, Wehrwirtschaft.

[7]) z. B.: „noch halbjährige Belassung in bisheriger Stelle" oder „alsbaldige Verwendung als Geschw.-Kommodore".

Efficiency Report for First Lieutenant Hubert Pölz (back side) – signed by the acting commander, 3rd Group, 3rd Ground-Attack Wing, Captain Fritz Eyer, and by Lieutenant Colonel Kurt Kuhlmey, Commodore, 3rd Ground-Attack Wing.

Dietrich Puttfarken

Bomber Pilot

"Sometimes he is a little too fast in making judgments and remarks."

Major Dietrich Puttfarken was born in Hamburg on April 30, 1920. He entered the *Luftwaffe* in November 1938 and was assigned on August 24, 1940 to the 1st Group, 51st Bomber Wing "Edelweiss" (*Kampfgeschwader 51 "Edelweiss"*), when he began flying missions against England in the Battle of Britain. On November 11, 1940, the chain of command for Second Lieutenant Dietrich Puttfarken submitted an efficiency report on him. Captain and Commander of the 1st Group, 51st Bomber Wing, Kurt von Greiff, wrote:[43]

> **Fitness Assessment:** Decent young officer who, presumably due to his early marriage, became more mature and independent than what is expected at his age. However, sometimes his naïve concepts show that his development has in no way been concluded. Must become more genuine and learn not to see everything from only his own standpoint. Mentally well talented. Shows initiative and his own thinking. However, sometimes he is a little too fast in making judgments and remarks. Strives to fill his present disparities in military and aviation areas, which are due to his accelerated training. His appearance at the front and his presentation of training material are correct and defined, but he must still become smoother. His talents as a pilot, which are quite good sometimes, tempt him to dare too much so that supervision is necessary. Controls the Ju 88 in instrument-flying day and night under not too difficult conditions. During his first combat missions against the enemy, he excelled due to his eagerness, vigilance and flight knowledge. A well liked comrade. Well mannered in social circles. Lieutenant Puttfarken is deeply and convincingly rooted in National Socialistic ideology. He is able to teach this philosophy and to pass on National Socialist thinking. Fulfills his position.

On February 1, 1941, Lieutenant Colonel and *Geschwader* Commodore Bruno Schulz-Heyn, simply added, "In agreement." Schultz-Heyn revisited the report on August 8, 1941 and again limited his comments to, "Nothing to be added."

On June 26, 1942, Colonel Paul Koester, the *Geschwader* Commodore, remarked, "Nothing to be added. [Puttfarken] was promoted to First Lieutenant on April 1, 1942."

Puttfarken received the *Luftwaffe* Honor Goblet on December 7, 1941 and the German Cross in Gold on July 28, 1942. On October 7, 1942, Dietrich Puttfarken won the Knight's Cross of the Iron Cross as a pilot in the 1st Squadron, 51st Bomber Wing. On November 21, 1942, he assumed command of the 11th Squadron, 51st Bomber Wing. In this capacity, he continued to fly missions on the Eastern Front, to include many anti-partisan operations. On March 25, 1944, Puttfarken assumed command of the 5th Squadron, 51st Bomber Wing and began flying long-range night-fighter missions over England, flying a Messerschmitt Me 410A-1. On the night of April 11-12, 1944, he shot down three British aircraft (a Spitfire, a Mosquito and a Stirling III bomber) over England. Dietrich Puttfarken was killed in action conducting intruder operations over England on the night of April 22-23, 1944. Prior to his death that night, he shot down two American B-24 Liberators of the USAAF's 2nd Bomb Division, returning from a mission bombing Hamm, Germany. Officially listed as missing in action (his plane was probably seriously damaged by return fire from the B-24s), his body – and that of his radio operator, Master Sergeant Willi Lux – was never found and presumed lost in the North Sea. Puttfarken was posthumously promoted to major.

During the war, Dietrich Puttfarken flew 269 combat missions and destroyed 30 aircraft on the ground, destroyed three key bridges over the Don River and sank an enemy submarine. He was credited with five nighttime aerial victories.[44]

I./Kampfgeschwader 51 .... O.U. , 11. Nov. 194o

(Dienststelle, Truppenteil)

Feldpostnummer: L 26464

Luftgaupostamt Paris

Lichtbild

Beurteilungsnotiz

über

den Leutnant und Staffeloffizier

(Dienstgrad, Dienststellung)

Dietrich Puttfarken geb.: 3o. 4. 192o

(Vor- und Zuname)

<u>Verheiratet</u>, ledig, verwitwet, geschieden (Zutreffendes unterstreichen)

Jetzige Verwendung: (z. B. Staffelkapitän seit) Flugzeugführer

(Eignungsbeurteilung nächste Seite)

Efficiency Report for Second Lieutenant Dietrich Puttfarken (first side) – dated November 11, 1940, on pre-printed form, with typed and hand-written comments.

Eignungsbeurteilung:

Anständiger junger Offizier,der wohl durch seine früh= zeitige Heirat gereifter und selbständiger wurde als sonst in seinem Alter vorauszusetzen ist.Gelegentlich naive Auffassun= gen zeigen jedoch,dass seine Entwicklung keineswegs abgeschlos= sen ist.Muss noch natürlicher werden und nicht alles von sich aus sehen.Geistig gut veranlagt.Zeigt Initiative und eigene Gedanken.Mitunter jedoch noch etwas zu vorschnell in Ansicht und Äusserungen.

Bemüht sich die vorhandenen Lücken auf militärischem und fliegerischem Gebiet,die in seiner schnellen Ausbildung begründet sind,auszufüllen.Sein Auftreten vor der Front und seine Unterichtserteilung sind korrekt und bestimmt,müssen aber noch gewandter werden.

Seine recht guten fliegerischen Anlagen verführen ihn gelegentlich dazu,sich zuviel zuzutrauen,sodass hier eine Be= treuung erforderlich ist.Beherrscht die Ju 88 im Blindflug bei Tag und Nacht unter nicht allzu schwierigen Verhältnissen.Hat sich bei seinen ersten Feindflügen durch seine Einsatzfreudig= keit,Umsicht und fliegerisches Können ausgezeichnet.

Gern gesehener Kamerad.Gesellschaftlich wohlerzogen.

Leutnant Puttfarken steht innerlich und überzeugt auf dem Boden der nationalsozialistischen Weltanschauung.Er ist befähigt weltanschaulichen Unterricht zu erteilen und das na= tionalsozialistische Gedankengut zu übermitteln.

Füllt seine Stelle aus.

Efficiency Report for Second Lieutenant Dietrich Puttfarken (second side).

Wie wird jetzige Stelle ausgefüllt? Füllt seine Stelle aus.

Geeignet zur Beförderung zum nächsthöheren Dienstgrad? –

Erworbene Lw.-Scheine: ELFS, Bl.Flug II K

Strafen: –

Verwendungsvorschläge: –

(Unterschrift)

Gefechtsstand, den 3. 2. 1941

(Dienstgrad und Dienststellung)

Hauptmann und Kommandeur der I./K.G. 51

Zusätze zur Beurteilungsnotiz: (Nur bei Vorlage an höhere Dienststellen)

Einverstanden.

Gefechtsstand, 20. 2. 41.

Anläßlich der Übergabe des Geschwaders:

Nichts hinzuzufügen.

Gefechtsstand, den 3o.8.41.

Oberstleutnant u. Geschwaderkommodore

Efficiency Report for Second Lieutenant Dietrich Puttfarken (third side) – signed by Captain and Commander, 1st Group, 51st Bomber Wing, Kurt von Greiff, and twice by Lieutenant Colonel Bruno Schulz-Heyn, Commodore, 51st Bomber Wing.

Zusatz zur Beurteilung vom 3o.8.1941:

Nichts hinzuzufügen. Wurde am 1.4.42 zum Oblt. befördert.

Gefechtsstand, den 26. 6. 1942

Koester.

Oberst und Geschwaderkommodore.

Efficiency Report for Second Lieutenant Dietrich Puttfarken (fourth side) – signed by Colonel Paul Koester, Commodore, 51st Bomber Wing.

Rudolf Rademacher

Fighter Pilot

"Somewhat disinterested and stubborn."

Second Lieutenant Rudolf "Rudi" Rademacher was born on June 13, 1913 in Lüneburg. He served in the German Army from November 1, 1934 to October 12, 1935 and then resumed his civilian career as a butcher – a trade that was held against him in his quest to become an officer. Rademacher joined the *Luftwaffe* on August 28, 1939 just before the outbreak of the war. After attending flight school from June 5, 1940 to May 30, 1941, he was finally assigned to the 3rd Squadron, 54th Fighter Wing "Green Hearts" (*Jagdgeschwader 54 "Grünherz"*) on December 1, 1941 and scored his first air victory (an Il-2 Sturmovik) on his fifth combat mission on January 9, 1942 northeast of Ostkaja. By February 12, 1942, Rademacher had earned the *Luftwaffe* Flying Clasp for Fighters in Bronze. On February 25, he shot down a Curtiss P-40; he would add another P-40 on March 5. He received the Iron Cross 2nd Class on March 22, 1942; on April 11, 1942, he earned the *Luftwaffe* Flying Clasp for Fighters in Silver. He earned the Iron Cross 1st Class on May 20, and the *Luftwaffe* Flying Clasp for Fighters in Gold on May 23. Rademacher won the *Luftwaffe* Honor Goblet on October 19, 1942. By the end of the year, he had achieved 22 victories. On March 1, 1943, Rademacher was reassigned to the 1st Squadron. He received the German Cross in Gold shortly thereafter, on April 30, 1943. On July 5, 1943, Rademacher shot down 7 enemy aircraft, but later missed four months of combat due to illness.

On September 16, 1943, Master Sergeant Rademacher's chain of command submitted him for promotion to wartime officer due to bravery in the face of the enemy. First Lieutenant Walter Nowotny wrote:[45]

> The squadron requests the promotion of Master Sergeant Rudi Rademacher to officer (during wartime) due to his courage against the enemy:
>
> **Reason for consideration:** Master Sergeant Rademacher is an old, experienced fighter pilot with an open, honest and well-grounded character who, by reason of his soldierly bearing, his military and flying knowledge and achievement, his above average intellectual talent and his teacher and leader characteristics, is without hesitation suitable to be an officer. Rademacher is well rooted in National Socialist philosophy and is able to evaluate and pass on his National Socialist thinking. He possesses his own initiative and a talent for improvisation. Physically, he is tall, strong, tough and has stamina. He has infantry experience from his peacetime service in the Army. He has achieved 57 shoot-downs and was awarded the German Cross in Gold on March 25, 1943. He has achieved excellent results in ground-attack and fighter-bomber missions.
>
> Master Sergeant Rademacher was already an officer candidate in the Army, but by reason of his civilian occupation [butcher], he was found unsuitable as an officer candidate for other than service reasons by a narrow-minded regimental commander and stricken from the officer candidate list. Due to this removal, he has felt let down and changed his attitude towards becoming an officer. This caused him to become somewhat disinterested and stubborn, but with proper leadership and guidance, he will be brought back to the correct attitude concerning the occupation of an officer, which is still within him.

The wing commodore, Hubertus von Bonin, writing five days later, said:

> As to his character, Master Sergeant Rademacher is without question a soldier who has excelled and has demonstrated exemplary accomplishments against the enemy. He will know how to rid himself of the described weaknesses without fail so that he will become a good squadron officer. The wing requests that Technical Sergeant Rademacher be commissioned an officer due to his courage against the enemy.

Rademacher resumed flying at the end of the year and reached the 61 victory mark. In 1944, he raised this total to 76 before being assigned to the 1st Squadron, Supplemental Group North (*Ergänzungsgruppe Nord*), an operational training unit, on September 1, 1944, as a flight instructor. He promptly shot down 4 four-engine bombers and 1 P-47 Thunderbolt. On September 18, he was severely wounded in action attacking a formation of bombers and had to bail out of his stricken Focke-Wulf 190A-8. Rudolf Rademacher received the Knight's Cross of the Iron Cross on September 30, 1944 with a victory total of 81.

In January 1945, Rademacher transferred to the 11th Squadron, 7th Fighter Wing (*Jagdgeschwader 7*) and began training with the Messerschmitt Me 262 jet fighter. He achieved 16 air victories in this aircraft – the highest total in a jet by any *Luftwaffe* fighter pilot. These included a Spitfire, 5 B-24 Liberator bombers, 3 P-51 Mustangs and 5 B-17 Flying Fortresses.[46]

During the war, Rademacher flew 500 combat missions and shot down 97 enemy aircraft, including 16 four-engine bombers. He claimed a further 23 victories, but had no witness to make these official. During his service in the 1st Squadron, 54th Fighter Wing, Rudi Rademacher was a member of the most famous flight in the *Luftwaffe*, composed of First Lieutenant Walter Nowotny, Master Sergeant Anton Döbele, Master Sergeant Karl Schnörrer and Rademacher, which shot down 450 enemy aircraft in Russia. After the war, he could not get flying out of his blood; on June 13, 1953, Rudi Rademacher died in a glider accident near Lüneburg.[47]

1.Staffel
I./Jagdgeschwader 54.

O.U., den 16.9.1943

Betr.: Antrag auf Beförderung des Ofw. Rudi R a d e m a c h e r zum Kriegsoffizier wegen Tapferkeit vor dem Feinde.

An
I./Jagdgeschwader 54.

Die Staffel bittet um Beförderung des Ofw. Rudi Rademacher zum Kriegsoffizier wegen Tapferkeit vor dem Feinde:

Begründung: Oberfeldwebel Rademacher ist ein alter, erfahrener Jagdflieger mit offenem, ehrlichem und gefestigtem Charakter, der auf Grund seiner soldatischen Haltung, seiner militärischen und fliegerischen Kenntnisse und Leistunge seiner überdurchschnittlichen geistigen Veranlagung, seine Erzieher-und Führereigenschaften uneingeschränkt zum Offizier geeignet ist. Rademacher steht fest auf dem Boden der nationalsozialistischen Weltanschauung und ist jederzeit in der Lage, das nationalsozialistische Gedankengut zu verwerten und weiter-zuvermitteln. Er besitz viel Eigeninitiative und Improvisationstalent. Er ist körperlich gross, kräftig, zäh und ausdauernd. Infanteristische Erfahrungen besitzt Rademacher aus seiner friedenmässigen Ausbildung im Reichsheer. Er errang bisher 57 Abschüsse und wurde am 25.3.43 mit dem Deutschen Kreuz in Gold ausgezeichnet. Besonders grosse Erfolge errang er durch zahlreiche Tiefangriffe und Jabo-Einsätze.

Ofw. Rademacher war schon beim Heer R.O.A., wurde abe auf Grund seines Berufes von einem engstirnigen Regimentskommandeur als ausserdienstlich zum R.O. ungeeignet von der R.O.A.-Liste gestrichen. Auf Grund dieser Streichung fühlte er sich herabgesetzt und änderte seine Einstellung zum Offiziersberuf. Er ist dadurch etwas gleichgültig und stur geworden, wird aber bei geeigneter Führung und Anleitung rasch zur richtigen Einstellung dem Offiziersberuf gegenüber, die so wieso noch in ihm liegt, zurückgeführt werden.

Oberleutnant u. Staffelkapitän

b.w.

Efficiency Report for Master Sergeant Rudolf Rademacher (front side) – dated September 16, 1943, and signed by First Lieutenant Walter Nowotny, Commander, 1st Squadron, 54th Fighter Wing.

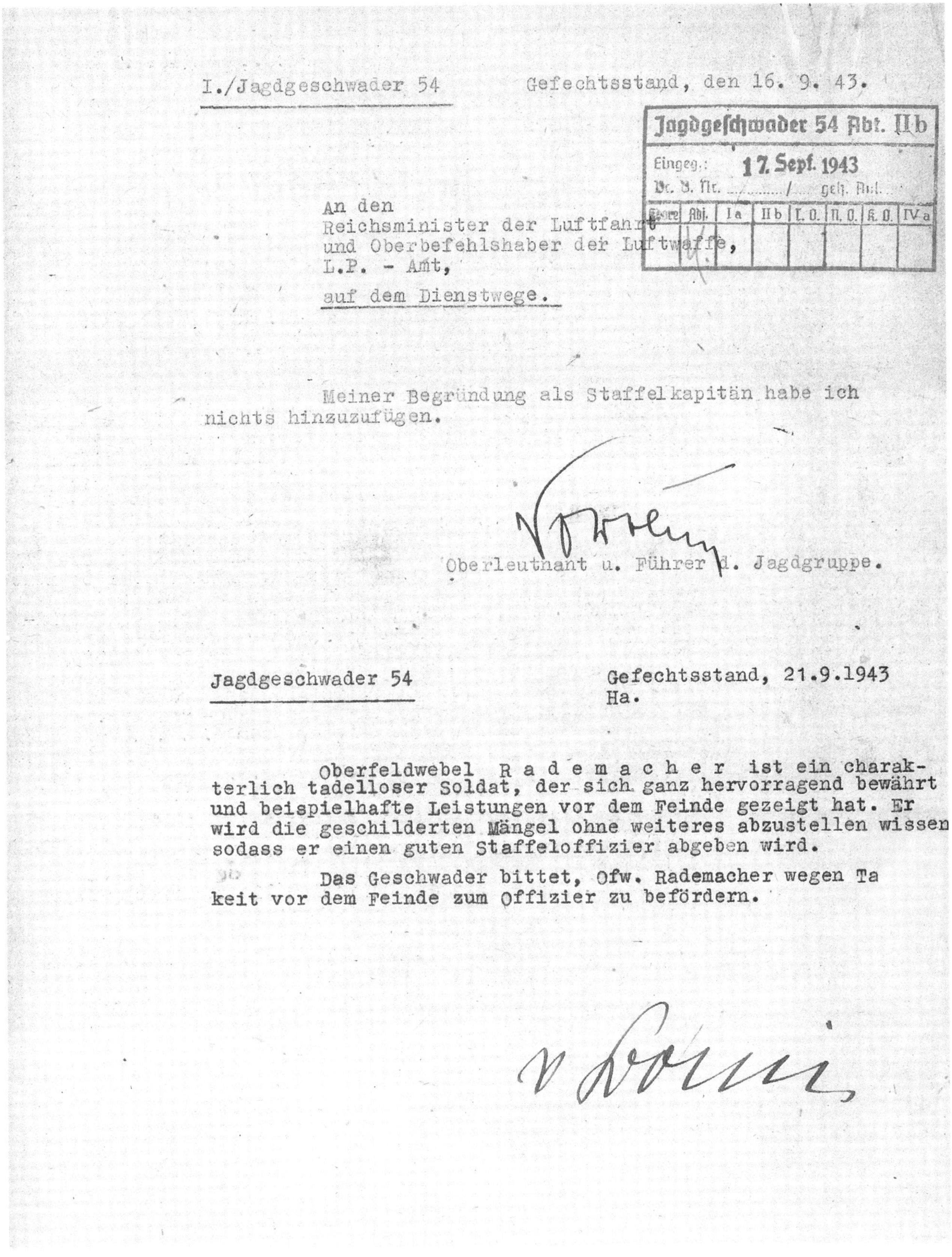

I./Jagdgeschwader 54 Gefechtsstand, den 16. 9. 43.

Jagdgeschwader 54 Abt. IIb
Eingeg.: 17. Sept. 1943
Br. B. Nr. ..../...... geh. Anl. ....

Kdre	Adj.	Ia	IIb	T.O.	N.O.	K.O.	IVa

An den
Reichsminister der Luftfahrt
und Oberbefehlshaber der Luftwaffe,
L.P. - Amt,
auf dem Dienstwege.

Meiner Begründung als Staffelkapitän habe ich nichts hinzuzufügen.

Oberleutnant u. Führer d. Jagdgruppe.

Jagdgeschwader 54 Gefechtsstand, 21.9.1943
Ha.

Oberfeldwebel R a d e m a c h e r ist ein charakterlich tadelloser Soldat, der sich ganz hervorragend bewährt und beispielhafte Leistungen vor dem Feinde gezeigt hat. Er wird die geschilderten Mängel ohne weiteres abzustellen wissen sodass er einen guten Staffeloffizier abgeben wird.

Das Geschwader bittet, Ofw. Rademacher wegen Ta keit vor dem Feinde zum Offizier zu befördern.

v Bonin

Efficiency Report for Master Sergeant Rudolf Rademacher (front side) – signed again by Nowotny and Hubertus von Bonin, Commodore, 54th Fighter Wing.

Hans Roehrig

Fighter Pilot

"Very good athlete."

Captain Hans Roehrig was born on November 4, 1919 at Hindenburg in Silesia. He was assigned to the 3rd Squadron, 210th Test Group (*Erprobungsgruppe 210*), a special combat test group, on September 23, 1940. He flew several fighter-bomber missions over England and, according to one source, recorded five aerial victories during this time.[48] On May 1, 1941, Roehrig transferred to the 3rd Squadron, 53rd Fighter Wing "Ace of Spades" (*Jagdgeschwader 53 "Pikas"*), as the *Luftwaffe* prepared for the upcoming Russian campaign. On July 4, 1941, he was injured when he crashed his Messerschmitt Me 109F-2 on take-off and did not record his initial victory with that unit until July 25, when he shot down a Russian DB-3 twin-engine bomber. By the time the 1st Group, 53rd Fighter Wing left Russia in late 1941, Roehrig had added a further two victories to his tally. Roehrig then relocated with the 3rd Squadron to the Mediterranean theater, and from bases in Sicily, he flew missions over British-held Malta.

In May 1942, the 1st Group once again moved to the Eastern Front and once again Roehrig hit a patch of bad luck. On June 30, 1942, Roehrig suffered minor injuries from glass splinters when his Messerschmitt Me 109F-4 was hit in the cockpit area during aerial combat, but was able to bring his aircraft safely back to his airfield at Kolpna. He was shot down again in aerial combat with Russian fighters on August 6, bailed out of his stricken Messerschmitt Me 109G-2, and was promptly shot at by Russian fighters while descending in his parachute. He landed unhurt and returned to his unit. Roehrig recorded his 10th aerial victory on August 20. In September, Roehrig finally hit his stride, recording 39 victories during the month. They included three victories – including 2 Il-2 Sturmovik ground-attack aircraft – on September 8, 3 Il-2 Sturmoviks on September 9, 3 fighters on September 12, 3 more fighters on September 18, 4 Yak-1 fighters on September 19, 5 fighters on September 20 and 3 Yak-1 fighters on September 23. In late September 1942, the 1st Group, 53rd Fighter Wing again relocated to the Mediterranean theater, where Second Lieutenant Roehrig was awarded the Knight's Cross of the Iron Cross on October 2, 1942. Roehrig quickly added two further victories to his total, when he shot down two RAF Spitfire fighters on October 12 in only one minute of combat. He received the *Luftwaffe* Honor Goblet on October 26, 1942. In November 1942, he was appointed the commander of the 9th Squadron, 53rd Fighter Wing. He successfully led the unit during the campaigns in Tunisia and Sicily, recording his 60th aerial victory on January 28, 1943 and being promoted to first lieutenant on February 1, 1943. He shot down his first four-engine bomber, a USAAF B-17 Flying Fortress, over the Straits of Messina on June 25, for his 68th victory.

In the latter half of June, acting commander, 3rd Group, 53rd Fighter Wing, Captain Franz Götz, wrote a short evaluation report on First Lieutenant Roehrig. In it, Götz stated:[49]

> **Fitness Evaluation:** Of short, strongly-trained stature. Very good athlete. Sincere character with humor, liveliness and fresh spirit. Excellent, experienced fighter pilot. 67 victories in the air. Leads his squadron with vigilance and courage. Good troop leader with unquestionable military general knowledge. Immaculate education and social behavior.
>
> **How has the current position been fulfilled?** Very well!
>
> **Suitable for promotion to the next higher service grade?** Suitable without hesitation.

It would be his final report. Hans Roehrig recorded his last victories, the 74th and 75th, on July 11, 1943, when he shot down two USAAF P-38 Lightning twin-engine fighters over Sicily. On July 13, 1943, Roehrig led a mission, escorting Junkers Ju 52 transport aircraft to drop German *Fallschirmjäger* on the Catania plains in Sicily, when RAF Spitfire fighters intercepted the formation. Hans Roehrig failed to return from the mission in his Messerschmitt Me 109G-4; his body was never found. He was posthumously promoted to the grade of captain. Hans Roehrig was credited with 75 victories. He recorded 56 victories over the Eastern Front, including 12 Il-2 Sturmoviks. Of his 19 victories recorded over the Western Front, one was a four-engine bomber and six were P-38 Lightnings.[50]

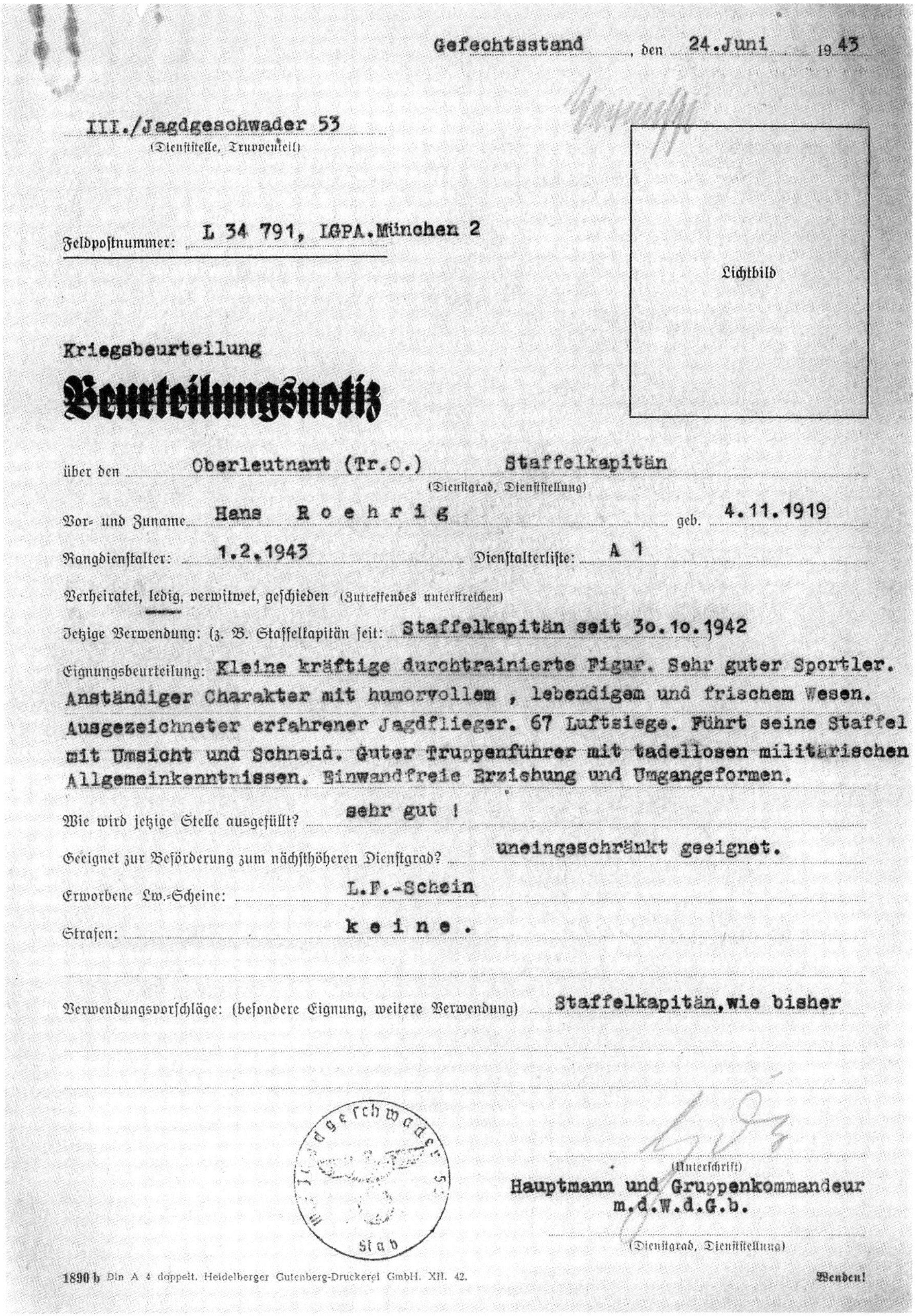

Gefechtsstand, den 24.Juni 1943

III./Jagdgeschwader 53
(Dienststelle, Truppenteil)

Feldpostnummer: L 34 791, LGPA.München 2

Lichtbild

Kriegsbeurteilung

Beurteilungsnotiz

über den Oberleutnant (Tr.O.) Staffelkapitän
(Dienstgrad, Dienststellung)

Vor- und Zuname Hans Roehrig geb. 4.11.1919

Rangdienstalter: 1.2.1943 Dienstalterliste: A 1

Verheiratet, ledig, verwitwet, geschieden (Zutreffendes unterstreichen)

Jetzige Verwendung: (z. B. Staffelkapitän seit: Staffelkapitän seit 30.10.1942

Eignungsbeurteilung: Kleine kräftige durchtrainierte Figur. Sehr guter Sportler. Anständiger Charakter mit humorvollem, lebendigem und frischem Wesen. Ausgezeichneter erfahrener Jagdflieger. 67 Luftsiege. Führt seine Staffel mit Umsicht und Schneid. Guter Truppenführer mit tadellosen militärischen Allgemeinkenntnissen. Einwandfreie Erziehung und Umgangsformen.

Wie wird jetzige Stelle ausgefüllt? sehr gut !

Geeignet zur Beförderung zum nächsthöheren Dienstgrad? uneingeschränkt geeignet.

Erworbene Lw.-Scheine: L.F.-Schein

Strafen: keine.

Verwendungsvorschläge: (besondere Eignung, weitere Verwendung) Staffelkapitän, wie bisher

(Unterschrift)

Hauptmann und Gruppenkommandeur
m.d.W.d.G.b.

(Dienstgrad, Dienststellung)

1890 b Din A 4 doppelt. Heidelberger Gutenberg-Druckerei GmbH. XII. 42.

Wenden!

Efficiency Report for First Lieutenant Hans Roehrig (one page only) – dated June 24, 1943, on pre-printed form from the Heidelberger-Gutenberg firm, with typed comments. Signed by Captain Franz Götz, acting commander, 3rd Group, 53rd Fighter Wing. Form has a place for a photo, but one was never affixed.

Herbert Röwer

Bomber Pilot

"Mentally above average, with diverse interests."

Second Lieutenant Herbert Röwer was born June 10, 1918 in Hörne/Halle, Westphalia. He joined the *Luftwaffe* on October 28, 1935. From 1939 to 1941, Technical Sergeant Röwer attended flight schools at Fassberg and Thorn before joining the 2nd Group, 3rd Bomber Wing "Blitz" (*Kampfgeschwader 3 "Blitz"*) on July 10, 1941. Only eight days later, flying a Junkers Ju 88A out of Deblin-Irena, he was forced to bail out of his aircraft during a reconnaissance mission. He won the War Service Cross 2nd Class with Swords on July 1, 1941; the Iron Cross 2nd Class on October 13, 1941; and the Iron Cross 1st Class on January 5, 1942. On January 26, Röwer, flying out of Schatalowka in a Junkers Ju 88, was forced to make an emergency landing between Russian and German lines when both engines failed, but he managed to safely return to friendly positions, where he was awarded the Wound Badge in Black on January 30, 1942. Röwer received the *Luftwaffe* Honor Goblet on July 29, 1942; he won both the Operational Flying Clasp for Bombers in Gold and the Eastern Front Medal on August 6, 1942. Promoted to master sergeant on September 1, 1942, Röwer received the German Cross in Gold on November 1, 1942 as a master sergeant-pilot in the 4th Squadron. On January 1, 1943, Röwer transferred from the 2nd Group to the newly formed 9th Squadron, 3rd Group. In this unit, which specialized in attacking enemy rail assets, he destroyed 59 locomotives, 14 munitions trains as well as 18 enemy tanks.

On April 27, 1943, Captain Ernst Fach, filling in for the 3rd Group Commander, submitted an efficiency report on Herbert Röwer. Fach wrote in part:[51]

> **Accomplishments against the enemy:** Master Sergeant Röwer has fully proven himself as a pilot in more than 230 combat missions against Russia due to his knowledge, his constantly balanced willingness for combat and his courage.
>
> **Short Assessment:** Tall, athletic, congenial appearance. Strict military bearing. Very good comprehension, mentally above average, with diverse interests. Well-rooted and balanced character, with a sound view of life, straight-forward and open. His military knowledge and accomplishments are very good. Secure and decisive towards the men under his command, accommodating and unpretentious towards superiors, good social manners, well-liked comrade.

Herbert Röwer was posted missing in action on May 5, 1943, when his Junkers Ju 88 was forced to make an emergency landing behind enemy lines east of Kharkov.

Herbert Röwer was awarded the Knight's Cross of the Iron Cross on July 3, 1943 after his death for service as a pilot in the 9th Squadron (Train), of the 3rd Bomber Wing "Blitz" and also received a posthumous promotion to second lieutenant.[52]

~~Nachweis der arischen Abstammung ist erbracht.~~ ~~An R. L. M. – L.P. 3, a.d.D.~~

Formblatt 1

Luftflotte: ~~Lw.-Kdo. Ost~~ Lfl. 4

Heimat-Luftgau: Königsberg I

Waffengattung*): Fliegertruppe Flugzeugführer

W. B. K.: Osnabrück

Truppenteil: III./Kampfgeschwader 3

(wird von L. P. ausgefüllt)

Geburtstag: 1o.6.1918

Name: R ö w e r

Geburtsort: H ö r n e

Vorname: Herbert

Beruf: Kaufmännischer Angestellter

Dienstgrad: Oberfeldwebel

Abiturient: ~~ja~~ — nein**)

Militärischer Werdegang:

Aktive Dienstzeit in der neuen Wehrmacht: von 28.1o.1935 bis jetzt

bzw. Kurzausbildung)V

Weitere Dienstverpflichtung auf ~~3 – 4 –~~ 12 ~~und mehr~~ Jahre 12 Jahre verpflichtet

Bei ehem. Soldaten, Dienstgrad bei Eintritt in die neue Wehrmacht: -.-

Friedensübungen: keine

Dienstzeit während des mobilen Verhältnisses: 3 Jahre, 2 Monate

1.9.39 – 31.1o.39 Gr.Kampffl.Sch.Faßberg
1.11.39– 31.8. 41 Gr.Kampffl.Sch.Thorn
1.9.41 – 31.12.42 II./Kampfgeschwader 3
1.1.43 – jetzt III./Kampfgeschwader 3

Beförderungen:
1.11.36 zum Gefreiten
1.4. 39 zum Unteroffizier
1.1o.4o zum Feldwebel
1.9. 42 zum Oberfeldwebel

Tag der Ernennung zum R.O.A : -.- bzw KO.A. 22.11.1942

Hat—nicht—~~mit Erfolg — ohne Erfolg~~**) an einem Kriegsoffizier-Nachwuchslehrgang

von -.- bis -.- teilgenommen.

*) Unter Waffengattung ist die Spezialausbildung mit anzugeben (Fliegertruppe — Flugzeugführer, Beobachter // Fallschirmtruppe — springendes Personal, Bodenpersonal // Flakartillerie — schwere Flak, leichte Flak, Scheinwerfer // Luftnachrichtentruppe — Funker, Fernsprecher).

**) Nichtzutreffendes ist zu streichen.

Vordrucklager Ludw. Flöttmann, Gütersloh. Vordruck-Nr. 770

Efficiency Report for Master Sergeant Herbert Röwer (front side) – dated April 27, 1943, on pre-printed form from the Ludwig Flöttmann firm in Gütersloh, with typed comments.

Zur Beförderung zum Offizier vorgeschlagen am: -.-

Bewährung vor dem Feinde: Ofw. Röwer hat sich in über 23o Feindflügen gegen Rußland als Flugzeugführer durch sein Können, seine stets gleichbleibende Einsatzfreudigkeit und Tapferkeit voll bewährt.

Auszeichnungen: K.V.K. II.Kl. mit Schwertern am 1.7.41, E.K. II. Kl. 13.1o.41, E.K. I. Kl. 5.1.42, Frontfl.Spange i. Gold 6.8.42, Verw. Abz. i.Schwarz 3o.1.42, Ehrenpokal f.bes. Leist.i.Luftkrieg 29.7.42, Ostmedaille 6.8.42, Deutsches Kreuz in Gold 1.11.1942.

Bestrafungen: keine

Kurze Beurteilungen: Große sportliche, sympathische Erscheinung. Straffe soldatische Haltung. Sehr gute Auffassungsgabe, steht geistig über dem Durchschnitt und ist vielseitig interessiert. Gefestigter und ausgeglichener Charakter mit einwandfreier Lebensauffassung, gerade und offen. Milit. Kenntnisse und Leistungen sind sehr gut. Auftreten gegenüber Untergebene sicher und bestimmt, gegenüber Vorgesetzte zuvorkommend und bescheiden, gute Umgangsformen, beliebter Kamerad.

Uk-Stellung während des Krieges:

von -.- bis -.-

Kurze Angabe des Grundes: -.-

Gruppengefechtsstand, den 27.4.1943
(Ort und Datum)

I. V.
Fach
(Unterschrift)
Hauptmann.

Efficiency Report for Master Sergeant Herbert Röwer (back side) – signed by Captain Ernst Fach, filling in for the 3rd Group Commander, 3rd Bomber Wing.

Erich Rudorffer

Fighter Pilot

"He is an example for the men under his command."

Major Erich Rudorffer was born November 1, 1917 at Zwochau near Leipzig, Saxony. He joined the *Luftwaffe* on April 16, 1936. Rudorffer was assigned to the 2nd Squadron, 2nd Fighter Wing "Richthofen" (*Jagdgeschwader 2 "Richthofen"*) on November 1, 1939 as a technical sergeant. He recorded his first victory, a French Curtiss Hawk 75 fighter, on May 14, 1940; he would score eight additional victories during the Battle of France and receive the Iron Cross 2nd Class on May 22, 1940 and the Iron Cross 1st Class on June 28, 1940. By May 1, 1941, now a second lieutenant, Rudorffer had achieved 19 victories, and was awarded the Knight's Cross of the Iron Cross. He then transferred to the 6th Squadron and finished the year with 40 kills. This included two Spitfires on July 7, a Spitfire and a Hurricane on July 9, two Spitfires on August 5, two Spitfires on August 19 and three Spitfires on September 21. Rudorffer assumed command of the 6th Squadron on July 17, 1941, was promoted to first lieutenant on October 1, 1941 and received the German Cross in Gold on December 20, 1941. His pace slowed in 1942 and he had but three victories prior to August, but flew in support of "Operation *Donnerkeil*" (Thunderbolt) in support of the German Navy's English Channel dash from Brest, France to Wilhelmshaven, Germany. Rudorffer was particularly successful over the Allied landings at Dieppe, France on August 19, 1942, when he shot down two Spitfire fighters in one minute. That November, the unit transferred to Tunisia, but Rudorffer did not move south until mid-December as he was in a Paris hospital recuperating from wounds.

On December 3, 1942, Rudorffer's chain of command submitted a recommendation for promotion to captain. First Lieutenant Adolf Dickfeld, serving as the acting 2nd Group commander, wrote:[53]

> First Lieutenant Rudorffer is a calm, modest person with an open, sincere character. He possesses good technical talents. His concept of service and his attitude as an officer are immaculate. Due to special accomplishments as a fighter pilot, he was promoted to Second Lieutenant (Wartime Officer) on October 28, 1940 after 19 victories. Within a short time, he has understood how to become part of the officer circle.
>
> As a flyer, again and again First Lieutenant R. [Rudorffer] has proven his eagerness for combat. On April 21, 1941, he shot down his 20th opponent and was awarded the Knight's Cross of the Iron Cross on May 6, 1941.
>
> On July 11, 1941, R. [Rudorffer] took over the 6th Squadron of J.G. 2, first as a substitute squadron leader, and on July 17, 1942 was appointed squadron leader. In December of 1941, he succeeded in his 40th air victory, for which he received the German Cross in Gold.
>
> R. [Rudorffer] understands from the standpoint of aviation, military requirements and human nature how to lead his squadron and has fully proven himself in this first independent position. He is an example for the men under his command and very well liked among his comrades. R. [Rudorffer] possesses his own initiative and knows how to help in every situation. R. [Rudorffer] is a National Socialist.

Lieutenant General Bruno Loerzer, 2nd Air Corps Commander, added his own comments on December 15, 1942:

> I am in full agreement with the good evaluation and second the preferential promotion to Captain (Wartime Officer)

Then Rudorffer hit a short rough patch. On December 17, his Focke-Wulf Fw 190A-4 sustained damage in aerial combat, and Rudorffer was forced to make an emergency landing. Three days later, his aircraft was again damaged by an enemy aircraft – a Spitfire. But his luck improved. While in Africa, Rudorffer shot down eight British aircraft (six Curtiss P-40 Tomahawk fighters and two P-38 Lightning fighters) in only 23 minutes on February 9, 1943 to raise his total to 61 aerial victories. On February 15, 1943, he shot down four P-38s and four Spitfires – in 55 minutes – to reach 69 kills. First Lieutenant Rudorffer assumed temporary command of the 2nd Group, 2nd Fighter Wing. After scoring a total of 27 victories in Tunisia, Rudorffer returned with his unit to the Channel Front in April 1943. In May 1943, Captain Rudorffer was appointed the 2nd Group Commander. He recorded two further victories, both Spitfires, before departing *Jagdgeschwader 2 "Richthofen"* with the mission of forming the 4th Group, 54th Fighter Wing "Green Hearts" (*Jagdgeschwader 54 "Grünherz"*) near Königsberg in June 1943.

However, the war forced a change in plans, and Rudorffer was transferred to the Eastern Front to assume command of the 2nd Group, 54th Fighter Wing, on August 1, 1943 after its commander, Heinrich Jung, failed to return from a mission on July 30. Once on the Eastern Front, Rudorffer's aerial victories took off. On August 24, 1943, he shot down five Russian aircraft on the first mission of the day and followed up with three more victories on a second mission. On September 14, 1943, he claimed five victories, bringing his total to 95. He scored seven victories in seven minutes on October 11, including his 100th; however, his greatest day in the air occurred on November 6, when in the course of 17 minutes, he shot down 13 enemy aircraft.

On April 7, 1944, Rudorffer shot down six enemy aircraft and was awarded the Oak Leaves to the Knight's Cross on April 11, 1944 for 134 victories. After a deserved leave away from the front, he returned to combat duty to claim five victories on July 3, six on July 26, five on August 25, six on September 25, seven on October 10 and 11 on October 28. For these and his overall exploits, Eric Rudorffer received the Swords to the Oak Leaves of his Knight's Cross for his 212th aerial victory on January 26, 1945. Ten days before, he was placed in command of the Me 262 jet fighter-equipped 1st Group, *Jagdgeschwader 7*. He became one of the first jet fighter aces by scoring 12 victories, including 10 four-engine bombers. Erich Rudorffer survived the war and continued his aviation career as a member of the new German *Bundesluftwaffe*.

Erich Rudorffer scored a total of 224 victories, 7th on the all-time list. Rudorffer flew over 1,000 combat missions, a sortie-to-victory ratio of 4.46 to 1. He was shot down 16 times and bailed out 9 times. Of his 138 Eastern Front kills, 58 were Il-2 Sturmoviks; he also shot down 11 four-engine bombers over Germany.[54]

Gefechtsstand, den 3. Dezember 1942
Wehrmachtteil: Luftwaffe

1.) Oberbefehlshaber Süd
2.) II./Jagdgeschwader Richthofen Nr.2
3.) W.B.K.: Liegnitz
4.) Vorgeschlagen gem.: R.d.L.u.Ob.d.L. (Luftwaffenpersonalamt) Az. 21 Nr.71 489/42 (2, I D) vom 16.10.42.
5.) Waffengattung: Fliegertruppe

V o r s c h l a g

zur Beförderung eines Offiziers (Kr.O.) zum nächsthöheren Dienstgrad.

Vor- und Zuname: Erich Rudorffer
Geburtsdatum: 1. 11. 1917
Jetziger Dienstgrad: Oberleutnant (Kr.O.)
Rangdienstalter: 1. 10. 1941
6.) Eingesetzt als: Staffelkapitän
7.) Geeignet zum: Staffelkapitän, später Gruppenkommandeur
Aktiver Wehrdienst: vom 16.4.36 - heute
Teilnahme an welchen Kämpfen: 8.1.40 - 9.5. 40 Verwendung im Operationsgebiet an der Westfront.

10.5.40 - 12.5.40 Durchbruch durch die südbelgischen Befestigungen und durch die Ardennen.

13.5.40-14.5.40 Durchbruchsschlacht zur Erzwingung des Maasüberganges.

15.5.40-19.5.40 Verfolgungskämpfe durch Südbelgien und die französische Grenzbefestigungen bis zur Oise.

20.5.40-4.6.40 Durchbruch zum Meer, Sicherung der linken Flanke der Angriffsgruppe und Unterstützung der Abwehrfront.

3.6.40 Großangriff auf Flughäfen im Raume Groß-Paris.

20.5.40-4.6.40 Einschließung der Feindkräfte in Flandern, Schlacht bei Dünkirchen.

5.6.40-10.6.40 Durchbruchsschlacht an der Somme und Verfolgungskämpfe bis zur Seine

5.6.40-13.6.40 Kämpfe um die Oise - u.- Aisne-Front

10.6.40-25.6.40 Verfolgungskämpfe bis über die Loire durch die Normandi u. die Bretagne (7.3.40-25.6.40 90 Feindflüge, 9 Abschüsse)

11.8.40-6.9.40 Planmäßige Bekämpfung der engl.Luftwaffe und ihrer Bodenorganisationen, der Lw.-Industrieziele, der Einfuhrhäfen und der Einfuhrtransporte.

13.8.40-18.8.40 Großangriff gegen die englischen Flughäfen.

16.8.40 Großangriff gegen die Flughäfen um Groß-London.

Recommendation for Promotion for First Lieutenant Erich Rudorffer (front side) – dated December 3, 1942, on blank paper, with typed comments.

7.9.40 Vergeltungsangriffe auf London u.die engl.Großstädte.

7.9.40-12.7.41 Teilnahme am Luftkrieg gegen England.
(11.8.40-12.7.41 76 Feindflüge, 16 Abschüsse)

13.7.41-20.11.42 Luftverteidigung im besetzten Gebiet Belgien und Nordfrankreich. (36 Feindflüge, 21 Abschüsse)

12.2.42 Schutz der Schlachtschiffe beim Durchbruch durch den Kanal.

Wird vorgeschlagen zur Beförderung zum: Hauptmann (Kr.O.)

Kurze Beurteilung durch den Regimentskommandeur, selbst.Batl.usw. Kdr.hinsichtlich dienstlicher Leistungen, Führerpersönlichkeit und Stellung im Kameradenkreise.

Oblt. Rudorffer ist ein ruhiger, bescheidener Mensch mit offenem, ehrlichem Charakter. Er besitzt eine gute technische Veranlagung. Seine Dienstauffassung und seine Haltung als Offizier sind einwandfrei. Infolge seiner besonderen Leistung als Jagdflieger wurde er nach 19 Abschüssen am 28.10.40 zum Leutnant (Kr.O.) befördert.
Er hat es in kürzester Zeit verstanden, sich in das Offizierkorps einzuleben.
Fliegerisch hat Oblt. R. immer erneut seine Einsatzfreudigkeit -wiesen. Am 21.4.41 schoß er seinen 20. Gegner ab und wurde am 6.5.4 mit dem Ritterkreuz des Eisernen Kreuzes ausgezeichnet.
R. übernahm am 11.7.41 die 6. Staffel des J.G.2 zunächst als stellvertretender Staffelkapitän und wurde am 17.7.41 zum Staffelkapitän ernannt. Er erzielte im Dezember 41 seinen 40.Luftsieg, wofür ihm das Deutsche Kreuz in Gold verliehen wurde.
R. versteht es, fliegerisch, militärisch und menschlich seine Staff zu führen und hat sich in dieser ersten selbständigen Stellung voll bewährt. Er ist seinen Untergebenen ein Vorbild, im Kameradenkreise sehr beliebt. R. besitzt eigene Initiative und weiß sich in jeder Lage zu helfen. R. ist Nationalsozialist.

Dickfeld
Oberleutnant und stellv.Gruppenkommandeur

Zusatz:

Ich bin mit der guten Beurteilung einverstanden und befürworte die bevorzugte Beförderung zum Hauptmann (Kr.O.).

Gefechtsstand, den 15 .12.1942
Der Kommandierende General
des II.Fliegerkorps

Loerzer
General der Flieger

Recommendation for Promotion for First Lieutenant Erich Rudorffer (back side) – signed by First Lieutenant Adolf Dickfeld, acting commander, 2nd Group, 2nd Fighter Wing, and by Lieutenant General Bruno Loerzer, 2nd Air Corps Commander.

Martin Schächter
Fallschirmjäger

"During an artillery attack on the division command post at the Invasion Front, he was buried alive and again wounded."

Major Martin Schächter was born in Petershagen in the district of Minden, North Rhine-Westphalia, on March 14, 1915. He entered the German Army on April 1, 1935 as an officer candidate with the 18th Engineer Battalion. One year later, he transferred to the *Luftwaffe* and began observer training. Schächter, who was promoted to second lieutenant on April 1, 1937, then spent several years in various bomber units to include the 4th Group, 152nd Bomber Wing "Hindenburg (*Kampfgeschwader 152 "Hindenburg"*), and the 3rd Group, 355th Bomber Wing (*Kampfgeschwader 355*).[55] On January 1, 1939, Martin Schächter joined the 1st Paratroop Regiment (*Fallschirmjäger-Regiment 1*) and fought in Poland in September 1939. He then joined the secret Assault Detachment Koch (*Fallschirmjäger-Sturm-Abteilung Koch*), which had the cover name "Test Detachment Friedrichshafen," on March 1, 1940 as the acting commander of the engineer company.

On the morning of May 10, 1940, Second Lieutenant Martin Schächter, leader of Assault Group Iron (*Eisen*) took off from Cologne-Butzweilerhof at 4:30 a.m. with 10 gliders and the mission of seizing the bridge over the Albert Canal at Canne on the route from Maastricht to Liège.[56] However, the glider with the 1st Squad was released too early and did not have enough height or speed to reach the landing zone, coming to ground instead on the high ground southwest of the bridge. As the other assault groups had already landed, the Belgians realized what was happening and blew up the bridge around 5:35 a.m. With poor visibility, the glider of the 9th Squad landed 220 yards south of the bridge at the village of Eben Emael, while the gliders carrying the 6th and 7th Squads landed on the middle high ground instead of the northern, as planned. Meanwhile, the Belgians hit the glider with the 3rd Squad with a high explosive round, setting it on fire, although the craft managed to land in the designated area. The paratroopers began clearing trenches in the landing area of defending troops, during which time Martin Schächter was seriously wounded in the head and legs, and Second Lieutenant Meissner assumed command of the group. For his actions that morning, Martin Schächter was awarded the Iron Cross 2nd Class, the Iron Cross 1st Class and the Knight's Cross of the Iron Cross on May 12, 1940. He was promoted to first lieutenant on May 16, 1940 (with a date of rank backdated to February 1, 1939). Schächter spent nine months in the hospital, leaving to join the 1st Paratroop Assault Regiment (*Fallschirmjäger-Sturm-Regiment 1*) in February 1941. He air-landed at Máleme, Crete during the German invasion of the island, on May 20, 1941, but was seriously wounded the following day. He again spent time in a hospital. Promoted to captain on February 1, 1942, he then was attached to the *Luftwaffe* headquarters in Berlin until September 1, 1943, when he joined the staff of the 3rd Paratroop Division (*3. Fallschirmjäger-Division*). During this assignment, he was once again wounded – although less seriously – when American artillery struck the division headquarters.

On October 30, 1944, the chain of command of the 3rd Paratroop Division submitted an efficiency report requesting preferential promotion to major for Martin Schächter. Major General Richard Schimpf, the division commander, wrote, in part:[57]

Reason for consideration:

Accomplishments in general. Captain Schächter is very superior to other officers as to the concept of duty, maturity and know-how. As Ib [Supply Officer] of the division and as acting company commander of an engineer company, he has demonstrated energy, talent for improvisation and his own initiative. In particular, at the Invasion Front, as the Ib [Supply Officer], he has decisively contributed to the constant ability of the division to fight. Thanks to his prudence and his high degree of know-how, the fighting units of the division were equipped with the necessary weapons, ammunition and equipment at the right time and, despite transportation difficulties, they were supplied with the necessary supplies.

Detailed information. During the seizure of Fort Eben Emael and the bridges over the Albert Canal, he has proven his military knowledge as a company leader. During these battles, he was heavily wounded in the head and legs and was awarded the Knight's Cross. During the battles for the Island of Crete, barely recuperated, he was again wounded. Although only ready for combat in a restricted manner, he urgently requested to return to the frontline but, due to his severe wounds, he could not serve as battalion leader. During an artillery attack on the division command post at the Invasion Front, he was buried alive and again wounded. Without concern for himself and even though he was not yet ready for combat, he again reported back to the division – proof of his great willingness for combat and strong will power.

With his accomplishments and his knowledge, he stands far above the average and is to be awarded a preferential promotion as an award for his attitude as a fighter.

Colonel General Kurt Student, the commander of the Parachute Army, added: " In agreement!"

Martin Schächter was promoted to major on January 1, 1945. He remained with the division until March 15, 1945, when he became a prisoner of war.[58]

3.Fallschirmjäger-Division
Abteilung IIa

Div.St.Qu., 30.10.1944

V o r s c h l a g

zur

b e v o r z u g t e n B e f ö r d e r u n g
gem.R.d.L.u.Ob.d.L.LP Nr. 71489/42 (2,ID) II.Ang.v.22.12.42 Absch.

zum Major

für Hauptmann (Tr.O.) S c h ä c h t e r Martin

Dienststellung: 2. Generalstabsoffizier i.V. Sachbearbeiter Ib

Rangdienstalter: 1.2.1942

Beförderungsdaten: zum Leutnant 1.4.1937 1.1.38
zum Oberleutnant 1.8.1939 1.2.39
zum Hauptmann 1.2.1942 1.2.42

Geburtsdatum: 14.3.1915 in Petershagen

Auszeichnungen: 15.9.1940 Verwundetenabzeichen in Silber
12.5.1940 E.K. II.Kl. - E.K. I.Kl. - Ritterkreuz zum Eisernen Kreuz

B e g r ü n d u n g :

A) Allgemeine Leistungen.
Hptm. Schächter ist in Pflichtauffassung, Reife und Können anderen Offizieren weit voraus. Als I b der Division und als Kompanieführer einer Pionierkompanie hat er Energie, Tatkraft, Improvisationsvermögen und Eigeninitiative gezeigt. Vor allem an der Invasionsfront als Ib hat er entscheidend für die ständige Kampfbereitschaft der Division beigetragen. Seiner Umsicht und seinem grossen Können ist es zu verdanken, dass die kämpfenden Einheiten der Division rechtzeitig mit den erforderlichen Waffen, Munition und Gerät ausgerüstet waren und trotz der grossen Beförderungsschwierigkeiten mit dem erforderlichen Nachschub versehen wurden.

B) Einzelangaben.
Bei der Einnahme des Forts Eben Emael und der Brücken über den Albert-Kanal hat er als Kompaniechef sein soldatisches Können unter Beweis gestellt. Er wurde bei diesen Kämpfen durch Kopf- und Beinschuss schwer verwundet und mit dem Ritterkreuz ausgezeichnet. Bei den Kämpfen um die Insel Kreta, kaum wieder hergestellt, wurde er erneut schwer verwundet. Obwohl nur bedingt einsatzfähig drängte er zum Einsatz in vorderster Front, konnte aber auf Grund seiner schweren Verwundung als Batl.Führer nicht eingesetzt werden. Bei einem Artillerieüberfall auf den Divisionsgefechtsstand an der Invasionsfront wurde er verschüttet und erneut verwundet. Ohne Rücksicht auf seine Person und obwohl nicht einsatzbereit meldete er sich wieder bei der Division. Ein Be -

Bitte wenden!

Request for Preferred Promotion for Captain Martin Schächter (front side) – dated October 30, 1944, on blank paper, with typed and hand-written comments.

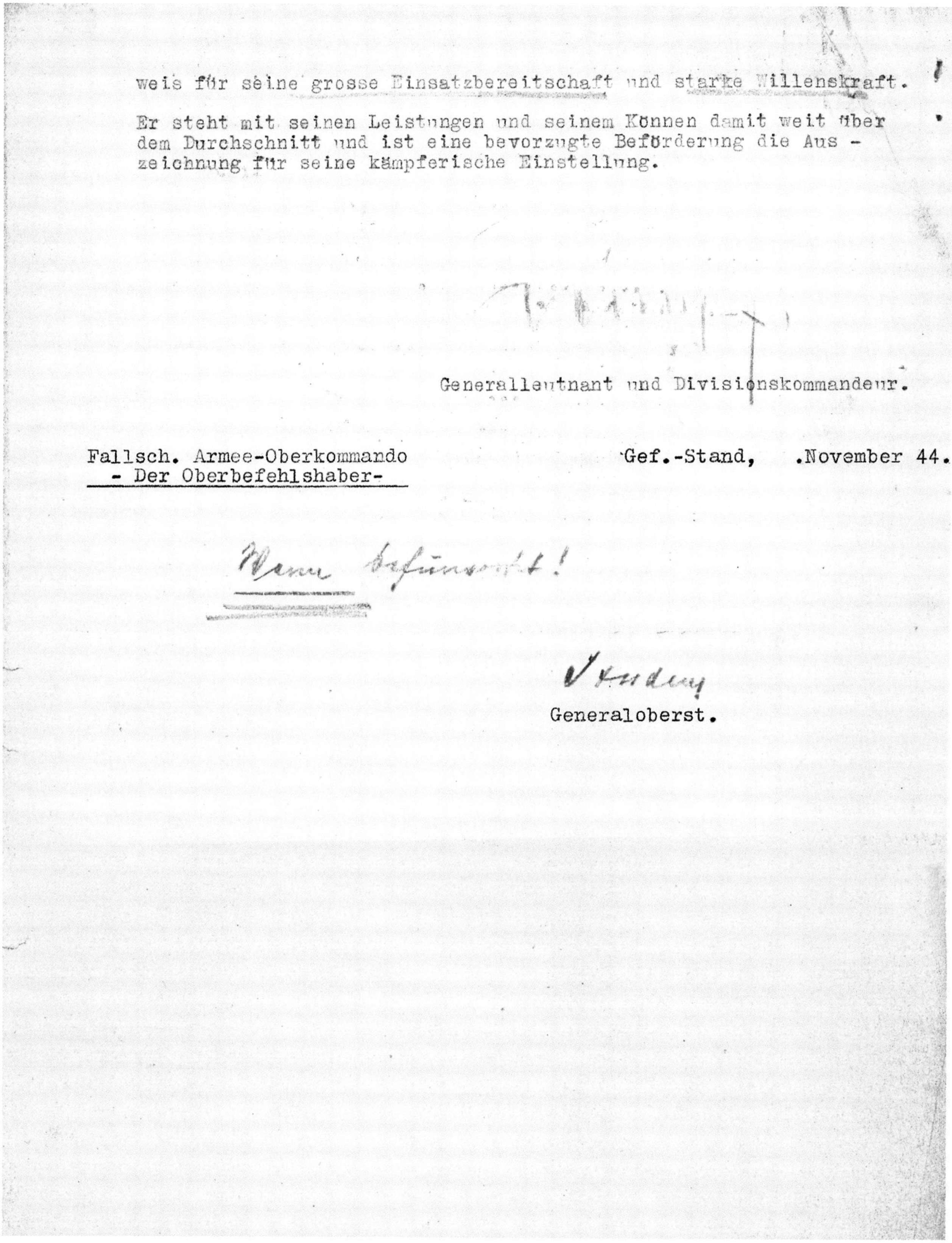

weis für seine grosse Einsatzbereitschaft und starke Willenskraft.

Er steht mit seinen Leistungen und seinem Können damit weit über dem Durchschnitt und ist eine bevorzugte Beförderung die Auszeichnung für seine kämpferische Einstellung.

Generalleutnant und Divisionskommandeur.

Fallsch. Armee-Oberkommando
- Der Oberbefehlshaber-

Gef.-Stand, .November 44.

Warm befürwortet!

Generaloberst.

Request for Preferred Promotion for Captain Martin Schächter (back side) – signed by Major General Richard Schimpf, commander of the 3rd Paratroop Division, and by Colonel General Kurt Student, commander of the Paratroop Army.

Wolfgang Schellmann

Fighter Pilot

"An exemplary military trainer and educator for his squadron."

Lieutenant Colonel Wolfgang Schellmann was born on March 2, 1911 at Kassel. He entered the Army on April 1, 1930 and transferred to the *Luftwaffe* on August 1, 1934. From March 1, 1935, Schellmann led the 2nd Squadron, 132nd Fighter Wing "Richthofen" (*Jagdgeschwader 132 "Richthofen"*); on December 19, 1937 he assumed command of the 1st Squadron of the 88th Fighter Group (*Jagdgruppe 88* [J/88]) of the Condor Legion, and led this unit during the Spanish Civil War against the Republican forces opposing Generalissimo Franco.[59] He scored his first aerial victory on January 17, 1938 – an I-16 "Rata." Schellmann became the second highest scorer of the German fighter pilots, with 12 kills, behind only Werner Mölders and was awarded the Spanish Cross in Gold with Swords and Diamonds. On his return from Spain in September 1938, Schellmann was assigned to the 1st Group, 331st Fighter Wing (*Jagdgeschwader 331*) and then from April 1, 1939, he served in a staff position in Berlin. At the outbreak of World War II, Schellmann was serving with the 1st Group, 77th Fighter Wing (*Jagdgeschwader 77*), participating in the invasion of Poland. Shortly thereafter, he was transferred to the staff of the 2nd Air Fleet. On December 15, 1939, Captain Schellmann was appointed the Commander, 2nd Group, 2nd Fighter Wing "Richthofen" (*Jagdgeschwader 2 "Richthofen"*). He scored his first victory in the war on May 15, 1940, when he shot down a RAF Hurricane fighter near Couly. By the end of the French campaign he had seven victories to his credit, including two over Dunkirk. Schellmann was appointed the commodore of *Jagdgeschwader 2 "Richthofen"* on September 3, 1940 during the Battle of Britain and was awarded the Knight's Cross of the Iron Cross on September 18, 1940 for 10 victories. On October 22, 1940, Schellmann was appointed the commodore of the 27th Fighter Wing (*Jagdgeschwader 27*) on the Channel Front. In the spring of 1941, he led the unit during the invasion of Yugoslavia and Greece.

Schellmann claimed one victory, a RAF Hurricane fighter (80th Fighter Squadron), over Tanagra, Greece, bringing his victory total to 24, including his Spanish Civil War victories. He then led the 27th Fighter Wing for "Operation Barbarossa," the invasion of Russia. On June 22, 1941, the first day of the invasion, he became a victim of a "taran" attack made by a Russian I-16 fighter in the vicinity of Kamenki near Grodno in Russia. (Another source says that it was not a taran attack, but that his aircraft struck pieces of an I-16 he had just shot down.) Schellmann bailed out of his stricken Messerschmitt Me 109E-7, but was never seen again.[60] It is thought by some sources that the Russian NKVD shot him. He was posthumously promoted to Lieutenant Colonel.

Wolfgang Schellmann was credited with 25 victories in over 150 combat missions, a sortie-to-victory rate of 6.00 to 1. He recorded 12 victories during the Spanish Civil War and 13 in World War II – 12 of which were on the Western Front.[61]

Early in his career, Schellmann received an officer efficiency report that foreshadowed his successes to come. On September 27, 1937, Major Max Ibel, Schellmann's group commander, wrote:[62]

> **General Evaluation:** Schellmann, due to his total personality, is an excellent troop officer, conscious of the goal of fulfilling his duties while at the same time lively and impulsive in his decisions. Without being obsessive, he possesses an above-average zeal for service. With his comrades and the men under his command, he enjoys a very good rapport. As a trainer of fighter pilots and teacher of his squadron, he possesses great know-how and a strong eagerness for action. An exemplary military trainer and educator for his squadron. His behavior outside the service and in society is immaculate. Sch. [Schellmann] has fulfilled his position very well.

Ibel added the following hand-written comments on February 8, 1938, indicating that Schellmann was posted to Spain as part of *Luftwaffe* support to Generalissimo Franco:

> First Lieutenant Schellmann was transferred for Exercise Rügen [*Übung Rügen*] on December 8, 1937.
>
> Nothing to be added to the evaluation.

On May 2, 1939, Major Karl Viek, the new group commander, added:

> Sch. [Schellmann] has fully proven himself as a squadron commander. Natural leader.

Seven days later, Lieutenant Colonel Gerd von Massow, the *Geschwader* commodore, wrote the following description of Schellmann from his point of view:

> Captain Schellmann is a fighter pilot and squadron commander far above the average. During the half year as a squadron commander, he has understood how to pass on his rich experience from [Exercise] Rügen to his squadron. Sch. [Schellmann] is not only a great master in practice, but also has the gift to pass on in writing his knowledge and experience in a useful manner. Enormously interested, very diligent, without false aspirations. A good comrade, well educated, with good social manners. Particularly suited for training as general staff officer. In every respect a personality who warrants attention.

Jagdgeschwader 135
I. Gruppe

Nr.: 1o

Beurteilung

zum 15. November 1937

über den Oberleutnant Wolfgang Schellmann

Dienststellung: Staffelkapitän der 2. Staffel

I. Geboren am: 2. 3. 11. Religion: ev.

in Kassel Kreis: Kassel

Verheiratet: nein Kinder: nein Söhne: Töchter:

Diensteintritt: 1. 4. 3o.

Laufbahn: aktiv seit 1.4.3o bis 25. 7. 34 beim Heer
Aktiv vom 1.8.34 bei der Luftwaffe

Rangdienstalter: 1. 1o. 35 (29)

Zeitpunkt der Übernahme der oben angegebenen Stellung: 15. 3. 37.

Besoldungsdienstalter: 1. 8. 33. C 8

II. Körperliche Eignung: mittelgross, sehr gute mil. Erscheinung

Wirtschaftliche Verhältnisse: geordnet, auf sein Gehalt angewiesen.

Bestrafungen: keine

Stammwaffe: Infantrie

Fliegerische Verwendung:

a) vor dem Weltkriege: nein

b) im Weltkriege: nein

c) im Reichsheer: vom 1.4.3o bis 3o. 9. 31 fliegerische Ausbildung bei der D.V.S., wird als aktive mil. Dienstzeit angerechnet

d) in der Luftwaffe:

Flugzeugführer: ja (Mil.-Flzg.-Führerschein)

Beobachter: nein

Sonderausbildung:

a) vor dem Kriege o. Reichswehr: Flugzeugführer-Ausbildung. (Jagdflieger)

b) in der Luftwaffe: Adjutant Jagdgruppe –
Mil.-Kraftfahrzeug-Führerschein I u. III.

Efficiency Report for First Lieutenant Wolfgang Schellmann (first page) – dated November 15, 1937.

III. Allgemeines Urteil. Schellmann ist nach seiner ganzen Persönlichkeit ein ausgezeichneter Truppenoffizier, zielbewusst in der Durchführung seiner Aufgaben, dabei lebhaft und impulsiv im Entschluss.

Er besitzt ohne Streberei einen überdurchschnittlichen Diensteifer.

Bei Kameraden und Untergebenen steht er in sehr gutem Ansehen.

Als Jagdflugzeugführer und als Lehrer seiner Staffel besitzt er grosses Können und eine starke Einsatzbereitschaft. Ein vorzüglicher militärischer Ausbilder und Erzieher seiner Staffel.

Ausserdienstliches Verhalten und gesellschaftliche Formen einwandfrei.

Sch. füllt seine Stelle - sehr gut - aus.

Bad-Aibling, den 29.9.37.

Ibel

Major und Gruppen Kdr.

Efficiency Report for First Lieutenant Wolfgang Schellmann (second page) – signed by Major Max-Josef Ibel, Commander, 1st Group, 135th Fighter Wing.

Oblt. Schellmann wurde am 8/12.37.
zur Übung Rügen versetzt
Zur Beurteilung nichts hinzuzufügen
Bad-Aibling, den 8/2.38.

Ibel
Major u. Gr. Kdeur.

Sch. hat sich als Staffelkapitän voll bewährt. Führernatur.

Döberitz d. 2.5.39.

Vieck
Major u. Gr. Kdr.

Hauptmann Schellmann

ist ein weit ueber dem Durchschnitt stehender Jagdflieger und Staffelkapitaen. Waehrend der halbjaehrigen Zeit als Staffelkapitaen hat er es verstanden,seine reichen Ruegen-e fahrungen an seine Staffel weiterzugeben. Sch. ist nicht nur ein grosser Koenner in der Praxis,sondern hat auch die Begabung, sein Wissen und seine Erfahrungen in brauchbarer Form schriftlich festzulegen.

Enorm interessiert,sehr fleissig,ohne falsches Strebertum. Guter Kamerad,wohlerzogen,gute gesellschaftliche Formen.

Zur Ausbildung als Generalstabsoffizier besonders geeignet. In jeder Weise eine Persoenlichkeit,die Beachtung verdient.

Doeberitz,den 9.5.39.

Persönlich geschrieben.

v. Massow

Oberstleutnant u. Kommodore
des
Jagdgeschwader Richthofen

Efficiency Report for First Lieutenant Wolfgang Schellmann (third page) – signed again by Major Max-Josef Ibel, by Major Karl Viek, Commander, 1st Group, 135th Fighter Wing, and by Lieutenant Colonel Gerd von Massow, Commodore, 135th Fighter Wing.

Wolfgang Schenck

Fighter/Destroyer/Stuka Pilot

"He appears to have lost his spirit for battle and is tired of being at the front."

Lieutenant Colonel Wolfgang "Bombo" Schenck was born in Windhuk, German Southwest Africa on February 7, 1913. Schenck was educated in Germany and later went to Tanganyika to become a coffee planter. In late 1936, he returned to Germany and joined the *Luftwaffe* as an officer candidate. After pilot training, he was assigned to the 132nd Fighter Wing "Richthofen" (*Jagdgeschwader 132 "Richthofen"*); he later joined the 1st Destroyer Wing (*Zerstörergeschwader 1*), equipped with the twin-engine Me-110 heavy fighter. Schenck participated in the German operations against Poland (where he received the Iron Cross 2nd Class on September 23, 1939), Norway, and France (and shot down two aircraft on May 11), but was shot down and seriously injured on May 16, 1940 – wounds which hospitalized him for 3 months. During his hospital stay, Schenck received the Iron Cross 1st Class on May 25. On September 4, 1940, Schenck assumed command of the 1st Squadron, 210th Test Group (*Erprobungsgruppe 210*) – an operational test unit – which was tasked to develop and perfect fighter-bomber tactics. Two months later, Schenck received the *Luftwaffe* Honor Goblet. Wolfgang Schenk won the Knight's Cross of the Iron Cross on August 14, 1941 as a first lieutenant and commander of the 1st Squadron, 210th Fast Bomber Wing (*Schnellkampfgeschwader 210*) – a fighter-bomber unit – having achieved 9 aerial victories and 200 ground-attack combat missions, which also included sinking 38,000 tons of shipping.

On September 24, 1941, he took over the Messerschmitt Me 210 test squadron at Rechlin (*Erprobungsstaffel Me 210*). In January 1942, he returned to the 1st Group, 1st Destroyer Wing and on March 3, 1942 assumed command of this formation. Over the next months in Russia, he raised his aerial victories to 18 and destroyed 15 Soviet tanks in ground-attack missions. Schenck became the 139th recipient of the Oak Leaves to the Knight's Cross on October 30, 1942 as a captain and Commander, 1st Group, 1st Destroyer Wing (*Zerstörergeschwader 1*), having flown 300 combat missions – many in the Messerschmitt Me 110. He spent three months thereafter on the *Luftwaffe* Operations Staff in Berlin and then became the Commodore, 2nd Ground-Attack Wing (*Schlachtgeschwader 2*) on January 3, 1943 in the Mediterranean theater. Wounded again in 1943, he recovered and later was made Inspector of Fighter-Bomber Pilots. He was promoted to major on August 1, 1943.

On October 11, 1943, Major General Alfred Bülowius, the commanding general of the 2nd Air Corps (*II. Fliegerkorps*) wrote a supplement to an efficiency report on Wolfgang Schenk, stating:[63]

> Major Schenck is not known to me personally, so I cannot render an opinion regarding his character and personality traits. During a previous duty subordination [in my command], various difficulties concerning him surfaced, which at the end led to court-martial proceedings, the results of which are not known to me due to his transfer. These difficulties were characterized by all kinds of objections toward mission orders, inexact or delayed execution of ordered missions, slackness, know-it-all attitude, fundamental rejection and grumbling in connection with orders. He was not up to the serious and special situation in Sicily and has not proven himself here as a leadership personality. He appears to have lost his spirit for battle and is tired of being at the front.

Nine days later, the commander of the 2nd Air Fleet (*Luftflotte 2*), Field Marshal Wolfram von Richthofen, hand-wrote, "Nothing to add."

This was a blistering attack by Bülowius and not softened by Field Marshal von Richthofen. Despite these damning comments, however, in June 1944 Schenk assumed command of Test Command "Schenck" (*Erprobungskommando Schenck*). This unit, sent to France, tested the Me-262-A jet as a fighter-bomber against advancing Allied ground forces.[64] In September 1944, the *Luftwaffe* renamed the unit the 1st Group, 51st Bomber Wing (*Kampfgeschwader 51 [J]*). Schenck was promoted again – to lieutenant colonel – on November 1, 1944. From December 5, 1944 to January 31, 1945, Schenck served as the commodore of the 51st Bomber Wing "Edelweiss" (*Kampfgeschwader 51 "Edelweiss"*), flying the Me-262-A2. He finally served as Inspector of Jet Aircraft. Schenck flew over 400 combat missions in World War II in a variety of aircraft, achieved 18 aerial victories and sank 40,000 tons of Allied shipping. After the war, he returned to Africa and began a career as a bush pilot.[65]

Generalkommando des
II.Fliegerkorps

Gefechtsstand, den 11.10.1943

Zusatz zur Beurteilungsnotiz

des Major (Tr.O.) S c h e n c k, Wolfgang.

Persönlich ist mir Major Schenck nicht bekannt geworden, sodaß ich über Charakter und Persönlichkeitswert ein Urteil nicht abgeben kann.

Während seiner vorübergehenden einsatzmäßigen Unterstellung sind verschiedene Schwierigkeiten mit ihm aufgetreten, die dann letzten Endes zu einem kriegsgerichtlichen Verfahren führten, über dessen Ausgang mir infolge seiner Versetzung nichts bekannt ist.

Einwendungen aller Art zu Einsatzbefehlen, ungenaue oder unpünktliche Durchführung befohlener Aufträge, Unlust und Besserwissen, grundsätzliche Ablehnung und Nörgelei an gegebenen Befehlen kennzeichnen diese Schwierigkeiten. Der ernsten und besonderen Lage in Sizilien war er nicht gewachsen, als Führerpersönlichkeit hat er sich hier nicht erwiesen. Er erscheint abgekämpft und frontmüde.

Der Kommandierende General
des II. Fliegerkorps

Generalleutnant

Der Chef der Luftflotte 2

20.10.43

Generalfeldmarschall

Supplement to an Efficiency Report for Major Wolfgang Schenck (one page only) – dated October 11, 1943, on blank paper with typed and hand-written comments. Signed by Major General Alfred Bülowius, the Commanding General of the 2nd Air Corps, and by Field Marshal Wolfram von Richthofen, Commander, 2nd Air Fleet.

Horst Schiller

Stuka Pilot

"Very passionate Stuka pilot of outstanding courage and untiring eagerness for combat."

Major Horst Schiller was born on September 6, 1917 in Berlin. He entered the *Luftwaffe* on March 6, 1936 and two years later joined the 10th Flying Group (*Fliegergruppe 10*), a ground-attack unit. By mid-1939, this unit was renamed the 1st Group, 1st Stuka Wing (*Sturzkampfgeschwader 1*), and with it, Schiller flew combat missions in Poland, France and England. In Poland, on September 1, 1939, at 4:34 a.m., Horst Schiller flew in the three Junkers Ju-87B Stuka dive-bomber formation (led by Second Lieutenant Bruno Dilley) of the 3rd Squadron, 1st Stuka Wing in the attack against the Dirschau Bridge (over the Vistula River) to destroy the ignition cables for the Polish explosive charges designed to cripple the structure. It was the initial strike of the German invasion of Poland, the first act of World War II in Europe.

On September 28, 1941, Major Helmut Sorge, the 1st Group, 1st Stuka Wing Commander, submitted a hand-written efficiency report on First Lieutenant Horst Schiller. It read, in part:[66]

> **Evaluation of suitability:** Slender, medium height, youthful and military appearance. Immaculate character, fresh lieutenant type, often full of youthful high spirits, but never forgetting his good education and in all "freedom of speech" issues, always maintains military form. Mentally above average, with clear military and far-reaching views, good tactical talent, skillful pilot, often contributes his own considerations, shows initiative and works independently and deliberate. Vis-à-vis superiors and subordinates, he stands up well, even in difficult tasks.
>
> Schiller has a certain tendency to generosity, which is welcome; however, he applies it to little things of the military life. He must fight this tendency. As adjutant and simultaneously "Major on the Staff," he has been trustworthy and circumspect and has worked with great understanding. Very passionate Stuka pilot of outstanding courage and untiring eagerness for combat. Since receiving his punishment, he has never again been guilty of relapsing.
>
> For his courage in Poland and Norway, he was awarded the Iron Cross 2nd and 1st Class. During further engagements in Africa, in the Mediterranean and the Balkans, he showed such great knowledge of aviation and personal courage that he was awarded the *Luftwaffe* Honor Goblet for extraordinary accomplishments in the air. Without doubt, during further engagements, the possibility exists that he will be recommended for the award of Knight's Cross.
>
> **How has the current position been fulfilled?** Very well.
>
> **Suitable for promotion to next higher service grade?** Has not yet come up, but he is already suited for it at this time.
>
> **Punishments:** July 1938 – six weeks of strict house arrest. In February 1939, the penalty was changed to three years probation.[67]
>
> **Recommendation for employment as:** Squadron commander of a Stuka squadron. Particularly well-suited for the career on the General Staff.

Schiller received the German Cross in Gold on January 22, 1943. He then transferred to the Mediterranean, where in March 1942 he assumed command of the 1st Squadron, 3rd Stuka Wing (*Sturzkampfgeschwader 3*). On November 12, 1943, Schiller assumed acting command of the 1st Group, 3rd Stuka Wing. On June 2, 1943, Schiller's aircraft was struck by Russian anti-aircraft fire northwest of Krymskaja. Observers saw a parachute descend behind enemy lines, but Horst Schiller was never seen again. He received the Knight's Cross of the Iron Cross on June 9, 1944 as well as a posthumous promotion to major. During the war, Horst Schiller flew 466 combat missions – including the first one of the *Luftwaffe* – sank one enemy destroyer and numerous transport ships. He destroyed an armored train, a coast artillery battery and 17 enemy tanks.[68]

17

I./Sturzkampfgeschwader 1 Gefechtsstand, den 28.9.1941

Feldpostnummer L 37 714
Luftgaupostamt München 2

B e u r t e i l u n g s n o t i z

über

den Oblt. Horst S c h i l l e r

geb. am 6.9.1915

Familienstand: ledig

Jetzige Verwendung: Adjutant

Eignungsbeurteilung nächste Seite.

Efficiency Report for First Lieutenant Horst Schiller (first page) – dated September 28, 1941, on blank paper, with typed and hand-written comments. Photo attached to report.

17

Eignungsbeurteilung: Schlanke, mittelgroße, jugendliche und sportliche Erscheinung.

Tadelloser Charakter, frischer Leutnantstyp, oft von jugendlichem Übermut, jedoch nie seine gute Erziehung vergessend und bei aller „Freiheit des Wortes" stets seine militärischen Formen wahrend. Gesellschaftlich gewandt.

Geistig über dem Durchschnitt stehend; [illegible] militärisch und weiter Blick; gute taktische Veranlagung, sehr gewandt, bringt oft eigene Anregungen, zeigt Initiative u. arbeitet selbständig u. überlegt. Gegenüber Vorgesetzten u. Untergebenen setzt er sich gut durch, auch bei schwierigen Aufträgen.

Er hat einen gewissen Hang zur Großzügigkeit, der i.a. gar sympathisch ist, den er jedoch gelegentlich auch auf kleine Dinge des militärischen Lebens überträgt. Diese Neigung muß er bekämpfen.

Als Adjutant u. gleichzeitig „Major beim Stab" hat er zuverlässig, umsichtig und mit viel Verständnis gearbeitet.

Sehr geschickter Flugzeugführer von überragender Tapferkeit und unermüdlicher Einsatzbereitschaft. Seit seiner Bestrafung hat er sich nie wieder einen Verstoß gegen die Flugdisziplin zuschulden kommen lassen.

Für seine Tapferkeit in Polen u. Norwegen wurde er mit dem EK I u. II ausgezeichnet. Bei weiteren Einsätzen in Afrika, im Mittelmeer, ~~bei~~ auf dem Balkan, auf Kreta zeigte er so hohes fliegerisches Können u. persönlichen Schneid, daß ihm ~~mit~~ der Ehrenpokal des Herrn Reichsmarschalls für bes. Leistungen im Luftkrieg verliehen wurde. Ohne Zweifel hat er bei weiterem Einsatz die Aussicht, für die Verleihung des Ritterkreuzes in Vorschlag gebracht zu werden.

Efficiency Report for First Lieutenant Horst Schiller (second page).

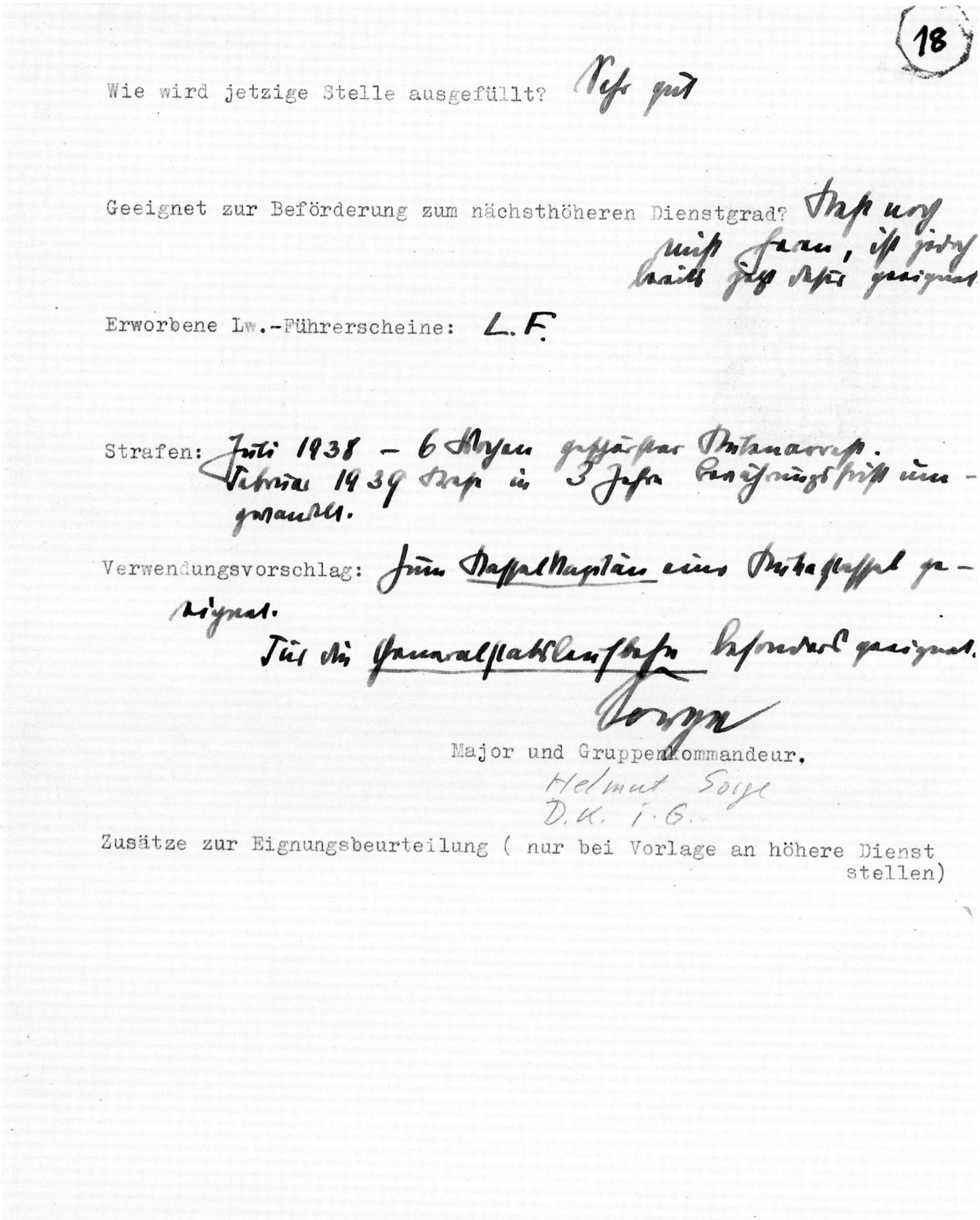

18

Wie wird jetzige Stelle ausgefüllt? Sehr gut

Geeignet zur Beförderung zum nächsthöheren Dienstgrad? Steht noch nicht heran, ist jedoch bereits jetzt schon geeignet.

Erworbene Lw.-Führerscheine: L.F.

Strafen: Juli 1938 – 6 Tagen geschärfter Stubenarrest. Februar 1939 Strafe in 3 Jahren Bewährungsfrist umgewandelt.

Verwendungsvorschlag: Zum Staffelkapitän einer Stukastaffel geeignet.

Für die Generalstabslaufbahn besonders geeignet.

Sorge

Major und Gruppenkommandeur.

Helmut Sorge
D.K. I.G.

Zusätze zur Eignungsbeurteilung (nur bei Vorlage an höhere Dienst stellen)

Efficiency Report for First Lieutenant Horst Schiller (third page) – signed by Major and Commander, 1st Group, 1st Stuka Wing, Helmut Sorge.

Horst Schimpke

Fallschirmjäger

"He is diligent, conscientious and eager to work."

Second Lieutenant Horst Schimpke was born in Berlin-Schöneberg on November 10, 1920. He entered the German Army's 206th Anti-tank Replacement Company in Allenstein on September 3, 1939. Transferring to the *Luftwaffe*, he underwent paratroop training in August 1940 before being assigned to the 3rd Company, Paratroop Anti-tank Detachment (*Fallschirm-Panzer-Jäger-Abteilung*); he was designated later in the year as an officer candidate. Schimpke jumped into Crete in May 1941 with the unit during the German invasion of the island, fighting at Máleme, Khaniá and Suda Bay. He was wounded in action and received the Iron Cross 2nd Class on June 8, 1941 and the Iron Cross 1st Class on June 21, 1941. Schimpke fought in North Africa from January 1 to March 27, 1942, as part of the defensive fighting at Maramarica and Cyrenaika; toward the middle of the year, he conducted security duties in the 3rd Air Fleet area and was promoted to technical sergeant on August 1, 1942. Late in the year, he deployed to Russia and fought there through the spring of 1943, making master sergeant on April 1, 1943.

In April 1943, the chain of command of the 1st Paratroop Division submitted an efficiency report on Horst Schimpke requesting he be commissioned a second lieutenant. Captain Gerhard Brückner, the 1st Paratroop Anti-Tank Detachment Commander, wrote in part:[69]

> **Evaluation:** Schimpke is a straight-forward, decent character, well liked by his comrades. He possesses an easy demeanor and has good general social manners. Mentally very alert and capable of satisfying high demands. Physically very flexible, good athlete. In service, he demonstrated very good knowledge and accomplishments. He is diligent, conscientious and eager to work. At the front, he shows an immaculate demeanor. In the training of his subordinates, he was exemplary. In the Eastern campaign, Master Sergeant Schimpke led an anti-tank gun platoon, which was engaged at the front line, to the fullest satisfaction of his superiors and he fully distinguished himself in that.

Brigadier General Richard Heidrich, the division commander, added:

> In agreement and seconded. Master Sergeant (Wartime Officer Candidate) Schimpke (Horst) is suitable for promotion to wartime officer without reservation.

The request was successful, and Horst Schimpke was commissioned a second lieutenant on August 1, 1943. On February 15, 1944, he became the acting commander of the 1st Company, 1st Paratroop Anti-Tank Detachment (*Fallschirm-Panzer-Jäger-Abteilung 1*). At the fighting at Cassino on March 17, 1944, his company destroyed 20 enemy tanks during the Allied attack. On September 5, 1944, Second Lieutenant Horst Schimpke received the Knight's Cross of the Iron Cross for this action. He survived the war.[70] Horst Schimpke died on March 6, 1980 in Bochum-Gerthe. He is buried at the *Friedhof Hiltrop* (Section 72, Grave 155-156).

Gen. Kdo. XI. Fl. Korps
~~Fliegerdivision 7~~ — W.B.K. ~~Rastenburg~~ (Ostpr.)

Waffengattung: Fallsch.Truppe
Springendes Personal
Truppenteil: Fallschirm-Panzer=jäger-Abteilung

Vorschlag

zur Beförderung zum Kriegsoffizier
gemäß D (Luft) 2200.

Name: Schimpke — Geburtstag: 1o.11.192o Ort: Berlin=Schöneberg
Vorname: Horst — Familienstand: ledig
Dienstgrad: O.Feldwebel — Beruf: Landw.Beamter
Verwendung: Zugführer — Konfession: evgl.

Militärischer Werdegang:
Aktive Dienstzeit von - bis -
Dienstzeit bei Kriegsbeginn: 43 Monate
Längere Dienstverpflichtung auf 3, 4 1/2 oder 12 und mehr Jahre: -

Beförderungen und Ernennungen:
zum Gefreiten: 1.9.194o — zum Feldwebel: 1.8.1942
zum Unteroffz. 1.1o.1941 — zum O.-Feldw.: 1.4.1943
Hat mit Erfolg an einem Vorauswahllehrgang für K.O.A. teil=genommen.
Tag der Ernennung zum R.O.A. - bzw. K.O.A. : 1.1o.1942
Ist im Waffeneinsatz gestanden, wo

Ist im Kampfeinsatz gestanden, wo: Luftlandeoperation Kreta Kämpfe bei Malemes, Chania u.an der Sudabucht vom 21.-27.5.41 Abwehrkampf in der Marmarica und Cyrenaika v. 15.1. - 2o.1.42 Zweite Gegenoffensive zur Wiedererlangung der Cyrenaika vom 21.1. - 6.2.42, Stellungskampf am Ostrand der Cyrenaika ; 17.7.-2.1o.42: Sicherung im besetzten Gebiet im Bereich des Luftflottenkommandos 3
Hat mit Erfolg an einem K.O.N.-Lehrgang vom 19.1o. - 19.12.42 teilgenommen.

Frontbewährung.
Offizierswahl hat stattgefunden am 1o.3.1943
Bildungsgang: Erziehung im Elternhaus, Volksschule 4 Jahre, Oberrealschule mit Abschluß Reife f. Obersekunda von 1931 - 1937, Erlernung der Landwirtschaft mit Abschlßprüfung vor der Landesbauernschaft, Tätigkeit als landw. Inspektor.

Request for Promotion to Officer for Master Sergeant Horst Schimpke (front side) – no exact date when report was begun, on blank paper, with typed comments. Later comments in pencil indicate that Schimpke was promoted to second lieutenant on August 1, 1943.

Bestrafungen vpr Diensteintritt: Keine

Bestrafungen nach Diensteintritt: Keine

Auszeichnungen: Eisernes Kreuz 2.Klasse verl. am 8.6.41
Eisernes Kreuz 1. Klasse verl. am 21.6.41
Verwundetenabzeichen in Schwarz: 4.7.41

Stand und Beruf des Vaters: Versicherungsangestellter

Familienname der Mutter: Haack

Anschrift der nächsten Angehörigen: Vater: Bruno Sch.
Berlin SW 29, Grimmstr. 17

Ausserdienstliche Eignung festgestellt durch:
beantragt bei: W.B.K.Rastenburg

Beurteilung:

Schimpke ist ein gerader, anständiger Charakter, bei Kameraden beliebt. Er besitzt ein freies Auftreten und hat gute Umgangsformen. Geistig sehr beweglich und für höhere Aufgaben fähig. Körperlich sehr gewandt, guter Sportsmann. Im Dienst hat er sehr gute Kenntnisse und Leistungen gezeigt. Er ist fleißig, gewissenhaft und tatkräftig. Vor der Front besitzt er ein tadelloses Auftreten. In der Ausbildung seiner Untergebenen war er vorbildlich. Im Osteinsatz hat der Ofw. Schimpke einen Pakzug, der in vorderster Linie eingesetzt war, zur vollsten Zufriedenheit seiner Vorgesetzten geführt und sich voll bewährt.

Hauptmann und Abteilungskommandeur.

Div.Gef.Std., den 1. 5. 1943

Stellungnahme des Divisionskommandeurs:

E i n v e r s t a n d e n und b e f ü r w o r t e t .
Obfw.(K.O.A.) S c h i m p k e (Horst) ist zur Beförderung zum Kriegsoffizier uneingeschränkt geeignet.

Generalmajor und Divisionskommandeur.

Request for Promotion to Officer for Master Sergeant Horst Schimpke (back side) – signed by Captain Gerhard Brückner, the 1st Paratroop Anti-Tank Detachment Commander, and by Brigadier General Richard Heidrich, Commander, 1st Paratroop Division.

Leonhard Schmidt

Fallschirmjäger

"Has always been an exemplary platoon leader and has consistently proved his unusual courage in the heaviest combat."

Captain Leonhard Schmidt was born on December 9, 1916 in Weissenstadt/Wunsiedel, Bavaria. He joined the 2nd Company, Regiment "General Göring" on November 3, 1937. In the spring of 1938, Schmidt attended airborne school at Stendal and joined the 2nd Company, 1st Paratroop Regiment (*Fallschirmjäger-Regiment 1*) on June 1, 1938. Schmidt deployed to Poland during the 1939 campaign, but saw no combat. However, the 3rd Company, to which he was now assigned, jumped into Stavanger, Norway to seize a key airfield at Stola; he won the Iron Cross 2nd Class on April 18, 1940 for this operation. On May 10, 1940, Schmidt and the 1st Paratroop Regiment fought at Dordrecht, Holland (to seize key bridges over the Maas River there, for which he received the Iron Cross 1st Class on May 25, 1940) and then reinforced General Eduard Dietl's mountain troops in northern Norway, at Narvik, from June 4 to July 6, 1940 – an operation that earned Schmidt the Narvik Battle Shield.

On May 20, 1941, Schmidt and the 3rd Company, 1st Paratroop Regiment jumped into Crete, east of Herákleion as part of the German airborne invasion of the island. He was wounded the same day. Schmidt and the regiment deployed to Russia on September 25, 1941 and fought east of Leningrad through November 15, 1941. On November 15, Schmidt was again wounded in action, this time near Schlüsselburg. He spent time in a field hospital where he was promoted to technical sergeant on January 1, 1942. He returned to Russia with his unit on October 25, 1942 and remained there until July 1, 1943. During this time, Schmidt's platoon distinguished itself in combat southwest of Orel in an attack on Promklewo.

In March 1943, Major Wolf-Werner von der Schulenburg, commander of the 1st Battalion, 1st Paratroop Regiment, submitted a request to promote Technical Sergeant Leo Schmidt to second lieutenant due to bravery in the face of the enemy. Von der Schulenburg wrote:[71]

> **Evaluation:** Technical Sergeant Schmidt has particularly excelled and distinguished himself in many missions. For the operation at Stavanger, Technical Sergeant Schmidt received the Iron Cross 2nd Class, and during the operation in Holland he got the Iron Cross 1st Class. He distinguished himself in the following operations in Narvik, Crete and Wyborgskaja through his consistent courage. In the severe battles southwest of Orel, during the period of March 1 to 17, 1943, Technical Sergeant Schmidt continuously proved his courage. Above that, he showed outstanding leadership qualities in leading his platoon.
>
> Schmidt's platoon participated decisively during the attack on Promklewo. Thanks to his personal risk-taking, the attack went on in such a smooth fashion that the enemy did not have the time to establish himself. The difficult task to take the village which was occupied by far superior forces, without the support of heavy weapons, could only be mastered by the extraordinary courage of the leader. Technical Sergeant Schmidt has to be named foremost here.
>
> On March 4, 1943, during an attack by the Russians at Baldysch, Technical Sergeant Schmidt succeeded in halting the enemy attack with a courageous counter-attack with a part of his platoon and the company troops. In dashing counter-attacks, Technical Sergeant Schmidt took 100 prisoners. Particularly through this counter-attack, the danger to Baldysch, and with that also for Dmitrowsk, was stopped and most of the attacking enemy could be destroyed. On March 5, 1943, during the attack on Aleschenka, Technical Sergeant Schmidt led the point platoon and again proved his personal courage and leadership qualities. Technical Sergeant Schmidt was greatly involved in the success of this difficult attack.
>
> On March 9, 1943, Schmidt once again distinguished himself in the counter-attacks against the Hills 266 and 262.3. Through his initiative, he and his section destroyed an enemy group that had slipped through the defenses.
>
> In summary, it can be said that Technical Sergeant Schmidt has always been an exemplary platoon leader and has consistently proved his unusual courage in the heaviest combat. The soldierly concept and the military appearance of Technical Sergeant Schmidt, during the years he was part of the battalion, have always been outstanding. Without reservation, Technical Sergeant Schmidt is suitable for becoming an officer.
>
> The battalion requests that Technical Sergeant Schmidt be promoted to officer due to his courage in the face of the enemy.

Von der Schulenburg's recommendation was successful, and Schmidt was commissioned a second lieutenant on April 20, 1943. He received the German Cross in Gold for these actions on June 24, 1943. His unit returned to Italy, where on December 15, 1943, Second Lieutenant Leonhard Schmidt became the acting commander of the 3rd Company, 1st Paratroop Regiment. In January 1944, Schmidt led his company on three instances of close combat northwest of Ortona in fighting against the British 8th Army. He then deployed to Cassino, where on February 18, 1944, he fought in close combat on Hills 593 and 450 against the Gurkhas of the 4th Indian Division. On April 3 and April 14, he again fought in close contact with attacking Allied forces. Schmidt was promoted to first lieutenant on July 1, 1944 and soon became the adjutant of the 2nd Battalion, 1st Paratroop Regiment. He would fight close combat operations on at least ten days that fall, as the *Fallschirmjäger* conducted a skillful withdrawal into northern Italy.

On December 5, 1944, he assumed temporary command of the 2nd Battalion. He was promoted to captain on April 20, 1945. On April 30, 1945, Captain Leonhard Schmidt received the Knight's Cross of the Iron Cross for his accumulated combat achievements in Italy.[72] He was taken prisoner on May 2, 1945. Leonhard Schmidt spent almost 7 years in the same *Fallschirmjäger* regiment, taking part in some of the heaviest fighting of the war in Europe.[73]

Generalkommando XI.Fl.-Korps
Fallschirmtruppe
I./Fallschirm-Jäger Rgt.1

W. B. K. Marktredwitz

V o r s c h l a g

zur Beförderung zum Kriegsoffizier
wegen Tapferkeit vor dem Feinde.

Name: Schmidt | Geburtstag: 9.12.16. | Ort: Weißenstadt
Vorname: Leo | Familienstand: verh. | Kinder: 1
Dienstgrad: Feldwebel | Beruf: Graphiker
Verwendung: Zugführer | Konfession: ev.
Militärischer Werdegang:

Dienstzeit seit: 1.11.37.
Dienstverpflichtung: keine

Beförderungen u. Ernennungen:

zum Gefreiten am 1.10.38. zum Oberjäger am 1.11.39.
" Obegefr. am 1.10.39. " Feldwebel am 1. 1.42.

Hat mit Erfolg an einem Vorauswahllehrgang für K.O.A. teilgenommen. entfällt

Tag der Ernennung zum K.O.A. "

Jst im Waffeneinsatz gestanden, wo Stavanger,Holland,Narvik,Kreta, Rußland 1941/42/43.
von ______ bis ______

Jst im Kampfeinsatz gestanden, wo wie oben
von ______ bis ______

Hat mit Erfolg an einem K.O.N.-Lehrgang von ______ bis ______ teilgenommen.

Offizierwahl hat stattgefunden am: entfällt

Bildungsgang:
8 Jahre Volksschule
2 Jahre Berufsschule

Bestrafungen vor Diensteintritt: keine

Bestrafungen nach Diensteintritt: keine

Auszeichnungen: EK II. u. I ,Narvikschild,Erdk.-Abz.d.Luftw., Verw.-Abzeichen (schwarz)

Stand u.Beruf des Vaters: Jnvalide

Familienname der Mutter: Lang

Anschrift der nächsten Angehörigen: Weißenstadt/Oberfr. Poststr.358

Ausserdienstliche Eignung festgestellt durch:
oder beantragt bei:

Request for Promotion to Officer for Technical Sergeant Leo Schmidt (front side) – no exact date when report was begun, on blank paper, with typed comments. Later comments in pencil indicate that Schmidt was promoted to second lieutenant on April 1, 1943.

Beurteilung:

Fw. Schmidt hat sich in den vielen Einsätzen besonders bewährt und ausgezeichnet. Fw.Sch. erhielt beim Einsatz Stavanger das EK 2 und beim Einsatz Holland das EK 1.Er zeichnete sich bei den folgenden Einsätzen in Narvik, Kreta und Wyborgskaja durch seine gleichbleibende Tapferkeit aus. Bei den schweren Kämpfen südwestlich Orel in der Zeit vom 1.-17.3.43. stellte Fw.Schm. seine Tapferkeit laufend unter Beweis. Darüber hinaus zeigte er bei der Führung seines Zuges hervorragende Führereigenschaften.

Beim Angriff auf Promklewo hatte der Zug Schm. mit entscheidenden Anteil. Seinem persönlichem Draufgängertum war es zu verdanken, daß der Angriff so zügig vonstatten ging und der Gegner keine Zeit fand, sich festzusetzen. Die schwierige Aufgabe, den von weit überlegenen Kräften besetzten Ort ohne Unterstützung von schweren Waffen zu nehmen, konnte nur durch die aussergewöhnlichen Tapferkeit der Führer gemeistert werden. Fw. Schm. ist hier an erster Stelle zu nennen.

Am 4.3.43. brachte Fw. Schm. bei einem Angriff des Russen bei Baldysch den feindlichen Angriff durch einen mit Teilen seines Zuges und dem Kp.-Trupp geführten kühnen Gegenstoß zum Stocken. Jm schneidigen Nachstoßen brachte Fw.Schm. 100 Gefangene ein. Hauptsächlich durch diesen Gegenstoß konnte die Gefahr für Baldysch und damit auch für Dmitrowsk gebannt und der angreifende Gegner fast restlos vernichtet werden.

Am 5.3.43. führte Schm. beim Angriff auf Aleschenka den Spitzenzug und stellte erneut seinen persönlichen Mut und seine Führereigenschaften unte Beweis. Am Gelingen dieses schwierigen Angriffs hat Fw.Schm. einen großen Anteil.

Am 9.3.43. zeichnete sich Schm. bei den Gegenangriffen gegen die Höhen 266 und 262,3 wiederum besonders aus. Durch eigene Jnitiative vernichtete er mit seinem Zuge eine durchgesickerte Kräftegruppe.

Zusammenfassend kann gesagt werden, daß Fw.Schm. sich in den schweren Kämpfen stets als vorbildlicher Zugführer gezeigt hat und daß er laufend Proben einer ungewöhnlichen Tapferkeit gab. Die soldatische Auffassung und das militärische Auftreten des Fw. Schm. sind in den Jahren seiner Zugehörigkeit zum Btl. stets hervorragend gewesen. Fw. Schm. ist zum Offz. uneingeschränkt geeignet.

Das Btl. bittet, Fw. Schm. wegen Tapferkeit vor dem Feinde zum Offz. befördern zu wollen.

Graf v. d. Schulenburg

Major u. Btl.-Kommandeur.

Request for Promotion to Officer for Technical Sergeant Leo Schmidt (back side) – signed by Major Wolf-Werner Graf von der Schulenburg, Commander, 1st Battalion, 1st Paratroop Regiment.

Otto Schmidt

Stuka Pilot

"In every respect, well-rooted character."

Captain Otto Schmidt was born in Brühlhof bei Kirchen an der Sieg, in the district of Altenkirchen on February 23, 1917. He joined the *Luftwaffe* on April 6, 1937, was promoted to second lieutenant on January 1, 1938 and flew in the Polish and French campaigns as a second lieutenant in the 1st Group, 76th Stuka Wing (*Sturzkampfgeschwader 76*) and subsequently with the 77th Stuka Wing (*Sturzkampfgeschwader 77*). Schmidt served for a period as the group adjutant and was promoted to first lieutenant on June 1, 1940.

On February 10, 1941, First Lieutenant Helmut Bruck, Commander, 1st Group, 77th Stuka Wing, submitted an efficiency report on Otto Schmidt. The report – which was hand-written, not typed – read, in part:[74]

> **Character:** In every respect, well-rooted character. Is true to the principles he sets for himself. Withdrawn in the circle of his comrades.
>
> **Personality values:** Excellent officer who acts deliberately. As a leader of a unit, still inexperienced. Demeanor within and outside of the service very correct.
>
> **Conduct before the enemy:** As "*Kettenführer*" [leader of three aircraft] in Poland, France and England. Iron Cross 1st Class.
>
> **Service accomplishments:** As squadron commander, works extremely well with the leader. Still lacking experience as an adjutant. However, is in command of very good empathy. Passionate flyer with an excellent expressed feeling for piloting.
>
> **Possibilities for use as:** Adjutant, squadron officer at any time. Very well suited to be a squadron commander, when he has gathered the necessary experience.

On August 25, 1941, Schmidt landed his aircraft behind enemy lines to rescue a radio operator from his unit, who had bailed out during combat. Schmidt assumed command of the 7th Squadron, 77th Stuka Wing on December 20, 1941. Schmidt won the German Cross in Gold on April 24, 1942. Promoted to captain on August 1, he flew his 500th combat mission on August 20, 1942 and received the Knight's Cross of the Iron Cross on September 3, 1942. From October 1942 to July 1943, Schmidt was detailed to the staff of *Luftwaffe* Command East. He returned to the front and took command on July 11, 1943 of the 2nd Squadron, 5th Stuka Wing (*Sturzkampfgeschwader 5*), which was designated the 5th Ground-Attack Wing (*Schlachtgeschwader 5*) that October. On November 4, 1943 he left the unit to join the 3rd Group, 77th Ground-Attack Wing (*Schlachtgeschwader 77*) in northern Russia, where he remained in combat until January 20, 1944. He then joined the staff of the 1st Air Fleet and on October 1, 1944 returned to Berlin to serve as a General Staff Officer on the Air War Academy at Berlin-Gatow. After the war, he remained in British captivity until 1947. Otto Schmidt flew 555 combat missions in Junkers Ju 87 aircraft. He destroyed 61 tanks, sank a freighter off Dunkirk and sank a Russian submarine in the Black Sea.[75]

I./Sturzkampfgeschwader 77

Beurteilungs-Notizen

für

Oblt. Otto Schmidt

seit dem 1.7.1938 bei I./Sturzkampfgeschwader 77

Charakter: In jeder Hinsicht gefestigter Charakter. Bleibt seinen sich selbst gestellten Grundsätzen treu. Im Kameradenkreis zurückhaltend.

Wert der Persönlichkeit: Verlässlicher Offizier, der überlegt zu handeln weiß. Als Führer eine Sicherheit und Erfahrung. Auftreten in u. außer Dienst sehr korrekt.

Bewährung vor dem Feinde: Als Kettenführer in Polen, Frankreich u. England. E.K. 1. Klasse.

Dienstliche Leistungen: Als Staffeloffizier arbeitet er hervorragend mit dem Führer zusammen. Als Adjutant fehlt Erfahrung. Besitzt jedoch sehr gutes Einfühlungsvermögen. Passionierter Flieger mit ausgesprochen gutem fliegerischen Gefühl.

Verwendungsmöglichkeit: Adjutant, Staffeloffizier jeder Art. Als Staffelkapitän sehr gut geeignet, wenn im Umgang mit Untergebenen die nötige Erfahrung gesammelt ist.

10.2.41.

Bruck, Oblt.

Efficiency Report for First Lieutenant Otto Schmidt (one page only) – dated February 10, 1941, on locally-produced pre-printed form, with hand-written comments. Signed by First Lieutenant Helmut Bruck, Commander, 1st Group, 77th Stuka Wing.

Heinz-Wolfgang Schnaufer

Night Fighter Pilot

"Somewhat shy."

Major Heinz-Wolfgang Schnaufer was born on February 16, 1922 in Calw, Württemberg. He joined the *Luftwaffe* on November 1, 1939 and was assigned to the 42nd Flight Training Regiment. From there, he attended two pilot schools, one at Guben and another at Alt-Lönnewitz. During this period, Heinz Schnaufer was promoted to officer candidate. On March 18, 1941, the commander of Pilot School (C) 3 (*Flugzeugführerschule (C) 3*), Colonel Eric Macard, submitted an efficiency report on Heinz Schnaufer, supporting his commissioning to second lieutenant. The report read, in part:[76]

> **Reason for Consideration:**
>
> **Disposition:** Decent, balanced character, calm, somewhat shy. Mentally and physically very well developed, is above average.
>
> **Militarily:** His soldierly appearance is very good, strict attitude. Good trainer. At the front he is a little too soft, but otherwise secure in giving orders. Good commando language, leadership qualities are present.
>
> **As a flyer:** In training towards the *Luftwaffe* Advanced Pilot's Certificate, he showed very useful flight accomplishments with a good feeling for flying. He will become a reliable pilot.
>
> **Outside of service:** Firmly rooted in National Socialism and is able to pass on the wealth of ideas of National Socialism. Good comrade with good manners.

The senior rater, Lieutenant General Helmuth Wilberg added simply: "Noted".

Heinz Schnaufer was promoted to second lieutenant on April 1, 1941 and assigned to the 2nd Group, 1st Night Fighter Wing (*Nachtjagdgeschwader 1*) in November 1941. On the night of June 1-2, 1942, he shot down his first enemy aircraft (which was heading toward Duisburg and Oberhausen), and by the end of the year had scored seven aerial victories. He received the Iron Cross 2nd Class on June 2, 1942 and the Iron Cross 1st Class on October 19, 1942. The year 1943 would prove much better; on one night, December 16-17, 1943, he scored four kills, while on May 29-30 and June 28-29, he scored three each. Schnaufer was promoted to first lieutenant on July 1, 1943, received the German Cross in Gold on July 3, 1943 and the *Luftwaffe* Honor Goblet on July 26, 1943. He assumed command of the 12th Squadron, 1st Night Fighter Wing on August 20, 1943. On December 31, 1943, after achieving 42 night victories, First Lieutenant Heinz Schnaufer received the Knight's Cross of the Iron Cross.

The following year proved even more significant. Schnaufer shot down three enemy aircraft on each of the following dates: February 15-16, April 24-25, May 12-13, July 28-29, October 9-10 and November 6-7. But on other nights, he achieved even greater results, scoring four kills on the nights of: April 24-25, May 24-25, June 21-22, August 12-13, and September 23-24. The year also saw him take command of the 2nd Group, 1st Night Fighter Wing on March 1, 1944, be promoted to major on May 1, 1944 and assume the position of Commodore, 4th Night Fighter Wing (*Nachtjagdgeschwader 4*) on November 1, 1944. All accomplishments came with rewards as Captain Heinz Schnaufer became the 507th recipient of the Oak Leaves to the Knight's Cross of the Iron Cross on June 24, 1944 and the 84th recipient of the Swords to the Oak Leaves on July 30, 1944. Schnaufer would go even further, winning the Diamonds to his Oak Leaves and Swords on October 16, 1944 – only the 21st recipient of this award.

In 1945, Heinz Schnaufer showed he had one more ace up his sleeve. On the night of February 21-22, 1945, Schnaufer shot down seven British Lancaster bombers in 19 minutes; he would achieve his 121st and final victory on the night of March 7-8, when he dispatched three more bombers. The *Luftwaffe* High Command then ordered Schnaufer to cease combat operations, but he disobeyed and flew several more missions. During the war, Heinz Schnaufer flew 164 combat missions, achieving 121 nighttime victories, of which 114 were four-engine bombers – equating to a sortie-to-victory ratio of 1.35 to 1. He was the most successful night fighter pilot in the *Luftwaffe*.

Schnaufer came close to death on several occasions during the war. On the night of August 17/18, 1943, during the Royal Air Force attack on the German weapons' research facility at Peenemünde, British Beaufighters, just-equipped with the Serrate device – a detector which enabled the pilot to find the location of a German night fighter by picking up its radar emissions. The Beaufighters shot down two aircraft in

Schnaufer's flight, but his Messerschmitt Me 110 escaped the trap – only to be shot at by German *flak* when he landed later at Wittmundhafen![77] Heinz Schnaufer survived the war, but on July 13, 1950 was involved in a traffic accident southwest of Bordeaux, France and died two days later in a hospital. He is buried in Calw.[78]

Geheim

Flugzeugführerschule (C) 3 Alt-Lönnewitz, 18.3.1941

Abt.IIa Az.:22

Br.B.Nr....374..../41 geh.

Betr.: Vorschlag zur Beförderung zum Leutnant.

Auf dem Dienstwege

an den R.d.L.u.Ob.d.L. (L.P.)

B e r l i n

Zur Beförderung zum Leutnant wird in Vorschlag gebracht :

Familienname: S c h n a u f e r Vorname : Heinz

geb. am: 16.2.1922 zu: Stuttgart Konfession : ev.

Dienstgrad: Oberfähnrich verwendet als : Flugzeugführer /LF (in Ausb.z. ELF)

Diensteintritt am : 15.11.1939 verh./led.: ledig

Ernennung zum Oberfähnrich bzw. 1.2.1941 Kinder ./.

Offz. Anwärter wann ? 1.4.1940

Wehrbez.Kdo. des Wohnortes : Potsdam I

Bestrafungen vor Diensteintritt: keine

Bestrafungen nach Diensteintritt: keine

Zum Offz. gewählt am : 15.3.1941

Beruf vor Diensteintritt: Schüler

Stand und Beruf des Vaters : Kaufmann

Mutter geborene : Frey

Anschrift der Eltern bezw. des Vormundes:

Vater : Alfred Schnaufer, Calw/Württbg.,Lederstr. 60

Bildungsgang : Volksschule, Gymnasium, N.P.E.A., Reifezeugnis

Mil. Werdegang :

15.11.39 – 8. 1.40	1./Fl.Ausb.Rgt.42	1.4.40	Fhj. ernannt
8. 1.40 – 19. 8.40	Flzgf.Sch.(A/B)3 Guben	1.4.40	Fhj.Gefr.
20. 8.40 –	Flzgf.Sch.(C) 3	1.7.40	Fhj.Uffz.
		1.9.40	Fähnrich
		1.2.41	Oberfähnrich

Begründung :

Seit seiner Beförderung zum Oberfähnrich weiter gut entwickelt.

Veranlagung : Anständiger, ausgeglichener Charakter, ruhig, etwas verschlossen. Geistig und körperlich sehr gut veranlagt, steht über dem Durchschnitt.

Militärisch : Sein soldatisches Auftreten ist sehr gut, stramme Haltung. Guter Exerzierer. Vor der Front ist er etwas zu weich, sonst aber sicher im Geben von Befehlen. Gute Kommandosprache. Führereigenschaften sind vorhanden.

Request for Promotion to Officer for Officer Candidate Heinz Schnaufer (front side) – dated March 18, 1941, on blank paper, with typed comments. Report is stamped "*Geheim*" (Secret) in red at the top.

Fliegerisch : Bei der Ausbildung zum ELF-Schein zeigte er bei gutem fliegerischen Gefühl sehr brauchbare fliegerische Leistungen. Er wird ein zuverlässiger Flugzeugführer werden.

Außer Dienst : Steht fest auf dem Boden des Nationalsozialismus und ist befähigt das Ideengut des Nationalsozialismus weiter zu geben. Guter Kamerad mit guten Formen.

Oberst und Kommandeur.

G e s e h e n .

Dresden, den 21. März 1941.

General der Flieger und
Höh.Fl.Ausb. Kdr. 4

Request for Promotion to Officer for Officer Candidate Heinz Schnaufer (back side) – signed by Colonel Eric Macard and Lieutenant General Helmuth Wilberg.

Herbert Schob

Destroyer Pilot

"Full of humor."

Herbert Schob was born May 12, 1915 at Leipzig. He entered the *Luftwaffe* in 1936, and after flight training joined the 4th Squadron, 134th Fighter Wing "Horst Wessel" (*Jagdgeschwader 134 "Horst Wessel"*). In June 1937, he joined the 4th Squadron, 1st Demonstration Wing (*Lehrgeschwader 1*). Schob fought in the Condor Legion in Spain, registering 6 kills. In March 1939, he returned to Germany; during the Polish campaign, he added two more aerial victories. On April 17, 1940, he shot down two British aircraft off the Norwegian coast, flying in the 3rd Squadron, 76th Destroyer Wing (*Zerstörergeschwader 76*). Schob took part in the Balkans campaign in 1941 and then flew on the Eastern Front. He destroyed 48 enemy aircraft on the ground, 128 supply vehicles, 15 artillery pieces, 2 anti-aircraft batteries and 3 trains, as well as achieving 3 aerial victories. Herbert Schob received the *Luftwaffe* Honor Goblet on November 27, 1941 and the German Cross in Gold on April 27, 1942. On June 18, 1942, he was assigned to the Destroyer Supplemental Group at Deblin (*Zerstörer-Ergänzungsgruppe*). In October, he attended an officer school and was commissioned a second lieutenant. Schob rejoined the 1st Squadron, 76th Destroyer Group on August 28, 1943 and assumed command of this formation on December 20, 1943. Over the next few months, he shot down 9 American planes, including two B-17 Flying Fortresses, part of the 8th Air Force's first attack on Berlin on March 6, 1944, but his Messerschmitt Me 110G-2 was hit by fire from escorting P-51 Mustangs; he was wounded, and he and his radio operator were forced to bail out. He returned to the wing in May as the operations officer.

On May 10, 1944, Schob's chain of command submitted a special efficiency report requesting that he be promoted to captain. His group commander wrote:[79]

> Average height, of stout appearance, but very flexible. Full of humor and an officer with immaculate character. With quick comprehension, he understands how to improvise and work on his own. Due to his 10 years of service, he has good troop service knowledge. He understands how to lead his squadron well on the ground and in the air. As a flyer, he is very talented. First Lieutenant Schob has proven himself in an excellent way in all war theaters, and he was recommended for the Knight's Cross. His social inexperience has improved. He understands how to present himself well as an officer, and he has earned the respect and recognition of his comrades and the men under his command.

Major Robert Kowalewski, the acting wing commodore, added the following comments:

> Nothing to be added to the above evaluation. Without hesitation, I consider First Lieutenant Schob suitable for promotion to captain.

On June 11, 1944, the 8th Fighter Division Commander, Colonel Gotthardt Handrick, added his own remarks:

> I do not know First Lieutenant Schob personally. Based on the reason for consideration given by the Group Commander and the evaluation by the Wing Commodore,

I consider First Lieutenant Schob suitable for promotion to Captain (wartime officer).

Herbert Schob received the Knight's Cross of the Iron Cross on June 9, 1944 after achieving 19 aerial victories in addition to his ground-attack accomplishments. He assumed command of the Supplemental Squadron, 76th Destroyer Wing, on June 15, 144 and led this unit until August 31, 1944. On that date, the unit was renamed the 1st Squadron, Fighter Group East (*Jagdgruppe Ost*), and Schob remained in command until November 1944, when he moved to the 300th Fighter Wing (*Jagdgeschwader 300*), and served as the operations officer. Herbert Schob died April 5, 1981 in Frankfurt/Main, Hesse. He is buried at the *Hauptfriedhof* in Frankfurt/Main (Section V, Grave 1070). Schob flew over 300 combat missions and scored 28 aerial victories. These included 6 in Spain and 17 in the West (including 10 four-engine bombers).[80]

RDA-Mob.

Vorschl.Dienststelle: Z.G.76
Lg.Kdo. :Gen.Kdo.I/J.K.
W.B.K. : Stralsund

Datum : 1o.5.44
Waffengattung: Fl.Truppe

Es wird vorgeschlagen zum Hauptmann (Kr.O.) mit Wirkung v.:1.7.44

Vor- und Zuname : Herbert S c h o b
Jetziger Dienstgrad: Oblt. (Kr.O.)

Geb.Datum : 12.5.1915
befördert am: 1.1o.1943
R.D.A. : 1. 3.1941

eingesetzt als: Staffelkapitän und Flugzeugführer
~~nicht~~/in Truppenführerstellung
auf Planstelle (Hptm.) gem.KStN 1157 (L) Bl.:a Zeile: 1

geeignet zum : Staffelkapitän

Art und Dauer der Verwendung im derzeitigen mobilen Einsatz einschl. Uk-Stellung und Arbeitsurlaub oder sonstigen Urlaubs über 3 Monate:

Von:	bis:	Dienststelle:	Dienststellung:
11.11.38	18. 3.4o	1. (Zerst.) Lehrgeschw.1 Barth	Flugzeugführer
19. 3.4o	31. 8.4o	3./Z.G.76	"
1. 9.4o	3o. 9.4o	6./N.J.G. 1	"
1.1o.4o	13.12.4o	8./N.J.G. 1	"
14.12.4o	2. 1.41	N.J.-Div.Stab	"
3. 1.41	31. 3.41	Flugbereitschaft des RLM T.K.	"
1. 4.41	3o.11.41	I./Z.G. 26, 2. Staffel	"
1.12.41	27. 4.42	I./N.J.G.4, 2. Staffel	"
28. 4.42	2. 5.42	II./Z.G. 2, 5. Staffel	"
3. 5.42	22. 7.42	2./Erg.Zerst.Gr.	"
23. 7.42	7. 2.43	1./Erg.Zerst.Gr.	"
8. 2.43	5.1o.43	Erg.Nahaufklärergruppe	"
6.1o.43	noch	I./Z.G.76	Flugz.F.u.Staffelf.

Strafen: keine

Auszeichnungen des jetzigen Krieges mit Verleihungsdaten:

8. 9.39 E.K. II
30. 6.4o E.K. I
30. 1.41 Narvikschild
30. 5.41 Fr.Fl.Sp.f.Jäger in Gold
8.12.41 Ehrenpokal
27. 4.42 Deutsches Kreuz in Gold
21. 5.42 Ärmelband Kreta
18. 9.42 Ostmedaille
5. 4.44 Verw.Abz.schwarz

Beurteilung durch den Disziplinarvorgesetzten:

Mittelgrosse, füllige Erscheinung, jedoch sehr beweglich. Humorvoller und charakterlich einwandfreier Offz. Von schneller Auffassung, vermag zu improvisieren und selbständig zu handeln. Auf Grund seiner 1o-jährigen Dienstzeit besitzt er gute truppendienstliche Kenntnisse. Er verstand es, seine Staffel am Boden und in der Luft gut zu führen. Fliegerisch sehr gut veranlagt. Oblt. Sch. hat sich auf allen Kriegsschauplätzen hervorragend bewährt, er wurde zum Ritterkreuz eingereicht. Seine gesellschaftliche Ungeübtheit hat sich gebessert. Er versteht es, sich als Offz. durchzusetzen und hat sich Achtung und Anerkennung bei Kameraden und Untergebenen erworben.

Opperdorf

Hauptmann und Gruppenkommandeur
m.d.W.d.G.b.

wenden!

Request for Promotion for First Lieutenant Herbert Schob (front side) – dated May 10, 1944, on blank paper, with typed comments. Signed by a captain and acting group commander.

Stellungnahme des Geschwaderkommodore:

Umseitiger Beurteilung ist nichts hinzuzufügen.
Ich halte Oblt. S c h o b zur Beförderung zum Hauptmann
für uneingeschränkt geeignet.

Major und Geschwaderkommodore.
m.d.W.d.G.b.

8. J a g d d i v i s i o n   Div.Gefechtsstand,den 11.6.1944.
-Kommandeur-

Oblt.S c h o b ist mir persönlich nicht bekannt.
Auf Grund der Beurteilung des Gruppenkommandeurs und der
Stellungnahme des Geschwaderkommodore halte ich Oblt.Schob
für die Beförderung zum Hauptmann (Kr.O.) geeignet.

Oberst.

Request for Promotion for First Lieutenant Herbert Schob (back side) – signed by Major Robert Kowalewski, acting commodore, 76th Destroyer Wing, and by Colonel Gotthardt Handrick, Commander, 8th Fighter Division.

Rudolf Schoenert
Night Fighter Pilot

"He always looks for new missions."

Major Rudolf Schoenert was born on July 27, 1911 in Glogau, Silesia. He joined the commercial shipping industry in 1928, became a pilot in 1933, and joined *Lufthansa* in 1936. After that, he entered the *Luftwaffe* and became a reserve second lieutenant in May 1938. Schoenert trained to fly large seaplanes before transferring to the 4th Squadron, 1st Night Fighter Wing (*Nachtjagdgeschwader 1*) on June 9, 1941. During the night of July 8-9, 1941, Schoenert shot down his first two enemy aircraft (that were probably on an RAF Bomber Command mission against Hamm). He won the Iron Cross 2nd Class the following day and the Iron Cross 1st Class on July 22, 1941. Schoenert became the acting commander, 5th Squadron on September 1, 1941. Schoenert received the *Luftwaffe* Honor Goblet on January 5, 1942. In May 1942, he assumed command of the 4th Squadron, 2nd Night Fighter Wing (*Nachtjagdgeschwader 2* won the German Cross in Gold on May 25, 1942. First Lieutenant Rudolf Schoenert received the Knight's Cross of the Iron Cross on July 25, 1942 after achieving 21 aerial victories at night. On October 1, 1942, he transferred to the command of the 2nd Squadron, 3rd Night Fighter Wing (*Nachtjagdgeschwader 3*), before rising to become the commander of the 2nd Group, 5th Night Fighter Wing (*Nachtjagdgeschwader 5*) on December 1, 1942.

On June 1, 1943, Schoenert's chain of command submitted an efficiency report on him. Major and acting *Geschwader* commodore, Fritz Schaffer, wrote the following:[81]

> Since the beginning of December 1942, Captain Sch. [Schoenert] has been tasked as the temporary stand-in for the group commander of 2nd Group, *Nachtjagdgeschwader 5*. He is a mature, steadfast personality and in possession of good character attributes. As an officer and pilot, he sets an example for the men under his command concerning diligence, willingness for action and achievement. Talent for improvisation and initiative are exceedingly present and are of good use for the entire group with positive results. With great interest, he always looks for new missions. For service with troops (Sch. [Schoenert] is a reserve officer) he strives with great success to further broaden his knowledge. As an officer and superior, he is respected and liked within the circle of his comrades. Captain Sch. [Schoenert] fulfills his position well.

Brigadier General Joachim-Friedrich Huth, the temporary stand-in for the commander of the 4th Fighter Division (*4. Jagddivision*) added a hand-written notation to the report:

> Excellent fighter pilot with rich experience and great technical knowledge. Is effective by setting an example and fully functions as the commander.

Schoenert "set an example" on the night of August 2/3, 1943, when he shot down a British Lancaster bomber over the North Sea as it flew on the RAF Bomber Command mission to destroy Hamburg.[82] On August 6, 1943, Schoenert moved to the Eastern Front and assumed command of the 1st Group, 100th Night Fighter Wing (*Nachtjagdgeschwader 100*) and by the end of October had shot down 32 Russian aircraft. Flying aptly named "Railroad Night Hunting" missions, he dispatched four enemy aircraft on each of three different nights, and three enemy planes on three each of three other nights. On January 1, 1944, Schoenert assumed command of the 10th Night Fighter Group – a test unit – and soon won the Oak Leaves to the Knight's Cross on April 11, 1944 (the 450th recipient). Two weeks prior to the award, Schoenert shot down a Lancaster during the disastrous RAF Bomber Command raid on Nuremburg.[83] At the end of the war on March 6, 1945, he took command of the 5th Night Fighter Wing. On the night of April 24-25, 1945, he shot down four Soviet bombers south of Berlin, before he was shot down – probably by a British night fighter – east of the Elbe.

Rudolf Schoenert flew 376 combat missions and shot down 65 enemy aircraft, a sortie-to-victory ratio of 5.78 to 1. Some 36 of his victories came on the Eastern Front. Rudolf Schoenert was generally credited with the concept, design and introduction into operational service of the *Schräge Musik* (literally slanting music, or jazz music), which were two 20-mm cannons mounted in the upper surface of the night fighter aircraft fuselage behind the pilot and pointing upward and slightly forward. Rudolf Schoenert died November 30, 1985 in Canada.[84]

Nachtjagdgeschwader 5 O.U., den 30.4. 1943.

Dienststelle, Truppenteil

Feldpostnummer: L 51248 Lgpa.Berlin

Beurteilungsnotiz Kriegsbeurteilung zum 1.Juni 1943.

Anlass: termingemässe Vorlage zum 1.Juni 1943.

über den Hauptmann (d.R.), Gruppenkommandeur II./N.J.G.5 m.d.W.d.G.b.

Dienstgrad, Dienststellung

Vor- und Zuname: Rudolf S c h o e n e r t geb. 27.7.1911

Rangdienstalter: 1.1.1943 Dienstalterliste: C

Verheiratet, ledig, verwitwet, geschieden (Zutreffendes unterstreichen)

Jetzige Verwendung: (z. B. Staffelkapitän seit seit Anfang Dezember 1942 m.d.W.d.G.b. des Gruppenkommandeurs II./N.J.G.5

Eignungsbeurteilung: siehe Rückseite

Wie wird jetzige Stelle ausgefüllt? gut

Geeignet zur Beförderung zum nächsthöheren Dienstgrad? ja, uneingeschränkt geeignet

Erworbene Lw.-Scheine? ELF-Schein, Blindflug C

Strafen: keine

Verwendungsvorschläge: (besondere Eignung, weitere Verwendung) Gruppenkommandeur einer Nachtjagdgruppe

Unterschrift

Major u. Geschwaderkommodore.

Dienstgrad und Dienststellung

m.d.W.d.G.b.

876a Maximilian-Verlag, Berlin SW 68, Ritterstr. 33 Wenden

Efficiency Report for Captain Rudolf Schoenert (front side) – dated April 30, 1943, on pre-printed form from the Maximilian Publishing firm in Berlin, with typed and one hand-written comments. Signed on this side by acting commodore, 1st Night Fighter Wing, Major Fritz Schaffer.

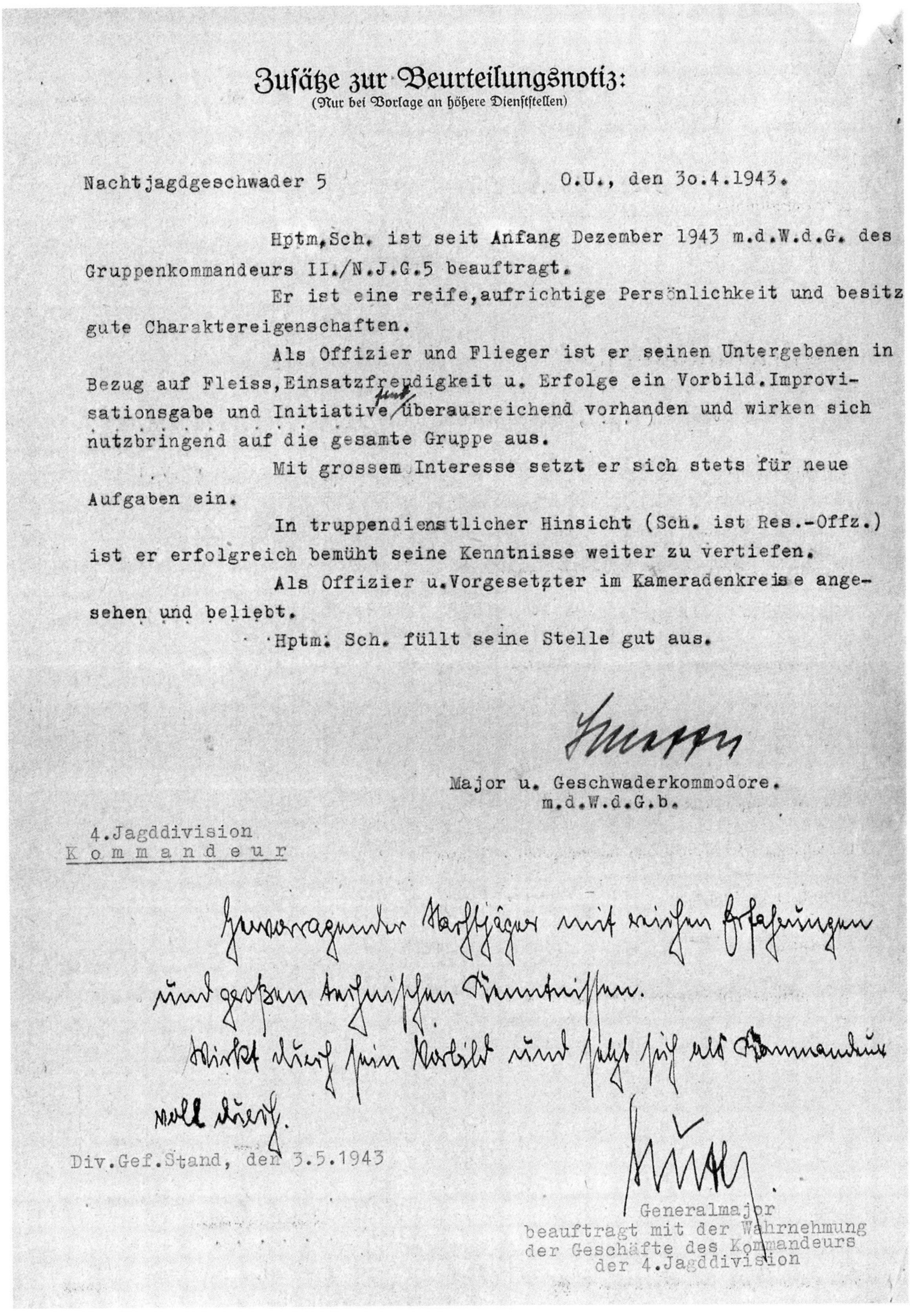

Zusätze zur Beurteilungsnotiz:

(Nur bei Vorlage an höhere Dienststellen)

Nachtjagdgeschwader 5 O.U., den 3o.4.1943.

Hptm.Sch. ist seit Anfang Dezember 1943 m.d.W.d.G. des Gruppenkommandeurs II./N.J.G.5 beauftragt.

Er ist eine reife,aufrichtige Persönlichkeit und besitz gute Charaktereigenschaften.

Als Offizier und Flieger ist er seinen Untergebenen in Bezug auf Fleiss,Einsatzfreudigkeit u. Erfolge ein Vorbild.Improvisationsgabe und Initiative sind überausreichend vorhanden und wirken sich nutzbringend auf die gesamte Gruppe aus.

Mit grossem Interesse setzt er sich stets für neue Aufgaben ein.

In truppendienstlicher Hinsicht (Sch. ist Res.-Offz.) ist er erfolgreich bemüht seine Kenntnisse weiter zu vertiefen.

Als Offizier u.Vorgesetzter im Kameradenkreise angesehen und beliebt.

Hptm. Sch. füllt seine Stelle gut aus.

Major u. Geschwaderkommodore.
m.d.W.d.G.b.

4.Jagddivision
Kommandeur

Hervorragender Nachtjäger mit reichen Erfahrungen und großen taktischen Kenntnissen.
Wirkt durch sein Vorbild und setzt sich als Kommandeur voll durch.

Div.Gef.Stand, den 3.5.1943

Generalmajor
beauftragt mit der Wahrnehmung
der Geschäfte des Kommandeurs
der 4.Jagddivision

Efficiency Report for Captain Rudolf Schoenert (back side) – signed again by Major Fritz Schaffer, and by Brigadier General Joachim-Friedrich Huth, acting commander of the 4th Fighter Division.

Walter Schuck
Fighter Pilot

"Slender build, but has endurance and hardiness."

First Lieutenant Walter Schuck was born in Frankenholz/Saar on July 30, 1920. In the fall of 1940, he reported to the Supplemental Group, 3rd Fighter Wing (*Jagdgeschwader 3*) and later transferred to the 7th Squadron, 5th Fighter Wing "Polar Sea" (*Jagdgeschwader 5 "Eismeer"*). He recorded his first aerial victory on May 15, 1942 in the far northern sector of the Eastern Front. He received the *Luftwaffe* Honor Goblet on March 29, 1943 and the German Cross in Gold on June 24, 1943, by which time he had achieved 54 aerial victories. Walter Schuck won the Knight's Cross of the Iron Cross on April 8, 1944, having achieved 84 kills by this date.

On June 5, 1944, Schuck's chain of command submitted a special evaluation requesting that he be commissioned a wartime officer. The bulk of the report was provided by Second Lieutenant Werner Gayko, the 9th Squadron Commander. Gayko wrote:[85]

> **Evaluation by the Squadron Commander:** Officer Candidate Schuck is of average mental capability, skillful and shows interest. Slender build, but has endurance and hardiness. Vivid, refreshing, open, true, decent, polite and ambitious character. Balanced personality. Good and well liked comrade. Excellent and passionate fighter pilot. Calculated daring, secure and calm in air battle are his particular assets. In more than 270 combat missions at the front, he has 94 confirmed aerial victories. Schuck has been awarded the Knight's Cross of the Iron Cross, the German Cross in Gold, *Luftwaffe* Honor Goblet, Iron Cross 1st Class, Iron Cross 2nd Class, Operational Flying Clasp for Fighters in Gold and the Black Wound Badge. As a soldier and superior, his appearance is without criticism. Willingness for increased responsibility and demands of service. Healthy, secure capability of judgment. His small shortcomings in the mental field are correctible through school subjects and, as compared to his successes, are relegated to the background. Despite his successes, he is always modest and correct.
>
> **Opinion of the Squadron Leader:** Due to his personality, his character attributes and his successes as a fighter pilot, I consider Officer Candidate Schuck fully eligible to become a wartime officer.

Colonel Otto Weiss signed for the 3rd Air Commander, but added no comments.

Schuck achieved his 100th victory on June 15, 1944, but perhaps his single best day was June 17, 1944 when he dispatched 12 enemy planes. On August 1, 1944, Schuck transferred to command the 10th Squadron and was promoted to second lieutenant. He won the Oak Leaves to the Knight's Cross on September 30, 1944 (the 616th recipient) after his 171st aerial victory. In early 1945, Walter Schuck trained on the Messerschmitt Me 262 jet aircraft and on March 24, 1945 assumed command of the 3rd Squadron, 7th Fighter Wing (*Jagdgeschwader 7*). He would shoot down 8 enemy aircraft flying the jet, including four B-17G Flying Fortresses on April 10, 1945, but was also shot down that day by American fighters and had to bail out. He finished the war with 500 combat missions and achieved 206 aerial victories, an incredible sortie-to-victory ratio of 2.42 to 1.[86]

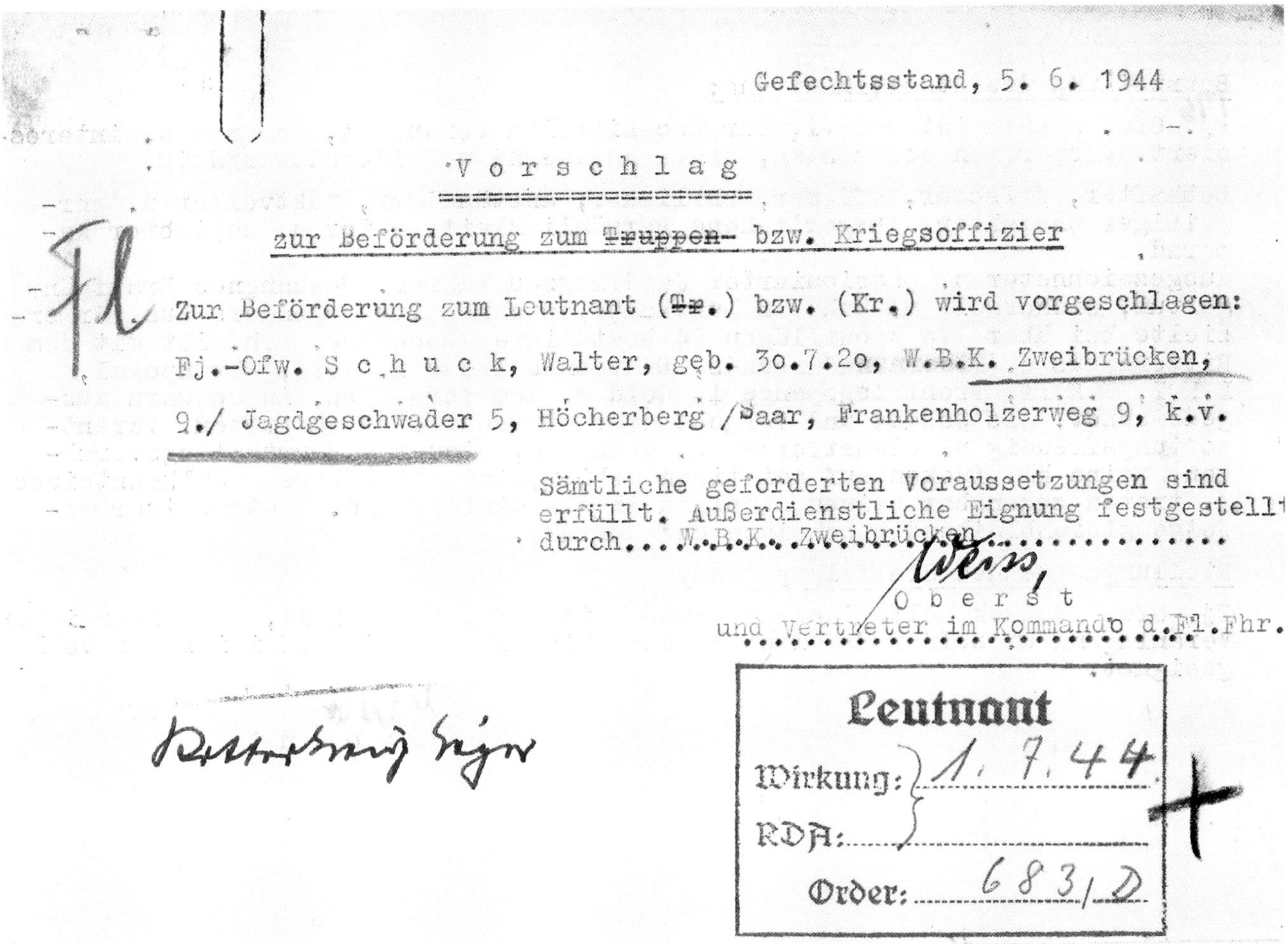

Gefechtsstand, 5. 6. 1944

V o r s c h l a g

zur Beförderung zum ~~Truppen-~~ bzw. Kriegsoffizier

Fl

Zur Beförderung zum Leutnant (~~Tr.~~) bzw. (Kr.) wird vorgeschlagen:

Fj.-Ofw. S c h u c k, Walter, geb. 3o.7.2o, W.B.K. Zweibrücken,

9./ Jagdgeschwader 5, Höcherberg /Saar, Frankenholzerweg 9, k.v.

Sämtliche geforderten Voraussetzungen sind erfüllt. Außerdienstliche Eignung festgestellt durch.....W.B.K. Zweibrücken...............

Weiss,
O b e r s t
und Vertreter im Kommando d.Fl.Fhr.

Leutnant
Wirkung: 1. 7. 44
RDA:
Order: 683/D

Request for Promotion to Officer for Officer Candidate Walter Schuck (front side) – dated June 5, 1944, on blank paper, with typed comments. Signed by Colonel Otto Weiss, acting commander for the 3rd Air Commander. Red stamp indicates that Schuck was promoted to second lieutenant on July 1, 1944.

Beurteilung des Staffelkapitäns:

Fj.-Ofw. Schuck ist geistig durchschnittlich veranlagt, gewandt u. interessiert. Körperlich schmächtig, aber ausdauernd u. widerstandsfähig.

Lebhafter, frischer, offener, ehrlicher, anständiger, taktvoller u. ehrgeiziger Charakter. Ausgeglichene Persönlichkeit. Guter u. beliebter Kamerad.

Ausgezeichneter u. passionierter Jagdflugzeugführer. Besonnenes Draufgängertum, Sicherheit u. Ruhe im Luftkampf, zeichnen ihn besonders aus. Er erzielte bei über 27o Frontflügen 94 bestätigte Abschüsse. Sch. ist mit dem Ritterkreuz d. Eisernen Kreuzes, Deutsches Kreuz i. Gold, Ehrenpokal, E.K.I, E.K.II, Frontflugspange i. Gold u. dem Verw. Abz. in schwarz ausgezeichnet. Als Soldat und Vorgesetzter einwandfreies Auftreten. Verantwortungsfreudig u. dienstfordernd. Gesundes, sicheres Beurteilungsvermögen. Seine kl. Lücken auf geistigem Gebiet, sind erlernbare Schulkenntnisse u. treten gegenüber seinen Erfolgen in den Hintergrund. Trotz seiner Erfolge gleichbleibend bescheiden und korrekt.

Stellungnahme des Staffelkapitäns:

Fj.-Ofw. Schuck halte ich auf Grund seiner Persönlichkeit, charakterlicher Veranlagung u. seiner Erfolge als Jagdflieger zum Kriegsoffizier für voll geeignet.

Gayko

Leutnant

Request for Promotion to Officer for Officer Candidate Walter Schuck (back side) – signed by Second Lieutenant Werner Gayko, Commander, 9th Squadron, 5th Fighter Wing.

Wolf-Werner Graf von der Schulenburg

Fallschirmjäger

"Despite his age and severe injuries suffered during the World War – one leg shortened by 5 cm – at the beginning of the war, he reported to the parachute troops."

Lieutenant Colonel Wolf-Werner Graf von der Schulenburg was born in Berlin-Charlottenburg on September 14, 1899. His father served as the chief of staff in World War I for an army group commanded by the Crown Prince. The younger von der Schulenburg joined the Army in 1917 and was very seriously wounded. As a result, operations left one of his legs two inches shorter than the other. Nevertheless, he was commissioned a second lieutenant on September 1, 1918. He rejoined the military in 1939, transferring to the *Luftwaffe's* 1st Paratroop Regiment (*Fallschirmjäger-Regiment 1*) – at age 40 – where he was promoted on April 1, 1940 to first lieutenant. His unit jumped into Moerdijk-Dordrecht, Holland in May 1940; for his actions during the seizure of some key bridges, von der Schulenburg received both the Iron Cross 2nd Class and 1st Class on May 23, 1940. Von der Schulenburg was promoted to captain on November 1, 1940. On May 20, 1941, the 1st Paratroop Regiment jumped into Crete east of Herákleion as part of the German airborne invasion of the island. Von der Schulenburg and the regiment deployed to Russia on September 25, 1941 and fought east of Leningrad through November 15, 1941. On November 19, 1941, von der Schulenburg was again promoted – to major. He was named acting commander of the 1st Battalion, 1st Paratroop Regiment on February 20, 1942. He returned to Russia with his unit on October 25, 1942. In February 1943, von der Schulenburg distinguished himself south of Orel during a Russian breakthrough of the 2nd *Panzer* Army, actions which led to the 78th Assault Division to recommend him for a Knight's Cross of the Iron Cross, which von der Schulenburg received on June 20, 1943.

Von der Schulenburg remained in Russia until July 1, 1943. He and his unit then deployed to Italy and fought at Tarent and Ortona. From November 1943 to mid-January 1944, he served as the acting commander of the 1st Paratroop Regiment; he then returned to the 1st Battalion as the commander and fought at Cassino, defending the high ground northwest of the town.

On April 4, 1944, Colonel Karl-Lothar Schulz, commander of the 1st Paratroop Regiment, initiated a request for a preferential promotion for Major von der Schulenburg. Schulz wrote:[87]

Reason for Consideration:

Accomplishments in general:

Since February 20, 1942, Major Graf von der Schulenburg has led the 1st Battalion, 1st Paratroop Regiment. During the missions of the regiment, Major Graf von der Schulenburg particularly distinguished himself through his outstanding personal courage and deliberate leadership. When in the winter in the East of 1942/43 the Russians succeeded with strong forces in a break-through at Dimitrowsk, Schulenburg was able to halt this to a stand-still, due to relentless personal engagement of himself with his battalion in severe offensive and defensive battles, while causing the heaviest losses to the enemy and thus avoiding the break-through to Orel-Bryansk.

During operations in Italy, Major Schulenburg and his battalion were in constant contact with the enemy in the withdrawal operations from the battle area of Tarent up to the Sangro position. Here again he proved his high military capabilities by clearing up even the most difficult situations with his leadership skills.

From mid-November 1943 to mid-January 1944, Schulenburg led the regiment as acting commander.

During the difficult defensive battles at Ortona, he demonstrated in this leadership position a clear view of difficult situations and a strength of decision-making.

In the battle area of Cassino, Schulenburg and his battalion excelled through decisive accomplishments in battle. When, during the first phase of the Cassino battles of February 8th to February 22, 1944, the enemy tried to force a breakthrough over the heights northwest of Cassino to the road from Cassino to Rome, the Battalion Schulenburg was a significant participant in the situation so that all breakthrough attempts were defeated with heavy losses for the enemy and in this way, the fall of Cassino was prevented.

Particular details:

Major Graf von der Schulenburg is an officer of high personal values. Exemplary willingness for combat as well as outstanding leadership and personal courage in battle mark him particularly. He is fully suitable to be a regimental commander.

Despite his age and the severe injuries suffered during the World War – one leg shortened by 5 cm – at the beginning of the war, he reported to the parachute troops and participated in all missions of the regiment. Based on his exemplary accomplishments, I deem Major Graf von der Schulenburg fully worthy of preferential promotion to lieutenant colonel and consider him suitable for this service grade without reservation.

Major General Richard Heidrich, the 1st Paratroop Division Commander, added a short note: "In agreement and seconded."

A few weeks later, on April 21, 1944, von der Schulenburg assumed command of the 13th Paratroop Regiment (*Fallschirmjäger-Regiment 13*) and deployed to Normandy. Shortly after the invasion, von der Schulenburg's regiment served as a battle group of the 17th SS *Panzer* Grenadier Division east of Marigny, France. A massive Allied armored attack inflicted heavy losses on one of the regiment's battalions; the following day, on July 14, 1944, Major Graf von der Schulenburg moved to the front to make a personal assessment of the situation. Leading the battalion forward in the hedgerows, an American infantryman apparently spotted the German officer and let loose with submachine gun fire. Struck several times, von der Schulenburg was instantly killed in action. He subsequently was promoted to lieutenant colonel on July 23, 1944.[88] Lieutenant Colonel Wolf-Werner Graf von der Schulenburg is buried at a German Military Cemetery at Marigny, France (Section 2, Row 22, Grave 821).

Fallschirm-Jäger Rgt.1 den 4.April 1944.
W.B.K.: Berlin X Waffengattung:Luftwaffe
Lg.Kdo. III

V o r s c h l a g

zur

b e v o r z u g t e n B e f ö r d e r u n g

Gemäß R.d.L.u.Ob.d.L. LP Nr. 71 489/42 (2,ID)
II.Ang. v. 22.12.42. Abschnitt B

für Major (z.V.) Wolf-Werner Graf von der Schulenburg

Dienststellung: Btl.-Kommandeur

Rangdienstalter: 1.9.42

Beförderungsdaten zu den beiden letzten
Offz.-Dienstgraden: Hauptmann: 1.11.40
Major: 1.9.42

Geburtsdatum: 14.9.99

Auszeichnungen: Spange zum E.K.II, E.K.I, Ritterkreuz zum E.K., Erdkampfabz. d. Lw., Kreta-Ärmelband.

Begründung:

A) Allgemeine Leistungen

Major Graf von der Schulenburg führt seit dem 20.2.1942 das I./Fsch.Jg.Rgt.1. Bei den Einsätzen des Regiments zeichnete sich Major Graf von der Schulenburg durch hervorragende persönliche Tapferkeit und überlegene Führung besonders aus. Als im Ostwinter 1942/43 dem Russen mit starken Kräften ein Durchbruch bei Dimitrowsk gelang, hat Sch. durch rücksichtslosen Einsatz seiner Person mit seinem Btl. unter schweren Angriffs- und Abwehrkämpfen diesen zum Stehen gebracht , dem Feind schwerste Verluste beigefügt und damit den Durchbruch nach Orel-Briansk verhindert.

Im Italieneinsatz war Major Sch. in den Kämpfen der Absetzbewegungen vom Kampfraum Tarent bis zur Sangrostellung mit seinem Btl. ständig am Feind. Hierbei stellte er wiederum seine hohen militärischen Fähigkeiten unter Beweis, indem er mit führungsmäßigem Geschick selbst schwierigste Lagen klärte.

Von Mitte November 1943 bis Mitte Januar 1944 führte Sch. vertretungsweise das Regiment.

In den schweren Abwehrkämpfen um Ortona zeigte er auch in dieser Führerstellung einen klaren Blick für schwierige Lagen und Entschlußkraft.

Im Kampfraum Cassino tat sich Sch. mit seinem Btl. durch entscheidende Kampfleistungen hervor. Als der Feind in der ersten Phase der Cassinokämpfe vom 8.-22.2.44 über die Höhen nordwestlich Cassino einen Durchbruch zur Strasse Cassino-Rom erzwingen wollte, war das Btl. Schulenburg maßgeblich daran beteiligt, daß alle Durchbruchsversuche unter schweren Verlusten für den Feind abgeschlagen wurden und damit der Fall Cassinos verhindert wurde.

-2-

Request for Preferred Promotion for Major Wolf-Werner Graf von der Schulenburg (front side) – dated April 4, 1944, on blank paper, with typed comments. Extensive underlining with blue pencil probably occurred at a higher headquarters review.

\- 2 -

B)Einzelangaben

Major Graf von der Schulenburg ist ein Offizier von hohem Persönlichkeitswert. Vorbildliche Einsatzfreudigkeit sowie hervor= ragende Führung und persönliche Tapferkeit im Kampf zeichnen ihn besonders aus. Er ist zum Regimentskommandeur voll geeignet.

Trotz seines Alters und seiner im Weltkrieg erlittenen schweren Verwundung - 5 cm verkürztes Bein - meldete er sich zu Beginn des Krieges zur Fallschirmtruppe und nahm an allen Einsätzen des Regiments teil. Auf Grund seiner beispielhaften Leistungen erachte ich Major Graf von der Schulenburg einer bevorzugten Beförderung zum Oberst= leutnant für voll würdig und halte ihn zu diesem Dienstgrad für un= eingeschränkt geeignet.

Oberst und Regimentskommandeur.

Stellungnahme des Divisionskommandeurs:

E i n v e r s t a n d e n und

b e f ü r w o r t e t .

Div.Gef.Stand,den 4.4.1944.

Generalleutnant und Div.Kommandeur.

Request for Preferred Promotion for Major Wolf-Werner Graf von der Schulenburg (back side) – signed by Colonel Karl-Lothar Schulz, Commander, 1st Paratroop Regiment, and by Major General Richard Heidrich, Commander, 1st Paratroop Division.

Franz Schwaiger

Fighter Pilot

"Inspiring and an example in every respect for the young pilots."

Second Lieutenant Franz Schwaiger was born in Ulm, Baden-Württemberg on February 1, 1918. In the summer of 1941, Schwaiger joined the 6th Squadron, 3rd Fighter Wing (*Jagdgeschwader 3*) on the Eastern Front and registered his first aerial victory on August 16, 1941. He received the Iron Cross 2nd Class on September 2, 1941 and the Iron Cross 1st Class on September 20, 1941. On April 8, 1942, in Africa, Franz Schwaiger's landing gear collapsed when his Messerschmitt Me 109F-4 was landing at Martuba. By the end of the year, Schwaiger had registered 8 kills; he achieved his 10th on May 29th, 1942 and his 20th – a LaGG-3 – on July 31, 1942. Perhaps because of this relatively slow start, Schwaiger transferred to the 2nd Squadron and a month later transferred again to the 3rd Squadron. Whatever the reason, his score started to rapidly increase and he reached 30 victories by August 20, 40 victories by September 29 and 50 victories by October 9. On October 29, 1942, Sergeant Franz Schwaiger received the Knight's Cross of the Iron Cross, having achieved 53 aerial victories. Schwaiger also won the German Cross in Gold on November 16, 1942 and the Operational Flying Clasp for Fighters in Gold on February 1, 1942.

Captain and Group Commander Klaus Quaet-Faslem submitted an efficiency report on Franz Schwaiger on February 28, 1943. In it, he wrote:

> Master Sergeant Schwaiger is a fully developed, matured person, decent and full of temperament. Clear judgment capability. As a soldier and pilot, he has proven himself due to his exemplary heroic willingness for combat. Untiring in combat, courageous and dashing. Inspiring and an example in every respect for the young pilots. He has succeeded in 55 aerial victories to date. Master Sergeant Schwaiger has the character and military attributes to become an officer and is being recommended due to his courage against the enemy.

Lieutenant Colonel and wing commodore Wolf-Dietrich Wilcke added:

> With the evaluation of the commander, I am in complete agreement. Master Sergeant Schwaiger is ready to become an officer right now.

Schwaiger then returned to Germany and completed officer training, before returning to his squadron in the summer of 1943. By this time the unit had transferred to the homeland defense of Germany; on March 9, 1944, Schwaiger assumed command of the 1st Squadron, 3rd Fighter Wing. On April 24, 1944, he shot down a P-51 Mustang, but his Messerschmitt Me 109G-5 received severe damage and he was forced to make a belly-landing at Rain am Lech, Bavaria. He reportedly safely exited the aircraft after it came to a halt, but he was strafed and killed by U.S. fighter aircraft as he crossed the open field in which he had landed. Franz Schwaiger scored 67 aerial victories during the war, of which 56 were on the Eastern Front.[89]

Anlage 9
zu D II 5

Gen.Kdo.VIII.Fliegerkorps (Höh. Kdo.-Beh.) — Ulm / Donau W.B.K.

Waffengattung: Fliegertruppe(Flugzeugführer)

Truppenteil: I. / Jagdgeschwader Udet

Vorschlag
zur Beförderung zum Kriegsoffizier

gemäß D. (Luft) 2200 D II 6

Name: Schwaiger Geburtstag: 1. 2. 1918 Ort: Ulm / Donau

Vorname: Franz Familienstand: ledig Kinder: keine

Dienstgrad: Feldwebel Beruf: Motorenschlosser

Verwendung: Flugzeugführer Konfession: r. kath.

Militärischer Werdegang:

Aktive Dienstzeit: von 7. 11. 1938 bis noch

" "

" "

Dienstzeit seit Kriegsbeginn:

Längere Dienstverpflichtung auf 3, 4 1/2 oder 12 und mehr Jahre: 4 1/2 Jahre

Beförderungen und Ernennungen:

zum Gefreiten 1. 10. 1939 zum Feldwebel (Wachtm.) 1. 9. 1942

zum Uffz. 1. 3. 1941

Tag der Ernennung zum R.-O.-A. nicht ernannt bzw. K.-O.-A. ---

Hat – nicht – ~~mit Erfolg – ohne Erfolg~~ – an einem K.-O.-A.-Lehrgang von bis teilgenommen.

Offizierwahl hat stattgefunden am: nein

Bildungsgang: Erziehung im elterlichen Hause, Ostern 1924 bis Ostern 1932 Volksschule Ulm/Donau, Ostern 1932 bis Ostern 1935 Gewerbeschule Ulm, von 1932 bis 1935 das Handwerk eines Motorenschlossers erlernt, Gesellenprüfung 1935 bestanden.

Lager-Nr. 1934 Heß, Braunschweig-München

Request for Promotion to Officer for Technical Sergeant Franz Schwaiger (front side) – dated February 28, 1943. Pencil annotation indicates that Schwaiger was promoted to second lieutenant on April 1, 1943.

Bestrafungen vor Diensteintritt: keine

Bestrafungen nach Diensteintritt: siehe Strafbuchauszug

Auszeichnungen: 2.9.41 EK.2, 20.9.41 EK.1, 1.2.42 Frontflugspange für Jäger in Gold, 29.10.42 Deutsches Kreuz in Gold, 2.11.42 Ritterkreuz.

Stand und Beruf des Vaters: Werkmeister

Familienname der Mutter: geb. Gengenbach

Anschrift der nächsten Angehörigen: Vater: Josef Schwaiger, Ulm / Donau, Scharnhorststraße 46

Außerdienstliche Eignung festgestellt durch: W.B.K. Ulm

Beurteilung: Feldwebel Schwaiger ist ein vollkommen ausgereifter, fertiger Mensch, ehrlich und temperamentvoll. Klares Urteilsvermögen.

Als Soldat und Flugzeugführer hat er sich durch vorbildlichen heldenhafte Einsatzfreudigkeit bewährt. Unermüdlich im Einsatz, tapfer und schneidig. Anfeuernd und für die jungen Flugzeugführer in jeder Hinsicht Vorbild. Er hat bisher 55 Abschüsse erzielt.

Fw. Schwaiger hat die charakterliche und militärische Eignung zum Offz. und wird zu diesem wegen Tapferkeit vor dem Feinde vorgeschlagen.

Gefechtsstand, 28. 2. 1943
(Ort und Datum)

Quaet-Faslem
(Unterschrift)
Hauptmann und Gruppenkommandeur.

Stellungnahme der Zwischenvorgesetzten:

Mit der Beurteilung durch Kommandeur voll einverstanden.
Feldwebel Schwaiger ist zum Offizier geeignet.

Wilcke

Oberstleutnant
u.
Geschwaderkommodore.

Request for Promotion to Officer for Technical Sergeant Franz Schwaiger (back side) – signed by Captain Klaus Quaet-Faslem, Commander, 1st Group, 3rd Fighter Wing, and by Lieutenant Colonel Wolf-Dietrich Wilcke, Commodore, 3rd Fighter Wing.

Georg Seelmann

Fighter Pilot

"Straight-forward, intelligent human being."

First Lieutenant Georg Seelmann was born on February 4, 1917 at Bamberg, Bavaria. He entered the *Luftwaffe* on November 3, 1937 and received pilot training at Herzogenaurach, Dornstadt and Schleissheim. Seelmann was assigned to the 2nd Squadron, 77th Fighter Wing "Ace of Hearts" (*Jagdgeschwader 77 "Herzas"*) on July 1, 1939 and flew combat missions during the Polish campaign beginning September 1. Seelmann received the Iron Cross 2nd Class on November 1, 1939. He gained his first aerial victory on May 14, 1940 during the French Campaign, when he shot down a French Morane-Saulnier MS 406 fighter near Charleroi. During the Battle of Britain, Seelmann claimed at least one RAF Spitfire fighter; he was awarded the Iron Cross 1st Class on September 28, 1940.

In October 1940, Seelmann's chain of command submitted a report through the 2nd Air Corps to Berlin requesting that Technical Sergeant Seelmann be promoted to second lieutenant. First Lieutenant Franz Hahn, the 2nd Squadron Commander, wrote in part:[90]

> Technical Sergeant Seelmann arrived at the 2nd Squadron, 1st Group, 77th Fighter Wing on July 1, 1939. He flew all missions in the squadron during the Poland Campaign, on border patrols in the West, during operations against France and now against England, and he has excelled as a fighter pilot due to his discipline and courage. He succeeded to have one enemy kill each in France and England. On November 1, 1939, he received the Iron Cross 2nd Class. As a superior, he understands how to succeed and demonstrates that he is up to all military questions. Seelmann is a straightforward, intelligent human being and lives up to all requirements which are posed to an officer.

Captain Johannes Janke, the 1st Group Commander, added the following on October 4, 1940:

> Nothing is to be added to the evaluation of the squadron commander. In operations against England, Technical Sergeant Seelmann has excelled particularly well, and on September 28, 1940 he received the Iron Cross 1st Class. Without restriction, he is suited for promotion to the rank of officer.

On November 21, 1940, his unit was designated the 11th Squadron, 51st Fighter Wing (*Jagdgeschwader 51*). Operating on the Eastern Front, in July 1941, Seelmann recorded 17 victories, including his 10th (a DB-3 bomber) on July 2 and his 20th victory (another DB-3) on July 16; he achieved his 30th victory (a Pe-2) on August 9. On August 30, a Russian bomber rammed Seelmann during aerial combat, and he bailed out of his stricken Messerschmitt Me 109F-2 ten miles behind Russian lines near Novgorod. He successfully evaded capture and returned to German lines. Second Lieutenant Georg Seelmann was awarded the Knight's Cross of the Iron Cross on October 6, 1941 for 37 aerial victories. In mid-December, he was transferred to the Supplemental Group (*Ergänzungsgruppe*) – an operational training unit of *Jagdgeschwader 51 "Mölders"* – to perform instructional duties. He then transferred to Supplemental Fighter Group East (*Ergänzung-Jagdgruppe Ost*) – another operational training unit – on February 25, 1942. He returned to the front on August 1 as the Commander, 11th Squadron, 51st Fighter Wing. He scored his final kill, an Il-2 Sturmovik, on August 2, 1942. However, the next day, Seelmann was shot down by return fire from Russian bombers and again had to bail out of his burning Messerschmitt Me 109F-2 southwest of Rzev, although on this occasion he was badly wounded. Two months later, on October 8, Seelmann was appointed the commander of the 4th Squadron, 51st Fighter Wing and the following month led the unit to the Mediterranean theater and bases in Tunisia. At the end of March 1943, Seelmann relinquished command of the 4th Squadron due to the lingering after-effects of his wounds the previous August. He was later assigned a non-combat role as Commander, 1st Squadron, 103rd Fighter Wing (*Jagdgeschwader 103*) – another operational training unit – in the summer of 1943. He survived the war.

Georg Seelmann was credited with 39 victories in 550 missions, a sortie-to-victory ratio of 14.10 to 1. He recorded three victories over the Western Front. George Seelmann died on September 18, 1987 at Lichtenfels in Upper Franconia. He is buried there in the *Stadtfriedhof* (Section 6, Row 14, Grave 1).[91]

1. Generalkommando des II. Fliegerkorps
2. I./Jagdgeschwader 77
3. W.B.K. Wehrbezirkskommando 2, Breslau
4. Vorgeschlagen gem. B.L.B. 194o Ziffer 485
5. Waffengattung: Fliegertruppe

Betr.: Vorschlag zur Beförderung zum Leutnant (d.B.)

Auf dem Dienstwege

an

R.d.L.u.Ob.d.L. (L.P.)

B e r l i n

Zur Beförderung zum Leutnant (d.B.) wird in Vorschlag gebracht:

Familienname, Vorname: S e e l m a n n , Georg

geb. am: 4. 2. 1917 zu: Bamberg Konf.: kath.

Dienstgrad: Feldwebel 6.verwendet als: Flugzeugführer =LF= (cm.)

7.Diensteintritt am: 3.11.1937 verh./led.: ledig

Ernennung zum Oberfähnrich bezw. Offz.Anw. wann: 31. 3. 1939 Kinder: keine

Bestrafung vor Diensteintritt: -.-

Bestrafung nach Diensteintritt: -.-

Zum Offizier gewählt am: 29.9.40

Beruf vor Diensteintritt: Schüler

Stand und Beruf des Vaters: Telegr. Bauführer

Mutter geborene: W e i h s

Anschrift der Eltern bezw.des Vormundes: Telegr.Bauführer
Josef S e e l m a n n
Bamberg , Josephstr.21

Bildungsgang: 5 Jahre Volksschule
9 Jahre humanistisches Gymnasium (April 1928 - Febr. 1937)
(Abitur Februar 1937)
7 Monate R.A.D. (1.4. - 23.1o.37)

Request for Promotion to Officer for Technical Sergeant Georg Seelmann (front side) – dated 1940. Pencil notation indicates that Seelmann was promoted to second lieutenant (reserve) on October 1, 1940.

8. Militärischer Werdegang:

Grundausbildung:	v. 3.11.37 - 31. 3.38	4./Fea 15
Flugzeugfhr.Sch.E	v. 1. 4.38 - 1. 8.38	Herzogenaurach
Flugzeugfhr.Sch.	v. 2. 8.38 - 31. 3.39	Dornstadt
Jagdfliegerschule	v. 1. 4.39 - 3o. 6.39	Schleißheim
I./Jagdgeschwader 77	v. 1. 7.39	

Beförderungen u.Ernennungen:

z.Gefr.	1.12.38
z.R.O.A.	31. 3.39
z.Uffz.	1. 6.39
z.Feldw.	1. 6.4o

9. Begründung: Der Feldwebel S e e l m a n n kam am 1. 7. 1939 in die 2. Staffel I./J.G. 77 . Er flog alle Einsätze der Staffel im Polenkrieg, in der Grenzüberwachung im Westen, beim Einsatz gegen Frankreich, jetzt gegen England mit und zeichnete sich durch Disziplin und Schneid als Jagdflieger aus. Es gelang ihm in Frankreich und England je ein feindliches Jagdflugzeug abzuschießen.
Am 1. November 1939 erhielt er das E.K. 2. Klasse.
Als Vorgesetzter weiß er sich durchzusetzen und zeigt sich allen militärischen Fragen gewachsen. Seelmann ist ein gerader, intelligenter Mensch und entspricht allen Anforderungen die an einen Offizier (d.B.) gestellt werden.

Oberleutnant u. Staffelkapitän.

I./Jagdgeschwader 77

Der Beurteilung des Staffelkapitäns ist nichts hinzuzufügen.

Feldwebel Seelmann hat sich im Einsatz gegen England ganz besonders ausgezeichnet und erhielt am 28.9.40 das E.K.I. Klasse.

Zum Offizier (d.B.) in jeder Hinsicht uneingeschränkt geeignet.

Gefechtsstand, 4. Okt. 1940

Hauptmann u. Gruppenkommandeur

Request for Promotion to Officer for Technical Sergeant Georg Seelmann (back side) – signed by First Lieutenant Franz Hahn, Commander, 2nd Squadron, 77th Fighter Wing, and by Captain Johannes Janke, Commander, 1st Group, 77th Fighter Wing.

Günther Sempert

Fallschirmjäger

"Mentally very active, skillful in quick comprehension."

Major Günther Sempert was born on October 20, 1918 at Wechselburg an der Mulde near Leipzig, Saxony. He entered the German Army on November 2, 1937 as an officer candidate with the 4th Anti-Tank Detachment. One year later he began officer training, subsequently fought in the Polish campaign – where he was wounded on September 9 – and was commissioned a second lieutenant on December 22, 1939. Sempert then assumed duties as a recruiting officer in Spremberg, but apparently desired more challenging duties and volunteered for airborne training, which he completed in August 1940. He transferred to the *Luftwaffe* and became a platoon leader in the 3rd Company, 7th Paratroop Anti-Tank Detachment (*Fallschirm-Panzer-Jäger-Abteilung 7*). Sempert, now a platoon leader in the 1st Company, jumped into Crete on May 20, 1941 as part of the German airborne invasion of the island. He was wounded the same day, but later fought at Máleme, Khaniá and Suda Bay. He received the Iron Cross 2nd Class on June 11, 1941 and the Iron Cross 1st Class on July 5, 1941. He was promoted to first lieutenant on December 1, 1941.

Sempert fought in North Africa from January 1 to March 27, 1942, as part of the defensive fighting at Maramarica and Cyrenaika. On April 25, 1942, he assumed command of the 5th Company, 7th Paratroop Anti-Tank Detachment. While visiting the invasion site at Dieppe – after the fighting – a round of ammunition exploded, causing him to lose an eye. On October 20, 1942, he deployed to Russia and fought there through March 31, 1943. He deployed to Italy, becoming the commander of the 4th Company, 1st Paratroop Anti-Tank Detachment (*Fallschirm-Panzer-Jäger-Abteilung 1*) on June 15, 1943. He was wounded in action on November 28, 1943.

During much of the fighting at Cassino, First Lieutenant Sempert served as the acting commander of the 1st Paratroop Anti-Tank Detachment. He was promoted to captain on May 5, 1944 and received the German Cross in Gold on June 14, 1944. Sempert remained in the fighting, wounded for a fifth time on August 11, 1944. On September 30, 1944, Günther Sempert received the Knight's Cross of the Iron Cross for his heroism and achievements during the battles at Cassino, where his unit was credited with destroying a total of 120 enemy armored vehicles.

The chain of command in the 1st Paratroop Division submitted a request on November 4, 1944 for a preferential promotion for Captain Günther Sempert. Captain Hannes Schwarzer wrote:[92]

General accomplishments:
Captain Sempert is an outstanding officer with distinct leadership qualities. Mentally very active, skillful in quick comprehension. His military attitude is secure and correct in every situation. With his exemplary military attitude, his just way and his exemplary willingness for combat, he is very well liked and respected by his comrades and subordinates. He is an energetic person, with very good knowledge in all military areas. Has good tactical knowledge. He willingly makes decisions and is aware of the responsibilities. His know-how and knowledge enable him to master even the most difficult situation in battle.

Detailed information:
Already during the fighting on Crete, Sempert excelled as an outstanding fighter and was awarded the Iron Cross 2nd Class and 1st Class. During the Russian Campaign, the company under his command was engaged in the centers of battle and destroyed 67 enemy bunkers. In 1943, he and his company played a significant role of the liberation of the Duce [Mussolini].[93] For the liberation of the Duce and for the engagement of his company in Southern Italy, where 16 enemy tanks were destroyed, he was awarded the German Cross in Gold. Of special note is how Sempert excelled in the 3rd Cassino Battle, where as the leader of the [anti-tank] detachment, he destroyed more than 120 enemy tanks and where he recognized in time the enemy breakthrough towards the unit on his right flank and, with skillful use of his anti-tank weapons, sealed it off. For the accomplishments in the 3rd Cassino Battle, he was awarded the Knight's Cross of the Iron Cross by the *Führer*.

Major General Richard Heidrich, the division commander, wrote the following as the senior rater the following day:

Opinion of the Division Commander:

In agreement and seconded. Captain Sempert (Günther), 1st Parachute Anti-Tank Detachment, is suitable for promotion to Major without reservation.

Sempert was promoted to major on January 30, 1945. He was wounded again on April 8, 1945, prior to becoming a prisoner of war on May 2, 1945.[94]

4

Fallschirm-Panzerjäger-Abteilung 1 Gef.Std., den 4.11.44

V o r s c h l a g

zur

b e v o r z u g t e n B e f ö r d e r u n g .

Gemäss R.d.L. u.Ob.d.L. LP. Nr. 71 489-42 (2,ID)
II.Ang. vom 22.12.42 Abschnitt A

für Hauptmann (Tr.O.) S e m p e r t, Günther

Dienststellung:	Abteilungsführer
Rangdienstalter:	1. Juni 1944 (Ord.Nr. 22)
Beförderungsdaten zu den beiden letzten Offz.-Dienstgraden:	a) Oberleutnant: 1.12.1941 b) Hauptmann: 1. 6.1944 (22)
Geburtsdatum:	2o. Oktober 1918
Auszeichnungen:	Eisernes Kreuz II.Klasse 8.6.41 Eisernes Kreuz I.Klasse 21.6.41 Erdkampfabzeichen der Luftwaffe 1.1o.42 Ärmelband "Kreta" 2o.5.1943 Deutsches Kreuz in Gold 14.6.44 Ritterkreuz des Eisernen Kreuzes 3o.9.44

B e g r ü n d u n g :

A) Allgemeine Leistungen:

Der Hauptmann Sempert ist ein hervorragender Offizier mit ausgepräg= ten Führereigenschaften. Geistig sehr rege,gewandt mit schneller Auf- fassungsgabe. Seine soldatische Haltung ist in jeder Lage sicher und korrekt. Durch seine vorbildliche soldatische Haltung, seine gerechte Art und seine beispielhafte Einsatzbereitschaft ist er bei seinen Kameraden und Untergebenen sehr beliebt und geachtet. Er ist eine energische Persönlichkeit mit sehr guten Kenntnissen auf allen militärischen Gebieten. Verfügt über gute taktische Kenntnisse. Ent- schlussfreudig und verantwortungsbewusst. Sein Können und Wissen befähigt ihn, auch die schwierigsten Lagen im Einsatz zu meistern.

Wenden.

Request for Preferred Promotion for Captain Günther Sempert (front side) – dated November 4, 1944, on blank paper, with typed comments. Extensive underlining with blue pencil probably occurred at a higher headquarters review.

B) Einzelangaben.

Schon beim Kampf auf Kreta bewährte sich Sempert als hervorragender Kämpfer und wurde mit dem Eisernes Kreuz II. und I.Klasse. Im Rußland-Einsatz 1942-43 war seine von ihm geführte Kompanie in den Brennpunkten eingesetzt und vernichtete 67 besetzte Feindbunker. 1943 war er mit seiner Kompanie massgeblich an der Befreiung des Duce beteiligt. Für die Befreiung des Duce und für den Einsatz seiner Kompanie in Süditalien, wo 16 Feindpanzer vernichtet wurden, wurde er mit dem Deutschen Kreuz in Gold ausgezeichnet. Besonders bewährte sich Sempert in der 3.Cassino-Schlacht, wo er als Führer der Abteilung mit unterstellten Einheiten über 12o Feindpanzer vernichtete und feindliche Einbrüche beim rechten Nachbarn rechtzeitig erkannte und durch geschickten Einsatz der Panzer-Abwehrwaffen abriegelte. Für die Leistungen in der 3.Cassino-Schlacht wurde er vom Führer mit dem Ritterkreuz des Eisernen Kreuzes ausgezeichnet.

I. V.

Schwarzer

H a u p t m a n n .

Stellungnahme des Divisionskommandeurs:

E i n v e r s t a n d e n und b e f ü r w o r t e t .
Hauptmann (Tr.O.) S e m p e r t (Günther), Fsch.Panzerjägerabteilung 1, ist zur Beförderung zum Major uneingeschränkt geeignet.

Div.Gef.Stand, den 5.11.1944.

Heidrich

Generalleutnant und Divisionskommandeur.

Request for Preferred Promotion for Captain Günther Sempert (back side) – signed by Captain Hannes Schwarzer, acting commander, 1st Paratroop Anti-Tank Detachment, and by Major General Richard Heidrich, Commander, 1st Paratroop Division.

Friedrich Seyffardt

Ground-Attack Pilot

"Overseeing and mastering every situation with great success."

First Lieutenant Friedrich "Fritz" Seyffardt was born on August 20, 1920 in Krautscheid in the Rhineland. He received pilot training in 1942 and then joined the 101st Ground-Attack Wing (*Schlachtgeschwader 101*) before transferring to the Destroyer Supplemental Group at Deblin-Irena. He then saw combat duty with the 1st Ground-Attack Wing (*Schlachtgeschwader 1*), which was renamed the 2nd Group, 2nd Ground-Attack Wing "Immelmann" (*Schlachtgeschwader 2 "Immelmann"*). During this period, the unit was equipped with Focke-Wulf Fw 190A-5 aircraft and based at Anapa in the North Caucasus supporting the 17th German Army in the Kuban. In early July, they moved north to Varvarovka to operate against Soviet forces along the Donez River southeast of Kharkov. Seyffardt won the Iron Cross 2nd Class on June 6, 1943 and the Iron Cross 1st Class on August 14, 1943. He received the German Cross in Gold on December 12, 1943 and the *Luftwaffe* Honor Goblet on January 17, 1944. On April 17, 1944, he received the Operational Flying Clasp for Ground-Attack Pilots in Gold with Pendant.

On June 14, 1944, his chain of command in the 2nd Group, 2nd Ground-Attack Wing "Immelmann" submitted an officer efficiency report of First Lieutenant Friedrich Seyffardt. The Group Commander, Major Heinz Frank, was the sole rater on the report and wrote the following:[95]

> **Short Evaluation** (Personal values, National Socialist attitude, accomplishments before the enemy, service accomplishments, mental and physical attributes and suitability, infantry experience, when and how obtained): Tall, slender appearance. Athletic, persevering, fully trained. On duty able to withstand great demands. Open, sincere, goal-oriented character. Dutiful, mature attitude, despite his young age. Good personal values. Mental attributes above average. Vivid and good general knowledge. His attitude toward the profession as an officer is immaculate. Towards superiors and subordinates always correct and definite. Well liked and popular among his comrades. Social manners are without criticism. Own initiative and talent for improvisation are present. He is firmly rooted in National Socialist philosophy and is capable to pass on National Socialist thoughts. First Lieutenant Seyffardt is an excellent fighter pilot, who has engaged in close to 500 missions, overseeing and mastering every situation with great success as a flight and squadron leader. He was a good example for his pilots as to risk-taking, cheerful readiness for combat and piloting know-how.
>
> **Strong Traits:** leadership nature, dare-devil, talent for improvisation.
>
> **Weak Traits:** none
>
> **Summarized evaluation:** above average
> (Above Average, Average, Below Average)
>
> **How is the current position being filled?** Very well fulfilled.

(Use only: Very well fulfilled, well fulfilled, fulfilled, not fulfilled)

Suitable for promotion to next higher service grade? Yes

Suitable for which next-higher position: Squadron Commander. First Lieutenant Seyffardt has been engaged for a total 5 months as acting squadron commander.

Known to the person submitting this review: since October 15, 1943.

Subordinated to the person submitting this review: since October 15, 1944.

Seyffardt continued to do well, flying in his Focke-Wulf FW 190, and the following day he became the commander of the 1st Squadron, 152nd Ground-Attack Wing (*Schlachtgeschwader 152*), which was renamed the 10th Squadron, 151st Ground-Attack Wing (*Schlachtgeschwader 151*) on October 15, 1944. On August 8, 1944, Fritz Seyffardt received the Knight's Cross of the Iron Cross (he was submitted for the award on May 25, 1944) for achievements as a pilot in the 5th Squadron, 2nd Ground-Attack Wing. He continued in this position until March 4, 1945, when he assumed command of the 12th Squadron of the wing. Fritz Seyffardt survived the war and was credited with flying 506 combat missions, during which he shot down 30 enemy aircraft as well as achieving numerous ground target hits.[96]

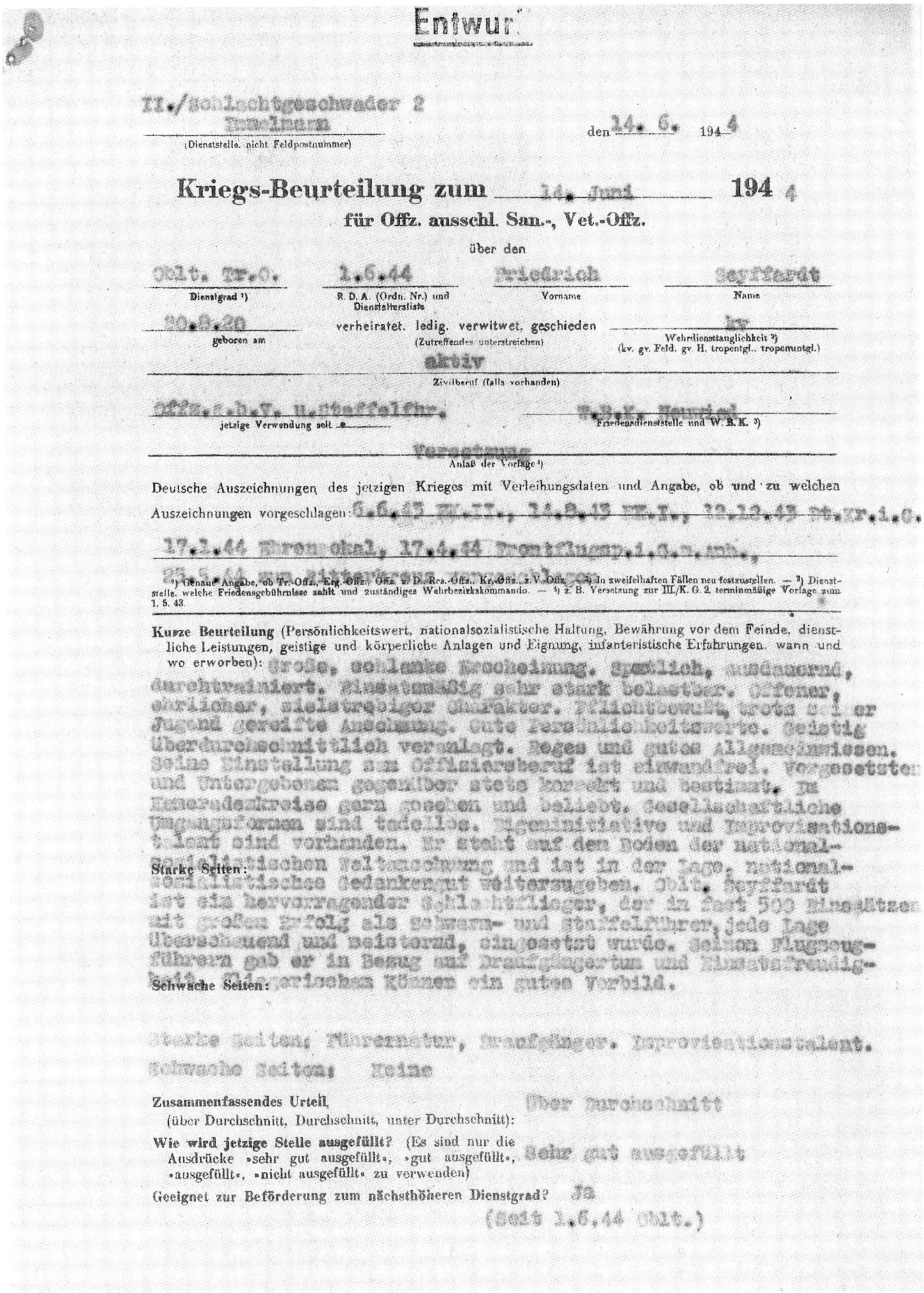

Entwurf

II./Schlachtgeschwader 2
Immelmann
(Dienststelle, nicht Feldpostnummer)

den 14. 6. 1944

Kriegs-Beurteilung zum 14. Juni **1944**
für Offz. ausschl. San.-, Vet.-Offz.

über den

Oblt. Tr.O.	1.6.44	Friedrich	Seyffardt
Dienstgrad [1])	R. D. A. (Ordn. Nr.) und Dienstaltersliste	Vorname	Name

20.8.20 — geboren am
verheiratet. ledig. verwitwet. geschieden (Zutreffendes unterstreichen)
kv — Wehrdiensttauglichkeit [2]) (kv. gv. Feld. gv. H. tropentgl., tropenuntgl.)

aktiv — Zivilberuf (falls vorhanden)

Offz.z.b.V. u.Staffelführ. — jetzige Verwendung seit
W.B.K. Neuwied — Friedensdienststelle und W.B.K. [3])

Versetzung — Anlaß der Vorlage [4])

Deutsche Auszeichnungen des jetzigen Krieges mit Verleihungsdaten und Angabe, ob und zu welchen Auszeichnungen vorgeschlagen: 6.6.43 EK.II., 14.8.43 EK.I., 12.12.43 Dt.Kr.i.G. 17.1.44 Ehrenpokal, 17.4.44 Frontflugsp.i.G.m.Anh., 23.5.44 zum Ritterkreuz vorgeschlagen

[1]) Genaue Angabe, ob Tr.-Offz., Erg.-Offz., Offz. z. D., Res.-Offz., Kr.-Offz., z.V.-Offz. — [2]) In zweifelhaften Fällen neu festzustellen. — [3]) Dienststelle, welche Friedensgebührnisse zahlt und zuständiges Wehrbezirkskommando. — [4]) z. B. Versetzung zur III/K. G. 2, terminmäßige Vorlage zum 1. 5. 43.

Kurze Beurteilung (Persönlichkeitswert, nationalsozialistische Haltung, Bewährung vor dem Feinde, dienstliche Leistungen, geistige und körperliche Anlagen und Eignung, infanteristische Erfahrungen, wann und wo erworben): Große, schlanke Erscheinung. Sportlich, ausdauernd, durchtrainiert. Einsatzmäßig sehr stark belastbar. Offener, ehrlicher, zielstrebiger Charakter. Pflichtbewußt, trotz seiner Jugend gereifte Anschauung. Gute Persönlichkeitswerte. Geistig überdurchschnittlich veranlagt. Reges und gutes Allgemeinwissen. Seine Einstellung zum Offiziersberuf ist einwandfrei. Vorgesetzten und Untergebenen gegenüber stets korrekt und bestimmt. Im Kameradenkreise gern gesehen und beliebt. Gesellschaftliche Umgangsformen sind tadellos. Eigeninitiative und Improvisationstalent sind vorhanden. Er steht auf dem Boden der nationalsozialistischen Weltanschauung und ist in der Lage, nationalsozialistisches Gedankengut weiterzugeben. Oblt. Seyffardt ist ein hervorragender Schlachtflieger, der in fast 500 Einsätzen mit großem Erfolg als Schwarm- und Staffelführer, jede Lage überschauend und meisternd, eingesetzt wurde. Seinen Flugzeugführern gab er in Bezug auf Draufgängertum und Einsatzfreudigkeit, fliegerischem Können ein gutes Vorbild.

Starke Seiten:

Schwache Seiten:

Starke Seiten: Führernatur, Draufgänger. Improvisationstalent.

Schwache Seiten: Keine

Zusammenfassendes Urteil (über Durchschnitt, Durchschnitt, unter Durchschnitt): Über Durchschnitt

Wie wird jetzige Stelle ausgefüllt? (Es sind nur die Ausdrücke »sehr gut ausgefüllt«, »gut ausgefüllt«, »ausgefüllt«, »nicht ausgefüllt« zu verwenden) Sehr gut ausgefüllt

Geeignet zur Beförderung zum nächsthöheren Dienstgrad? Ja (Seit 1.6.44 Oblt.)

Efficiency Report for First Lieutenant Friedrich Seyffardt (front side) – dated June 14, 1944, on pre-printed form, with typed comments.

Eignung für welche nächsthöhere Verwendung[5])? für welche besondere oder anderweitige Verwendung[6])? Vorschlag für Verwendung in nächster Zeit[7])?	Staffelkapitän. Oblt. Seyffardt war insgesamt 5 Monate als Staffelführer eingesetzt.
Sprachkenntnisse (keine Schulkenntnisse) a) abgelegte Prüfungen: (z. B.: Dolmetscherprüfung 1. 10. 42) b) Beherrschung der Sprache: (z. B.: durch Aufenthalt im Ausland)	Keine
Eröffnung zu welchen Punkten, wann, wie (mündlich oder schriftlich) und durch wen?	"-"
Strafen sind mit vollem Straftenor sowie Vermerk über Vollstreckung abschriftlich als Anlage der Kriegsbeurteilung beizuheften.	Keine
Dem Beurteilenden bekannt seit / unterstellt seit	15.10.43
Ausbildung a) erworbene Scheine: (L. F., E. L. F., L. B. usw.) b) Sonderausbildung: (z. B. Bild-Offz., Techn. Offz., Meß-Offz., Funk-Drahtnachr.-Offz., W. K. S.)	LF "-"

Unterschrift | Major und Gruppenkommandeur (Dienstgrad und Dienststellung)

Beitrag des Chefs des Generalstabes der vorgesetzten Kommandobehörde (nur bei Genst.-Offz. in Stabsstellungen und zur Dienstleistung zum Generalstab kommandierten Offizieren):

Zusätze vorgesetzter Dienststellen:

[5]) Gilt für alle Offz., für Truppen-Offz. hinsichtlich Eignung zur Führung des nächsthöheren Verbandes, für Genst.-Offz. hinsichtlich Eignung zum Chef oder Ia, Ic der Luftfl., Flieger-Korps, Flak-Korps, Fl.-Div., Flak-Div., zur Versetzung in den Genst., zur Kommandierung in den Genst. — [6]) z. B.: Höherer Adjutant, Erzieher, Lehrer auf Spezialgebieten, auf Grund von Sprachkenntnissen im Attachédienst; für Genst.-Offz. hinsichtlich Eignung für Verwendung im Quartiermeisterdienst, im Ic-Dienst, im Transportwesen, als Lehrer für Genst.-Lehrgang (Taktik bzw. Qu.-Dienst); besondere Anlagen für Kriegsgeschichte, Wehrwirtschaft. — [7]) z. B.: „noch halbjährige Belassung in bisheriger Stelle" oder „alsbaldige Verwendung als Geschw.-Kommodore".

Efficiency Report for First Lieutenant Friedrich Seyffardt (back side) – signed by Major Heinz Frank, Commander, 2nd Group, 2nd Ground-Attack Wing.

Walter Sigel

Stuka Pilot

"Tendency to salesmanship behavior, which manifests itself in his frequent attempts to 'trade off' something from clearly spelled out orders."

Colonel Walter Sigel was born on January 12, 1906 in Ulm. He entered *Lufthansa* training in 1932, but shortly thereafter did his military training in the 10th Infantry Regiment of the Army. On May 10, 1935, officer candidate Sigel transferred to the *Luftwaffe* and two years later became a squadron commander in the 1st Group, 167th Stuka Wing (*Sturzkampfgeschwader 167*). The unit underwent several re-designations and on May 1, 1939 became the 1st Group, 76th Stuka Wing (*Sturzkampfgeschwader 76*), with Sigel as the group commander. On August 15, 1939, he was seconds away from becoming a fatality during the "Catastrophe of Neuhammer," when – on a practice bombing maneuver – 13 Stukas plunged through thick ground fog and crashed, killing all 26 crewmen. Sigel, in a follow-on echelon, pulled out in time to avoid certain death. He led his group in Poland, Belgium and France. He received the Iron Cross 2nd Class on September 17, 1939, the Iron Cross 1st Class on June 20, 1940 and the Knight's Cross of the Iron Cross on July 21, 1940.

Sigel continued to get in the fight over the English Channel, followed by the 1941 Balkan campaign and action over Crete in May 1941. On June 20, 1941, Lieutenant Colonel Oskar Dinort, the Commander, 2nd Stuka Wing "Immelmann" (*Sturzkampfgeschwader 2 "Immelmann"*), submitted an officer efficiency report on Major Walter Sigel. Dinort, who was the only rater on this report, hand-wrote the following:[97]

> **Character:** Basically decent character with tendency to salesmanship behavior, which manifests itself in his frequent attempts to 'trade off' something from clearly spelled out orders, at the same time sometimes stubborn and easily hurt.
>
> **Personal values:** Personality with expressed self-confidence. Passionate Stuka officer. Willingness for combat with great sense of responsibility. Dominant. Compassionate. Works on himself when he receives definite instructions. National Socialist.
>
> **Conduct before the enemy:** Distinguished himself fully during the Poland Campaign, in the West and Southeast as a Stuka group commander. Dashing, circumspect and persevering. Was awarded the Knight's Cross of the Iron Cross in the West due to a number of outstanding deeds. Excellent participation in the battles against English air forces at Crete.
>
> **Accomplishments in Service:** Still is lacking some military knowledge, most probably due to his fast ascent. When instructed, he takes pain to educate his unit to soldierly strictness. Excellent Stuka pilot with good teaching capabilities. Knows well to improvise. Good talent for giving orders.
>
> **Possible employment:** Continue as Stuka group commander. Good suitability for commander of a Stuka school.

From April 1942 to May 1943, Sigel was the Commodore, 3rd Stuka Wing (*Sturzkampfgeschwader 3*), supporting the Africa Corps in North Africa. During this time he flew a Junkers Ju 87D, and among other missions, participated in the first battle of Alamein. On September 2, 1942, as a lieutenant colonel, he became the 116th recipient of the Oak Leaves to the Knight's Cross. He was promoted to colonel on June 1, 1943 and assumed the key posting of Inspector of Ground-Attack Units. Some months later, he assumed command of an ad hoc *Luftwaffe* anti-partisan formation in northern Italy before leading the *Luftwaffe* effort to attack the Allied Anzio landing in early 1944. In April 1944, he was named Air Commander Norway (*Fliegerführer Norwegen*). On May 8, 1944, during an inspection flight in a Fieseler Stork Fi 156, Colonel Walter Sigel crashed into the Trondheim Fjord and was killed. He is buried at a German Military Cemetery at Trondheim-Havstein, Norway (Row 6, Grave 5).

During the war, Walter Sigel flew over 300 combat missions in a Stuka.[98]

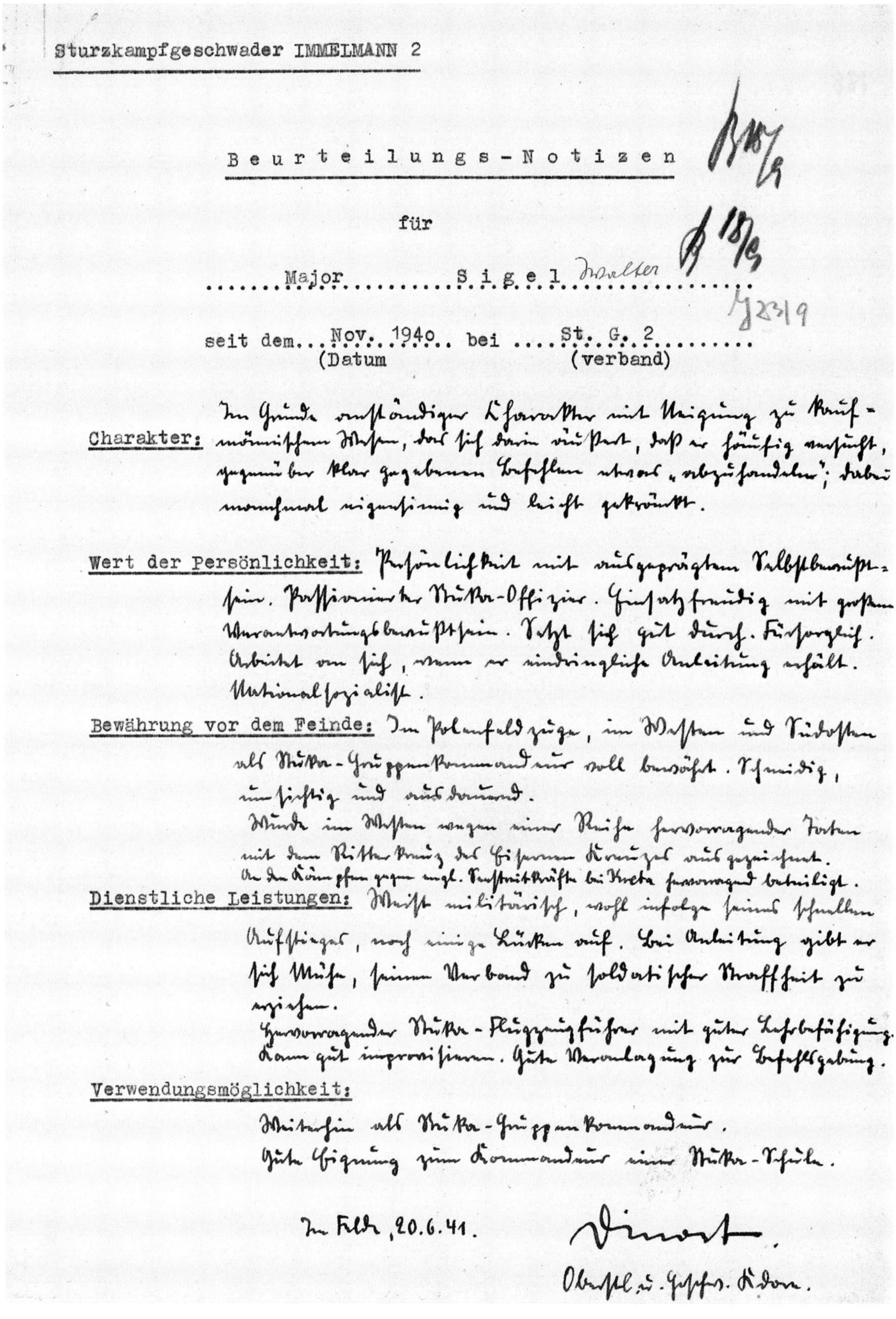

Sturzkampfgeschwader IMMELMANN 2

Beurteilungs-Notizen

für

Major Sigel Walter

seit dem Nov. 1940 bei St. G. 2
(Datum) (verband)

Charakter: Im Grunde anständiger Charakter mit Neigung zu kaufmännischem Wesen, das sich darin äußert, daß er häufig versucht, gegenüber klar gegebenen Befehlen etwas „abzuhandeln"; dabei manchmal eigensinnig und leicht gekränkt.

Wert der Persönlichkeit: Persönlichkeit mit ausgeprägtem Selbstbewußtsein. Passionierter Stuka-Offizier. Einsatzfreudig mit großem Verantwortungsbewußtsein. Setzt sich gut durch. Fürsorglich. Arbeitet an sich, wenn er eindringliche Anleitung erhält. Nationalsozialist.

Bewährung vor dem Feinde: Im Polenfeldzuge, im Westen und Südosten als Stuka-Gruppenkommandeur voll bewährt. Schneidig, umsichtig und ausdauernd.
Wurde im Westen wegen einer Reihe hervorragender Taten mit dem Ritterkreuz des Eisernen Kreuzes ausgezeichnet.
An den Kämpfen gegen engl. Seestreitkräfte bei Kreta hervorragend beteiligt.

Dienstliche Leistungen: Weist militärisch, wohl infolge seines schnellen Aufstieges, noch einige Lücken auf. Bei Anleitung gibt er sich Mühe, seinen Verband zu soldatischer Straffheit zu erziehen.
Hervorragender Stuka-Flugzeugführer mit guter Lehrbefähigung. Kann gut improvisieren. Gute Veranlagung zur Befehlsgebung.

Verwendungsmöglichkeit:

Weiterhin als Stuka-Gruppenkommandeur.
Gute Eignung zum Kommandeur einer Stuka-Schule.

Im Felde, 20.6.41.

Dinort.

Oberstlt. u. Geschw. Kdore.

Efficiency Report for Major Walter Sigel (one page only) – dated June 20, 1941, on blank paper, with typed and hand-written comments. Signed by Lieutenant Colonel Oskar Dinort, Commodore, 2nd Stuka Wing.

Eduard Skrzipek

Bomber Pilot

"Still lacking social manners, particularly in social gatherings."

Captain Eduard Skrzipek was born on June 26, 1917 in Beuthen-Rossberg, Silesia. He entered the *Luftwaffe* on November 1, 1937 and attended various flight schools at Guben, Landau and Tutow. He joined the 2nd Group, 27th Bomber Wing "Boelcke" (*Kampfgeschwader 27 "Boelcke"*) on January 3, 1940. He received the Iron Cross 2nd Class on September 15, 1940 and the Iron Cross 1st Class on September 30, 1940, for missions flown as part of the 3rd Air Fleet during the Battle of Britain. On the night of November 14/15, Skrzipek participated in the Luftwaffe bombing of Coventry, England.

On December 12, 1940, the chain of command in the 27th Bomber Wing submitted an efficiency report on Second Lieutenant Eduard Skrzipek. Captain Reinhard Günzel, the 2nd Group Commander, wrote the following comments:[99]

> **Service Appearance:** Military in his appearance, however, sometimes he lets himself go slightly.
>
> **Behavior outside of service:** Strives to obtain still lacking social manners, particularly in social gatherings.
>
> **Awards:** September 15, 1940 Iron Cross 2nd Class; September 30, 1940 Iron Cross 1st Class
>
> **Punishments:** none
>
> **Behavior vis-à-vis superiors, subordinates and position within the circle of comrades (does the person under review show leadership qualities):** The still present lack of skill in dealing with superiors during his short time of being part of the officer corps will be left behind by him in a short time. By his subordinates, he is recognized as the superior. He has adapted well to the circle of comrades. Possesses leadership qualities.
>
> **Clearly outstanding character attributes:** Definitely reliable.
>
> **Particular military capabilities and recommendations for possible engagement:** Experienced pilot. Skillful in giving instructions. Is being recommended for continued service as a pilot in a bomber squadron, may later serve as a flight instructor.
>
> **Summarized evaluation (is the person under review "above average," "average" or "below average" by using a strict measuring scale):** Physically and mentally well gifted. His service accomplishments are respectively good, so that he can be counted among the average of his year group. Has shown readiness for action in all missions against the enemy and has executed his orders with great results.

The commodore of the 27th Bomber Wing, Lieutenant Colonel Gerhard Ulbricht, simply stated: "Nothing to be added."

The commanding general of the 4th Air Corps (*IV. Flieger-Korps*), Major General Kurt Pflugbeil reviewed the report, signed it, but made no comments.

In 1941, Skrzipek and his unit transferred to Romania and flew during "Operation Barbarossa" in southern Russia. In 1942, the 2nd Group, as part of the 8th Air Corps, flew in support of German Army units at Stalingrad. He was wounded in action during a mission over Stalingrad by a Russian fighter on August 23, 1942. Eduard Skrzipek won the Knight's Cross of the Iron Cross on April 16, 1943 as a first lieutenant and pilot in the 5th Squadron, 27th Bomber Wing "Boelcke." He continued to fly missions in southern Russia; on June 24, 1944, Captain Eduard Skrzipek became the 509th recipient of the Oak Leaves to the Knight's Cross as the Commander, 14th Squadron, 27th Bomber Wing. Eduard Skrzipek was killed while conducting a test flight near Pilsen (now Plzen, Czech Republic), for the *Luftwaffe* Test Group Rechlin on February 25, 1945. He is buried in the central city cemetery of Plzen, in a section (Block 77) containing the remains of 584 German soldiers. The 14th Squadron specialized in attacking enemy rail assets, and during the war, Eduard Skrzipek destroyed 22 transport trains, 45 enemy aircraft on the ground and shot down another three in the air.[100]

Luftflotte 3 W.B.K.: Naumburg

Waffengattung: Fliegertruppe

Truppenteil: II./ Kampfgeschwader
"Boelcke" Nr.27

B e u r t e i l u n g

Name: S k r z i p e k

Vorname: Eduard, Peter

Dienstgrad: Leutnant der Reserve R.D.A.: 1.11.4o

Geburtsdatum und -ort: 26.6.1917 Beuthen/Oberschlesien

Beruf: Schüler

Abiturient: ja

Aktive Dienstzeit: von: 1.11.1937 bis: 2.1.194o
bei: Fea 12 Schönwalde; Fl.Waffenschule E Neustadt; Fl.Ausb.Reg 71 Guben; Flugzeugführerschule C Landau; Gr.K.Fl.Schule Tutow. Seit 3.1.194o bei II./ K.G.Boelcke Nr.27

Bisherige dienstliche Verwendung als Offizier:
von: 1.11.194o bis: als: Flugzeugführer

Sonderausbildung:
Flugzeugführer mit erweitertem Lw. Flugzeugführerschein (Land) und Blindflugschein II (Kr.)

Sprachkenntnisse:

Schulkenntnisse: englisch, französisch

Wort und Schrift:

Efficiency Report for Second Lieutenant (Reserve) Eduard Skrzipek (first page) – dated December 31, 1940, on blank paper, with typed comments.

- 2 -

Dienstliches Auftreten:

In seinem Auftreten militärisch, lässt sich noch zeitweise etwas gehen.

Ausserdienstliches Verhalten:

Ist bemüht, sich noch fehlende Umgangsformen besonders im gesellschaftlichen Verkehr anzueignen.

Auszeichnungen:

15.9.4o E.K.2.Klasse, 3o.9.4o E.K.1.Klasse

Bestrafungen:

Keine

Verhalten gegenüber Vorgesetzten, Untergegenen und Stellung im Kameradenkreis (besitzt der beurteilte Führereigenschaften):

Während seiner kurzen Zugehörigkeit zum Offizierkorps noch anhaftende Ungeschicklichkeiten im Auftreten gegenüber Vorgesetzten wird er bald ablegen. Bei seinen Untergebenen wird er als Vorgesetzter anerkannt. Hat sich gut in den Kameradenkreis eingelebt. Besitzt Führereigenschaften.

Wesentlich hervortretende Charaktereigenschaften:

Unbedingt zuverlässig.

Efficiency Report for Second Lieutenant (Reserve) Eduard Skrzipek (second page)

Besondere militärische Fähigkeiten und Vorschläge für Verwendungsmöglichkeiten:

Erfahrener Flugzeugführer. Geschickt in der Erteilung des Unterrichts. Wird für Verwendung weiterhin als Flugzeugführer einer Kampfstaffel, später vielleicht als Fluglehrer vorgeschlagen.

Zusammenfassendes Urteil:

(Steht der Beurteilte bei Anlegung eines strengen Massstabes "über dem Durchschnitt", "im Durchschnitt" oder "unter dem Durchschnitt")

Körperlich und geistig gut veranlagt. Seine dienstlichen Leistungen sind entsprechend gut, sodass er zum Durchschnitt seines Jahrgangs gerechnet werden kann.

Hat sich bei allen Feindeinsätzen einsatzfreudig gezeigt und erfolgreich seine Aufträge ausgeführt.

Bourges, den 31.12.1940
(Ort und Datum)

Günzel
Hauptmann und Gruppenkommandeur
(Unterschrift)
(Name und Dienstgrad)

Kampfgeschwader Boelcke Nr.27 Den 7.Januar 1941.
Der Kommodore.

Nichts hinzuzufügen.

Ulbricht
Major

Efficiency Report for Second Lieutenant (Reserve) Eduard Skrzipek (third page) – signed by Captain Reinhard Günzel, the 2nd Group Commander, 27th Bomber Wing, and Lieutenant Colonel Gerhard Ulbricht, Commodore, 27th Bomber Wing.

Der Kommandierende General
des IV.Flieger-Korps.

Generalleutnant.

Efficiency Report for Second Lieutenant (Reserve) Eduard Skrzipek (fourth page) – signed by Major General Kurt Pflugbeil, Commanding General, 4th Air Corps.

Rudolf Smola

Stuka Pilot

"Natural leader."

Captain Rudolf "Bazi" Smola was born on July 27, 1944 in Vienna, Austria. He began World War II assigned as a second lieutenant and platoon leader in the 99th Mountain Infantry Regiment of the German Army and subsequently volunteered to fly with Army reconnaissance. He qualified as an observer, and flew a minimum of 130 short-range reconnaissance missions in the skies of Russia, for which he received the Iron Cross 2nd Class on July 13, 1941 and the Iron Cross 1st Class on August 24, 1941. He also won the *Luftwaffe* Honor Goblet on November 26, 1942 and the German Cross in Gold on March 31, 1943. Smola then transferred to the 1st Group, 101st Ground-Attack Wing (*Schlachtgeschwader 101*) and subsequently returned to the Eastern Front as the Commander, 5th Squadron, 2nd Ground-Attack Wing "Immelmann" (*Schlachtgeschwader 2 "Immelmann"*). His unit performed magnificently in the defense of the Crimea in 1944, shooting down 36 enemy aircraft, destroying 20 aircraft on the ground and destroying a large number of tanks northeast of Sevastopol. During the fight, Smola personally shot down three and destroyed 14 enemy aircraft on the ground. First Lieutenant Rudolf Smola received the Knight's Cross of the Iron Cross on July 27, 1944 for these accomplishments and for flying a total of 532 combat missions.

On October 10, 1944, Captain Karl Kennel, the Commander of the 2nd Group, *Schlachtgeschwader 2 "Immelmann,"* submitted an efficiency report on First Lieutenant Rudolf Smola, and wrote:[101]

> **Short Evaluation** (Personal values, National Socialist attitude, accomplishments before the enemy, service accomplishments, mental and physical attributes and suitability, infantry experience, when and how obtained)**:** Congenial, engaging personality. Self-assured and energetic. Open, sincere, single-minded and clean character. Mentally very well talented, educated and interested in many disciplines. Of average height, athletic appearance, fit and able to bear any burden. His service knowledge and accomplishments are good. Through personal élan and exemplary eagerness for action, he is a protective and acknowledged leader for his men. Due to his experience in 532 combat missions, he understands how to skillfully lead his unit in battle. Through his fresh and energetic style, he has attained excellent success in leading attacks. Smola acts in a military and correct way towards his superiors and the men under his command and is well liked by his peers. Firmly rooted in the philosophy of National Socialism and is able to pass on his National Socialistic thinking.
>
> **Strong Traits:** Personal initiative, natural leader. Very good unit commander. Very good tactical knowledge.
>
> **Summary Assessment:** Above Average
> (Above Average, Average, Below Average)
>
> **How well is the current position being fulfilled:** Well fulfilled.
> (Use only: Very well fulfilled, well fulfilled, fulfilled, not fulfilled)
>
> **Suitable for promotion to the next higher service grade:** Yes.
>
> **Suitable as:** Group Commander.
>
> **Subordinated to the person submitting this review:** since July 27, 1944.

Shortly thereafter, Smola was tabbed to be the acting commander of the 4th Group, 151st Ground-Attack Wing (*Schlachtgeschwader 151*). On March 4, 1945, he transferred to become Commander, 1st Group, 3rd Ground-Attack Wing (*Schlachtgeschwader 3*). On March 27, 1945, infantry ground fire struck Smola's aircraft three miles north of Zinten near Heiligenbeil in East Prussia (now Mamonowo/Bagrationowski, Russia); it crashed behind enemy lines and burned, killing Captain Rudolf Smola. During the war, he had flown over 600 combat missions and had achieved 17 aerial victories.[102]

II./Schlachtgeschwader 2 Immelmann — den 1. 1o. 194 4

(Dienststelle, nicht Feldpostnummer)

Kriegs-Beurteilung zum 1. Oktober 1944

für Offz. ausschl. San.-, Vet.-Offz.

über den

Oblt.(Tr.O.)	1.1o.1941	Rudolf	S m o l a
Dienstgrad [1]	R. D. A. (Ordn. Nr.) und Dienstaltersliste	Vorname	Name

3.8.1917 — geboren am

verheiratet, ledig, verwitwet, geschieden (Zutreffendes unterstreichen)

kv — Wehrdienstauglichkeit [2] (kv. gv. Feld, gv. H. tropentgl., tropenuntgl.)

./. — Zivilberuf (falls vorhanden)

Heeresstandortverwaltung Kufstein WBK Kempten — Friedensdienststelle und W. B. K. [3]

Staffelkapitän — jetzige Verwendung seit

D (Luft) 2ooo II 2 b — Anlaß der Vorlage [4]

Deutsche Auszeichnungen des jetzigen Krieges mit Verleihungsdaten und Angabe, ob und zu welchen Auszeichnungen vorgeschlagen:

EK II.Kl. 13.7.41 Frontfl.Sp.in Gold 31.12.42
EK I.Kl. 28.8.41
Ritterkreuz 27.7.44 Ehrenpokal 26.11.42 Frontfl.Sp.in Gold
D.Kr.in Gold 31.3.43mit Anhänger 13.4.44

[1] Genaue Angabe, ob Tr.-Offz., Erg.-Offz., Offz. z. D., Res.-Offz., Kr.-Offz., z.V.-Offz. — [2] In zweifelhaften Fällen neu festzustellen. — [3] Dienststelle, welche Friedensgebührnisse zahlt und zuständiges Wehrbezirkskommando. — [4] z. B. Versetzung zur III./K. G. 2, terminmäßige Vorlage zum 1. 5. 43.

Kurze Beurteilung (Persönlichkeitswert, nationalsozialistische Haltung, Bewährung vor dem Feinde, dienstliche Leistungen, geistige und körperliche Anlagen und Eignung, infanteristische Erfahrungen, wann und wo erworben):

Sympathische, einnehmende Persönlichkeit. Selbstbewusst und energisch. Offener, ehrlicher, zielstrebiger und lauterer Charakter. Geistig sehr gut veranlagt, vielseitig gebildet und interessiert. Mittelgrosse, sportliche Erscheinung, durchtrainiert und belastungsfähig. Seine dienstlichen Kenntnisse und Leistungen sind gut. Durch persönlichen Schneid und vorbildliche Einsatzfreudigkeit ist er seinen Männern ein geschätzter und anerkannter Führer. Auf Grund seiner Erfahrung in 532 Feindflügen versteht er es, seinen Verband geschickt im Angriff zu führen. Es hat durch seine frische und energische Art in der Angriffsführung hervorragende Erfolge erzielt. S. tritt Vorgesetzten und Untergebenen gegenüber soldatisch und korrekt auf und ist im Kameradenkreise sehr beliebt.
Steht fest auf dem Boden der nationalsozialistischen Weltanschauung und ist befeähigt nationalsozialistisches Gedankengut zu vermitteln.

Starke Seiten:

Schwache Seiten:

Starke Seiten: Eigeninitiative, Führernatur. Sehr guter Einheitsführer. Sehr gutes taktisches Verständnis.

Zusammenfassendes Urteil (über Durchschnitt, Durchschnitt, unter Durchschnitt): Über Durchschnitt

Wie wird jetzige Stelle ausgefüllt? (Es sind nur die Ausdrücke »sehr gut ausgefüllt«, »gut ausgefüllt«, »ausgefüllt«, »nicht ausgefüllt« zu verwenden): Gut ausgefüllt

Geeignet zur Beförderung zum nächsthöheren Dienstgrad? Ja

Efficiency Report for First Lieutenant Rudolf Smola (front side) – dated October 1, 1944, on pre-printed form, with typed comments.

Eignung
für welche nächsthöhere Verwendung[5]? —
für welche besondere oder anderweitige Verwendung[6]? —
Vorschlag für Verwendung in nächster Zeit[7]? Gruppenkommandeur

Sprachkenntnisse (keine Schulkenntnisse)
a) abgelegte Prüfungen:
(z. B.: Dolmetscherprüfung 1. 10. 42) keine
b) Beherrschung der Sprache:
(z. B.: durch Aufenthalt im Ausland)

Eröffnung zu welchen Punkten, wann, wie (mündlich oder schriftlich) und durch wen? keine

Strafen sind mit vollem Straftenor sowie Vermerk über Vollstreckung abschriftlich als Anlage der Kriegsbeurteilung beizuheften. keine

Dem Beurteilenden ~~bekannt seit~~ **unterstellt seit** 27. Juli 1944

Ausbildung
a) erworbene Scheine:
(L. F., E. L. F., L. B. usw.) LF, Beobachter
b) Sonderausbildung:
(z. B. Bild-Offz., Techn. Offz., Meß-Offz., Funk-Drahtnachr.-Offz., W. K. S.)

Kennel
Unterschrift

Hauptmann und Gruppenkommandeur
Dienstgrad und Dienststellung

Beitrag des Chefs des Generalstabes der vorgesetzten Kommandobehörde (nur bei Genst.-Offz. in Stabsstellungen und zur Dienstleistung zum Generalstab kommandierten Offizieren):

Zusätze vorgesetzter Dienststellen:

[5]) Gilt für alle Offz., für Truppen-Offz. hinsichtlich Eignung zur Führung des nächsthöheren Verbandes, für Genst.-Offz. hinsichtlich Eignung zum Chef oder Ia, Ic der Luftfl., Flieger-Korps, Flak-Korps, Fl.-Div., Flak-Div., zur Versetzung in den Genst., zur Kommandierung in den Genst. — [6]) z. B.: Höherer Adjutant, Erzieher, Lehrer auf Spezialgebieten, auf Grund von Sprachkenntnissen im Attachédienst; für Genst.-Offz. hinsichtlich Eignung für Verwendung im Quartiermeisterdienst, im Ic-Dienst, im Transportwesen, als Lehrer für Genst.-Lehrgang (Taktik bzw. Qu.-Dienst); besondere Anlagen für Kriegsgeschichte, Wehrwirtschaft. — [7]) z. B.: »noch halbjährige Belassung in bisheriger Stelle« oder »alsbaldige Verwendung als Geschw.-Kommodore«.

Efficiency Report for First Lieutenant Rudolf Smola (back side) – signed twice by Captain Karl Kennel, Commander, 2nd Group, 2nd Ground-Attack Wing.

Willi Sölter

Bomber Pilot

"Within a very short time, his group has sunk 15,000 tons commercial shipping capacity and one destroyer and has also damaged an additional 93,000 tons and two destroyers."

Major Willi Sölter was born on July 18, 1913 in Hann. Münden, Lower Saxony. He flew combat missions over England, the Soviet Union, Italy and the Mediterranean. Sölter won the German Cross in Gold on December 29, 1941 as a first lieutenant. On July 1, 1943, Sölter became the acting commander of the 1st Group, 77th Bomber Wing (*Kampfgeschwader 77*), based at Grieslienen, East Prussia.

On May 22, 1944, the chain of command submitted a request for a preferential promotion to major for Captain Sölter. The acting wing commodore Major Wilhelm Stemmler wrote:[103]

> The wing requests the naming of Captain Willi Sölter – 1st Group.77th Bomber Wing – to group commander of this group. On July 1, 1943, Captain Sölter was tasked as temporary acting commander of the 1st Group, 77th Bomber Wing, according to regulations. Based on his accomplishments to date as acting group leader, he has demonstrated full suitability to be group commander. In addition, Captain Sölter is being recommended for preferential promotion to major on July 1, 1944.
>
> During a total of 232 combat missions, he has attained outstanding success and was awarded the German Cross in Gold on December 29, 1941. Since the awarding of the German Cross, Captain Sölter has flown an additional 90 combat missions, and since March 15, 1944 he has again been engaged with the 1st Group, 77th Bomber Wing in aerial torpedo missions. In these engagements, within a very short time, his group has sunk 15,000 tons commercial shipping capacity and one destroyer and has also damaged an additional 93,000 tons and two destroyers.

Captain Willi Sölter won the Knight's Cross of the Iron Cross on August 9, 1944 for previous accomplishments as the commander of the 1st Group, 77th Bomber Wing. He assumed command of the 1st Group, 26th Bomber Wing "Lions" (*Kampfgeschwader 26 "Löwen"*) in July 1944 and led the formation until it was disbanded in February 1945. Willi Sölter died on July 13, 1995 at Uetze/Celle in Lower Saxony. He is buried there at the *Kirchlichen Friedhof* (Section 36, Row 3, Grave 3).[104]

Kampfgeschwader 77 Gefechtsstand, den 22.5.1944
IIa Nr. 655 /44 o.

Bezug: D.R.d.L.u.Ob.d.L., L.P.Amt, Az.21, Nr.71489/42 (2, I D) - II.Ang.- vom 22.12.42.

Betr.: Bevorzugten Beförderung von Offizieren; hier: Ernennung zum Gruppenkommandeur und bevorzugte Beförderung zum Major des Hauptmann (Tr.O.) Willi S ö l t e r , I./K.G.77.

2. Fliegerdivision
Eingang: 26 MAI 1944

Gen. Kdo. X. Fl. Korps
Eing. 7 JUNI 1944
Br.B.Nr.
Az. Anl.

An den
Reichsminister der Luftfahrt
und
Oberbefehlshaber der Luftwaffe
- Luftwaffenpersonalamt -

über 2.Fliegerdivision, IIa.

Das Geschwader bittet um Ernennung des Hauptmann (Tr.) Willi S ö l t e r - I./K.G.77 - zum Gruppenkommandeur dieser Gruppe. Hptm.Sölter ist gemäß R.d.L.u.Ob.d.L., L.P. Nr. 43947/43 (1 I C) am 1.7.1943 mit der Wahrnehmung der Geschäfte des Kommandeurs der I./K.G.77 beauftragt worden. Er hat auf Grund seiner bisherigen Leistungen als Verbandsführer seine volle Eignung zum Gruppenkommandeur bewiesen. Hauptmann S ö l t e r wird ferner für eine bevorzugte Beförderung zum Major am 1.7.1944 vorgeschlagen.
Er hat bei insgesamt 232 Feindflügen hervorragende Erfolge erzielt und wurde bereits am 29.12.1941 mit dem Deutschen Kreuz in Gold ausgezeichnet. Seit der Verleihung des Deutschen Kreuzes hat Hauptmann Sölter weitere 90 Feindflüge geflogen und befindet sich seit 15.3.44 mit der für den LT-Einsatz umgerüsteten I./K.G.77 erneut im Einsatz. Hierbei hat seine Gruppe bei 4 LT-Angriffen innerhalb kurzer Zeit 15000 BRT Handelsschiffsraums und 1 Zerstörer versenkt sowie weitere 93.000 BRT und 2 Zerstörer beschädigt.

- 1 Beurteilung i.verschl.Umschl.-

Major und Kommodore
m.d.W.d.G.b.

Request for Preferred Promotion for Captain Wilhelm Sölter (one page only) – dated May 22, 1944, on blank paper, with typed comments. Signed by Major Wilhelm Stemmler, the acting commodore of the 77th Bomber Wing. Stamped blocks indicate that the request was received at the 2nd Air Division on May 26, and at the 10th Air Corps on June 7.

Waldemar Stadermann

Bomber Pilot

"Secure and calm in every situation."

Second Lieutenant Waldemar Stadermann, the son of a master shoemaker, was born January 3, 1916 in Gotha-Siebleben. Stadermann entered the *Luftwaffe* on April 16, 1936. He attended flight schools at Weimar-Nohra, Halberstadt and Ludwigslust before joining the 2nd Group, 77th Bomber Wing (*Kampfgeschwader 77*) on July 1, 1938. During the Polish campaign, flying Dornier Do 17Zs out of Brünn, Stadermann flew 38 combat missions; he added another 42 missions during the French campaign. During the Battle of Britain, now equipped with a Junkers Ju 88, Waldemar Stadermann flew 59 missions, and during the unit's service in Russia, he flew 73 missions. Stadermann was promoted to second lieutenant on February 1, 1941.

On April 14, 1941, Stadermann's chain of command in the 2nd Group, 77th Bomber Wing submitted a special efficiency report requesting that his official status be changed from wartime office to full active career officer. Captain and Group Commander Dietrich Peltz wrote the following in support of this request:[105]

> **Personality attributes:** Particularly valuable soldier and officer with leadership qualities. Strong-willed, disciplined, understands how to assert himself. Secure appearance at the front. Good social manners. Rooted in National Socialist ideology.
>
> **Character tendencies:** Open, bright character with good tendencies. Is energetic, works to improve himself. Surpasses difficulties due to his own initiative. Very well liked by his superiors and the men under his command. Helpful and polite. His outstanding military disposition and attitude are meaningful for his nature.
>
> **Military attributes:** Exemplary soldier, appearance at the front secure and good. It must be particularly stressed that he is an outstanding pilot with know-how. Secure and calm in every situation.
>
> **Mental attributes:** Mentally well-positioned, interested, good general education. Seeks to understand and learn something every chance he has. Still must learn how to concentrate on what is the most important matter for himself.
>
> **Physical attributes:** Of medium built, good appearance, good talent.
>
> **Other matters** (particularly regarding proving himself vis-à-vis the enemy, in the current service position and regarding suitability for promotion to next higher service grade)**:** Outstanding enthusiasm for action. In the face of the enemy (112 missions!) he has proven himself in numerous flights. Belongs to the best pilots of the group. Particularly suited as a troop officer. Not yet eligible for promotion to next higher service grade.

On November 12, 1941, Second Lieutenant Waldemar Stadermann won the Knight's Cross of the Iron Cross for his actions in Russia as a pilot in the 6th Squadron, *Kampfgeschwader 77*. After briefly being based at Ansbach, Germany, the unit deployed to Comiso, Sicily. Waldemar Stadermann was killed in action February 15, 1942 over Malta.[106] He is buried at the German Military Cemetery at Cagliari, Italy (Block 1, Grave 48).

II./ Kampfgeschwader 77 Gefechtsstand, den 14.4.1941

V o r s c h l a g

zur Überführung des Lt. Stadermann (Kriegsoffizier)

zu den aktiven Friedensoffizieren.

Familienname, Vorname: S t a d e r m a n n , Waldemar

geb. am: 3. Januar 1916 zu: Gotha Konfession: Gottgl.

Verheiratet, ~~ledig, verwitwet, geschieden.~~

Dienstgrad: Leutnant Rangdienstalter: 1. 2. 1941

Diensteintritt: 16. 4. 1936

Militärische Dienstzeiten (bei Unterbrechungen) und Werdegang:

v. 16. 4.1936 bis 30. 4.1937 Fea. 23, Oschatz
v. 1. 5.1937 " 31. 8.1937 Fl.Schule Weimar-Nohra
v. 1. 9.1937 " 28. 2.1938 Flzg.Fhr.Sch. Halberstadt
v. 1. 3.1938 " 30. 6.1938 C-Schule Ludwigslust
v. 1. 7.1938 " heute II./K.G. 77

jetzige Verwendung: Flugzeugführer

für welche weitere Verwendung geeignet: Staffeloffizier

Bestrafungen vor Diensteintritt: " K e i n e "

Bestrafungen während der milit. Dienstzeiten: " K e i n e "

Bildungsgang (Schulabschluss):

v. 3. 1.1916 bis April 1922 im elterlichen Hause erzogen
v. April 1922 " März 1926 Volksschule Sieblében
v. -"- 1926 " März 1932 Oberrealschule Gotha
v. -"- 1932 " -"- 1936 Gothaer Versicherungsbanken
v. -"- 1936 " heute aktiver Wehrdienst

Zivilberuf: Versicherungsangestellter

Beruf des Vaters: Schuhmachermeister

Erworbene Lw.-Scheine: ELF-Schein/ Bl. II

Request for Transfer for Second Lieutenant Waldemar Stadermann from Wartime Officer to Career Status (first page) – dated April 4, 1941, on blank paper, with typed comments.

Beurteilung:

1. Persönlichkeitswert:

Besonders wertvoller Soldat und Offizier mit Führereigenschaften. Willensstark, diszipliniert, versteht sich durchzusetzen. Sicheres Auftreten vor der Front. Gute gesellschaftliche Formen. Steht auf dem Boden der nationalsozialistischen Weltanschauung.

2. Charakterliche Eignung:

Offener, aufgeschlossener Charakter mit sehr guten Anlagen. Besitzt Energie, arbeitet an sich. Überwindet Schwierigkeiten auf Grund eigener Initiative. Bei Vorgesetzten und Untergebenen sehr beliebt. Hilfsbereit und taktvoll. Seine hervorragende soldatische Einstellung und Haltung ist für sein Wesen bestimmend.

3. Militärische Veranlagung:

Vorbildlicher Soldat, Auftreten vor der Front sicher und gut. Überragender Flugzeugführer mit besonders hervorzuhebendem Können. Sicher und ruhig in jeder Situation.

4. Geistige Veranlagung:

Geistig gut veranlagt, interessiert, gute Allgemeinbildung. Sucht bei jeder Gelegenheit aufzunehmen und zu lernen. Muss noch lernen, sich auf das für ihn wesentliche zu konzentrieren.

5. Körperliche Veranlagung:

Mittelgrosse, gute Erscheinung, gut veranlagt.

6. Sonstiges (insbesondere über Bewährung vor dem Feinde, in der jetzigen Dienststellung und über Eignung zur Beförderung zum nächsthöheren Dienstgrad):

Hervorragende Einsatzfreude. Vor dem Feinde (112 Einsätze!) bei zahlreichen Flügen bewährt. Gehört zu den besten Flugzeugführern der Gruppe. Zur Übernahme als Truppenoffizier besonders geeignet.
Steht zur Beförderung zum nächsthöheren Dienstgrad noch nicht heran.

Hauptmann und Gruppenkommandeur.

Request for Transfer for Second Lieutenant Waldemar Stadermann from Wartime Officer to Career Status (second page) – signed by Captain Dietrich Peltz, Commander, 2nd Group, 77th Bomber Wing.

Heinrich Sterr

Fighter Pilot

"Has an enthusiastic heart."

First Lieutenant Heinrich "Bazi" (Rascal) Sterr was born on September 24, 1919 in Ortenburg, Bavaria. He joined the 6th Squadron, 54th Fighter Wing "Green Hearts" (*Jagdgeschwader 54 "Grünherz"*) at the beginning of 1942 and shot down his first enemy aircraft on April 6, 1942. By the end of the year, Sterr had chalked up 10 aerial victories, but then his score started to mount. By the end of March 1943, flying a Focke-Wulf Fw 190A-4, he had 31 kills; on June 17, 1943 the total had reached 40. During this period, he received the *Luftwaffe* Honor Goblet on April 30. Sterr shot down his 60th enemy aircraft on July 30, 1943 and his 75th on August 11, 1943. He won the German Cross in Gold on August 30, 1943.

On September 12, 1943, the chain of command of the 2nd Group, 54th Fighter Wing "Green Hearts" completed an efficiency report on Master Sergeant Heinz Sterr. Captain Eric Rudorffer, the Group Commander, wrote:[107]

> Master Sergeant Sterr is a trustworthy, balanced, calm character. His attitude in every respect is immaculate. He is firmly rooted in the National Socialist ideology. As a fighter pilot, Sterr has proven himself in an excellent way. In all situations, he has demonstrated reliability, courage and exemplary spirit for the attack. He has 75 aerial victories. Sterr is capable of sweeping along the pilots in his flight and to lead them to success in this way. He was recommended for the Knight's Cross of the Iron Cross and promises to attain considerably greater successes. His military appearance is without criticism. Sterr is in the position to prove himself as a superior and to relate opinions and experiences to the men under his command. As to general education, Master Sergeant Sterr seems not to have quite reached the average of an officer. On the other hand, he has demonstrated an excellent military accomplishment, a pronounced personality suitable for leadership and an immaculate character attitude. Without reservation, Master Sergeant Sterr is suitable for promotion to wartime officer.

Major Hubertus von Bonin, the commodore of the 54th Fighter Wing, also weighed in with these remarks:

> Master Sergeant Sterr is a particularly outstanding fighter pilot who has demonstrated exemplary accomplishments. Particularly, he is able to train his pilots and help them to succeed. His military attitude is immaculate, his attitude is without criticism. Due to all of his attributes, he will be able to know how to get rid of any deficiencies still present. Master Sergeant Sterr is fully suitable for promotion to wartime officer.

Sterr continued to fly well. On October 8, 1943, he shot down two aircraft, bringing his total to 86 aerial victories, but during the fight his Focke-Wulf Fw 190A-6 was heavily damaged and he was forced to bail out. Severely injured in the process, he did not return to the front until March 1944, but achieved his 100th victory by March 29 and was named the commander of the 6th Squadron. While on convalescent leave, he received the Knight's Cross of the Iron Cross on December 5, 1943. In June 1944, his unit was re-designated the 12th Squadron, 4th Group, 54th Fighter Wing "Green Hearts" and sent to the Western Front, taking part in the battle of Arnhem. Soon thereafter, Heinrich Sterr assumed command of the new 16th Squadron in the wing.

On September 29, 1944, Second Lieutenant Sterr's chain of command in the 4th Group, 54th Fighter Wing "Green Hearts" submitted another efficiency report on him requesting a direct promotion to captain – thus skipping the grade of first lieutenant! Major and Group Commander Wolfgang Späte wrote:[108]

> Due to his courage against the enemy, Second Lieutenant Sterr was promoted to officer. Shortly after he had become an officer, he was tasked with the command of a squadron and demonstrated that he was up to this task from the beginning in a surprising and good manner. Considering his age, he is of above-average maturity and balance, is equipped with secure and cleverly thought-through judgment, is passionate and unselfish in combat, has an enthusiastic heart, and he can be called the example of a fighter squadron leader. As much as he is able to always bring the troops under his command to successful engagement in the air (he was already the leader of a battle unit the size of a squadron), he also guarantees the strict and correct leadership of his unit. (His experience as a troop trainer has been a great asset in this connection.) For his pilots, he is not only a leader and example concerning pilot skills, but he also knows to maximize this with aggression and willingness for combat, which is the foundation of his own aerial victories. With 128 confirmed aerial victories, Sterr is poised to be awarded the Oak Leaves to the Knight's Cross. Since June 1, 1944, Sterr has been the squadron leader. His squadron, which is one of the best and most successful of the Wing, has also proven itself under his leadership in the most difficult situations in the East and the West. In dealing with superiors and with the men under his command, Sterr is flexible and secure, with particularly pronounced empathy. His social manners are very good. Decisiveness and the joy of making decisions are present. He is a convinced National Socialist.

Brigadier General Walter Grabmann, the 3rd Fighter Division Commander, added the following comments:

> Due to the evaluation by the group commander, I second the preferential promotion of Second Lieutenant Sterr to Captain with an interim promotion to First Lieutenant.

Major General Josef "Beppo" Schmid, the commanding general of the 1st Fighter Corps, added the following positive evaluation on October 10, 1944:

> Courageous, successful officer with the genuine élan of a fighter pilot; he succeeded in 128 aerial victories. Owner of the Knights Cross. Proven as squadron leader in an outstanding way. Without reservation, he is suited for preferential promotion to Captain with an interim promotion to First Lieutenant.

But Sterr's days were numbered. He was shot down and killed on November 26, 1944 by a P-51 Mustang, while attempting to land at Vörden in his Focke-Wulf Fw 190A-8. He is buried at a German Military Cemetery at Hofkirchen (Row 23, Grave 6-68). Heinrich Sterr was submitted for the Oak Leaves to his Knight's Cross, but the award was never formally approved. At the time of his death, Sterr had 129 aerial victories of which 4 had occurred in the west.[109]

II./Jagdgeschwader 54 Gefechtsstand, den 12. 9.1943

B e u r t e i l u n g

über den Oberfeldwebel Heinz S t e r r .

Obfw. S t e r r ist ein ehrlicher, ausgeglichener, ruhiger Charakter. Seine Haltung ist in jeder Beziehung einwandfrei. Er steht fest auf den Boden der nationalsozialistischen Weltan - schauung.

Als Jagdflieger hat sich Sterr ausgezeichnet bewährt. In allen Lagen hat er Zuverlässigkeit, Schneid und vorbildlichen Angriffsgeist gezeigt. Er erzielte 75 Abschüsse. Sterr besitzt die Fähigkeit, die mit ihm im Schwarm fliegenden Flugzeugführer mitzureißen und sie dadurch auch zu Erfolgen zu führen. Er ist zur Beleihung mit dem Ritterkreuz des Eisernen Kreuzes vorgeschlagen und verspricht, zu noch wesentlich größeren Erfolgen zu kommen.

Das militärische Auftreten ist einwandfrei. Sterr ist in der Lage, sich als Vorgesetzter durchzusetzen und Anschauungen und Erfahrungen auch an Untergebene zu übermitteln. Es fehlt an Gewandtheit. In der Allgemeinbildung dürfte Obfw. Sterr den Durchschnitt eines Offiziers noch nicht ganz erreichen. Dem - gegenüber steht eine ausgezeichnete kämpferische Leistung, eine ausgeprägte zum Führer geeignete Persönlichkeit und eine ein - wandfreie charakterliche Haltung.
Obfw. Sterr ist zur Beförderung zum Kriegsoffizier uneingeschränkt geeignet.

Rudorffer

Hauptmann und Führer der Jagdgruppe.

Request for Promotion to officer for Master Sergeant Heinz Sterr (front side) – dated September 12, 1943, on blank paper, with typed comments. Signed by Captain Eric Rudorffer, Commander, 2nd Group, 54th Fighter Wing.

Jagdgeschwader 54 — Gefechtsstand, 16.9.1943

Oberfeldwebel S t e r r ist ein ganz hervorragender Jagdflieger, der sich durch seine vorbildlichen Leistungen ausgezeichnet hat. Vor allen Dingen ist er in der Lage, seine Flugzeugführer zu erziehen und zu Erfolgen zu bringen.

Seine militärische Haltung ist einwandfrei, seine Anschauung tadellos. Seiner ganzen Veranlagung nach wird er die noch vorhandenen Mängel abzustellen wissen.

Oberfeldwebel Sterr ist zur Beförderung zum Kriegsoffizier voll geeignet.

Request for Promotion to officer for Master Sergeant Heinz Sterr (back side) – signed by Major Hubertus von Bonin, Commodore, 54th Fighter Wing.

z Uz 4 26.11.44

B e f ö r d e r u n g s v o r s c h l a g.

zur bevorzugten Beförderung eines Offiziers (Kr.O.)

Vorschl.Dienststelle: IV./Jagdgeschwader 54
Luftflotte : Gen.Kdo.I.Jagdkorps Datum: 29.9.44
W.B.K. : München II Waffengattung: Flg.-Tr.

Es wird vorgeschlagen zum Hauptmann Kr.O. mit Wirkung vom: 1.1o.44

Vor- und Zuname : Heinz Sterr Geb.Datum: 24.9.19
Jetziger Dienstgrad : Leutnant(Kr.O.) befördert am: 1.11.43 R.D.A.: 1.1.41

Eingesetzt als : Staffelkapitän
in Truppenstellung
auf Planstelle (Staffelkapitän) gem. KSTN 1143 (L)
Blatt a Zeile 1

Geeignet zum : Gruppenkommandeur

Art und Dauer der Verwendung im derzeitigen mobilen Einsatz einschl. UK-Stellung und Arbeitsurlaub oder sonstigen Urlaub über 3 Monate:

on:	bis:	Dienststelle:	Dienststellung:
.Sept.4o	Mai 4o	Flg.H.Komp. Crailsheim	Ausbilder
1.Juni 4o	April 41	A/B 111 Öls	Flugschüler
1.Mai 41	Juni 41	Jagdvorschule Kamens	Flugschüler
1.Juli 41	15.Sept.41	Jagdschule Magdeburg	Flugschüler
15.Sept.41	3o.Dez. 41	E.-Gruppe Neukuren	Flugschüler
1.Jan.42	1.April 44	6./Jagdgeschwader 54	Flzgführer
2.Apr. 44	6.Juni 44	6./Jagdgeschwader 54	Staffelführer
7.Juni 44	jetzt	16./Jagdgeschwader 54	Staffelkapitän

Strafen: k e i n e

Auszeichnungen des jetzigen Krieges mit Verleihungsdaten:

EK II	3o. 6.42
EK I	8. 1.43
Ehrenp.	22. 4.43
D.K.i.G.	23. 7.43
Ritterkr.	5.12.43
Bronze Fr.Fl.Spange f.J.	1o. 4.42
Silber "	22. 7.42
Gold "	14. 9.42

Beurteilung durch den Disziplinarvorgesetzten:

Lt. Sterr wurde wegen Tapferkeit vor dem Feinde zum Offizier befördert. Kaum Offizier geworden, wurde er mit der Führung einer Staffel beauftragt und zeigte sich dieser Aufgabe in überraschend guter Weise in jeder Hinsicht von Anfang an gewachsen. Für sein Alter von überdurchschnittlicher Reife und Ausgeglichenheit, ausgestattet mit sicherem und klug abwägendem Urteilsvermögen, leidenschaftlich und unbedenklich im Einsatz, mit begeisterungsfähigem Herzen, ist er als Vorbild eines Jagdstaffel-Kapitäns zu bezeichnen. So wie er taktisch den von ihm in der Luft geführten Verband stets zum erfolgreichen Einsatz bringt (er war bereits als Führer von Gefechtsverbänden in Geschwaderstärke eingesetzt), ist er andererseits auch der Garant für eine straffe und korrekte Führung seiner Einheit in truppendienstlicher Hinsicht. (Seine Erfahrung als Truppenausbilder kommt ihm hierbei zustatten.) Seinen Flugzeugführern ist er nicht nur in fliegerischer Hinsicht Führer und Vorbild, sondern weiß sie auch mit der Angriffsfreude und Einsatzbereitschaft zu erfüllen, die die Grundlage seiner eigenen Abschußerfolge bildet. St. steht mit 128 anerkannten Abschüssen

w e n d e n !

Request for Preferred Promotion for Second Lieutenant Heinz Sterr (front side) – dated September 29, 1944, on blank paper, with typed comments. Blue pencil markings probably done at a higher headquarters.

zur Auszeichnung mit dem Eichenlaub zum Ritterkreuz heran. Seit 1.6.44 ist St. als Staffelkapitän bestätigt worden. Seine Staffel, die eine der besten und erfolgreichsten des Geschwaders ist, hat sich unter seiner Führung auch in schwierigsten Lagen im Osten und im Westen bewährt.

Im Verkehr mit Vorgesetzten und Untergebenen zeigt St. sich gewandt und sicher, mit besonders ausgeprägtem Einfühlungsvermögen. Seine gesellschaftlichen Umgangsformen sind sehr gut.
Entschlußkraft und -freude sind vorhanden. Überzeugter Nationalsozialist.

Major u. Gruppenkommandeur.

Stellungnahme der nächsthöheren Disziplinarvorgesetzten:

3. J a g d d i v i s i o n Divisionsgefechtsstand, den 4.10.1944.
Der Kommandeur

Auf Grund der Beurteilung durch den Gruppenkommandeur befürworte ich die bevorzugte Beförderung des Leutnant S t e r r zum Hauptmann mit Zwischenbeförderung zum Oberleutnant.

Der Kommandierende General Korpsgefechtsstand, 10.10.44
des I. Jagdkorps

Tapferer, erfolgreicher Offizier mit echt jagdfliegerischem Schwung; erzielte 128 Abschüsse. Ritterkreuzträger.

Als Staffelkapitän vor dem Feinde hervorragend bewährt.

Zur bevorzugten Beförderung zum Hauptmann mit Zwischenbeförderung zum Oberleutnant uneingeschränkt geeignet.

Request for Preferred Promotion for Second Lieutenant Heinz Sterr (back side) – signed by Major Wolfgang Späte, Commander, 4th Group, 54th Fighter Wing, by Brigadier General Walter Grabmann, the 3rd Fighter Division Commander, and by Major General Josef "Beppo" Schmid, the Commanding General of the 1st Fighter Corps.

Walter Stimpel

Stuka Pilot

"He always understands how to comprehend the essential."

Major Walter Stimpel was born on November 29, 1917 in Oelsen near Pirna. He entered the *Luftwaffe* on April 1, 1936 and was promoted to second lieutenant on January 1, 1938. After receiving required training, he joined the 165th Stuka Wing (*Sturzkampfgeschwader 165*) and began World War II as the adjutant for the 2nd Group, 77th Stuka Wing (*Sturzkampfgeschwader 77*). With this unit, Walter Stimpel fought in Poland, France, the English Channel, Yugoslavia and finally Russia. Stimpel received the Iron Cross 2nd Class on September 13, 1939 and the Iron Cross 1st Class on June 14, 1940. Stimpel was wounded in action and received the Black Wound Badge on July 10, 1941. He won the German Cross in Gold on November 24, 1941. At the beginning of 1942, he assumed command of the 6th Squadron, 77th Stuka Wing. He excelled in this position, and on June 7, 1942, First Lieutenant Walter Stimpel received the Knight's Cross of the Iron Cross. He also received the Operational Flying Clasp for Bombers in Gold with Pendant on September 18, 1942. In November 1942, Stimpel was assigned to the Air War Academy, where he studied to be a General Staff Officer. From the summer of 1943 to the end of the war, Walter Stimpel served with *Luftwaffe* Command Southeast, before joining the *Luftwaffe* Operations Staff. He was promoted to major on February 1, 1944.

On March 28, 1945, with the Soviet Army within 50 miles of Berlin, the chain of command for Walter Stimpel at the *Luftwaffe* Operations Staff continued to submit efficiency reports. Lieutenant Colonel Kurt von Greiff, the section chief, wrote the following:[110]

> **Short Evaluation** (Personal values, National Socialist attitude, accomplishments before the enemy, service accomplishments, mental and physical attributes and suitability, infantry experience, when and how obtained)**:** As to character and capabilities, particularly outstanding, youthful personality, mature and accomplished far above his age. Loyalty, sense of duty and military demeanor combine in the best possible way with a modest, yet definite and skillful appearance. Mentally flexible, above average and strives to enhance his good knowledge in all military as well as general areas. He always understands how to comprehend the essential. During his dual service as liaison officer of the *Luftwaffe* High Command to the *Reichsführer-SS* – who at the time was also serving as an army group commander – and as a liaison officer for an air fleet to this army group at the same time, he has performed with skill and energy. Against the enemy, he is a proven officer, particularly at the front (owner of the Knight's Cross). Among his comrades, he is respected and well liked. Fully rooted in the National Socialistic ideology. An officer who deserves special recognition and advancement.
>
> **Summary Assessment:** Above Average
> (Above Average, Average, Below Average)
>
> **How well is the current position being fulfilled:** Very well fulfilled [a hand-written "very" was added.]
> (Use only: Very well fulfilled, well fulfilled, fulfilled, not fulfilled)
>
> **Suitable for promotion to the next higher service grade:** Not yet under discussion.
>
> **Suitable as:** Employ in operational officer duties. Group Commander in a ground-attack group.
>
> **Known to the person submitting this review:** since summer 1944.
>
> **Subordinated to the person submitting this review:** since December 4, 1944.

The Chief of the *Luftwaffe* Operations Staff, Brigadier General Eckhard Christian, added his own comments:

> Despite his young age, Major i.G. Stimpel is a particularly good officer on the General Staff, who should be employed in independent positions, such as the Operations Officer for an Air Division.

Walter Stimpel survived the war. He is credited with flying over 400 combat missions in the Junkers Ju 87 Stuka, sinking a supply ship on the Dnepr River and 5 freighters in the Black Sea.[111]

E n t w u r f

Luftwaffenführungsstab Ia H.Qu., den 28. 3. 1945
(Dienststelle, nicht Feldpostnummer)

Kriegs-Beurteilung zum 1. April **194**5
für Offz. ausschl. San.-, Vet.-Offz.

über den

Major i.G.	1.2.44 A 1	Walter	Stimpel
Dienstgrad [1])	R. D. A. (Ordn. Nr.) und Dienstaltersliste	Vorname	Name

29.11.1917 — verheiratet, ledig, verwitwet, geschieden — kv
geboren am — (Zutreffendes unterstreichen) — Wehrdiensttauglichkeit [2]) (kv, gv Feld, gv H, tropentgl., tropenuntgl.)

/
Zivilberuf (falls vorhanden)

VO des OKL zum Reichsf. SS — Breslau-Schöngarten; WBK Breslau III
jetzige Verwendung seit 4.12.44 — Friedensdienststelle und W. B. K. [3])

Termin 1.4.45 gemäß D (Luft) 2000
Anlaß der Vorlage [4])

Deutsche Auszeichnungen des jetzigen Krieges mit Verleihungsdaten und Angabe, ob und zu welchen Auszeichnungen vorgeschlagen: 13.9.39 EK II, 14.6.40 EK I, 10.7.41 Verw.Abz. Schw. 24.11.41 DK in Gold, 9.6.42 Ritterkreuz des EK, 18.9.42 Anhänger (300) ~~zur FFSp. (K) in Gold, 18.9.42 Ostmedaille, 15.3.43 Krimschild~~

[1]) Genaue Angabe, ob Tr.-Offz., Erg.-Offz., Offz. z. D., Res.-Offz., Kr.-Offz. z. V.-Offz. — [2]) In zweifelhaften Fällen neu festzustellen. — [3]) Dienststelle, welche Friedensgebührnisse zahlt und zuständiges Wehrbezirkskommando. — [4]) z. B.: Versetzung zur III./K.G. 2, terminmäßige Vorlage zum 1. 5. 43.

Kurze Beurteilung (Persönlichkeitswert, nationalsozialistische Haltung, Bewährung vor dem Feinde, dienstliche Leistungen, geistige und körperliche Anlagen und Eignung, infanteristische Erfahrungen, wann und wo erworben):

Nach Charakter und Fähigkeiten besonders hervorstechende jugendliche Persönlichkeit, die weit über ihr Alter hinaus reif und fertig ist. Treue, Pflichtbewusstsein und soldatische Einstellung verbinden sich bei ihm in glücklichster Weise mit bescheidenem und doch bestimmtem und gewandtem Auftreten.
Geistig beweglich und weit über dem Durchschnitt ist er bemüht, seine guten Kenntnisse auf allen militärischen und ausserdienstlichen Gebieten zu erweitern. Versteht es, stets das Wesentliche zu erfassen.
Hat infolgedessen seinen Posten als Verb.Offz. des OKL beim Reichsführer ~~Stärke Seiten:~~ SS - und während dessen Verwendung als Oberbefehlshaber einer Heeresgruppe gleichzeitig als Verb.Offz. einer Luftflotte zu dieser Heeresgruppe - mit Geschick und Tatkraft voll ausgefüllt. Vor dem Feind bewährter, besonders fronterfahrener Offizier. (Ritterkreuzträger)
Im Kameradenkreise geachtet und beliebt.
Steht voll auf dem Boden der nationalsozialistischen Weltanschauung.
~~Schwache Seiten:~~
Ein Offizier, der besondere Beachtung und Förderung verdient.

S17636

Zusammenfassendes Urteil (über Durchschnitt, Durchschnitt, unter Durchschnitt): Über dem Durchschnitt.

Wie wird jetzige Stelle ausgefüllt? (Es sind nur die Ausdrücke „sehr gut ausgefüllt", „gut ausgefüllt", „ausgefüllt", „nicht ausgefüllt" zu verwenden): Gut ausgefüllt.

Geeignet zur Beförderung zum nächsthöheren Dienstgrad? Steht noch nicht heran.

B 3614. M.-V 7. 3 44

Efficiency Report for Major Walter Stimpel (front side) – dated March 28, 1945, on pre-printed form, with typed and one hand-written comment. "S17636" is probably an administrative file number.

Eignung Verwendung im Ia-Dienst.
für welche nächsthöhere Verwendung [5])?
für welche besondere oder anderweitige Verwendung [6])? Gruppen-Kdr. einer Schlachtgr.
Vorschlag für Verwendung in nächster Zeit [7])?

Sprachkenntnisse (keine Schulkenntnisse) –
a) abgelegte Prüfungen:
(z. B.: Dolmetscherprüfung 1. 10. 42)
b) Beherrschung der Sprache:
(z. B.: durch Aufenthalt im Ausland)

Eröffnung zu welchen Punkten, wann, wie (mündlich oder schriftlich) und durch wen? –

Strafen sind mit vollem Straftenor sowie Vermerk über Vollstreckung abschriftlich als Anlage der Kriegsbeurteilung beizuheften. –

Dem Beurteilenden **bekannt seit** Sommer 44
unterstellt seit 4.12.44

Ausbildung
a) erworbene Scheine:
(L. F., E. L. F., L. B. usw.) ELF, LB
b) Sonderausbildung:
(z. B. Bild-Offz., Techn. Offz., Meß-Offz., Funk-Drahtnachr.-Offz., W. K. S.)

Unterschrift: [signature] — Oberstlt.i.G. u. Abt.Chef
Dienstgrad und Dienststellung

Beitrag des Chefs des Generalstabes der vorgesetzten Kommandobehörde (nur bei Genst.-Offz. in Stabsstellungen und zur Dienstleistung zum Generalstab kommandierten Offizieren):

Zusätze vorgesetzter Dienststellen:

Der Chef des Lw.Führungsstabes

Major i.G. Stimpel ist trotz seiner Jugend ein besonders guter Genealstabsoffizier, der in selbständigen Stellungen verwendet werden sollte, Ia einer Fliegerdivision.

S 17637 [signature]

Generalmajor.

[5]) Gilt für alle Offz., für Truppen-Offz. hinsichtlich Eignung zur Führung des nächsthöheren Verbandes, für Genst.-Offz. hinsichtlich Eignung zum Chef oder I a, I c der Luftfl., Flieger-Korps, Flak-Korps, Fl.-Div., Flak-Div., zur Versetzung in den Genst., zur Kommandierung in den Genst. — [6]) z. B.: Höherer Adjutant, Erzieher, Lehrer auf Spezialgebieten, auf Grund von Sprachkenntnissen im Attachédienst, für Genst.-Offz. hinsichtlich Eignung für Verwendung im Quartiermeisterdienst, im I c-Dienst, im Transportwesen, als Lehrer für Genst.-Lehrgang (Taktik bzw. Qu.-Dienst); besondere Anlagen für Kriegsgeschichte, Wehrwirtschaft. — [7]) z. B.: „noch halbjährige Belassung in bisheriger Stelle" oder „alsbaldige Verwendung als Geschw.-Kommodore".

Efficiency Report for Major Walter Stimpel (back side) – signed by Lieutenant Colonel Kurt von Greiff, and Brigadier General Eckhard Christian, both of the *Luftwaffe* Operations staff.

Heinz Strüning
Night Fighter Pilot

"Could be a little more lively sometimes."

Captain Heinz Strüning was born in Neviges, Rhineland, on January 13, 1912. Strüning entered the *Luftwaffe* in 1935 and on August 2, 1939 was assigned as a sergeant to the 5th Squadron, 26th Destroyer Wing "Horst Wessel" (*Zerstörergeschwader 26 "Horst Wessel"*). Strüning transferred to the destroyer squadron of the 30th Bomber Wing (*Kampfgeschwader 30*) on April 11, 1940 and flew in the Norwegian campaign. On July 1, 1940, he entered night fighter training with the 1st Squadron, 2nd Night Fighter Wing (*Nachtjagdgeschwader 2*). Strüning won the Iron Cross 2nd Class on July 15, 1940 and the Iron Cross 1st Class on November 25, 1940 – this latter award coming one day after he claimed his first aerial victory, a Wellington bomber over the North Sea. He received the *Luftwaffe* Honor Goblet on June 15, 1941 and by the end of the year had accumulated 9 long-range (intruder) aerial victories over England. These included a Hudson and a Wellington on February 15, 1941 (that were probably from an RAF Bomber Command mission against the Holten oil plant at Sterkrade) and two Blenheim bombers over Grantham on August 19, 1941 (returning from RAF "circus" [coordinated fighter and bomber attacks] operations against Hazebrouck). He transferred to the 7th Squadron, 2nd Night Fighter Wing on November 1, 1941.

Strüning continued on a brisk pace the following year, registering two Boston bombers in a span of one minute on May 31, 1942, and received the German Cross in Gold on July 29, 1942. Strüning then transferred to the 8th Squadron, 1st Night Fighter Wing (*Nachtjagdgeschwader 1*) on September 23, 1942. Heinz Strüning won the Knight's Cross of the Iron Cross on October 29, 1942 as a pilot in the 3rd Squadron, 1st Night Fighter Wing. A month later, he transferred to Sicily and flew 20 night missions over the Mediterranean. In May 1943, he returned to homeland defense with the 2nd Squadron, 1st Fighter Wing. Strüning shot down 2 Halifax bombers early on May 14, 1943 that were on an RAF Bomber Command raid on Bochum. He shot down a De Haviland Mosquito on the night of May 27-28, 1943 and destroyed three bombers (a Lancaster, a Stirling and a Halifax), part of a 630-aircraft RAF Bomber Command attack against Wuppertal in just thirteen minutes early on June 25, 1943.[112] With these accomplishments, he became the commander of the 3rd Squadron on July 1, 1943.

On July 7, 1943, Heinz Strüning's chain of command submitted an efficiency report on him. Captain Hans-Dieter Frank, the acting group commander, wrote the following:[113]

Short Evaluation (Personal values, National Socialist attitude, Accomplishments before the enemy, service accomplishments, mental and physical attributes and suitability, infantry experiences, when and how obtained)**:** Second Lieutenant Strüning has belonged to the 1st Group, 1st Night Fighter Wing since May 8, 1043. Decent character with good general education. Decent, adaptable human being. Calm, always full of humor. Well meaning and polite. Immaculate soldierly attitude. Understands how to prevail. Has a good talent as squadron leader. Possesses the confidence of superiors and subordinates.

Well-rooted in National Socialist philosophy and able to pass on its concepts.

Very passionate flyer. Calm, prudent pilot, who demonstrates that he can master even extraordinary situations. Has proven himself in 18 day flights and 223 night combat flights against the enemy, with 9 kills with long-range night fighters, 25 in short-range night fighters.

Strong Traits: Excellent accomplishments in combat.

Weak Traits: Tends to treat subordinates too softly due to his own good nature.

Summarized Evaluation: above average
(Above Average, Average, Below Average)

How well is the current position being fulfilled? Well fulfilled.
(Use only: Very well fulfilled, well fulfilled, fulfilled, not fulfilled)

Suitable for promotion to next higher service grade? Yes

Suitable as: Squadron Commander.

Subordinated to the person submitting this review: since May 8, 1943.

Major Werner Streib, the acting wing commodore, added this short note to the report:

> Decent character. Outstanding frontline officer. Could be a little more lively sometimes. Fully suitable for promotion to first lieutenant.

Now flying a Heinkel He 219, Strüning shot down 3 British Halifax bombers – part of 660 that attacked Mönchengladbach and Rheydt – in just twenty-five minutes early on August 31, 1943, bringing his total to 40 aerial victories.[114] He shot down 3 enemy four-engine aircraft on the night of June 21-22, 1944 (part of 133 RAF Bomber Command aircraft that attacked the synthetic-oil plant at Wesseling) and another Mosquito on the night of July 18-19, thirty miles west of Berlin.[115] Captain Heinz Strüning became the 528th recipient of the Oak Leaves to the Knight's Cross on July 20, 1944 as the Commander, 3rd Squadron, 1st Night Fighter Wing. He transferred to the 9th Squadron, 1st Night Fighter Wing on September 1, 1944. Captain Heinz Strüning was killed in action on the night of December 24-25, 1944, when his Messerschmitt Me 110G-4 was shot down by a long-range British night fighter near Bergisch-Gladbach. While attempting to bail out, he struck the undercarriage of the plane and was killed. Authorities found his body two months later. During his career, Heinz Strüning shot down 56 enemy aircraft, including 2 Mosquitoes; all his victories were at night.[116]

I./ Nachtjagdgeschwader 1 (Dienststelle, nicht Feldpostnummer) O.U., den 7.Juli 1943

Anlage 1
zu Nr. 610

Kriegs-Beurteilung zum -. **194**

für Offz. ausschl. San.-, Vet.-Offz.

über den

Leutnant (Kr.O.) — Dienstgrad [1]
1.8.1942 D — R. D. A. (Ordn. Nr. und Dienstaltersliste)
Heinz — Vorname
S t r ü n i n g — Name

13.1.1912 — geboren am
verheiratet, ledig, verwitwet, geschieden (Zutreffendes unterstreichen)
k.v. tropentgl. — Wehrdiensttauglichkeit [2] (kv, gv Feld, gv H, tropentgl., tropenuntgl.)

Kaufmännischer Angestellter — Zivilberuf (falls vorhanden)

Staffelführer 3./N.J.G.1 — jetzige Verwendung seit 1.7.1943
Fl.Horst Werl, W.B.K.: S o e s t — Friedensdienststelle und W. B. K. [3]

D.R.d.L.u.Ob.d.L. LP-Amt Az. 21 Nr. 71 489/42 (2, I D) - II.Ang. v.22.12.1942 — Anlaß der Vorlage [4]
Bevorzugte Beförderung

Deutsche Auszeichnungen des jetzigen Krieges mit Verleihungsdaten und Angabe, ob und zu welchen Auszeichnungen vorgeschlagen: 15.7.40 E.K.II, 25.11.40 E.K. I, 15.6.41 Ehrenpokal, 29.7.1942 Deutsche Kreuz in Gold, 29.10.1942 Ritterkreuz.

[1]) Genaue Angabe, ob Tr.-Offz., Erg.-Offz., Offz. z. D., Res.-Offz., Kr.-Offz., z. V.-Offz. — [2]) In zweifelhaften Fällen neu festzustellen. — [3]) Dienststelle, welche Friedensgebührnisse zahlt und zuständiges Wehrbezirkskommando. — [4]) z. B. Versetzung zur III./K. G. 2, terminmäßige Vorlage zum 1. 5. 43.

Kurze Beurteilung (Persönlichkeitswert, nationalsozialistische Haltung, Bewährung vor dem Feinde, dienstliche Leistungen, geistige und körperliche Anlagen und Eignung, infanteristische Erfahrungen, wann und wo erworben): Lt. Strüning gehört seit dem 8.5.43 zur I./N.J.G.1.
Anständiger Charakter mit guter Allgemeinbildung. Gutmütiger, anpassungsfähiger Mensch.Ruhiges, immer heiteres Wesen. Zuvorkommend und höflich. Einwandfreie, soldatische Haltung. Versteht sich durchzusetzen. Besitzt als Staffelführer gute Anlagen. Hat das Vertrauen Vorgesetzter und Untergebener.
Steht auf dem Boden nationalsozialistischer Weltanschauung und kann deren Gedankengut weitergeben.
Fliegerisch sehr passioniert. Ruhiger, umsichtiger Flugzeugführer, der sich auch aussergewöhnlichen Lagen gewachsen zeigt. Vor dem Feinde in 18 Tag- und 223 Nachteinsätzen bewährt, dabei 9 Abschüsse in der Fernnachtjagd, 25 in der Nahnachtjagd.

Starke Seiten: Hervorragende Einsatzbewährung.

Schwache Seiten: Neigt auf Grund eigener Gutmütigkeit dazu, Untergebene zu weich zu behandeln.

Zusammenfassendes Urteil (über Durchschnitt, Durchschnitt, unter Durchschnitt): über Durchschnitt

Wie wird jetzige Stelle ausgefüllt? (Es sind nur die Ausdrücke „sehr gut ausgefüllt", „gut ausgefüllt", „ausgefüllt", „nicht ausgefüllt" zu verwenden) gut ausgefüllt

Geeignet zur Beförderung zum nächsthöheren Dienstgrad? ja

2169 b *Heidelberger Gutenberg-Druckerei GmbH. Den Haag 5-43* K 287

Efficiency Report for Second Lieutenant Heinz Strünning (front side) – dated July 7, 1943, on pre-printed form from the Heidelberger-Gutenberg firm in Den Haag, with typed comments.

Eignung
für welche nächsthöhere Verwendung [5]?
für welche besondere oder anderweitige Verwendung [6]?
Vorschlag für Verwendung in nächster Zeit [7]? — zum Staffelkapitän

---

Sprachkenntnisse (keine Schulkenntnisse)
a) abgelegte Prüfungen:
(z. B.: Dolmetscherprüfung 1. 10. 42) — keine
b) Beherrschung der Sprache:
(z. B.: durch Aufenthalt im Ausland)

Eröffnung zu welchen Punkten, wann, wie (mündlich oder schriftlich) und durch wen?

Strafen sind mit vollem Straftenor sowie Vermerk über Vollstreckung abschriftlich als Anlage der Kriegsbeurteilung beizuheften.

Dem Beurteilenden unterstellt seit ~~bekannt seit~~ 8.5.1943

Ausbildung
a) erworbene Scheine:
(L. F., E. L. F., L. B. usw.) — E.L.F./II
b) Sonderausbildung:
(z. B. Bild-Offz., Techn. Offz., Meß-Offz., Funk-Drahtnachr.-Offz., W. K. S.)

[signature] — Unterschrift

Hauptmann m.d.W.d.G.b. — Dienstgrad und Dienststellung

Beitrag des Chefs des Generalstabes der vorgesetzten Kommandobehörde (nur bei Genst.-Offz. in Stabsstellungen und zur Dienstleistung zum Generalstab kommandierten Offizieren):

Zusätze vorgesetzter Dienststellen: Der Geschwaderkommodore

Anständiger Charakter.
Hervorragender Frontoffizier. Könnte manchmal etwas lebhafter sein. Zur Beförderung zum Oberleutnant voll geeignet.

m.d.W.d.G.b.

[signature]

Major

[5] Gilt für alle Offz., für Truppen-Offz. hinsichlich Eignung zur Führung des nächsthöheren Verbandes, für Genst.-Offz. hinsichtlich Eignung zum Chef oder I a, I c der Luftfl., Flieger-Korps, Flak-Korps, Fl.-Div., Flak-Div., zur Versetzung in den Genst., zur Kommandierung in den Genst. — [6] z. B.: Höherer Adjutant, Erzieher, Lehrer auf Spezialgebieten, auf Grund von Sprachkenntnissen im Attachédienst: für Genst.-Offz. hinsichtlich Eignung für Verwendung im Quartiermeisterdienst, im Ic-Dienst im Transportwesen als Lehrer für Genst.-Lehrgang (Taktik bzw. Qu.-Dienst); besondere Anlagen für Kriegsgeschichte, Wehrwirtschaft. — [7] z. B.: „noch halbjährige Belassung in bisheriger Stelle" oder „alsbaldige Verwendung als Geschw.-Kommodore"

Efficiency Report for Second Lieutenant Heinz Strünning (back side) – signed by Captain Hans-Dieter Frank, the acting group commander, and Major Werner Streib, the acting commodore of the 1st Night Fighter Wing.

Karl (Tyczka) Tannert

Fallschirmjäger

"Tannert with a few men of his headquarters and the signal platoon retook the village on his own initiative, averting a danger to the flank of the regiment and the entire division."

Lieutenant Colonel Karl Stefan (Tyczka) Tannert was born on December 22, 1910 in Psaar near Loben, Upper Silesia. He served in the border protection services before joined the German Army in 1933. On June 21, 1939, he transferred to the *Luftwaffe* and volunteered for airborne school. Promoted to second lieutenant on June 26, 1939, two months later on August 15, 1939, Tyczka joined the 1st Battalion, 1st Paratroop Regiment (*Fallschirmjäger-Regiment 1*). He fought in Poland in 1939 and in Denmark (helping to seize a key bridge at Masnedö), Holland (at the attack on the bridges at Dordrecht) and Norway (Narvik) in 1940, winning the Iron Cross 2nd Class on April 18, 1940 and the Iron Cross 1st Class on May 18, 1940. At Narvik, his aircraft was shot down, and Tyczka helped save several crewmen in the deep snow, suffering frostbite before rescued several days later. Now a first lieutenant (he was promoted on August 1), Tyczka assumed command of the 1st Company, 1st Paratroop Regiment on September 1, 1940.

On May 20, 1941, his company jumped into action east of Heráklion during the German airborne invasion of Crete. The following day he was seriously wounded as his unit attempted to seize the airfield near the city. He returned to his unit in time to deploy to Russia. From November 9-19, he fought at Gorodok and Wyborg, and although wounded on November 15, he remained with his troops, preventing a Russian breakthrough. The following month, the chain of command submitted him for the award of the Knight's Cross of the Iron Cross, but the award was not approved. On February 18, 1942, Karl Tyczka adopted the family name of Tannert. He was promoted to captain on March 1, 1942, and on March 11, he received the German Cross in Gold. On March 1, 1943, Tannert assumed command of the 1st Battalion, 6th Paratroop Regiment (*Fallschirmjäger-Regiment 6*), but he soon transferred to the 3rd Battalion, 2nd Paratroop Regiment (*Fallschirmjäger-Regiment 2*) as the acting commander. Tannert returned to Russia, fighting near Kirowograd and Nowgorodka, once again defending against a significant Russian armored onslaught. This time, Karl Tannert did receive the Knight's Cross of the Iron Cross – on April 5, 1944.

On June 9, 1944, the chain of command in the 2nd Paratroop Regiment submitted Captain Karl Tannert for a preferential promotion to major. Colonel Hans Kroh, the regimental commander, stated:[117]

Reason for consideration:

Accomplishments in general:
Captain Tannert has distinguished himself in an outstanding way as acting battalion commander during the fighting at Rome and in particular in Russia. Within a short time, Captain Tannert understood how to form a well-trained, militarily effective unit out of a newly established unit.

In detail:
As of April 1943, Captain Tannert has been in acting command of the 3rd Battalion, 2nd Paratroop Regiment. This battalion, which was established and trained by him, was led by him with great skill during the mission at Rome.

During the fighting in the winter of 1943/44, he led the battalion in December of 1943 in the area of Shitomir with great offensive power and captured Jelnitsch, a suburb of Radomyschl. The ordered offensive objective was reached in a very short time.

After transferring by air into the area of Kirowograd, Tannert and his battalion participated in an outstanding manner in storming Nowgorodka.

The large enemy attack on January 5, 1944 east of Kirowograd near Nowo-Andrejewka, with approximately 500 tanks and 3 rifle divisions went almost half-way through Tannert's battalion. During this battle, Captain Tannert maintained his position with the few still remaining men into the evening and maintained his command in the area of Nowo-Andrejewka. Due to Captain Tannert's holding of the position, it was possible for the regiment to form a new defensive line and to delay the advance of the tanks long enough until the city of Kirowograd was cleared in an orderly way.

When the enemy advanced on January 7, 1944 into the village of Nowo-Fedorowka, which belonged to the neighboring division to his left, Tannert with a few men of his headquarters and the signal platoon retook the village on his own initiative, averting a danger to the flank of the regiment and the entire division. For this accomplishment, Tannert received the Knight's Cross of the Iron Cross.

The division commander Major General Bernhard Ramcke added:

> The proposal by Colonel Kroh for the preferential promotion of Captain Tannert is seconded in its full extent. During offensive and defensive battles, Tannert has excelled as an outstanding battalion leader.

On June 15, 1944, the acting commander of the Paratroop Army, Lieutenant General Kurt Student, added one sentence: "The preferential promotion is warmly approved by me."

On August 29, 1944, Karl Tannert assumed acting command of the 2nd Paratroop Regiment. He was promoted to major the same day and took part in the German defense of Brest, France. On September 16, in the surrounded city, General Ramcke recommended Tannert for the Oak Leaves to the Knight's Cross and a promotion to lieutenant colonel, before the surrender of the fortress. Tannert went into American captivity on September 20, 1944. He was promoted to lieutenant colonel on January 1, 1945, but the award of the Oak Leaves was never confirmed.[118]

Fallsch.Jg.Rgt.2 O.U., den 9.6. 1944

V o r s c h l a g

zur

be v o r z u g t e n B e f ö r d e r u n g

Gem.R.d.L.Ob.d.L. LP Nr. 71489/42 (2,ID) II.Ang.
v. 22.12.1942

für Hauptmann (Tr.O.) T a n n e r t , Karl Stefan

Diensstellung: Batl.-Kdr. - 20.1.44
Rangdienstalter: 1.3.42 (343)
Beförderungsdaten zu den beiden
letzten Offz.-Dienstgraden: zum Oblt.am 1. 6.39
zum Hptm.am 1. 3.42

Geburtsdatum: 22.12.1910
Auszeichnungen: 18.4.40 E.K. II
18.5.40 E.K. I
11.3.42 Deutsches Kreuz in Gold
5.4.44 Ritterkreuz
14.8.41 Narvikschild
20.9.42 Erdkampfabzeichen der LW.
22.7.42 Medaille "Winterschlacht im Osten"
4.5.39 Medaille zur Erinnerung an den 1.Okt.1939

Begründung:

A.) Allgemeine Leistungen:

Hauptmann Tannert hat sich im Einsatz Rom und besonders in Russland als Batl.-Fhr.hervorragend bewährt. Hauptmann Tannert versteht es, aus einer neuaufgestellten Truppe in kurzer Zeit eine gut ausgebildete, soldatisch erzogene schlagkräftige Einheit zu machen.

B.) Einzelangaben:

Hauptmann Tannert führt seit April 1943 das III./2 Fallsch.Jg.Rgt.2 Dieses von ihm aufgestellte und ausgebildete Batl. führte er beim Einsatz Rom mit gutem Geschick.

Im Wintereinsatz 1943/44 führte er das Batl. im Dezember 1943 im Raume von Shitomir mit grossem Angriffsschwung und nahm Jelnitsch, einen Vorort von Radomyschl. Das befohlene Angriffsziel wurde in kürzester Zeit erreicht.

Nach der Verlegung im Lufttransport im Raum von Kirowograd war T. mit seinem Batl. hervorragend beim Sturm auf Nowgorodka beteiligt.

Der am 5.1.44 geführte feindliche Grossangriff ostwärts Kirowograd bei Nowo-Andrejewka mit etwa 500 Panzern und 3 Schützendivisionen ging ging etwa zur Hälfte durch das Batl.Tannert. Hptm.Tannert hielt sich hierbei mit wenigen ihm noch verbliebenen Männern bis zum Abend und zum befohlenen Absetzen in der Ortschaft Nowo-Andrejewka. Durch das Aushalten von Hptm. Tannert war es dem Rgt. möglich, eine neue Verteidigungslinie auszubauen und den Panzervorstoss so lange aufzuhalten,bis die

Request for Preferred Promotion for Captain Karl Tannert (first page) – dated June 9, 1944, on blank paper, with typed comments.

28

Stadt Kirowograd ordnungsgemäss geräumt war.

Als am 7.1.44 der Feind in das zur linken Nachbardivision gehörende Dorf Nowo-Fedorówka eindrang, nahm T. mit wenigen Männern seines Stabes und Nachrichtenzuges in selbstständigem Entschluss den Ort zurück und schaltete damit eine gefährliche Flankenbedrohung für das Rgt. und die ganze Division aus. T. erhielt für diese Tat das Ritterkreuz.

Oberst u. Rgt.-Kdr.

Stellungnahme des Div.Kdr.

O.U.,den 9.6.44.

Dem Vorschlag des Obersten Kroh für die bevorzugte Beförderung Hptm. Tannert wird in vollem Umfange zugestimmt.T. hat sich in Angriffs-u. Abwehrkämpfen als hervorragender Btl.-Fhr.hervorgetan.

Ramcke.

Generallt.u.Div.Kdr.

b.w.

Request for Preferred Promotion for Captain Karl Tannert (second page) – signed by Colonel Hans Kroh, Commander, 2nd Paratroop Regiment, and by Major General Bernhard Ramcke, Commander, 2nd Paratroop Division.

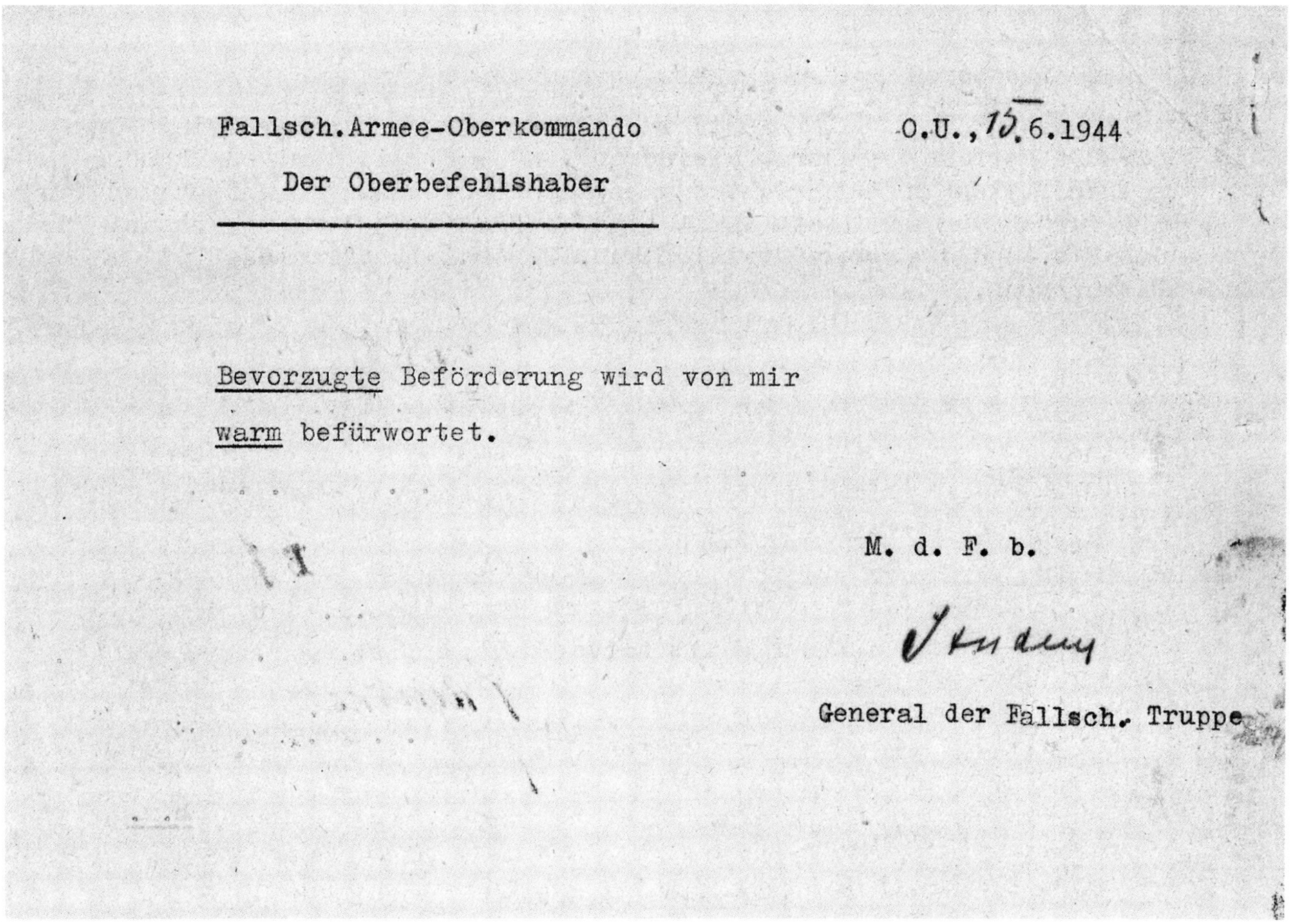

Fallsch. Armee-Oberkommando

Der Oberbefehlshaber

O.U., 15.6.1944

Bevorzugte Beförderung wird von mir warm befürwortet.

M. d. F. b.

General der Fallsch. Truppe

Request for Preferred Promotion for Captain Karl Tannert (third page) – signed by Lieutenant General Kurt Student, Commander, Paratroop Army.

Gerhard Thyben

Fighter Pilot

"Due to his young age, still somewhat unbalanced."

Gerhard Thyben was born February 24, 1922 in Kiel. He began his military service on July 15, 1940. He was promoted to private first class on July 1, 1941 and to staff sergeant on April 1, 1943. He joined the 6th Squadron, 3rd Fighter Wing "Udet" (*Jagdgeschwader 3 "Udet"*) in Russia on January 26, 1943 and soon thereafter, on February 26, 1943, achieved his first aerial victory. Thyben won the Iron Cross 2nd Class on May 25, 1943. On July 7, 1943, he shot down four enemy aircraft raising his total to 22; he won the Iron Cross 1st Class on July 10, 1943.

On August 1, 1943, Major Kurt Brändle, 2nd Group Commander, *Jagdgeschwader 3 "Udet,"* submitted an efficiency report on Thyben, which read:[119]

> Lively and temperamental, possesses self-confidence and independent thinking. Due to his young age, still somewhat unbalanced, but promises to become a good wartime officer after further schooling. In 150 combat flights against the enemy, he has succeeded in 31 victories.

That month, with his total at 32 kills, Thyben and his unit transferred west, where on February 11, 1944 he shot down three P-38 Lightnings. During this period, he won the *Luftwaffe* Honor Goblet on August 30, 1943 and the German Cross in Gold on October 23, 1943. In April 1944, Second Lieutenant Thyben transferred to the 5th Squadron, 54th Fighter Wing "Green Hearts" (*Jagdgeschwader 54 "Grünherz"*), reaching his 50th victory on June 23. By July 7, he had 60 kills, and by September 4, he had 70 victories. The month proved a good one; Thyben scored four kills on September 6, September 15 and September 25. He also shot down six aircraft on September 16. September 30 saw Thyben reach 100 kills, now as the commander of the 7th Squadron. By October 30, 1944, Thyben had 115 kills; he received the Knight's Cross of the Iron Cross on December 6, 1944. By December 22, now in action in the skies over Courland, Gerhard Thyben reached his 130th victory. He continued that pace in 1945 and achieved his 150th victory on February 17. On April 8, 1945, Thyben became the 822nd recipient of the Oak Leaves to the Knight's Cross, with 156 aerial victories to his credit. He shot down his final – 157th – enemy aircraft on May 8, 1945 over the Baltic Sea, very probably the final *Luftwaffe* confirmed aerial victory in the conflict. During the war, he flew 385 combat missions, of which 22 were fighter-bomber sorties that resulted in the destruction of two enemy aircraft on the ground and 7 vehicles. In the air, 5 of his victories occurred in the West; in his victories on the Eastern Front, he shot down 28 Il-2 Sturmoviks. According to his efficiency report, he served 11 days of severe arrest, although there is no crime listed.[120]

Formblatt 1

Luftflotte: Lfl.Kdo.4

Heimat-Luftgau: Lg.Kdo.VI

Waffengattung*): Fliegertruppe
Flugzeugführer

W.B.K.: Kiel

Truppenteil: II./Jagdgeschwader Udet
6.Staffel

(wird von L. P. ausgefüllt)
B 2

Geburtstag: 24.2.1922

Name: T h y b e n

Geburtsort: Kiel

Vorname: Gerhard

Beruf: Maschinenbaupraktikant

Dienstgrad: Unteroffizier

Abiturient: ~~ja~~ — nein**)

Ständiger Wohnsitz vor der Einberufung: Kiel, Graf-Spee-Str.14

Militärischer Werdegang:

Aktive Dienstzeit in der neuen Wehrmacht: von 15.7.1940 bis jetzt
bzw. Kurzausbildung)

Weitere Dienstverpflichtung auf 3 = 4½ = 12 u. mehr Jahre nein (2jähr. aktiv)

Bei ehem. Soldaten, Dienstgrad bei Eintritt in die neue Wehrmacht: ./.

Friedensübungen: ./.

Dienstzeit während des mobilen Verhältnisses: ./.

Beförderungen: 1.7.1941 zum Gefreiten
1.4.1943 zum Unteroffizier

Tag der Ernennung zum R. O. A.: ./. bzw. K. O. A.

Hat — nicht — ~~mit Erfolg — ohne Erfolg~~ — **) an einem Kriegsoffizier-Nachwuchslehrgang

von ./. bis ./. teilgenommen.

*) Unter Waffengattung ist die Spezialausbildung mit anzugeben (Fliegertruppe — Flugzeugführer, Beobachter, Fallschirmtruppe — springendes Personal, Bodenpersonal / / Flakartillerie — schwere Flak, leichte Flak, Scheinwerfer / / Luftnachrichtentruppe — Funker, Fernsprecher).

**) Nichtzutreffendes ist zu streichen.

B287. 12. 40

Efficiency Report for Sergeant Gerhard Thyben (front side) – dated August 1, 1943, on pre-printed form, with typed comments.

Zur Beförderung zum Offizier vorgeschlagen am: ./.

Bewährung vor dem Feinde: seit 26.1.1943 bei der 6./ J.G.Udet in Rußland eingesetzt. 15o Feindflüge, 31 Abschüsse.

Auszeichnungen: E.K.II 25.5.43
E.K. I 1o.7.43 , zum Ehrenpokal und zum Deutschen Kreuz in Gold eingereicht.

Bestrafungen: 11 Tage geschärfter Arrest

Kurze Beurteilung: Lebhaft und temperamentvoll, besitzt Selbstbewußtsein und Selbständigkeit. Infolge seiner Jugend noch etwas unausgeglichen, gibt sich jedoch große Mühe und verspricht nach weiterer Schulung ein guter Kriegsoffizier zu werden. In 15o Feindflügen erzielte er 31 Abschüsse.

Uk-Stellung während des Krieges:

von ./. bis ./.

Kurze Angabe des Grundes: ./.

Gefechtsstand, den 1. Aug. 1943
(Ort und Datum)

(Unterschrift)
Major u.selbst.Gruppenkommandeur

Efficiency Report for Sergeant Gerhard Thyben (back side) – signed by Major Kurt Brändle, Commander, 2nd Group, 3rd Fighter Wing.

Cord Tietjen

Fallschirmjäger

"Skillful trainer."

Captain Cord Tietjen was born on November 10, 1914 in Danzig-Langfuhr. Tietjen joined the German Army's 20th Engineer Battalion on October 20, 1936. The following year, he attended the airborne school at Stendal, in just the third airborne training course (he was the 338th graduate of the school). In 1938, Tietjen was selected to be an officer candidate, separated from the Army and transferred to the *Luftwaffe*. He then was seconded to a special demolitions unit at Ahlhorn at the beginning of 1939, was promoted to second lieutenant on May 7 and named a platoon leader in the 5th Company, 1st Paratroop Regiment (*Fallschirmjäger-Regiment 1*).

In June 1939, the acting commander of the 2nd Battalion, 1st Paratroop Regiment, Captain Fritz Prager, initiated an efficiency report on Second Lieutenant Cord Tietjen. The report was not in a pre-printed format, but rather typed categories for each rated area, and then the document was completed by hand in ink. Prager wrote:[121]

Has the person under review fulfilled the requirements posed to him? Yes

Service-related capabilities: good section commander, skillful trainer

Concept of service: excellent

Appearance at the front: very good

Accomplishments as leader, parachute soldier, trainer, teacher, etc. in particular fields: Accomplishments in all service branches particularly good.

Particular capabilities: [no entry made]

Particular knowledge: engineer service

Position within the circle of comrades: well liked

Proposed for use in active service: platoon leader of a parachute company

Behavior outside of the service: immaculate

Capable to be an active officer: particularly capable

Lieutenant Colonel, and regimental commander, Bruno Bräuer, simply added: "In agreement."

Tietjen served with the 5th Company, 1st Paratroop Regiment in Poland during the Polish campaign and jumped into Holland in May 1940. At Moerdijk, Tietjen stormed a Dutch bunker at the north end of the key railroad bridge over the Maas River and blew it up. He continued to disrupt Dutch defensive positions. During the fighting, he was wounded in the knee by a grenade fragment. He received the Iron Cross 2nd Class and 1st Class on May 23, 1940. The following day, Second Lieutenant Cord Tietjen received the Knight's Cross of the Iron Cross. Tietjen assumed command of the 1st Company, 7th Paratroop Engineer Battalion (*Fallschirm-Pionier-Bataillon 7*) on September 1, 1940; he was promoted to first lieutenant on October 28, 1940. On May 20, 1941, Tietjen and his unit jumped into Crete as part of the German airborne invasion of the island. Landing in Prison Valley south of Kirtomados, the engineers battled the 8th Greek Regiment. On February 21, 1942, Tietjen became the commander of the 2nd Company, Corps Paratroop Engineer Battalion (*Korps-Fallschirm-Pionier-Bataillon*) and led this unit at El Alamein in the Ramcke Brigade. On November 5, 1942, British forces captured Cord Tietjen. The *Luftwaffe* Personnel Office promoted him to captain on March 1, 1943; he remained in British captivity until 1947. Cord Tietjen died on June 18, 2005 at Arnsberg, North Rhine-Westphalia. He is buried there in the *Friedhof* on Sunderner Street (N 101, Grave 87).[122]

Luftgau VI Wehrbezirkskommando K i e l
Flieger-Division 7
Waffengattung: Fallschirm-Jäger
Truppenteil: II./Fallschirm-Jäger Rgt.1

B e u r t e i l u n g

über den

Leutnant d.R. T i e t j e n , Cord

Geburtsdatum: 1o. November 1914

Leutnant d.R. T i e t j e n hat vom 2o. Oktober 1936 bis 3o. September 1938 die 2-jährige Dienstzeit abgeleistet und ist gemäß A.H.M. 1937 Bl. 14 Ziffer 294 auf ein 3. Dienstjahr weiterverpflichtet.

Efficiency Report for Second Lieutenant (Reserve) Cord Tietjen (first page) – dated June 27, 1939, on blank paper, with typed and hand-written comments.

1. Hat der Beurteilte die gestellten Anforderungen erfüllt:

Ja.

2. Dienstliche Befähigung:

guter Zugführer, geschickter Ausbilder.

Dienstauffassung:

vorzüglich

Auftreten vor der Front:

sehr gut

Leistungen als Führer, Fallschirmschütze, Ausbilder, Lehrer usw. bzw. auf fachlichem Gebiet (für Sanitätsoffizier d.B. und Offiziere (W) d.B.):

Leistungen in allen Dienstzweigen bes. gut.

Besondere Eignung:

Besondere Kenntnisse: Pionierdienst.

Stellung im Kameradenkreise:

beliebt und geachtet.

Efficiency Report for Second Lieutenant (Reserve) Cord Tietjen (second page)

Vorschlag für Mob.-Verwendung:
(z.B. "Zugführer bei einer 8,8 cm Batterie" oder
"Führer einer Fernsprechbetriebskompanie" oder
"Führer einer Aufklärungsstaffel (H) " usw.

Zugführer Fernspr.-Betr.-Komp.

3. Ausserdienstliches Verhalten:

einwandfrei.

4. Auszufüllen bei Beförderungsübungen:

(Liegt Eignung zum nächsthöheren Dienstgrad vor):

5. Auszufüllen bei Beförderungsübungen, die erstmalig ohne Erfolg abgeleistet worden sind.

Ist Wiederholung der Beförderungsübung erfolgversprechend oder zwecklos:

6. Eignung zum aktiven Offizier: ~~bed. geeignet.~~

a) als Trup enoffizier

b) als (Ergänzungs-) Offizier:

II./Fallschirm-Jäger Rgt. 1

Prager

Hauptmann und Bataillonsführer.

E i n v e r s t a n d e n !

Stendal, den 27.6.1939

Bräuer

Oberstleutnant und Rgt.-Kommandeur.

Efficiency Report for Second Lieutenant (Reserve) Cord Tietjen (third page) – signed by Captain Fritz Prager, Commander, 2nd Battalion, 1st Paratroop Regiment, and Lieutenant Colonel Bruno Bräuer, Commander, 1st Paratroop Regiment.

Erich Timm

Fallschirmjäger

"Dazzling élan."

Lieutenant Colonel Erich Timm was born in Königsberg, Prussia on February 15, 1913. He entered the Police in 1933, before transferring to the *Luftwaffe* on July 25, 1935 with a grade of second lieutenant. Shortly thereafter, he became the battery commander of the 4th Battery, 32nd *Flak* Regiment in Berlin, and subsequently the battery commander of the 106th Light *Flak* Battery in Salzwedel. His unit participated in the invasion of Holland in May 1940 as part of the 7th Air Division (*7. Flieger-Division*); for his leadership in this campaign, First Lieutenant Timm received both the Iron Cross 2nd Class and the Iron Cross 1st Class on May 17, 1940. He was subsequently awarded the *Luftwaffe Flak* Badge on April 15, 1941. On April 26, 1941, he assumed command of the 1st Company of the Parachute *Flak*-Machine-gun Battalion for the upcoming invasion of Crete. He was severely wounded on the first day of fighting – May 20, 1941. He was subsequently awarded the *Luftwaffe* Honor Goblet for special leadership in the air war on October 7, 1941. His wounds forced Captain Timm (promoted on June 1, 1941) to recuperate until February 1943, when he assumed command of the 100th Special *Luftwaffe* Field Battalion (*Luftwaffe-Feld-Bataillon z.b.V. 100*) in Russia.

Sufficiently fit, Timm commanded this unit until assuming command of the 1st Battalion, 12th Paratroop Assault Regiment on August 1, 1943 in Italy. On November 24, 1943, Lieutenant General Kurt Student recommended Timm for promotion to major. The report listed his numerous awards, previous promotions and the fact that he had been serving as the battalion leader since March 23, 1943. Student, who signed the report in his traditional green pencil, characterized Erich Timm as follows:

> Straight-forward, honest character. Upright, open personality; dutiful, passionate. Mentally good average, understands to think clearly and consequential. Shows tactical understanding. Quite good physical capabilities, strong and tough. His soldierly attitude and his military appearance are correct and without criticism. Extremely correct in all matters of his service. Well liked among his comrades. Due to his just and caring nature, he is respected and liked by his superiors and men under his command. Captain Timm is well rooted in National Socialist philosophy. On March 23, 1943, Captain Timm took over a battalion completely unknown to him, while in heavy defensive battles in a critical situation on the Eastern Front. Thanks to his forceful action, circumspection and his dazzling élan, his battalion in several days of severe battles was able to repel an enemy that was far superior in numbers as well as weaponry and to cause the enemy heavy losses. Captain Timm showed the same good efforts as the leader of a battalion in the battle for Rome. The reorganization of the battalion after the release of Captain Timm from service on the Eastern Front has proven that he is an excellent leader and educator for his officers, sergeants and enlisted men not only in battle, but also in his capacity as a trainer. Without reservation, he is suited to be named Battalion Commander and at the same time receive a preferential promotion to Major. The command selection and promotion receive my warmest agreement.

The recommendation was successful and he was promoted to major and became the acting commander of the regiment, which in January 1944 became heavily engaged at the Anzio-Nettuno beachhead as part of the 4th Paratroop Division. On February 16, 1944, the division launched a secondary attack – to support the Hermann Göring Division's main attack at Cisterna – to eliminate the beachhead. Contrary to expectations for a supporting attack, the 4th Paratroop Division broke through the British 56th Division and gained two miles. On May 23, 1944 Timm's unit attempted to counterattack the flank of the Allied breakout attempt near the town of Velletri, before giving way to the Allied assault. On June 1, 1944 the official *Wehrmacht* dispatches highlighted the regiment and Major Timm as "especially outstanding." On July 20, 1944, he assumed command of the regiment.

The 4th Paratroop Division then conducted a fighting retreat north, taking up defensive positions near Florence at the end of August. A month later, in brutal combat at the Futa Pass, the 12th Paratroop Assault Regiment was reduced to less than 50% strength.

Erich Timm was awarded the Knight's Cross of the Iron Cross on October 3, 1944 by Lieutenant General Alfred Schlemm (the commander of the 1st Parachute Corps) for his numerous accomplishments in the defense of Italy shortly after being awarded the *Luftwaffe* Ground Combat Badge. He achieved his final wartime grade, lieutenant colonel, on January 1, 1945, but he and his regiment could not stem the Allied tide as it crossed the Po River and surged north. His unit surrendered to Allied forces on April 28, 1945; he remained a prisoner of war for five months. He rejoined the German armed forces (*Bundeswehr*) in 1956, retiring in 1971 as a colonel. Erich Timm died October 6, 1997 in Erftstadt.[123]

Generalkommando
XI. Fliegerkorps
IIa

O.U., 24.11.1943

V o r s c h l a g
zur
bevorzugten Beförderung

gem. R.d.L.u.Ob.d.L.Nr. 71 489/42 (2,ID) II.Ang.v.22.12.42 Abschn.A.

für Hauptmann (Tr.O.) T i m m, Erich

Dienststellung: Btl. Führer des I./Sturm-Rgt. (seit 23.3.43)

Rangdienstalter: 1.7.1941

Beförderungsdaten zu den letzten beiden Offz.Dienstgraden: 1.8.38 zum Oblt. 1.7.41 " Hptm.

Geburtsdatum: 15.2.1913

Auszeichnungen: E.K.1.u.2.Kl., Ehrenpokal d.Luftwaffe, Ärmelband Kreta, Verwundetenabzeichen schwarz, Flak-Kampfabzeichen.

Begründung:

Gerader, ehrlicher Charakter. Aufrechte, offene Persönlichkeit; pflichtbewußt, passioniert. Geistig guter Durchschnitt, versteht klar und folgerichtig zu denken. Zeigt taktisches Verständnis.

Recht gute körperliche Veranlagung, kräftig und zäh. Seine soldatische Haltung und sein militärisches Auftreten sind korrekt und einwandfrei. Peinlich genau in allen Dingen seines Dienstes.

Im Kameradenkreise beliebt. Bei Vorgesetzten und Untergebenen wegen seiner Gerechtigkeit und Fürsorge angesehen und beliebt.

Hptm. Timm steht auf dem Boden der nationalsozialistischen Weltanschauung.

Hptm. Timm übernahm am 23.3.43 ein in schweren Abwehrkämpfen stehendes, ihm völlig unbekanntes Btl. in kritischer Lage. Seiner Tatkraft, Umsichtigkeit und seinem mitreißenden Schwung ist es zu verdanken, dass sein Btl. in mehrtägigen schweren Kämpfen einen zahlen-und waffenmässig weit überlegenen Feind abweisen und ihm schwere Verluste beibringen konnte.

Die gleichen sehr guten Leistungen zeigte Hptm. Timm als Führer eines Btl. beim Kampf um Rom.

Die von Hptm. Timm nach Ablösung aus dem Osteinsatz durchgeführte Reorganisation des Btl. hat bewiesen, dass er nicht nur im Kampf, sondern auch in der Ausbildung ein hervorragender Führer und Erzieher seiner Offiziere, Unteroffiziere und Mannschaften ist.

Zur Ernennung zum Btl.Kdr. und gleichzeitigen bevorzugten Beförderung zum Major uneingeschränkt geeignet.

Ernennung und Beförderung werden von mir wärmstens befürwortet.

Der Kommandierende General

General der Flieger.

Request for Preferred Promotion for Captain Erich Timm (one page only) – dated November 24, 1943, on blank paper, with typed comments. Signed by Lieutenant General Kurt Student, Commander of the 11th Air Corps.

Kurt Ubben

Fighter Pilot

"He has understood how to master the most difficult situations."

Major Kurt Ubben, nicknamed "Kuddel," was born on November 18, 1911 at Dorstadt in the Harz. He joined the Navy in 1931 and received his training on the sailing ship *Gorch Foch*. In 1935, Ubben transferred to the *Luftwaffe* and by 1938 was serving with the *Küstenjagdstaffel Kiel*, a coastal protection unit. At the outbreak of World War II, Master Sergeant Ubben was serving with the 5th Squadron, 186th Fighter Group (*Jagdgruppe 186*), slated to be based aboard the German Navy's aircraft carrier *Graf Zeppelin*, at that time still under construction. Flying a Messerschmitt Me 109E-3, Ubben gained his first aerial victory on May 10, 1940, when he shot down a Dutch Fokker D-XXI fighter over De Kooy, Holland during an attack on a Dutch airfield; he received the Iron Cross 2nd Class the same day. His unit also flew close-escort for Ju-88 bombers over Dunkirk.

In June 1940, Ubben transferred with the 2nd Group, *Jagdgruppe 186* to Stavanger, Norway, where they initially provided air cover for the battleship *Scharnhorst* at Trondheim. On July 5, the group was absorbed into 3rd Group, 77th Fighter Wing (*Jagdgeschwader 77*), when it became obvious that the completion of the *Graf Zeppelin* would be delayed, and they deployed to Berlin. On July 22, Ubben was appointed 8th Squadron Commander, 77th Fighter Wing, and received the Iron Cross 1st Class on August 1, 1940; by the end of the year, the unit was stationed on the Channel Front at Cherbourg, France. In early April 1941, the unit transferred to take part in the invasion of the Balkans, where Ubben claimed an RAF Hurricane fighter shot down over Lamia, Greece on April 19. However, during the engagement, his Messerschmitt Me 109E-7 was badly damaged by a direct anti-aircraft hit, and he made a forced-landing behind Allied lines. A fellow pilot in his unit landed a Fieseler Stork and flew him back to base. On May 22, First Lieutenant Ubben helped attack the Royal Navy's "Force C" between the islands of Kythera and Antikythera and scored a hit on the British battleship *Warspite*. Ubben also claimed a British motor torpedo boat sunk during this period.

Ubben and his unit participated in the invasion of Russia in June 1941. He claimed his 19th and 20th aerial victories – two I-153s in three minutes – on July 25, and his 30th, a DB-3 on August 29. Kurt Ubben was awarded the Knight's Cross of the Iron Cross on September 4, 1941, for 32 aerial victories; he had destroyed a further 26 aircraft on the ground, as well as 15 tanks. The next day, he was appointed the commander of the 3rd Group, 77th Fighter Wing. He scored his 50th kill (a Polikarpov I-15 single-engine biplane fighter) on October 19, a total that included 3 MiG-3s in eight minutes on October 9. His Messerschmitt Me 109F-4 experienced engine problems on December 4, forcing him to make a belly-landing at Mariupol, which caused 20% damage to the plane, but he continued increasing his total; Ubben shot down four Russian aircraft on December 9, which propelled him to his 61st victory, and he received the German Cross in Gold the same day.

On December 14, 1941, Major General Kurt Pflugbeil, the commander of the 4th Air Corps (*IV. Flieger-Korps*), submitted a request to the *Luftwaffe* Commander-in-Chief, through the Personnel Office, for a preferred promotion for First Lieutenant Ubben. Pflugbeil wrote:[124]

> I request that First Lieutenant Ubben (Kurt), who since August 1941 has been acting for the commander of the 3rd Group, JG 77, be preferentially promoted to

> Captain in recognition of his outstanding accomplishments against the enemy and his excellent achievements in leading the troops. First Lieutenant Ubben, who has an official date of rank of June 1, 1939, was awarded the Knight's Cross of the Iron Cross on September 4, 1941 for 28 aerial victories. In the meantime, he has increased his aerial victories to 61, and this makes him by far the most accomplished of his squadron. As a squadron commander as well as group commander, he has understood how to master the most difficult situations through his own example and model as a soldier and fighter pilot, and he has been able to sweep his troops along with him to the highest accomplishments.

Ubben won the Oak Leaves to the Knight's Cross (the 80th recipient of the award) on March 12, 1942 for 69 aerial victories. The 3rd Group transferred in October to North Africa, at a time when Ubben had reached 92 victories. He continued his success in the new theater gaining his 100th and 101st aerial victories (Curtiss P-40 Tomahawk fighters) on January 14, 1943. In October 1943, he led the group to Romania, where it was tasked with the aerial protection of the Ploesti oilfields; he shot down a B-17 Flying Fortress on October 1, 1943. It would be his last aerial victory. On March 10, 1944, Major Ubben was appointed the commander of the 2nd Fighter Wing "Richthofen" (*Jagdgeschwader 2 "Richthofen"*) in France, replacing the recently killed Lieutenant Colonel Egon Mayer. On April 27 1944, Ubben engaged USAAF fighters near Fère-en-Tardenois (west of Rheims), France. In the ensuing combat, Ubben's Focke-Wulf Fw 190A-8 was shot down. He bailed out, but his parachute failed to open, either due to an improperly fastened harness or to insufficient altitude.

Karl Ubben achieved 110 aerial victories in approximately 500 combat missions, a sortie-to-victory ratio of 4.54 to 1. He recorded 90 victories over the Eastern Front; included in his total is one four-engine bomber and seven P-38 fighters.[125] He is buried at the German Military Cemetery at St. Desir-de-Lisieux, France (Section 3, Row 40, Grave 1239).

Geheim

Generalkommando
des IV. Flieger-Korps

Den 14.Dezember 1941.

24. Dez. 1941

Az. 21 Adj./IIa

Nr. 1457/41 geh.

Bezug: R.d.L.u.Ob.d.L., L.P. Az.21 Nr.44200/41 geh. (2,ID) vom 27.10.41.

Betr.: Bevorzugte Beförderung des Oblt. U b b e n (Kurt), III./J.G.77.

Dem

Reichsminister der Luftfahrt und
Oberbefehlshaber der Luftwaffe
- Luftwaffenpersonalamt -

B e r l i n

L.P. Eing. 22. DEZ. 1941 56322/41 g.

Ich bitte, Oblt. U b b e n (Kurt), seit August 1941 beauftragt mit der Wahrnehmung der Geschäfte des Kommandeurs der III./J.G.77, als Anerkennung für seine hervorragende Bewährung vor dem Feinde und seine ausgezeichneten Leistungen in der Truppenführung bevorzugt zum Hauptmann zu befördern.

Oblt. Ubben, der ein R.D.A. seines Dienstgrades vom 1.6.39 hat, wurde nach seinem 28.Luftsiege am 4.9.1941 mit dem Ritterkreuz des Eisernen Kreuzes ausgezeichnet. Er hat inzwischen die Zahl seiner Luftsiege auf 61 erhöht und steht damit weit an der Spitze des Geschwaders.

Als Staffelkapitän wie als Gruppenkommandeur hat er es verstanden, durch sein Beispiel und Vorbild als Soldat und Jagdflieger auch die schwierigsten Verhältnisse zu meistern und die Truppe zu den höchsten Leistungen mitzureißen.

Der Kommandierende General
des IV. Flieger - Korps

Generalleutnant

Request for Preferred Promotion for First Lieutenant Kurt Ubben (one page only) – dated December 14, 1941, on blank paper, with typed comments. Signed by Major General Kurt Pflugbeil, Commander, 4th Air Corps. It arrived at the *Luftwaffe* Personnel Office on December 22, 1941. It appears as though two different officers (possibly Generals Karl Bodenschatz and Karl Barlen) reviewed the report on December 24 and annotated in gray and purple pencil that date. Someone else highlighted portions of the report in blue pencil.

Rudolf Weigel
Stuka Pilot

"Slightly conceited."

Captain Rudolf Weigel was born May 10, 1913 in Ludwigshafen, Rhineland-Pfalz, and joined the *Luftwaffe* on October 1, 1932. Weigel served as a flight leader in the 5th Squadron, 77th Stuka Wing in the 1939 Polish campaign. He also fought in the French campaign in 1940, where he was credited with sinking two ships off Dunkirk. Weigel was then transferred to the 7th Squadron and hence flew in the 1941 Balkan campaign and then in Russia. Rudolf Weigel was awarded the Knight's Cross of the Iron Cross on April 27, 1942, after flying 271 combat missions and destroying 10 anti-aircraft batteries and 20 artillery batteries. He was subsequently promoted to second lieutenant on August 1, 1942. Weigel was promoted again – to first lieutenant – on November 11, 1942.

On March 1, 1943, Captain, and acting commander of the 3rd Group, *Sturzkampfgeschwader 77*, Eberhard Jakob, wrote:[126]

> **Fitness Assessment:** Mentally well talented, average general education. Tall physique, robust and strong. Open, decent character, who is slightly conceited. Well-liked among his comrades. In flight engagements, he is relentless, courageous and a daredevil. Very good bomber and gunner. Personal initiative and a talent for improvisation are present, but not yet mature. "Foot soldier type." His military attitude and appearance are without criticism. His attitude towards the profession of an officer should be less conditional. Weigel is rooted in National Socialist ideology and understands how to explain its concepts. Since April 27, 1942, he has been a Knight's Cross holder.
>
> **How is the current position being fulfilled:** Well.
>
> **Suitable for promotion to the next higher service grade?** Not yet.
>
> **Suggestions for employment (particular aptitudes, other utilization):** Due to his injured right wrist, he is no longer suitable as a Stuka pilot. Very well suited as a flight instructor for light airplanes (A/B School!)

On the reverse, Jakob added on April 8, 1943: "For the time from March 1 to April 8, 1943, I have nothing to add."

On May 6, the acting commodore of *Sturzkampfgeschwader 77*, Major Helmut Bruck, wrote: "I have nothing to add to the above report."

From January 1944 to January 1945, Weigel served as a squadron commander and flight instructor in the 5th Squadron, 102nd Ground-Attack Wing (*Schlachtgeschwader 102*). He then joined the Focke-Wulf Fw 190-equipped 9th Anti-Tank Ground-Attack Wing (*Panzer-Schlachtgeschwader 9*), a unit designed to stop massive enemy tank attacks. It would soon get its opportunity.

At 5:00 a.m., April 16, 1945, nearly half a million Russian artillery shells thundered down on German forward positions along the Oder and Neisse rivers, fifty miles east of Berlin. Ninety-minutes later, Soviet Marshal Georgi Zhukov's tanks and infantry began pouring across both sides of the Frankfurt-on-Oder strongpoint still held by the German Ninth

Army. Savage battles developed between tank and anti-tank gun, while overhead two thousand Russian planes bombed and harassed the defenders, as the *Luftwaffe* also threw all it had into the battle. By nightfall, although a five-mile deep breach had been torn into the front near Wriezen, held by the ill-experienced *Luftwaffe's* 9th Paratroop Division, the 1st Byelorussian Front's offensive against Berlin was stalled by tenacious German resistance on the Seelow Heights, two miles west of the Oder, with great losses of troops and tanks for the Russians. Over the next two days, Zhukov committed his reserves and finally smashed through the German defenders. Sometime during this tumultuous 3-day period, Captain Rudolf Weigel – the "Foot soldier type" – in his Focke Wulf Fw 190, seeing what was happening to his comrades-in-arms, was indeed "relentless" and bored in to attack, but he was shot down near Wriezen – most likely on April 17. He was declared missing in action and was never seen again. At the time of his disappearance, Rudolf Weigel had flown 500 combat missions.[127]

III./Sturzkampfgeschwader 77, Gefechtsstand, 1.3.1943

B e u r t e i l u n g s n o t i z

über den Oberleutnant

Vor- und Zuname: Rudolf W e i g e l geb.am : 1o.5.1913

verheiratet , ledig , verwitwet , geschieden (Zutreffendes unterstr.)

Rangdienstalter: 1.11.1942 Dienstaltersliste: Kr.O.

Jetzige Verwendung: Staffeloffizier, Kettenführer.
stellv. Staffelführer von Nov. 42 bis Jan. 43.

Eignungsbeurteilung: Geistig gut veranlagt, durchschnittliche Allgemeinbildung. Körperlich gross, robust und kräftig.

Offener, anständiger Charakter, der von sich etwas eingenommen ist. Im Kameradenkreis beliebt.

Im fliegerischen Einsatz ist er hart, mutig und draufgängerisch. Sehr guter Werfer und Schütze. Eigeninitiative und Improvisationsgabe zwar vorhanden, doch noch nicht ausgeprägt. "Landsknechtstyp".

Seine soldatische Haltung und sein Auftreten sind einwandfrei. Seine Auffasung vom Offiziersberuf dürfte bedingungsloser sein.

W. steht auf den Boden nat.soz. Weltanschauung und versteht dessen Gedankengut zu vermitteln.

Ritterkreuzträger seit 27.4.42.

Wie wird jetzige Stelle ausgefüllt?: gut

Geeignet zur Beförderung zum nächsthöheren Dienstgrad?: noch nicht.

Erworbene Lw.-Scheine: LF - Scheine

Strafen: keine.

Verwendungsvorschläge: (besondere Eignung, weitere Verwendung)

Wegen Verletzung des rechten Handgelenkes zum Sturzkampfflieger nicht mehr geeignet. Als Fluglehrer auf leichten Flugzeugen sehr gut geeignet (A/B Schule!).

m.d.W.d.G.d.Kommandeurs b

Jakob

Unterschrift

H a u p t m a n n .

(Dienstgrad u.Dienststellung)

W e n d e n - !

Efficiency Report for First Lieutenant Rudolf Weigel (front side) – dated March 1, 1943, on local pre-printed form, with typed and hand-written comments. Signed by Captain Eberhard Jakob, acting commander of the 3rd Group, 77th Stuka Wing.

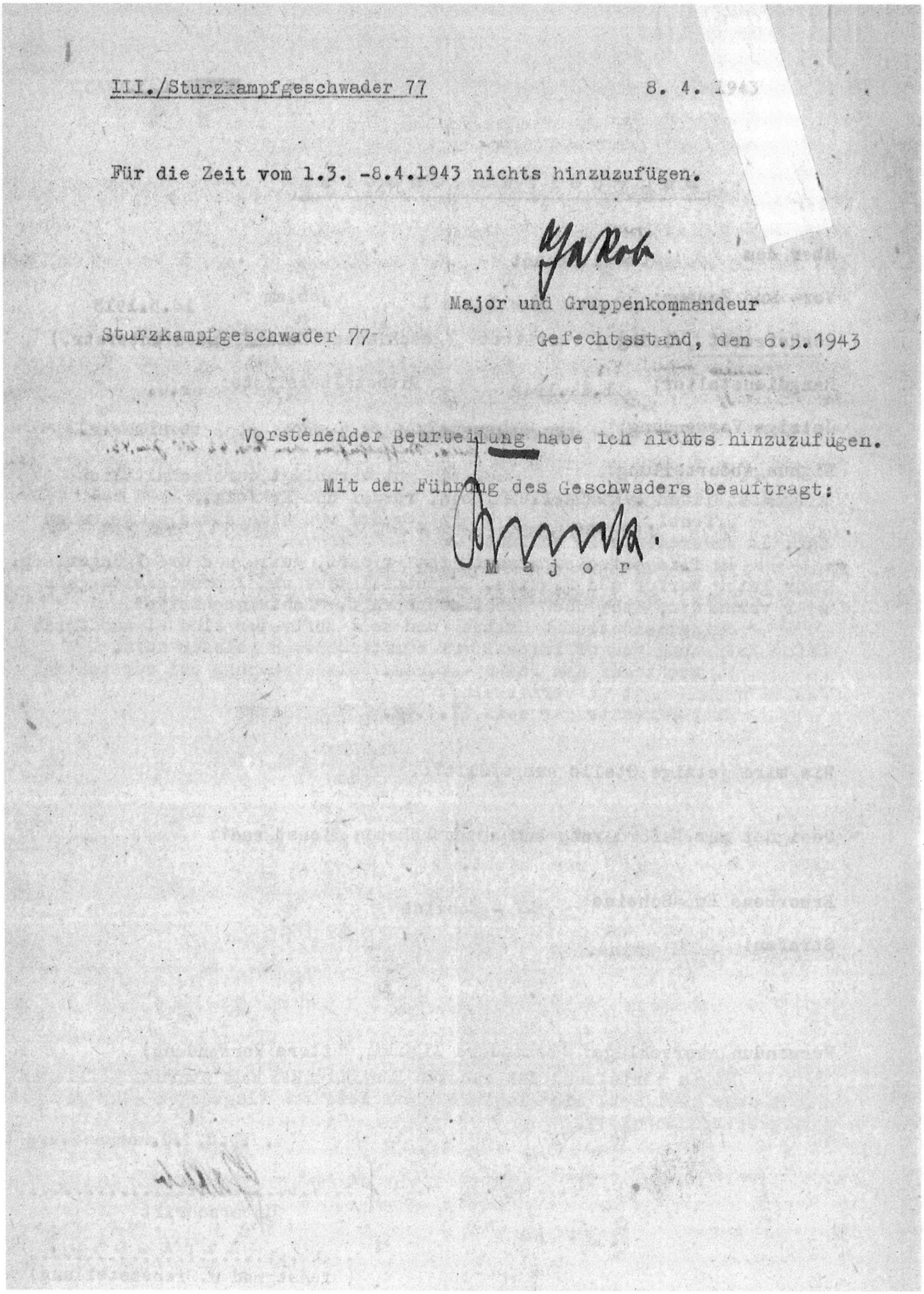

III./Sturzkampfgeschwader 77 8. 4. 1943

Für die Zeit vom 1.3. -8.4.1943 nichts hinzuzufügen.

Major und Gruppenkommandeur

Sturzkampfgeschwader 77 Gefechtsstand, den 6.5.1943

Vorstehender Beurteilung habe ich nichts hinzuzufügen.

Mit der Führung des Geschwaders beauftragt:

M a j o r

Efficiency Report for First Lieutenant Rudolf Weigel (back side) – signed again by Captain Eberhard Jakob and by Major Helmut Bruck, acting commodore of the 77th Stuka Wing.

Ernst Weismann

Fighter Pilot

"Confronts all things in life without worry."

First Lieutenant Ernst Weismann was born on February 22, 1922 in Zell/Amstetten, Austria. He entered the *Luftwaffe* on November 15, 1939. After flight training, Weismann was assigned to the Supplemental Group of the 51st Fighter Wing (*Ergänzungsgruppe, Jagdgeschwader 51*) on December 21, 1940. On March 8, 1941, he joined the 12th Squadron, 51st Fighter Wing. As an officer candidate, he scored his first two aerial victories – SB-2 bombers – on June 22, 1941 in Russia. He scored his third victory, a DB-3, on August 8 and shot down another DB-3 on August 9. He dispatched a Pe-2 on August 27 and an I-18 fighter on September 23. Officer Candidate Weismann shot down an I-18 on October 3 and gained his 8th kill – a Pe-2 – on October 7.

On October 14, 1941, Weismann's chain of command submitted a special efficiency report in support of a request for promotion to second lieutenant. Second Lieutenant Georg Seelmann, the acting squadron commander, wrote:[128]

> **Character:** Officer Candidate Weismann is a decent and true character. He is spirited and alert and confronts all things in life without worry. During operations against Russia, his character has gained a maturity which he was lacking before. His initial frivolity and inconsistency are gone and have made a place for clear and secure objectives. Also, he has a certain toughness that cannot be denied, which is expressed in his accomplishments.
>
> **Mental Disposition:** Spirited and alert, he is well liked in his circle of comrades. He likes light, entertaining literature and possesses good school training and general education.
>
> **Physical Attributes:** Strong and well-built soldier. He is a good athlete, prefers skiing and swimming.
>
> **Military Appearance:** In view of his short period of service, Weismann possesses good military general knowledge. His appearance at the front is secure and definite.
>
> **Evaluation as a Flyer:** Officer Candidate Weismann demonstrated in the Eastern Campaign that he is a thoughtful and good fighter pilot. A great number of flights against the enemy and eight aerial victories are proof of his knowledge. Also as a pair-leader, he has performed on his own with successful results. He promises to become a good flight leader.
>
> **Summarized Evaluation:** Most recently, Weismann has changed very much to his advantage. His frivolity and inconsistency have made place for endurance and toughness, which justify a promotion to Second Lieutenant. Officer Candidate Weismann promises to become a skillful officer and fighter pilot.

By December 4, 1941, Weismann reached his 20th kill – a LaGG-3 – and received the *Luftwaffe* Honor Goblet on February 5, 1942. On March 30, 1942, his Messerschmitt Me 109E-7 crashed into an Me 110 on takeoff at Schatalovka, destroying the aircraft, but leaving Weismann uninjured. He scored his 30th victory – a MiG-3 – on March 31, 1942. However, on April 10, 1942, his Messerschmitt Me 109F-2 experienced another takeoff accident, again destroying the aircraft and severely injuring Weismann. He returned to duty that summer, won the German Cross in Gold on June 9, 1942 and scored his 40th victory on July 7, 1942 (one of five enemy aircraft he shot down that day). Two days later, Weismann shot down another enemy aircraft, which proved to be the 800th victory for the 4th Group, 51st Fighter Wing. He reached his 50th victory with a MiG-3 on July 20, 1942. In the first thirteen days of August, Weismann added nineteen more victories, but his own luck ran out. On August 13, 1942, Second Lieutenant Ernst Weismann – in his Messerschmitt Me 109F-2 – was shot down in combat with Russian fighters north of Rzev. His wingman observed Weismann landing safely – but behind enemy lines. He was declared missing in action and was never seen again. Ernst Weismann was given a posthumous award of the Knight's Cross of the Iron Cross on August 21, 1942 as well as a promotion to first lieutenant. His 69 total victories in 280 combat missions equate to a sortie-to-victory ratio of 4.05 to 1.[129]

IV./Jagdgeschwader 51 — 14.Oktober 1941

Betr.: Vorschlag zur Beförderung zum Leutnant

Auf dem Dienstwege

An den R.d.L.u.Ob.d.L. (L.P.)

B e r l i n

Zur Beförderung zum Leutnant wird in Vorschlag gebracht :

Familienname: Weismann — Vorname: Ernst

geb. am: 22.2.22 zu: Zell a/Ybbs Konfession: ev.

Dienstgrad: Oberfähnrich verwendet als: Flugzeugführer

Diensteintritt am: 15.11.1939 verh./led.: led.

Ernennung zum Oberfähnrich: 1.2.1941 Kinder: keine

Offz. Anwärter wann? 1.4.194o

Wehrbez. Kdo. des Wohnortes: Amstetten

Bestrafungen vor dem Diensteintritt: keine

Bestrafungen nach Diensteintritt: s. Strafbuchauszug

Zum Offz. gewählt am: 13.1o.1941

Beruf vor Diensteintritt: Schüler

Stand und Beruf des Vaters: Studienrat

Mutter geborene: Meck

Anschrift der Eltern bzw. Vormundes:

Vater Max Weismann Waidhofen a/Ybbs
Am Berghof 3

Bildungsgang: Erziehung im Elternhaus
Sept. 28 bis Sept. 32 Volksschule in Waidhofen
Sept. 32 bis Sept. 39 Oberschule in Waidhofen

Mil. Werdegang:

15.11.39 – 7. 1.4o A.Fl. Ausb.Rgt. 51 Grundausbildung
8. 1.4o – 19.8.4o Schüler Fl.Ausb.Rgt.51 AB Schule
2o. 8.4o – 2o.12.4o Jagdfl.Schule 1 Jagdausbildung
21.12.4o – 7. 3.41 Ergänzungsgruppe J.G.51
8. 3.41 – 12./J.G. 51

1. 4.4o	zum Fahnenjunker	ernannt
1. 4.4o	zum Fhj.-Gefr.	bef.
1. 6.4o	zum Fhj.-Uffz.	bef.
1. 9.4o	zum Fähnrich	bef.
1. 2.41	zum Ob.-Fhr.	bef.

Begründung: s. Beurteilung

Request for Promotion to Officer for Officer Candidate Ernst Weismann (front side) – dated October 14, 1941, on blank paper, with typed comments.

Beurteilung des Oberfähnrich
W e i s m a n n

Charakter:

Oberfähnrich Weismann hat einen anständigen und ehrlichen Charakter. Er ist frisch und aufgeweckt und steht allen Dingen des Lebens unbekümmert gegenüber.

Durch den Einsatz gegen Rußland hat sein Charakter eine Reife erfahren, die ihm seither mangelte. Sein anfänglicher Leichtsinn und seine Wankelmütigkeit sind verschwunden und haben einer klaren und sicheren Zielsetzung Platz gemacht. Auch eine gewisse Zähigkeit ist ihm nicht abzusprechen, die in seinen Leistungen zum Ausdruck kommt.

Geistige Anlagen:

Frisch und aufgeweckt ist er beliebt in Kameradenkreisen. Er liebt leichte, unterhaltende Literatur und verfügt über eine gute Schul- und Allgemeinbildung.

Körperliche Anlagen:

Kräftig und gut gebauter Soldat. Er ist guter Sportler, bevorzugt Skilaufen und Schwimmen.

Militärisches Auftreten:

Im Hinblick auf die Kürze seiner Dienstzeit verfügt Oberfähnrich Weismann über ein gutes militärisches Allgemeinwissen. Sein Auftreten vor der Front ist sicher und bestimmt.

Fliegerische Beurteilung:

Oberfähnrich Weismann hat sich im Ostfeldzug als überlegter und guter Jagdflieger gezeigt. Eine große Anzahl von Feindflügen und 8 Abschüsse sind ein Beweis seines Könnens. Auch als Rottenführer hat er selbständig und erfolgreich gehandelt. Er verspricht ein guter Schwarmführer zu werden.

Gesamturteil:

Oberfähnrich Weismann hat sich in der letzten Zeit sehr zu seinem Vorteil verändert. Sein Leichtsinn und seine Flatterhaftigkeit haben einer Ausdauer und Zähigkeit Platz gemacht, die eine Beförderung zum Leutnant rechtfertigen. Oberfähnrich Weismann verspricht ein tüchtiger Offizier und Jagdflieger zu werden.

Seelmann

Leutnant u. Staffelführer.

Request for Promotion to Officer for Officer Candidate Ernst Weismann (back side) – signed by Second Lieutenant Georg Seelmann, acting commander, 12th Squadron, 51st Fighter Wing. Someone highlighted portions of the report in blue pencil.

Theodor Weissenberger

Fighter Pilot

"Without a doubt, belongs with the best fighter group commanders."

Major Theodor Weissenberger was born December 21, 1914 in Mühlheim am Main in Hesse. An ardent civilian glider pilot, he joined the *Luftwaffe* and after pilot training reported to the 1st Squadron (Z), 77th Fighter Wing (*Jagdgeschwader 77*) in Norway on September 1, 1941. Weissenberger scored his first aerial victory on October 24, 1941 and received the Iron Cross 2nd Class on November 6, 1941. While serving in this Destroyer squadron, Weissenberger – in addition to shooting down 23 enemy aircraft – destroyed 15 locomotives, 10 barracks, 2 anti-aircraft gun emplacements, 1 radio station and 1 train station. He received the Iron Cross 1st Class on February 17, 1942, the *Luftwaffe* Honor Goblet on May 28, 1942 and the German Cross in Gold on September 6, 1942. Transferring to the 6th Squadron, 5th Air Wing "Polar Sea" (*Jagdgeschwader 5 "Eismeer"*) on September 19, 1942, Second Lieutenant Weissenberger received the Knight's Cross of the Iron Cross on November 13, 1942 after achieving his 38th aerial victory. A master of shooting down multiple aircraft on a single day, Weissenberger scored 5 or more kills on: September 27, 1942, October 30, 1942, March 10, 1943, March 12, 1943, April 13, 1943, June 8, 1943, July 4, 1943, July 25, 1943, October 13, 1943, February 1, 1944, and March 25, 1944. On June 15, 1943, Weissenberger was named Commander, 7th Squadron, 5th Fighter Wing. On August 2, 1943, he became the 266th recipient of the Oak Leaves to the Knight's Cross. Weissenberger assumed command of the 6th Squadron, 5th Fighter Wing on September 30, 1943, before moving up to be the Commander, 2nd Group, 5th Fighter Wing on April 20, 1944. One month later (May 18), he scored his 175th aerial victory. Weissenberger then moved to the Western Front, assuming command of the 1st Group, 5th Fighter Wing, and by July 25, 1944 he had reached 200 kills.

Despite these achievements and the entrusted level of responsibility as a group commander, Weissenberger was still a first lieutenant, and the Chief of Staff, *Luftflottenkommando Reich* (Air Fleet *Reich*), Andreas Nielsen, wrote a letter to the *Luftwaffe* Personnel office requesting a promotion. The letter read:[130]

Dear General,

Due to my responsibility as his former air commander, I would like to speak for First Lieutenant Weissenberger, who at present is the leader of a fighter group on the Western Front. Weissenberger has 180, or by this time even more, aerial victories. For an endless time he has been group leader and has been awarded the Oak Leaves to the Knight's Cross. I cannot rid myself of the impression that he has been forgotten regarding a promotion, particularly since he is already over 30 years old.

I would be grateful if the General could have this case reexamined, since it appears unbearable to me that a person with such awards, who without a doubt belongs with the best fighter group commanders and who is this old, has been neglected in comparison with other leaders in comparable positions. I can only imagine that in this case, due to the pressure of ongoing business, some care was lacking.

With a Heil Hitler!
I am, General, your faithful,
Nielsen

The letter, which appeared to have been read by Generals Köhler and Bonatz in the Personnel Office, worked – and Weissenberger was swiftly promoted to captain, and his official date of rank was backdated to June 1, 1944. On December 1, 1944, Weissenberger assumed command of the 1st Group, 7th Fighter Wing (*Jagdgeschwader 7*) and on January 15, 1945, he became Commodore, 7th Fighter Wing – a Messerschmitt Me 262 jet-equipped unit. Weissenberger would score 8 victories while flying the Me 262, including 3 B-17 Flying Fortresses on an 8th Air Force mission to bomb Berlin. Weissenberger scored a total of 208 aerial victories, of which 33 were in the West and included 7 four-engine bombers. Weissenberger was submitted for the award of the Swords to his Oak Leaves, but the request was never completely formally approved. Theodor Weissenberger died in a racecar crash on June 10, 1950 at the Nürburgring.[131]

Luftflottenkommando Reich
Der Chef des Generalstabes

St.Qu., den 12.7.44

17. JULI 1944

Sehr geehrter Herr General !

Ich möchte aus meiner Verantwortung als sein früherer Fliegerführer heraus mich für den Oberleutnant W e i s s e n b e r g e r einsetzten, der z.Zt. an der Westfront Kommandeur einer Jagdgruppe ist.

Weissenberger hat wohl 180 oder z.Zt. mehr Abschüsse und ist schon eine endlose Zeit Gruppenkommandeur, ausgezeichnet mit dem Eichenlaub zum Ritterkreuz. Ich kann mich des Eindrucks nicht erwehren, als wenn er in der Beförderung vergessen worden ist, zumal er m.E. bereits über 30 Jahre alt ist.

Ich wäre dankbar, wenn Herr General diesen Fall überprüfen liessen, da es mir untragbar erscheint, dass ein mit solchen Auszeichnungen versehener Mann, der zweifellos mit zu den besten Jagdgruppenkommandeuren gehört und in vorgeschrittenem Lebensalter steht, gegenüber anderen Kommandeuren in derselben Lage benachteiligt wird. Ich kann mir nur vorstellen, dass hier im Drange der Geschäfte eine mangelnde Fürsorge vorliegt.

Mit H e i l H i t l e r !
bin ich Ihr, Herr General,

ergebenster

Nielsen

Gel. eines Tel. Gesprächs mit Nielsen am 17.7. mitgeteilt.

Mit Wirkung vom 1.6.44 bevorzugt zum Hauptmann (Kr) befördert worden. RDA. 1.6.44 Order 673/D vom 5.6.44

Request for Promotion for First Lieutenant Theo Weissenberger (one page only) – dated July 12, 1944, on letterhead paper, with typed comments. Signed by Major General Andreas Nielsen, Chief of Staff, Air Fleet *Reich*. The letter appears to have been annotated by Generals Köhler and Bonatz in the *Luftwaffe* Personnel Office.

Walter Werner

Fallschirmjäger

"His outstanding courage during the Second Cassino Battle marks the typical resolute soldier in his personality."

Second Lieutenant Walter Werner was born on July 11, 1917 in Brand-Erbisdorf near Freiberg in Saxony. He spent his first few years in the *Luftwaffe* as a mechanic and then received engineer training, serving with support troops in Poland, France, the Balkans and Russia in 1941. He then reported to the 13th Company, 1st Supplemental Paratroop Regiment (a training and replacement unit), before transferring to the 1st Company, 1st Paratroop Engineer Battalion (*Fallschirm-Pionier-Bataillon 1*). With the paratroops, he returned to Russia as a sergeant on October 28, 1942 and remained in the fighting there until March 31, 1943. On April 25, 1943, Werner received the Iron Cross 2nd Class. His unit returned to Italy on July 22, 1943. In early 1944, the engineer battalion – including Werner's platoon in the 1st Company – dug in at Cassino, where Werner established several strongpoints on March 11, 1944. Despite massive Allied bombing, Werner's engineers repelled numerous attacks in the city. He received the Iron Cross 1st Class on April 1, 1944. Werner continued the fight and was wounded on May 4, 1944 when a rocket exploded. On June 9, 1944, Technical Sergeant Walter Werner received the Knight's Cross of the Iron Cross.

On July 22, 1944, Major Ernst Frömming, the commander of the 1st Paratroop Engineer Battalion, initiated a request to promote Technical Sergeant Walter Werner to second lieutenant due to his bravery in the face of the enemy at Cassino. Frömming wrote:[132]

> Calm, deliberate, mature character. Secure, capable of making decisions, goal-oriented. Definitely conscientious and reliable. Courageous and unsparing in combat. Mentally of average disposition. Vivid and circumspect. Physically well gifted. Short, strong appearance. Capable of taking care of all demands. His National Socialist philosophy is without doubt. Disseminates National Socialist ideology among the men under his command.
>
> During his time with the battalion, Technical Sergeant Werner has understood how to advance from the lowest enlisted soldier to his current service grade due to his diligence and his courage in battle. His accomplishments in infantry and engineer service have been termed good in all reports. Werner demonstrates his particular capabilities and far-reaching action during combat. As early as the battles at Leningrad and during the Russian Campaign 42/43, Werner excelled through particular courage. Decisive, always clearly recognizing the situation, he has always been that person who keeps his men together in battle and who leads them in selfless combat. Always eager in service and knowledgeable in all engineer/technical details, he consistently strives to only accomplish the whole and the good matter at hand. His outstanding courage during the Second Cassino Battle marks the typical resolute soldier in his personality who, without regard for himself in leading the battle against the enemy, understood how to achieve success; and due to that fact, he was an outstanding participant in the defense of the town of Cassino. Because of his courage in the face of the enemy, Werner is recommended for preferential promotion to officer as a skillful and risk-taking engineer platoon leader.

Walter Werner was promoted to second lieutenant on August 22, 1944. He survived the war. Walter Werner died on June 25, 1997 at Neustadt am Rübenberge. His gravestone lies at the *Friedhof Lahe*, in Hannover, (Section 143, Grave 48).[133]

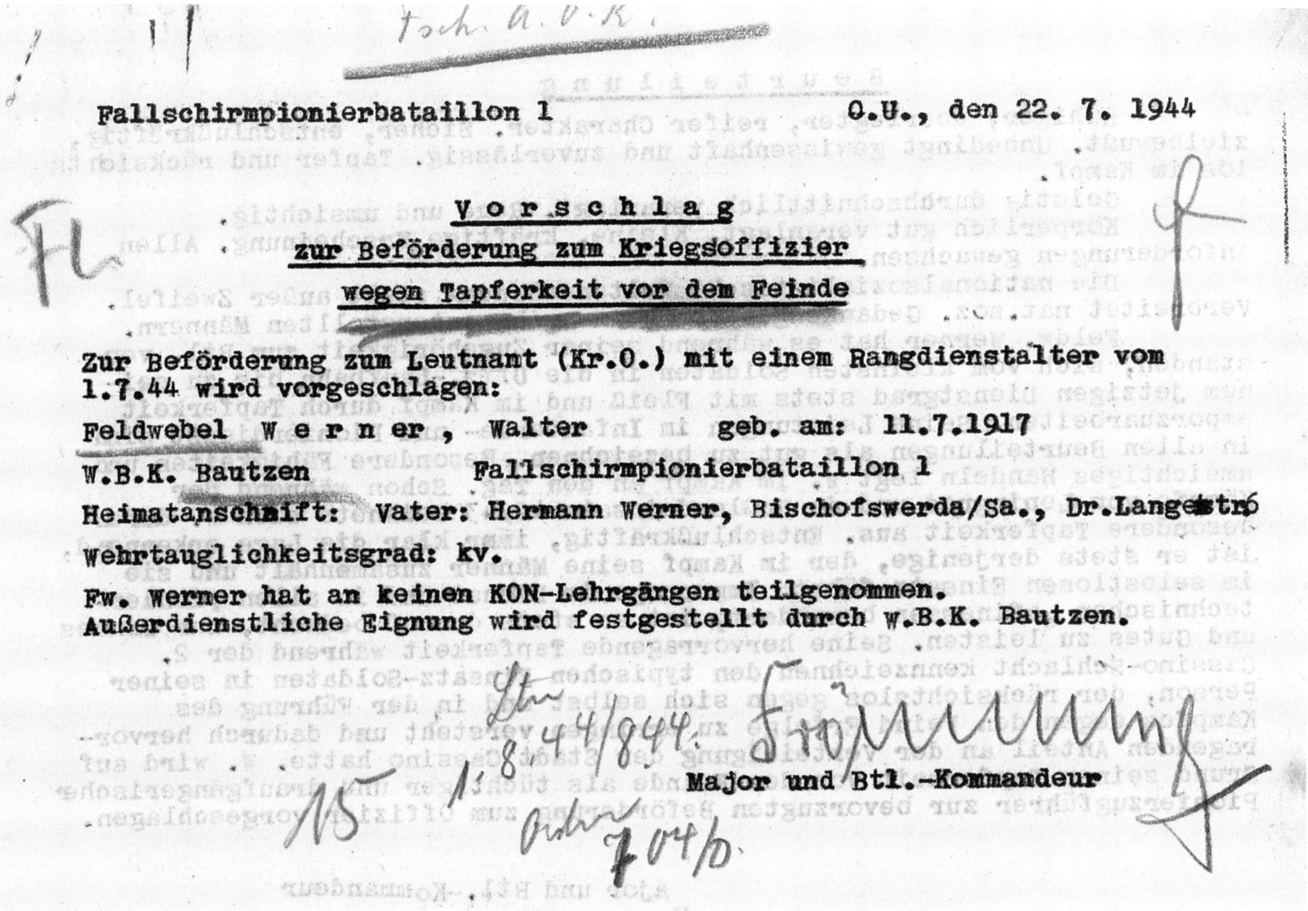

Fallschirmpionierbataillon 1 O.U., den 22. 7. 1944

Vorschlag
zur Beförderung zum Kriegsoffizier
wegen Tapferkeit vor dem Feinde

Zur Beförderung zum Leutnant (Kr.O.) mit einem Rangdienstalter vom 1.7.44 wird vorgeschlagen:

Feldwebel W e r n er , Walter geb. am: 11.7.1917

W.B.K. Bautzen Fallschirmpionierbataillon 1

Heimatanschrift: Vater: Hermann Werner, Bischofswerda/Sa., Dr.Langestr.

Wehrtauglichkeitsgrad: kv.

Fw. Werner hat an keinen KON-Lehrgängen teilgenommen.
Außerdienstliche Eignung wird festgestellt durch W.B.K. Bautzen.

Frömming
Major und Btl.-Kommandeur

Request for Promotion to Officer for Technical Sergeant Walter Werner (front side) – dated July 22, 1944, on half-page blank paper, with typed comments. Signed by Major Ernst Frömming, Commander, 1st Paratroop Engineer Battalion.

B e u r t e i l u n g

Ruhiger, überlegter, reifer Charakter. Sicher, entschlußkräftig, zielbewußt. Unbedingt gewissenhaft und zuverlässig. Tapfer und rücksichtslos im Kampf.

Geistig durhhschnittlich veranlagt. Rege und umsichtig.

Körperlich gut veranlagt. Kleine, kräftige Erscheinung. Allen Anforderungen gewachsen.

Die nationalsozialistische Weltanschauung steht außer Zweifel. Verbreitet nat.soz. Gedankengut bei seinen ihm unterstellten Männern.

Feldw. Werner hat es während seiner Zugehörigkeit zum Btl. verstanden, sich vom kleinsten Soldaten in die Uffz.-Laufbahn bis zu seinem jetzigen Dienstgrad stets mit Fleiß und im Kampf durch Tapferkeit emporzuarbeiten. Seine Leistungen im Infanterie- und Pionierdienst sind in allen Beurteilungen als gut zu bezeichnen. Besondere Fähigkeiten und umsichtiges Handeln legt W. im Kampf an den Tag. Schon während der Kämpfe vor Leningrad und im Rußlandeinsatz 42/43 zeihnete sich W. durch besondere Tapferkeit aus. Entschlußkräftig, immr klar die Lage erkennend, ist er stets derjenige, der im Kampf seine Männer zusammnhält und sie im selbstlosen Einsatz führt. Immerrege im Dienst und in allen pioniertechnischen Rafinessen bewandert, ist er stets darauf bedacht, nur Ganzes und Gutes zu leisten. Seine hervorragende Tapferkeit während der 2. Cassino-Schlacht kennzeichnet den typischen Einsatz-Soldaten in seiner Person, der rücksichtslos gegen sich selbst und in der Führung des Kampfes gegen den Feind Erfolge zu erringen versteht und dadurch hervorragenden Anteil an der Verteidigung der Stadt Cassino hatte. W. wird auf Grund seiner Tapferkeit vor dem Feinde als tüchtiger und draufgängerischer Pionierzugführer zur bevorzugten Beförderung zum Offizier vorgeschlagen.

ajor und Btl.-Kommandeur

Request for Promotion to Officer for Technical Sergeant Walter Werner (back side) – signed again by Major Ernst Frömming.

Heinz Wernicke

Fighter Pilot

"Would rather have others tell him what to do than to reach for his own initiative."

Second Lieutenant Heinz Wernicke was born in Berlin on October 17, 1920. In early 1942, he joined the 3rd Squadron, 54th Fighter Wing "Green Heart" (*Jagdgeschwader 54 "Grünherz"*) on the Eastern Front as a staff sergeant. He scored his first aerial victory in the summer of 1942 before being assigned to the Supplementary Group East (*Ergänzungsgruppe Ost*) – an operational training unit. Wernicke returned to the 6th Squadron of the 54th Fighter Wing at the beginning of 1943; by mid-year he had reached 15 kills, when he again did a short tour as an instructor and then attended officer training.

On July 4, 1943, Second Lieutenant Horst Ademeit, the 6th Squadron Commander, submitted an efficiency report on Technical Sergeant Wernicke, which said in part:[134]

> **Mental and physical attributes:** Mental interests above average. Physically of short build, but tough and capable.
>
> **Character traits:** Decent, but slightly aloof character, fills his position in his environment, would rather have others tell him what to do than to reach for his own initiative and, due to that, he appears a little tired. Among his comrades, Wernicke is well liked because of his decent, friendly attitude and since he never goes his separate ways.
>
> **Use in service:** fighter pilot
>
> **Special education:** as fighter pilot
>
> **Service knowledge and accomplishments:** Wernicke is well suited as a fighter pilot. He has the necessary passion and a positive attitude towards the service. Although he built understanding slowly, he has now shown good results. In his appearance as a superior, he lacks experience. To become an officer, he is still lacking service-oriented knowledge. His behavior vis-à-vis superiors is without criticism.
>
> **Punishments:** See extract from the penalty register.
>
> **Conduct:** good
>
> **Suitable for promotion to next higher service grade:** To become an officer, further training is still necessary.
>
> **Suitable as:** fighter pilot

Heinz Wernicke won the *Luftwaffe* Honor Goblet on April 24, 1943 and the German Cross in Gold on June 5, 1944. By August 15, 1944, he reached his 88th victory, and gained his 100th a month later flying a Focke-Wulf Fw 190A-8. On September 30, 1944, Heinz "Piepl" Wernicke received the Knight's Cross of the Iron Cross, having reached 112 aerial victories. He was then named commander of the 1st Squadron, *Jagdgeschwader 54 "Grünherz,"* but his accomplishments were drawing to a close.

On December 27, 1944, Heinz Wernicke shot down a Yak-9 fighter, his 117th and last victory. Moments later, Wernicke's aircraft slammed into that of his wingman, and both pilots were killed over Doblen, Courland (Dobele, Latvia). Heinz Wernicke's 117 aerial victories were all on the Eastern Front.[135]

W
D

II./Jagdgeschwader 54
6.Staffel

Befehlsstelle, den 4. 7. 1943

Feldpostnummer L 37 824 D
Luftgaupostamt Königsberg

B E U R T E I L U N G ,

des ....Feldwebel Heinz W e r n i c k e , (K.O.A.)........

a) Geistige und körperliche Anlagen ..Geistig interessiert, über dem Durchschnitt, körperlich klein, aber zäh und leistungsfähig.........

b) Charaktereigenschaften ..(siehe Rückseite)........

c) Dienstliche Verwendung ....J a g d f l i e g e r........

d) Besondere Ausbildung ....J a g d f l i e g e r........

e) Dienstliche Kenntnisse und Leistungen ..Als Jagdflieger ist Wernicke gut geeignet. Er hat die nötige Passion und eine positive Einstellung zum Dienst. Nach zunächst etwas langsam erworbener Erfahrung sind nunmehr gute Erfolge eingetreten. Im Auftreten als Vorgesetzter fehlt es ihm an Übung.

f) Strafen ....siehe Strafbuchauszug (Fortsetzung umseitig)

g) Führung ..Gut........

h) Eignung: 1. Zur Beförderung zum nächsthöheren Dienstgrad ..zum Offizier erst nach weiterer Ausbildung..

2. Zur Ernennung ..%........

3. Für welche Verwendung ....Jagdflieger........

II./Jagdgeschwader 54 · 6. Staffel

Ademeit

Leutnant und Staffelführer.

Efficiency Report for Technical Sergeant Heinz Wernicke (front side) – dated July 4, 1943, on locally-produced pre-printed form, with typed and hand-written comments. Signed by Second Lieutenant Horst Ademeit, Commander, 6th Squadron, 54th Fighter Wing.

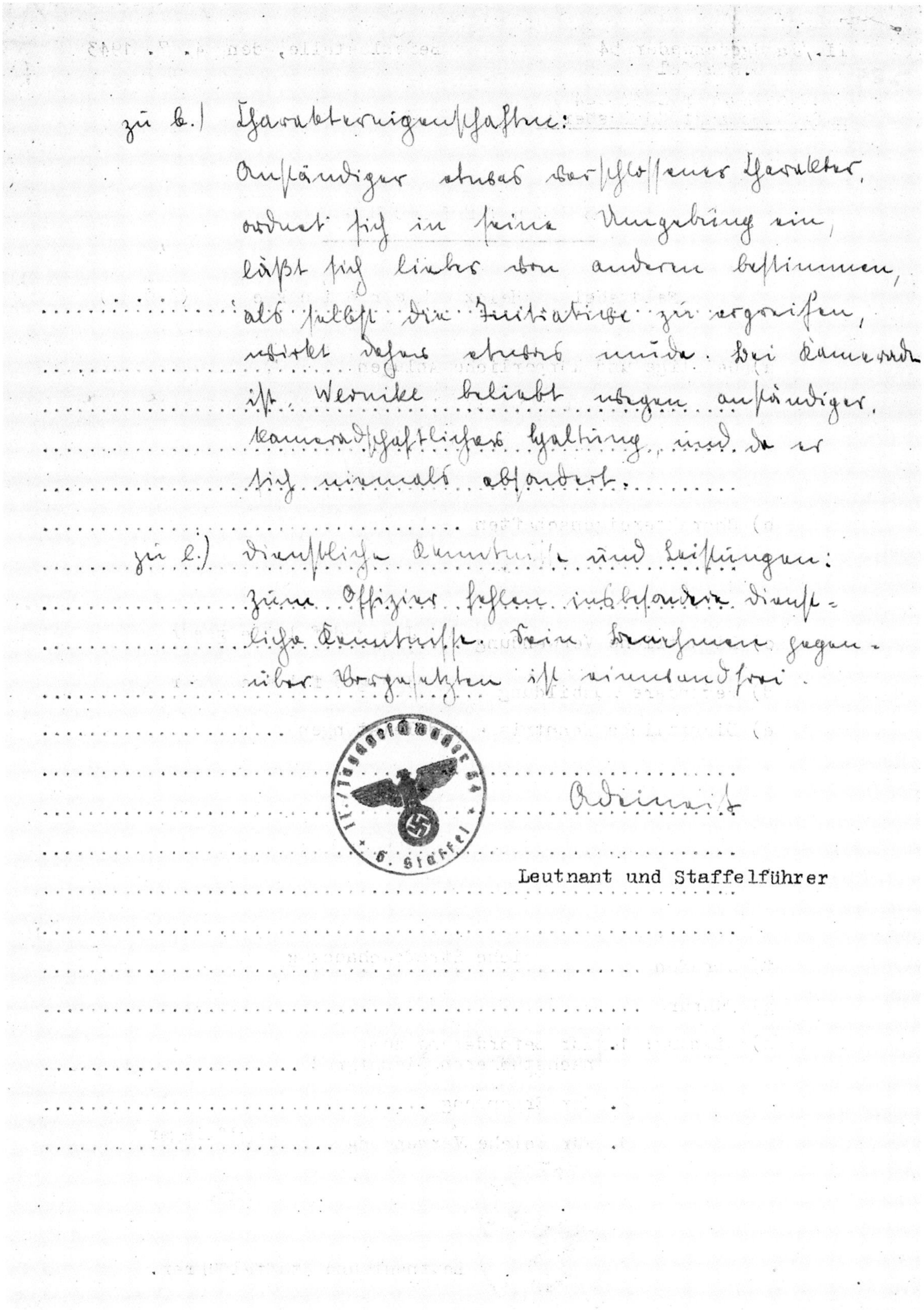

zu b.) Charaktereigenschaften:
Anständiger etwas verschlossener Charakter, ordnet sich in seine Umgebung ein, läßt sich lieber von anderen bestimmen, als selbst die Initiative zu ergreifen, wirkt daher etwas müde. Bei Kameraden ist Wernike beliebt wegen anständiger kameradschaftlicher Haltung, und da er sich niemals absondert.

zu c.) dienstliche Kenntnisse und Leistungen:
Zum Offizier fehlen insbesondere dienstliche Kenntnisse. Sein Benehmen gegenüber Vorgesetzten ist einwandfrei.

Ademeit
Leutnant und Staffelführer

Efficiency Report for Technical Sergeant Heinz Wernicke (back side) – signed again by Horst Ademeit.

Otto Wessling

Fighter Pilot

"For the men under his command, he is a thoroughly just superior."

First Lieutenant Otto Wessling was born in Bad Harzburg on September 23, 1913. He joined the *Luftwaffe* in 1937 and after flight training subsequently transferred to the 9th Squadron, 3rd Fighter Wing (*Jagdgeschwader 3*) in March 1940 – as a private first class – and achieved his first aerial victory, a Hurricane, west of St. Omer, France on June 30, 1940. He had already received the Iron Cross 2nd Class on June 22; this first victory earned him the Iron Cross 1st Class on July 1, 1940. On July 10, 1940, Wessling added a Blenheim bomber 12 miles west of Arras and followed that by downing a Spitfire on September 27. On February 5, 1941, Sergeant Wessling shot down a Hurricane west of Calais.

On May 15, 1941, Captain Walter Oesau, the 3rd Group Commander of the 3rd Fighter Wing, submitted an efficiency report on Technical Sergeant Otto Wessling, which read in part:[136]

> Wessling, who was born on September 23, 1913 at Bad Harzburg, attended the secondary high school there and passed the final exam of the intermediate level [2-3 years less education than meeting the *Abitur*]. In civilian life, Wessling is an interior architect. Wessling is very talented, mentally very alert and capable. He possesses good judgmental capabilities. Wessling is a mature, open and honest character. He stands by his opinions and defends them in a very definite way. He makes a good appearance with immaculate behavior and good manners as well as a demeanor which is without criticism. Due to his polite and always accommodating ways, Wessling is very well liked by his superiors as well as his comrades. For the men under his command, he is a thoroughly just superior. Coupled with a military attitude and demeanor which is without criticism, Wessling has made himself fully aware of the National Socialist philosophy and understands how to pass this matter on to the men under his command. Wessling is up to all the tasks which are demanded from him, and he executes them conscientiously. His accomplishments as a flyer are very good. Wessling is a passionate, calm and secure fighter pilot, with a good combination of risk-taking and deliberation, and these attributes made him into a courageous and decisive pilot. Up to now, Wessling has recorded 197 combat missions, 93 of which were flights over England, and during those he garnered 6 aerial victories. Wessling is suitable to become a wartime officer.

Six days later, Wessling shot down a Blenheim north of St. Pol. By the end of 1941, he had increased his total to 12 victories. He shot down his 19th and 20th enemy aircraft – two I-61 fighters in a five-minute span – on March 20, 1942. At 30 victories, he transferred to the 2nd Squadron, 3rd Fighter Wing "Udet" on April 6, 1942 and received the German Cross in Gold on May 25, 1942. By June 13, 1942, he reached his 34th victory and then raced to his 40th victory on June 29, on the way shooting down 4 MiG-1 fighters on June 22. Wessling scored his 50th kill – an Il-2 Sturmovik over Stalino – on July 21, 1942, his third kill of the day. On that date, Russian ground fire hit his Messerschmitt Me 109F-4, wounding him and causing a forced landing behind enemy lines. It would take him several days to reach the safety of German lines. On August 28, 1942, Wessling shot down his 60th enemy aircraft, a MiG-1, north of Stalingrad; two minutes later, he scored another kill. On September 4, 1942, Master Sergeant Otto Wessling – now with 68 confirmed kills – received the Knight's Cross of the Iron Cross.

Wessling then spent time with Supplemental Group East (*Ergänzungsgruppe Ost*) as a flight instructor and then received officer training. On June 1, 1943, Wessling was assigned to the 10th Squadron, 3rd Fighter Wing "Udet" in the Mediterranean; he became the squadron commander on July 17. On July 2, he shot down two B-24 Liberators. He followed that by shooting down 3 British Spitfires on July 12, and added 2 more B-24 Liberators on July 16 and a P-38 Lightning on July 18. On July 21, 1943, an Allied bombing raid on his airfield at Leverano, in southern Italy, severely wounded Wessling, putting him out of action until September 10, 1943, when he returned to command the 11th Squadron.

At the end of September 1943, the 4th Group, *Jagdgeschwader 3 "Udet,"* transferred to the home defense of Germany, and Wessling hit a dry spell, which lasted until March 23, 1944, when he shot down a B-17 Flying Fortress over Hamm, Germany, and added a P-38 Lightning four minutes later. On March 29, Wessling shot down a B-17 Flying Fortress and a P-51 Mustang in just a six-minute stretch. He added a B-17 and a B-24 in a five-minute period over Braunschweig on April 8 and a B-24 north of Rügen the following day. On April 11, 1944, it appeared that Wessling had really hit his stride, when he downed 3 B-17 Flying Fortresses; he would add 3 more B-17s over the next eight days, but these would be his last aerial victories. On April 19, 1944, First Lieutenant Otto Wessling was killed in action over Eschwege, Hesse – during an air raid by 53 B-17 Flying Fortresses of the 1st Bomb Division, 8th Air Force, on the airfield there – when his Messerschmitt Me 109G-6 was shot down. After his death, he was posthumously awarded the Oak Leaves to the Knight's Cross (the 530th *Wehrmacht* recipient) on July 20, 1944. His 83 total victories included 19 in the West (12 four-engine bombers). He is buried in the military section in the Bad Harzburg *Stadtfriedhof* (Row 2, Grave 449).[137]

III/J.G.3

Gefechtsstand, den 15.5.1941.

B e u r t e i l u n g

des Feldwebel Otto Wessling.

W., geboren am 23.9.1913 zu Bad Harzburg, besuchte dort die höhere Mittelschule und bestand die Abschlussprüfung der mittleren Reife. Er ist im Zivilberuf Innenarchitekt.
W. ist sehr begabt, geistig sehr rege und gewandt. Er verfügt über gute Urteilsfähigkeit bei sehr guter Allgemeinbildung.
W. hat einen ausgereiften, offenen und ehrlichen Charakter. Er steht zu seinen Ansichten und vertritt sie in sehr bestimmter Form. Er ist eine gute Erscheinung mit tadellosem Benehmen und guten Umgangsformen sowie einwandfreiem Auftreten.
Wegen seiner höflichen und stets zuvorkommenden Art ist W. sowohl bei seinen Vorgesetzten als auch bei seinen Kameraden sehr beliebt. Seinen Untergebenen ist W. ein durchaus gerechter Vorgesetzter.
Bei einwandfreier soldatischer Einstellung und Haltung hat sich W. mit dem nationalsozialistischen Gedankengut voll vertraut gemacht und versteht es auch dieses seinen Untergebenen zu vermitteln.
W. ist allen ihm gestellten Aufgaben gewachsen und führt sie gewissenhaft aus.
Seine fliegerischen Leistungen sind sehr gut. W. ist ein passionierter, ruhiger und sicherer Jagdflieger, bei dem Draufgängertum und Überlegung gut vereint sind und ihn zu einem mutigen und entschlossenen Flieger machen.
Bis jetzt hat W. 197 Feindflüge, davon 93 Englandflüge und hat dabei 6 Luftsiege errungen.
W. ist zum Kriegsoffizier geeignet.

Oesau

Hauptmann und Gruppenkommandeur

Efficiency Report for Technical Sergeant Otto Wessling (one page only) – dated May 15, 1941, on blank paper, with typed comments. Signed by Captain Walter Oesau, Commander, 3rd Group, 3rd Fighter Wing.

Walter Wolfrum

Fighter Pilot

"Serial victories are not rare for him."

First Lieutenant Walter Wolfrum was born May 23, 1923 in Schmölz near Kronach in Upper Franconia. He was assigned to the 5th Squadron, 52nd Fighter Wing (*Jagdgeschwader 52*) in January 1943, shooting down his first enemy aircraft on his 62nd combat mission on May 25, 1943. But this slow climb then picked up steam. By September 6, 1943, Wolfrum had 10 kills; on December 11, 1943, he had reached 20. On March 26, 1944, Wolfrum achieved his 51st aerial victory; he received the *Luftwaffe* Honor Goblet on April 20, 1944. He shot down 28 enemy aircraft in May – he was named Commander, 1st Squadron on May 16 – and was awarded the German Cross in Gold on May 18, 1944. This string included six victories on May 20, eleven on May 30 and six more on May 31, what the *Luftwaffe* termed "*Serienabschüsse*" (serial victories). The following day, June 1, 1944, Wolfrum reached 100 victories. However, the following month, on July 16, 1944, in combat with ten Russian fighters, Wolfrum's Messerschmitt Me 109G-6 was shot down and he was seriously wounded. On July 27, 1944, Second Lieutenant Walter Wolfrum received the Knight's Cross of the Iron Cross, with his score at 126 aerial victories.

On August 31, 1944, Colonel Dietrich Hrabak, the commodore of *Jagdgeschwader 52*, submitted a special efficiency report requesting a preferential promotion for Walter Wolfrum. It read:[138]

> The Wing requests that Second Lieutenant (Tr.O.) Wolfrum (Walter), former squadron leader of the 1st Squadron, *Jagdgeschwader 52*, be promoted preferentially to First Lieutenant. Second Lieutenant Wolfrum led the 1st Squadron from May 16, 1944 up to the time he was wounded on July 16, 1944. With prudence and energy, this young officer stood up for his squadron and was its leader in the air and on the ground. Quite extraordinary, he is an excellent fighter pilot, who has succeeded in 126 aerial victories in 406 combat missions. Serial victories are not rare for him. However, he also understands how to take young pilots into combat with the enemy so that they also made kills in a relatively short period of time. Due to his outstanding courage before the enemy and his constant willingness for combat, I deem Second Lieutenant Wolfrum worthy to be promoted to First Lieutenant according to the above mentioned regulations.

Major General Hans Seidemann, the Commander 8th Air Corps (*VIII. Fliegerkorps*) added his own short, but positive, remarks on September 8, 1944:

> I second the above application. Second Lieutenant Wolfrum has proven to be a courageous fighter pilot of the highest quality. He deserves preferential promotion to First Lieutenant.

The request was accepted, and Walter Wolfrum was promoted to first lieutenant with a date of rank backdated to September 1, 1944. Wolfrum returned to the front in February 1945, once again assumed command of the 1st Squadron and scored an additional eleven kills. He was captured at the end of the war by the Russians, but released due to his wounds in July 1945.

His 137 victories in 424 combat missions equates to a sortie-to-victory ratio of 3.09 to 1. All his victories occurred over the Eastern Front and included 16 Il-2 Sturmoviks. A further 40 kills were unconfirmed. Wolfrum was wounded in action four times and made 12 forced landings during the war.[139]

37410

Jagdgeschwader 52
Adjutant

Im Felde, den 31. 8. 1944

Einschreiben

Bezug: R.d.L.u.Ob.d.L.,L.P. Az. 21 Nr. 71 489/42 (2,I D) II.Ang. vom 22.12.42.

Betr.: Bevorzugte Beförderung des Lt.(Tr.O.) W o l f r u m (Walter) zum Oberleutnant (Tr.O.).

Anl. : 1 verschl. Umschlag enth. Kriegsbeurteilung.

An
Generalkommando des
VIII.Flieger - Korps,
II/Adj.

Gen. Kdo. VIII. Fliegerkorps
II./Adjutant
Eingang
6 SEP. 1944
Br. B. Nr. / geh. Kdos.

Das Geschwader bittet, Lt.(Tr.O.) W o l f r u m (Walter), ehemals Staffelführer der 1./J.G. 52, bevorzugt zum Oberleutnant befördern zu wollen.

Lt. W. führte ab 16.5.44 bis zu seiner Verwundung am 16.7.44 die 1. Staffel. Mit Umsicht und Tatkraft setzte sich dieser junge Offizier für seine Staffel ein und war ihr ein Führer in der Luft und auf der Erde. Ganz besonders aber ist er selbst ein hervorragender Jagdflieger, der in 406 Feindflügen 126 Abschüsse erringen konnte. Serienabschüsse sind bei ihm keine Seltenheiten. Aber auch junge Flugzeugführer weiß er an den Feind zu bringen, sodaß auch sie in verhältnismäßig kurzer Zeit zu Abschüssen kamen.

Auf Grund seiner hervorragenden Tapferkeit vor dem Feinde und seiner steten Einsatzbereitschaft halte ich Lt. W. für würdig, gemäß o.a. Bezug bevorzugt zum Oberleutnant zu befördern.

Hrabak

Request for Preferred Promotion for Second Lieutenant Walter Wolfrum (front side) – dated August 31, 1944, on blank paper, with typed comments. Signed by Colonel Dietrich Hrabak, Commodore, 52nd Fighter Wing. Stamp indicates the report arrived at the 8th Air Corps on September 6.

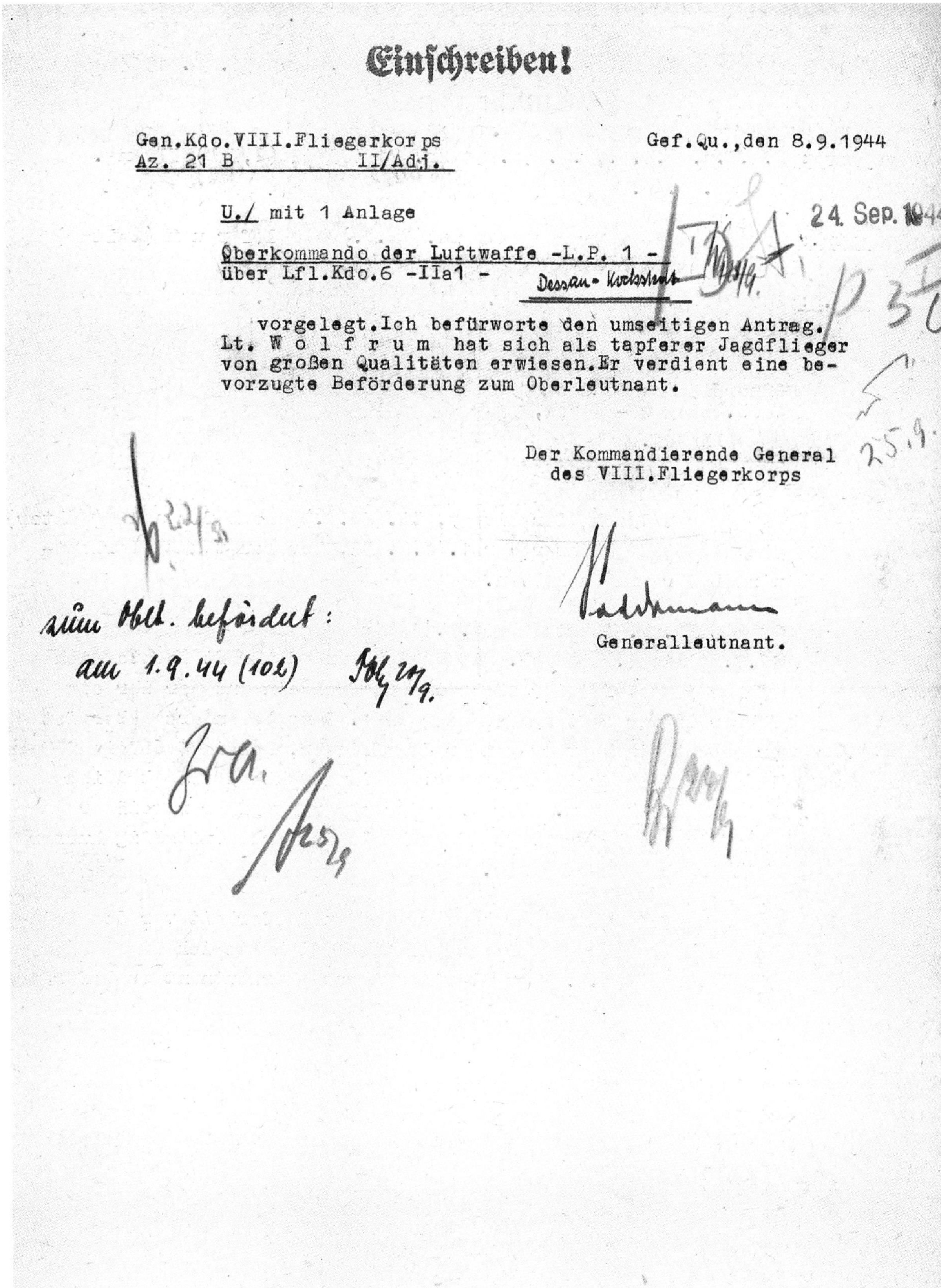

Einschreiben!

Gen.Kdo.VIII.Fliegerkorps
Az. 21 B II/Adj.

Gef.Qu., den 8.9.1944

24. Sep. 1944

U./ mit 1 Anlage

Oberkommando der Luftwaffe -L.P. 1 -
über Lfl.Kdo.6 -IIa1 -

vorgelegt. Ich befürworte den umseitigen Antrag. Lt. W o l f r u m hat sich als tapferer Jagdflieger von großen Qualitäten erwiesen. Er verdient eine bevorzugte Beförderung zum Oberleutnant.

Der Kommandierende General
des VIII.Fliegerkorps

Generalleutnant.

zum Oblt. befördert:
am 1.9.44 (102)

Request for Preferred Promotion for Second Lieutenant Walter Wolfrum (back side) – signed by Major General Hans Seidemann, Commander, 8th Air Corps.

Otto Würfel

Fighter Pilot

"Physically able to bear a burden."

Second Lieutenant Otto Würfel was born December 3, 1920 in Uelzen, Saxony. Würfel joined the *Luftwaffe* on October 3, 1939. He was promoted to private first class on October 1, 1940 and to sergeant on October 1, 1941. He joined the 9th Squadron, 51st Fighter Wing "Mölders" (*Jagdgeschwader 51 "Mölders")* in the middle of 1942 and won the Iron Cross 2nd and 1st Class on the same day, September 15, 1942. He scored his first victory – an Il-2 Sturmovik – on August 27, 1942. On October 15, 1942, he received the Operational Flying Clasp for Fighters in Gold, and by the summer of 1943 he had scored 9 aerial victories. He then spent a short tour as a flight instructor with Supplemental Group East (*Ergänzungsgruppe Ost*), before returning to his unit on September 3, 1943 – having been promoted to technical sergeant on September 1. Over the next five months, Würfel scored 70 victories. He was promoted to master sergeant on November 1, 1943 due to bravery in the face of the enemy.

On November 28, 1943, Lieutenant Colonel Karl-Gottfried Nordmann, Commodore, *Jagdgeschwader 51 "Mölders,"* submitted an efficiency report on Master Sergeant Otto Würfel, who at that time had achieved his 50th victory. It read, in part:[140]

> **Accomplishments confronting the enemy:** Master Sergeant Würfel excelled against the enemy in 225 combat missions up to now, with 50 aerial victories.
>
> **Short evaluation:** Master Sergeant Würfel has proven to be a very good soldier during his time with the group, and he has accumulated good flying and military accomplishments. As to his character, he is open and trustworthy, conscientious in his service and well liked by his comrades. His attitude and behavior towards his superiors is without criticism. Physically able to bear a burden, he possesses an immaculate military appearance and the necessary secure attitude to succeed. He is firmly rooted in National Socialist ideology. As a pilot, Würfel has always demonstrated his untiring preparedness for battle. Engaged as a leader of a two- and four-aircraft formation, due to his circumspection and risk-taking way of flying – as well as tactically correct leadership during flights as escort and during "free hunting" missions of his squadron – he has enabled them to be successful.

Würfel received the *Luftwaffe* Honor Goblet on December 13, 1943 and was reassigned to the 8th Squadron, *Jagdgeschwader 51 "Mölders."* On February 21, 1944, he downed six enemy aircraft, but the following day, his Focke-Wulf Fw 190A-5 rammed another German fighter during a fierce aerial battle and he parachuted down northwest of Rogatschew, Russia. Captured by the Russians, he became a prisoner of war at Camp 280/5 near Stalino. His incarceration proved too much, and the fighter pilot, who was "physically able to bear a burden," finally succumbed to typhus in the camp on December 22, 1944. Würfel was designated to receive the Knight's Cross of the Iron Cross on May 4, 1944 and was subsequently promoted to second lieutenant. His final total of aerial victories was 79, all on the Eastern Front.[141]

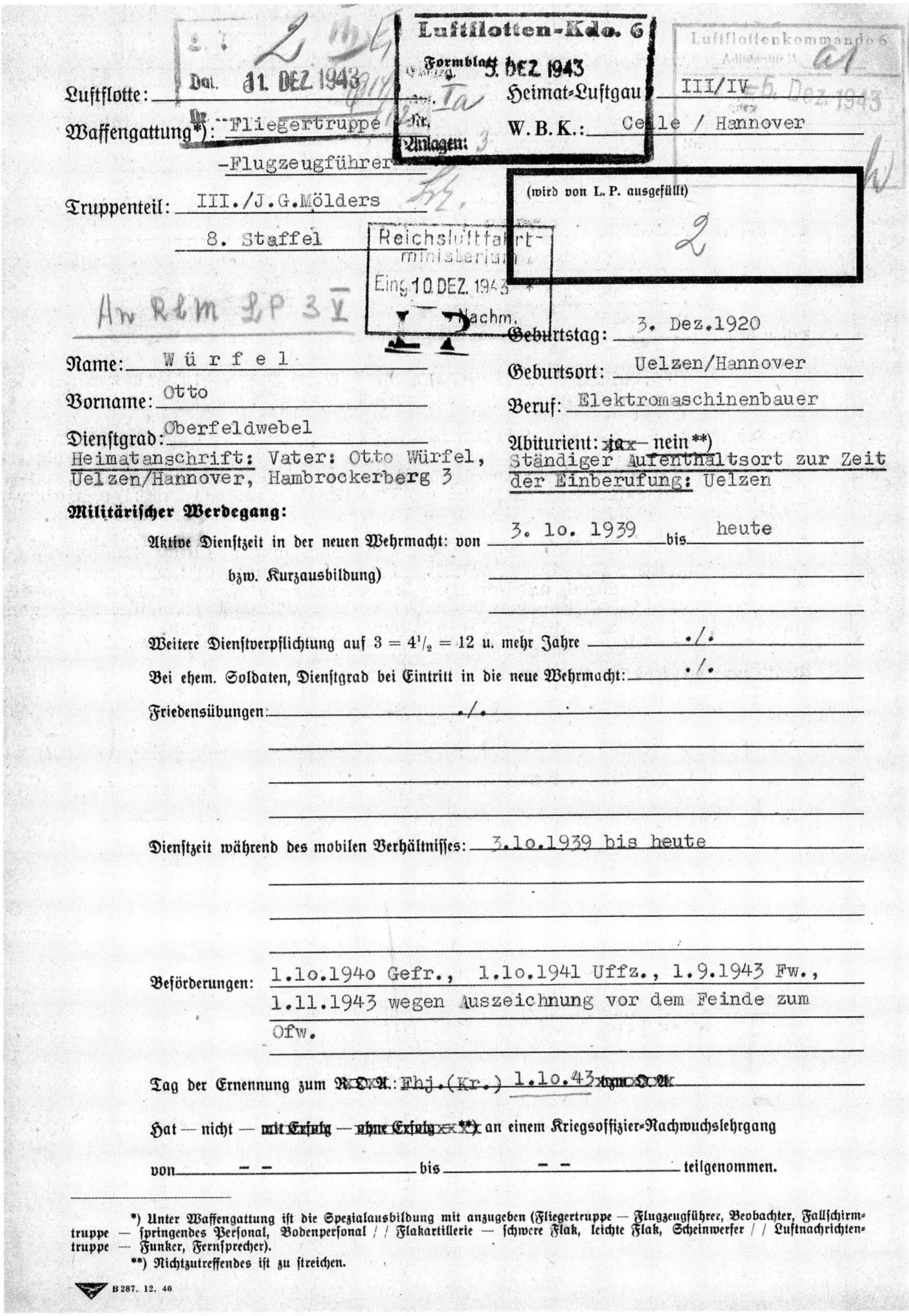

Luftflotten-Kdo. 6
Formblatt 3. DEZ 1943
Ia
Anlagen: 3

Dat. 11. DEZ 1943

Luftflottenkommando 6
a1
5. Dez. 1943

Luftflotte:

Heimat-Luftgau: III/IV

Waffengattung*): Fliegertruppe -Flugzeugführer

W.B.K.: Celle / Hannover

(wird von L. P. ausgefüllt) 2

Truppenteil: III./J.G.Mölders 8. Staffel

Reichsluftfahrtministerium Eing. 10 DEZ. 1943 Nachm.

An RLM LP 3 V

Name: W ü r f e l

Geburtstag: 3. Dez.1920

Vorname: Otto

Geburtsort: Uelzen/Hannover

Dienstgrad: Oberfeldwebel

Beruf: Elektromaschinenbauer

Abiturient: ~~ja~~ – nein**)

Heimatanschrift: Vater: Otto Würfel, Uelzen/Hannover, Hambrockerberg 3

Ständiger Aufenthaltsort zur Zeit der Einberufung: Uelzen

Militärischer Werdegang:

Aktive Dienstzeit in der neuen Wehrmacht: von 3. 10. 1939 bis heute

bzw. Kurzausbildung)

Weitere Dienstverpflichtung auf 3 = 4½ = 12 u. mehr Jahre ./.

Bei ehem. Soldaten, Dienstgrad bei Eintritt in die neue Wehrmacht: ./.

Friedensübungen: ./.

Dienstzeit während des mobilen Verhältnisses: 3.10.1939 bis heute

Beförderungen: 1.10.1940 Gefr., 1.10.1941 Uffz., 1.9.1943 Fw., 1.11.1943 wegen Auszeichnung vor dem Feinde zum Ofw.

Tag der Ernennung zum ~~R.O.A.~~: Fhj.(Kr.) 1.10.43 ~~bzw. O.A.~~

Hat — nicht — ~~mit Erfolg~~ — ~~ohne Erfolg~~ **) an einem Kriegsoffizier-Nachwuchslehrgang

von – – bis – – teilgenommen.

*) Unter Waffengattung ist die Spezialausbildung mit anzugeben (Fliegertruppe — Flugzeugführer, Beobachter, Fallschirmtruppe — springendes Personal, Bodenpersonal / / Flakartillerie — schwere Flak, leichte Flak, Scheinwerfer / / Luftnachrichtentruppe — Funker, Fernsprecher).

**) Nichtzutreffendes ist zu streichen.

B 287. 12. 40

Efficiency Report for Master Sergeant Otto Würfel (front side) – dated November 28, 1943, on pre-printed form, with typed comments. Stamps indicate that the report arrived at the 6th Air Fleet headquarters on December 5 and the *Luftwaffe* Personnel Office on December 10.

Zur Beförderung zum Offizier vorgeschlagen am: ./.

Bewährung vor dem Feinde: Ofw. Würfel bewährte sich vor dem Feinde in bisher 225 Feindflügen mit 5o Luftsiegen ausgezeichnet.

Auszeichnungen: 15.9.42 E.K.2, 15.9.42 E.K.1, 15,1o.1942 Frontflugspange für Jäger in Gold, Vorschlag zur Verleihung des Ehrenpokals und Deutschem Kreuz in Gold ist eingereicht.

Bestrafungen: Keine.

Kurze Beurteilung: Ofw.Würfel hat sich während seiner Zugehörigkeit zur Gruppe als sehr guter Soldat gezeigt, der fliegerisch und militärisch gute Leistungen aufzuweisen hat. Er ist von aufgeschlossenem ehrlichem Charakter, gewissenhaft im Dienst und bei seinen Kameraden sehr beliebt. Seine Haltung und Benehmen gesetzten gegenüber ist einwandfrei. Körperlich belastungsfähig, besitzt er einwandfreies militärisches Auftreten und die nötige Sicherheit sich durchzusetzen. Er steht fest auf dem Boden der nat.-soz. Weltanschauung.
In fliegerischer Hinsicht hat W. stets seine unermüdliche Einsatzbereitschaft unter Beweis gestellt. Als Rotten- und Schwarmführer eingesetzt, hat er durch umsichtiges und draufgängerisches Fliegen sowie taktisch richtiges Führen seines Schwarmes bei Begleitschutzaufträgen und freier Jagd seiner Staffel oft zum Erfolg verholfen.

Uk-Stellung während des Krieges:

von ./. bis ./.

Kurze Angabe des Grundes: ./.

Gefechtsstand, den 28.11.1943.
(Ort und Datum)

[signature]
(Unterschrift)

Oberstleutnant u.Geschwaderkommodore.

Efficiency Report for Master Sergeant Otto Würfel (back side) – signed by Lieutenant Colonel Karl-Gottfried Nordmann, Commodore, 51st Fighter Wing.

Hilmar Zahn
Fallschirmjäger

"Understands exceedingly well how to make gunnery training interesting and diversified."

Captain Hilmar Zahn was born on September 6, 1919 in Wiesbaden-Rambach. He served in the German Labor Service in 1937 before joining the 5th Company, 5th Infantry Regiment of the German Army in Bad Kreuznach. Zahn transferred to the *Luftwaffe* on April 1, 1938 and started down the path to becoming a non-commissioned officer. He served in several *Luftwaffe* construction units through 1942 when he was commissioned a second lieutenant of the reserves and attended airborne school. On June 3, 1942, he became a platoon leader in the 5th Company, 1st Paratroop Regiment (*Fallschirmjäger-Regiment 1*) and deployed to Russia on October 26, 1942. On February 15, 1943, while leading a reconnaissance patrol near Aleksejewka, he was wounded in action. He received the Iron Cross 2nd Class on March 3, 1943. Zahn left a hospital in Germany some months later and was assigned to the Paratroop Replacement Battalion at Stendal. He then transferred to Italy, where he once again became a platoon leader in the 5th Company.

On June 2, 1943, Second Lieutenant Hilmar Zahn's chain of command in the 2nd Battalion, 1st Paratroop Regiment, submitted a special report, requesting that he be named an active duty officer. The report was composed entirely by Major, and battalion commander, Kurt Gröschke. It read, in part:[142]

1. Personal assets: Second Lieutenant Zahn is a self-confident and energetic officer, who masters every situation.

2. Character traits: Zahn is an officer with an agreeable, fresh spirit and decent behavior. Due to his free and open character, he is highly appreciated in the officer corps.

3. Mental traits: His general education is good and wide-reaching. Mentally he is very flexible and vivid.

4. Military talent: Zahn makes a clear and military appearance. Factual, goal-oriented and clear in his thinking.

5. Physical traits: Zahn is a parachute soldier and physically very robust. His athletic accomplishments are above average.

6. Other: Second Lieutenant Zahn has excelled during battalion operations in the East as a platoon leader, particularly as reconnaissance and assault troop leader. For several weeks now, Zahn has been in charge of the heavy company and understands exceedingly well how to make gunnery training interesting and diversified. Leadership capabilities are present. Without hesitation, suitable for promotion to first lieutenant. His National Socialist attitude is above criticism.

The report helped Zahn with his next promotion, and he became a first lieutenant of reserves on July 14, 1943. Zahn then became the acting commander of the 5th Company, 1st Paratroop Regiment and fought at Ortona and Cassino. On

February 18, 1944, he received the Iron Cross 1st Class, but was seriously wounded on March 21, 1944 – a wound that resulted in the amputation of his right leg. While in the hospital, Hilmar Zahn received his active commission and was designated an active duty first lieutenant on May 10, 1944 and an active duty captain on June 16, 1944. In between these promotions, Hilmar Zahn received the Knight's Cross of the Iron Cross on June 9, 1944.

On March 23, 1945 – with a prosthetic leg – Captain Hilmar Zahn returned to command the 5th Company, 1st Paratroop Regiment and fought near Bologna, before he became a prisoner of war on May 8, 1945. In addition to the aforementioned awards, Hilmar Zahn received the Parachutist's Badge on July 22, 1942, the *Luftwaffe* Ground Combat Badge on March 5, 1944 and the Wound Badge in Gold on June 3, 1944. He survived the war.[143]

8

II./Fallschirmjäger-Rgt.1 , den 2.6.43

Feldpost-Nr. L 36 006 a Paris

V o r s c h l a g

zur Überführung des Kriegsoffiziers Lt.Zahn
zu den aktiven Friedensoffizieren.

Familienname, Vorname: Z a h n , Hilmar

geb. am : 6.9.1919 zu: Rambach Konfession: ev.

ledig

Dienstgrad: Leutnant (Kr.O.) Rangdienstalter: 1.4.42

Diensteintritt: 2.11.37

Militärische Dienstzeiten und Werdegang:

Vom 2.11.37	-	31.3.38	5./I.R. 1o7
" 1. 4.38	-	25.2.40	Horst-Kp. Mannheim
" 26.2.40	-	15.3.4o	Lw.Bau-Kp. 28/X/XII.
" 16.3.4o	-	31.5.4o	" " " 1/10/XII
" 1.6.4o	-	13.9.41	" " " 1/2/XVII
" 14.9.41	-	27.1.42	" " " 1/2/XVII
" 28.1.42	-	3o.4.42	Kampfschule der Lw.Gr.Born
" 1 .5.42	-	2. 6.42	Fallschirmschule Wittstock.(F.-Lehrgang)
" 3. 6.42	-		II./Fallschirmjäger-Rgt.1

Beförderungen und Ernennungen:

1.11.38	Gefreiter	8.8.41	Kr.Offz.Anw.
1.1o.39	Ob.-Gefreiter	1.4.42	Leutnant (Kr.O.)
1.1. 40	Uffz.-Anw.		
1.2. 40	Unteroffizier		
1.2. 41	Feldwebel		

Jetzige Verwendung: Zugführer

für welche weiteren Verwendungen geeignet: Kp. Führer

Bestrafung währende der militärischen Dienstzeit: keine

Bildungsgang: Erziehung im elterlichen Hause ; 1925 - 1933 Volksschule zu Rambach ; 1933 - 1936 Malerlehrling ; 1.4.37 - 24.10.37 RAD.

Zivilberuf: Maler und Anstreicher

Beruf des Vaters: Bankangestellter

Erworbene Lw.Scheine: Fallschirmschützenschein

2116 Beurteilung: umseitig

Request for Transfer for Second Lieutenant Hilmar Zahn from Wartime Officer to Career Status (front side) – dated June 2, 1943, on blank paper, with typed comments. Extensive underlining with blue pencil probably occurred at a higher headquarters review. "2116" in blue pencil is probably an administrative file number.

Beurteilung.

1. Persönlichkeitswert: Lt. Zahn ist ein selbstbewußter und energischer Offizier,der jeder Situation gewachsen ist.
2. Charakterliche Eignung: Z. ist ein Offizier mit erfreulicher Frische und anständiger Gesinnung. Durch sein freies und offenes Wesen wird er im Offz.-Korps sehr geschätzt.
3. Geistige Veranlagung: Seine Allgemeinbildung ist gut und umfassend. Geistig ist er sehr wendig und rege.
4. Militärische Veranlagung: Z. ist eine klare und soldatische Erscheinung. Sachlich , zielbewußt und klar im Denken.
5. Körperliche Veranlagung: Z. ist Fallschirmschütze und körperlich sehr widerstandsfähig.Seine sportliche Leistungen liegen über dem Durchschnitt.
6. Sonstiges: Lt. Zahn hat sich beim Osteinsatz des Btl. als Zugführer , besonders als Späh - und Stoßtruppführer hervorragend bewährt.

Z. führt seit einigen Wochen die schwere Kp. und versteht es ganz besonders die Schießausbildung interessant und vielseitig zu gestalten. Führereigenschaften sind vorhanden.

Zur Beförderung zum Oberleutnant uneingeschränkt geeignet.

Seine nationalsozialistische Gesinnung ist einwandfrei.

Major und Btl.-Kommandeur.

2117

Request for Transfer for Second Lieutenant Hilmar Zahn from Wartime Officer to Career Status (back side) – signed by Major Kurt Gröschke, Commander, 2nd Battalion, 1st Paratroop Regiment.

Eugen-Ludwig Zweigart

Fighter Pilot

"He possesses a clear manner of giving orders."

First Lieutenant Eugen-Ludwig Zweigart was born at Saargemünd in Lothringen on May 3, 1914. He joined the Army in 1935 and later transferred to the *Luftwaffe* and underwent flight training. In the fall of 1940, Staff Sergeant Zweigart was assigned to the 9th Squadron, 54th Fighter Wing "Green Hearts" (*Jagdgeschwader 54 "Grünherz"*). On November 10, he scored his first aerial victory when he shot down an RAF Blenheim twin-engine bomber near De Kooy, Holland, but he did not score his next victory (an I-153 fighter) until the first day of the Russian campaign. On November 11, 1941, he was shot down in his Messerschmitt Me 109F-2 and made a forced landing near Sablin in northern Russia. By December 1, 1941, Technical Sergeant Zweigart had nine victories to his credit; he increased his victory total to 15 by the end of April 1942 and, six months later, by the end of October, his total kills stood at 44. He received the *Luftwaffe* Honor Goblet on October 26, 1942 and the German Cross in Gold on November 17, 1942. On December 29, 1942, he shot down four enemy aircraft to raise his score to 54 and on January 22, 1943, Master Sergeant Eugen-Ludwig Zweigart was awarded the Knight's Cross of the Iron Cross as a pilot in the 5th Squadron, *Jagdgeschwader 54 "Grünherz."* Shortly after the award of the decoration, he was transferred to conduct instructional duties, but he returned to the 9th Squadron – now based on the Western Front conducting homeland defense – in May 1943. Zweigart recorded his 58th victory (a Spitfire) northwest of Ijmuiden, Holland on July 25, but was shot down two days later in aerial combat with USAAF four-engine bombers over Noorden, Nieuwkoop, Holland. He was able to bail out of his stricken Messerschmitt Me 109G-6, although he was wounded.[144]

On July 29, 1943, the 9th Squadron Commander, Captain Ekkehard Bob, submitted a special efficiency report, requesting that Eugen Zweigart be promoted to commissioned officer. Bob supported the request by writing:[145]

> Zweigart is mentally and physically talented with good general knowledge. Physically he is tough, with endurance, and he is a good athlete. He has an open, decent character with a refreshing but calm bearing. In his appearance vis-à-vis superiors and subordinates, he is thoroughly a soldier. Extremely correct and polite. He is a leadership personality, who understands how to sweep along comrades and subordinates in a manner that has earned him respect. Due to his awareness of his responsibility, his exemplary understanding of service and his self-reliance, on several occasions as acting squadron commander he led the squadron on missions to the fullest satisfaction of his superiors. He possesses a clear manner of giving orders and knows how to assert himself at the front. Zweigart has been with the squadron since August 31, 1940. He came to the squadron as a young, passionate fighter pilot and sergeant and, through his untiring willingness for combat, his eagerness and his dash, has become the most successful NCO pilot. During 371 flights at the front, so far he has 57 aerial victories. Through his untiring spirit for attack he is a shining example for all flight leaders. Therefore, he was awarded the Knight's Cross by the Führer on January 22, 1943.

Eugen Zweigart was transferred to the 7th Squadron on October 16, 1943 (and with them shot down two B-17 Flying Fortresses in a span of nine minutes on February 20, 1944) and to the 8th Squadron in March 1944. On March 6, he claimed three more B-17 bombers shot down. Finally in May, he transferred to the 3rd Group staff, *Jagdgeschwader 54 "Grünherz."* On June 8, 1944, Zweigart was shot down in a Focke-Wulf Fw 190A-8 in aerial combat with P-51 Mustangs near Le Cambaux, Normandy. According to one source, Zweigart bailed out, but was then shot and killed while suspended in his parachute. He is buried at the German Military Cemetery at St. Desir-de-Lisieux, France (Section 1, Row 45, Grave 984).

Eugen-Ludwig Zweigart was credited with 69 aerial victories, of which 53 were over the Eastern Front. Of his 16 victories over the Western Front, 11 were four-engine bombers.[146]

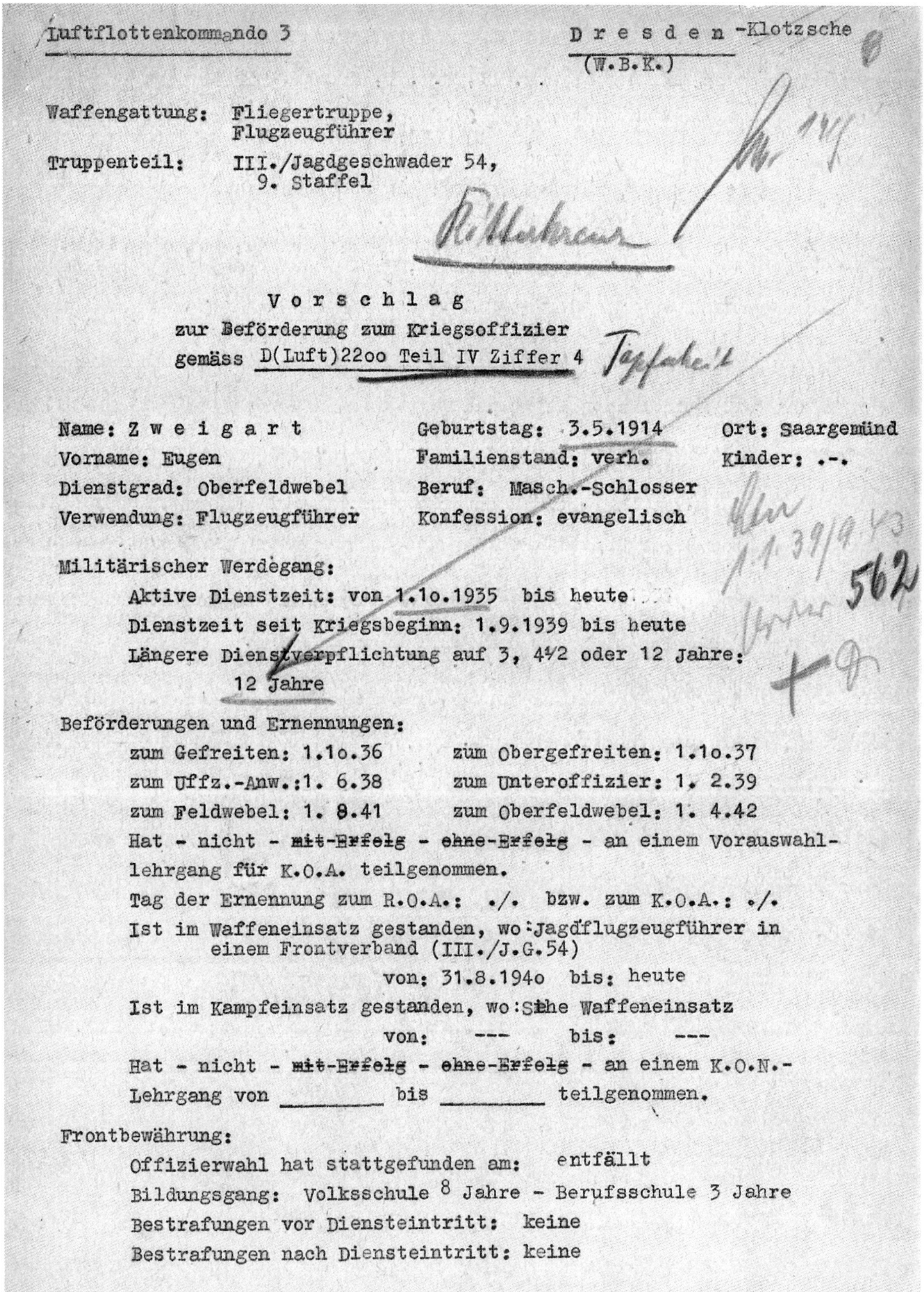

Luftflottenkommando 3 | D r e s d e n -Klotzsche (W.B.K.)

Waffengattung: Fliegertruppe, Flugzeugführer
Truppenteil: III./Jagdgeschwader 54, 9. Staffel

V o r s c h l a g
zur Beförderung zum Kriegsoffizier
gemäss D(Luft)22oo Teil IV Ziffer 4

Name: Z w e i g a r t   Geburtstag: 3.5.1914   Ort: Saargemünd
Vorname: Eugen   Familienstand: verh.   Kinder: .-.
Dienstgrad: Oberfeldwebel   Beruf: Masch.-Schlosser
Verwendung: Flugzeugführer   Konfession: evangelisch

Militärischer Werdegang:
Aktive Dienstzeit: von 1.1o.1935 bis heute
Dienstzeit seit Kriegsbeginn: 1.9.1939 bis heute
Längere Dienstverpflichtung auf 3, 4½ oder 12 Jahre:
12 Jahre

Beförderungen und Ernennungen:
zum Gefreiten: 1.1o.36   zum Obergefreiten: 1.1o.37
zum Uffz.-Anw.: 1. 6.38   zum Unteroffizier: 1. 2.39
zum Feldwebel: 1. 8.41   zum Oberfeldwebel: 1. 4.42
Hat - nicht - ~~mit Erfolg~~ - ~~ohne Erfolg~~ - an einem Vorauswahl-lehrgang für K.O.A. teilgenommen.
Tag der Ernennung zum R.O.A.: ./. bzw. zum K.O.A.: ./.
Ist im Waffeneinsatz gestanden, wo: Jagdflugzeugführer in einem Frontverband (III./J.G.54)
von: 31.8.194o bis: heute
Ist im Kampfeinsatz gestanden, wo: Siehe Waffeneinsatz
von: --- bis: ---
Hat - nicht - ~~mit Erfolg~~ - ~~ohne Erfolg~~ - an einem K.O.N.-Lehrgang von ________ bis ________ teilgenommen.

Frontbewährung:
Offizierwahl hat stattgefunden am: entfällt
Bildungsgang: Volksschule 8 Jahre - Berufsschule 3 Jahre
Bestrafungen vor Diensteintritt: keine
Bestrafungen nach Diensteintritt: keine

Request for Promotion to Officer for Master Sergeant Eugen Zweigart (front side) – dated July 29, 1943, on blank paper, with typed comments.

Auszeichnungen: E.K. II, E.K. I, Frontflugspange für Jäger
in Bronze, Silber und Gold, Ehrenpokal für
besondere Leistungen im Luftkrieg, Deutsches
Kreuz in Gold, Ritterkreuz des Eisernen Kreuzes,
Medaille "Winterschlacht im Osten 1941/42"

Stand und Beruf des Vaters: Eisenbahnschaffner

Familienname der Mutter: geb. Klein

Anschrift der nächsten Angehörigen: Ehefrau: Lotte Zweigart
Weixdorf/Dresden, Hindenburgstrasse 34

Ausserdienstliche Eignung festgestellt durch:
oder beantragt bei:

B e u r t e i l u n g :

Zweigart ist geistig und körperlich gut veranlagt mit gutem Allgemeinwissen. Er ist körperlich zäh und ausdauernd und ein guter Sportler. Er hat einen offenen, anständigen Charakter mit frischem aber ruhigem Wesen. In seinem Auftreten gegenüber Vorgesetzten und Untergebenen ist er durch und durch Soldat - l äusserst korrekt und zuvorkommend. Er ist eine Führerpersönlichkeit, die es versteht Kameraden und Untergebene mitzureissen, sodass er überall die ihm gebührende Achtung geniesst. Durch sei Verantwortungsbewusstsein, seine vorbildliche Dienstauffassung und seine Selbständigkeit führte er in Vertretung des Staffelkapitäns die Staffel mehrmals im Einsatz zur vollsten Zufriedenheit seiner Vorgesetzten. Er besitzt eine klare Befehlsgebung und weiss sich vor der Front durchzusetzen.
Zweigart ist seit dem 31.8.194o bei der Staffel. Er kam als junger, passioniertter Jagdflieger und Unteroffizier zur Staffel und hat es durch seine unermüdliche Einsatzfreudigkeit, seinen Eifer und sein Draufgängertum zum erfolgreichsten Uffz.-Flugzeugführer gebracht. In 371 Frontflügen schoss er bisher 57 feindliche Flugzeuge ab. Durch seinen unermüdlichen Angriffsgeist ist er allen Flugzeugführern ein leuchtendes Vorbild. So wurde ihm vom Führer am 22.1.1943 das Ritterkreuz verliehen.

Im Felde, den 29.7.1943

Bob

Hauptmann und Staffelkapitän

Request for Promotion to Officer for Master Sergeant Eugen Zweigart (back side) – signed by Captain Hans-Ekkehard Bob, Commander, 9th Squadron, 54th Fighter Wing.

RATER BIOGRAPHIES

The following are abbreviated biographies of the raters and senior raters, who signed the documents found in this book. When a rater was also the subject of an evaluation found in this book, the reader will find his expanded biography in the previous section, not in this section.

Horst Ademeit

Major Horst Ademeit was born on February 8, 1912 at Breslau in Silesia. He learned to fly before the war and, as a reservist, was trained as a fighter pilot. By spring 1940, Ademeit was serving with the 3rd Squadron, 54th Fighter Wing "Green Hearts" (*Jagdgeschwader 54 "Grünherz"*). His significant positions included: Commander, 6th Squadron, 54th Fighter Wing "Green Hearts," March 7, 1943-January 18, 1944; Commander, 1st Group, 54th Fighter Wing "Green Hearts," January 18, 1944-August 1, 1944; and acting commodore, 54th Fighter Wing "Green Hearts," August 1, 1944-August 7, 1944. Ademeit won the Iron Cross 2nd Class on September 7, 1940, the Iron Cross 1st Class on September 5, 1941, the *Luftwaffe* Honor Goblet on December 8, 1941 and the German Cross in Gold on February 25, 1942. He received the Knight's Cross of the Iron Cross on April 16, 1943 and the Oak Leaves to the Knight's Cross on March 2, 1944. On August 7, 1944, Ademeit was engaged in aerial combat with a Russian Il-2 Sturmovik over enemy lines near Dünaberg, Courland, in his Focke-Wulf Fw 190A-5 and failed to return from this mission. He remains missing to this day, possibly shot down by Russian ground fire and forced to make an emergency landing. Horst Ademeit was promoted to major after his death. He was credited with 166 victories in over 600 missions, of which 164 were over the Eastern Front.[1]

Hans-Ekkehard Bob

Major Hans-Ekkehard Bob was born on January 24, 1917 at Freiburg/Breisgau in Baden. He joined the *Luftwaffe* on December 1, 1936 as an officer candidate, spending his first year at the *Luftskriegsschule* Wildpark Werder for basic military training, and beginning flight training on June 1, 1937. At the beginning of 1938, he attended the Officer's Academy. Bob then transferred the 133rd Fighter Group (*Jagdfliegergruppe 133*) based at Wiesbaden, and later moved to the 334th Fighter Wing (*Jagdgeschwader 334*), equipped with Messerschmitt Me 110 *Zerstörer* twin-engine fighters, based at Gablingen. He then transferred to the newly formed 3rd Squadron, 21st Fighter Wing (*Jagdgeschwader 21*), based at Jesau – redesignated the 9th Squadron, 54th Fighter Wing "Green Hearts" (*Jagdgeschwader 54 "Grünherz"*). His promotions included: Second Lieutenant (*Leutnant*), September 1, 1938; First Lieutenant (*Oberleutnant*), August 1, 1940; and Major (*Major*), August 1, 1943. Bob's significant wartime positions included: Commander, 7th Squadron, 54th Fighter Wing "Green Hearts," October 10, 1940-November 28, 1940; Commander, 9th Squadron, 54th Fighter Wing "Green Hearts," November 28, 1940-August 1, 1943; Commander, 4th Group, 51st Fighter Wing "Mölders" (*Jagdgeschwader 51 "Mölders"*), August 1, 1943-May 9, 1944; and Commander, 2nd Group, 3rd Fighter Wing "Udet" (*Jagdgeschwader 3 "Udet"*), May 9, 1944-August 1944. Bob received the *Luftwaffe* Honor Goblet on September 28, 1940. *Reichsmarschall* Hermann Göring awarded him the Knight's Cross of the Iron Cross on March 7, 1941 at Le Mans, France. He received the German Cross in Gold on December 24, 1942. In August 1944, Bob transferred to *Erprobungskommando 262*, an experimental jet unit, where he received training on the Messerschmitt Me 262 jet fighter. He later joined units responsible for training former bomber pilots on single-engine fighters. Bob next became a member of Fighter Unit 44 (*Jagdverband 44*), the Me 262-equipped unit led by Lieutenant General Adolf Galland. After the war, Bob initially took employment as a farm laborer before establishing a transport business. In 1956, he founded a company manufacturing drilling equipment. Hans-Ekkehard Bob flew approximately 700 combat missions and claimed 60 victories, 37 on the Eastern Front, for a sortie-to-victory ratio of 1.62 to 1.[2]

Hubertus von Bonin

Lieutenant Colonel Hubertus von Bonin was born in Potsdam, Brandenburg on August 3, 1911. His significant assignments included: Commander, 5th Squadron, 26th Fighter Wing "Schlageter" (*Jagdgeschwader 26 "Schlageter"*), June 28, 1939-December 24, 1939; Commander, 3rd Squadron, 88th Fighter Group [Spain] (*Jagdgruppe 88* [J/88]), December 5, 1938-May 22, 1939; Commander, 1st Group, 26th Fighter Wing "Schlageter," January 1, 1940-May 9, 1940; Commander, 1st Group, 54th Fighter Wing "Green Hearts" (*Jagdgeschwader 54 "Grünherz"*), May 10, 1940-June 30, 1941; acting commander, 2nd Group, 51st Fighter Wing (*Jagdgeschwader 51*), July 11, 1941-August 8, 1941; Commander, 4th Fighter School (*Jagdfliegerschule 4*), July 11, 1941-October 1, 1941; Commander, 3rd Group, 52nd Fighter Wing (*Jagdgeschwader 52*), October 1, 1941-July 5, 1943; and Commodore, 54th Fighter Wing "Green Hearts," July 6, 1943-December 15, 1943. He was awarded the Knight's Cross of the Iron Cross on December 21, 1942. He also received the Spanish Cross in Gold with Swords. In addition, he won the German Cross in Gold on October 27, 1942. Major Hubertus von Bonin was killed in action over Gorodok, Russia on December 15, 1943 when his Focke-Wulf FW 190A-5 was shot down. He was buried at a German military cemetery at Orsha. Von Bonin was posthumously promoted to lieutenant colonel. Hubertus von Bonin scored 77 aerial victories, including 4 in Spain, 9 in the West and 64 over the Eastern Front. Hubertus von Bonin was one of three brothers who flew for the *Luftwaffe*. Jürgen Oskar von Bonin was killed in action as an observer in a transport wing, while Eckart-Wilhelm von Bonin, a Knight's Cross winner and night fighter, survived.[3]

Kurt Brändle

Major Kurt Brändle was born January 19, 1912 at Ludwigsburg, Württemberg. He entered the *Luftwaffe* in 1937 and by 1939 belonged to the 4th Squadron, 53rd Fighter Wing "Ace of Spades" (*Jagdgeschwader 53, "Pikas"*). He shot down his first two aircraft in May 1940, but crashed into a Dornier Do 17 bomber during takeoff and was hospitalized. His significant assignments included: Commander, 5th Squadron, 53rd Fighter Wing, September 1, 1940-April 15, 1942; and Commander, 2nd Group, 3rd Fighter Wing "Udet" (*Jagdgeschwader 3 "Udet"*), April 15, 1942-November 3, 1943. He won the Iron Cross 2nd Class on April 20, 1940, the Iron Cross 1st Class on September 3, 1940, the German Cross in Gold on February 25, 1942, the Knight's Cross of the Iron Cross on July 1, 1942 and the Oak Leaves to the Knight's Cross on August 27, 1942. He was killed in action on November 3, 1943 west of Amsterdam just after shooting down two P-47 Thunderbolts. He is buried at the German Military Cemetery at Ysselsteyn, Netherlands (Block CW, Row 1, Grave 25). Brändle is credited with 180 aerial victories in 700 combat missions, a sortie-to-victory ratio of 3.88 to 1. Twenty-five of his kills were in the West and included 1 four-engine bomber.[4]

Bruno Bräuer

Lieutenant General Bruno Bräuer was born February 4, 1893 in Willmannsdorf in Silesia. He entered the Army in 1908 and became an infantryman. Bräuer served in World War I with the 155th West Prussian Infantry Regiment, winning the Iron Cross 2nd and 1st Class. He left the Army after the war and entered the Police, where he later became the commander of the 1st Battalion Land Police Group "General Göring," the forerunner of the *Luftwaffe's Hermann Göring Regiment* and later *Hermann Göring Division*. Bräuer became a paratrooper in 1936 and transferred to the *Luftwaffe*. His significant positions included: Commander, 4th Battalion, Regiment "General Göring," September 1, 1937-April 1, 1938; Commander, 1st Battalion, 1st Paratroop Regiment (*Fallschirmjäger-Regiment 1*), April 1, 1938-November 23, 1938; Commander, 1st Paratroop Regiment, January 1, 1939-September 6, 1942; Commandant of Fortress Crete (*Kommandant der Festung Kreta*), February 23, 1943-June 1, 1944; and Commander, 9th Paratroop Division (*9. Fallschirmjäger-Division*), March 2, 1945-April 18, 1945. His promotions included: Lieutenant Colonel (*Oberstleutnant*), January 1, 1938; Colonel (*Oberst*), January 1, 1939; Brigadier General (*Generalmajor*), September 1, 1941; Major General (*Generalleutnant*), September 6, 1942; and Lieutenant General (*General der Fallschirmjäger*), June 1, 1944. He received the Knight's Cross of the Iron Cross on May 24, 1940 and the German Cross in Gold on April 13, 1942. A Greek tribunal sentenced him to death on February 9,

1946 for war crimes on Crete. Bruno Bräuer was executed by a Greek firing squad at Athens-Xaidari, Greece at 5:00 a.m. on May 20, 1947. He is buried at the German Military Cemetery at Máleme, Crete (Block 3, Grave 851.)[5]

Helmut Bruck

Colonel Helmut Bruck was born February 16, 1913 in Kittliztreben/Bunzlau. He entered the *Luftwaffe* as an officer candidate on August 1, 1935 and attended flight school at Magdeburg. His significant assignments included: acting commander, 1st Group, 77th Stuka Wing (*Sturzkampfgeschwader 77*), August 20, 1940-1941; Commander, 1st Group, 77th Stuka Wing, 1941-February 19, 1943; Commodore, 77th Stuka Wing, February 20, 1943-October 18, 1943; Commodore, 77th Ground-Attack Wing (*Schlachtgeschwader 77*), October 18, 1943-December 7, 1944; and Commodore, 151st Ground-Attack wing (*Schlachtgeschwader 151*), December 7, 1944-March 31, 1945. Bruck won the Iron Cross 2nd Class on September 13, 1939, the Iron Cross 1st Class on May 21, 1940, the Knight's Cross of the Iron Cross on September 4, 1941 and the Oak Leaves to the Knight's Cross on December 20, 1943. He also received the German Cross in Gold on October 20, 1942. His promotions included: Captain (*Hauptmann*), April 1, 1941; Major (*Major*), March 1, 1943; Lieutenant Colonel (*Oberstleutnant*), November 1, 1943; and Colonel (*Oberst*), April 1, 1944. He flew 973 combat missions during the war. Helmut Bruck died on August 25, 2001 in Veitlahm/Mainleus near Kulmbach, Bavaria.[6]

Gerhard Brückner

Gerhard Brückner won the German Cross in Gold on October 1, 1944 as the commander of the 1st Paratroop Anti-Tank Detachment (*Fallschirm-Panzer-Jäger Abteilung 1*). Brückner's assignments included: Commander, Paratroop Anti-Tank Detachment (*Fallschirm-Panzer-Jäger Abteilung*), September 1, 1942-September 10, 1943; and Commander, 1st Paratroop Anti-Tank Detachment, September 10, 1943-October 1944.[7]

Alfred Bülowius

Lieutenant General Alfred Bülowius was born on January 14, 1892 in Königsberg, East Prussia. He joined the Army in 1911 and served in World War I in the 41st Infantry Regiment before transferring to Bomber Wing 3, where he became a pilot. He left the Army in 1920 and briefly served in the Police before rejoining the Army in 1925. For the next nine years he served primarily in an air defense capacity; he transferred to the *Luftwaffe* on September 1, 1934. His significant positions included: Commodore 1st Demonstration Wing (*Lehr-Geschwader 1*), November 17, 1939-June 18, 1940 and June 21, 1940-October 21, 1940; Higher Flight Training Commander 7, October 21, 1940-January 14, 1941; Higher Commander Bomber and Stuka Schools, Prague, January 15, 1941-August 1, 1942; Commander *Luftwaffe* Command Don, August 2, 1942-October 31, 1942; Commander 1st Air Division (*1. Flieger-Division*), November 1, 1942-June 25, 1943; Commander 2nd Air Corps (*II. Fliegerkorps*), June 26, 1943-June 30, 1944; Commander 2nd Fighter Corps (*II. Jagdkorps*), July 1, 1944-October 15, 1944; Commander, 16th Air District (*Befehlshaber Luftgau XVI*), October 16, 1944-January 21, 1945; Commander, 15th Air District (*Befehlshaber Luftgau XV*), January 22, 1945-February 3, 1945; and Commander Staff Dresden in Air District 3, February 22, 1945-April 1945. His promotions included: Colonel (*Oberst*), January 1, 1939; Brigadier General (*Generalmajor*), June 1, 1941; Major General (*Generalleutnant*), March 1, 1943; and Lieutenant General (*General der Flieger*), December 1, 1944. Bülowius was shot down, wounded in action and captured by the French on June 18, 1940, but was repatriated two days later. He received the Knight's Cross of the Iron Cross on July 4, 1940 and the German Cross in Gold on December 21, 1942. Alfred Bülowius died on August 9, 1968 in Detmold, North Rhine-Westphalia. He is buried at the *Waldfriedhof Kupferberg* in Detmold (Section C, Grave 338).[8]

Eckhard Christian

Brigadier Eckhard Christian was born December 1, 1907 in Berlin-Charlottenburg, Brandenburg. He initially entered the German Navy on April 1, 1926, serving on several warships and specializing in torpedoes. Christian transferred to the *Luftwaffe* on October 1, 1934 with the grade of first lieutenant and received observer training before assuming duties as an aerial observer on the pocket battleship *Admiral Scheer*. His significant positions included: Operations Officer, 10th Air Corps (*X. Fliegerkorps*), March 8, 1940-June 2, 1940; Commander, 2nd Group, 26th Bomber Wing (*Kampfgeschwader 26*), August 21, 1940-January 14, 1941; General Staff Officer, Supreme Command (OKW), January 15, 1941-August 24, 1943; Operations Officer, *Luftwaffe* Operations Staff (*Ia des Luftwaffen-Führungsstabes*), August 25, 1943-August 31, 1944; Chief, *Luftwaffe* Operations Staff

(*Chef des Luftwaffen-Führungsstabes*), September 1, 1944-April 22, 1945; and Liaison Officer from *Luftwaffe* High Command (OKL) to OKW Staff North, April 22, 1945-May 8, 1945. Christian received the German Cross in Silver on May 10, 1945. His promotions included: Major (*Major*), June 1, 1940; Lieutenant Colonel (*Oberstleutnant*), March 1, 1942; Colonel (*Oberst*), March 1, 1943; and Brigadier General (*Generalmajor*), September 1, 1944. Eckhard Christian married Gerda Daranowsky, one of Adolf Hitler's secretaries, in 1943, but they later divorced. Eckhard Christian died on January 3, 1985 in Bad Kreuznach, Rhineland-Pfalz. He is buried at Bad Münster am Stein-Ebernburg, *Friedhof Ebernburg* (Section 8, Grave 20).[9]

Adolf Dickfeld

Colonel Adolf Dickfeld was born on February 20, 1910 at Jüterborg in Mark Brandenburg. He joined the *Luftwaffe* on March 1, 1937 and was promoted to second lieutenant on December 1, 1939. At the outbreak of the war, Dickfeld was assigned to the 3rd Group, 52nd Fighter Wing (*Jagdgeschwader 52*). On January 25, 1942, Adolf Dickfeld won the German Cross in Gold. Second Lieutenant Dickfeld was awarded the Knight's Cross of the Iron Cross on March 19, 1942; he was awarded the Oak Leaves to the Knight's Cross on May 19, 1942, for 101 victories. His promotions included: First Lieutenant (*Oberleutnant*), April 1, 1942; and Major (*Major*), May 18, 1943. His significant assignments included: Commander, 2nd Group, 2nd Fighter Wing "Richthofen" (*Jagdgeschwader 2 "Richthofen"*), November 7, 1942-January 8, 1943; and Commander, 2nd Group, 11th Fighter Wing (*Jagdgeschwader 11*), April 17, 1943-December 1943.[10]

Oskar Dinort

Brigadier General Oskar Dinort was born in Berlin-Charlottenburg on June 23, 1901. He entered the Army on February 11, 1919. In the late 1920s Dinort participated in secret flight training in the Soviet Union; he transferred to the *Luftwaffe* on May 1, 1934. Dinort's significant assignments included: Commander, 3rd Group, 134th Fighter Wing (*Jagdgeschwader 134*), January 4, 1936-March 15, 1937; Commander, 1st Group (Z), 1st Demonstration Wing (*Lehrgeschwader 1*), April 1, 1937-August 31, 1937; Commander, 1st Group, 165th Stuka Wing (*Sturzkampfgeschwader 165*), September 15, 1937-May 1, 1939; Commander, 1st Group, 2nd Stuka Wing "Immelmann" (*Sturzkampfgeschwader 2 "Immelmann"*), May 1, 1939-October 16, 1939; Commodore, 2nd Stuka Wing "Immelmann," October 16, 1939-October 11, 1941; Commodore, Target-Towing Wing (*Fliegerzielgeschwader*), August 1, 1942-August 31, 1943; and Commander, 3rd Flying School Division (*Fliegerschuldivision 3*), September 3, 1944-May 8, 1945.[11] His promotions included: Major (*Major*), March 1, 1937; Lieutenant Colonel (*Oberstleutnant*), July 19, 1940; Colonel (*Oberst*), September 1, 1941; and Brigadier General (*Generalmajor*), April 1, 1945. He won the Knight's Cross of the Iron Cross on June 20, 1940 and the Oak Leaves to the Knight's Cross on July 14, 1941.[12] Oskar Dinort died in Cologne-Riehl, North Rhine-Westphalia, on May 29, 1965. He is buried at the *Südfriedhof* in Cologne (Section 51, Grave 306).

Fritz Eyer

Captain Fritz Eyer's key assignments included: Commander, 6th Squadron, 2nd Stuka Wing "Immelmann" (*Sturzkampfgeschwader 2 "Immelmann"*), 1942-1943; Commander, 2nd Group, 102nd Stuka Wing (*Sturzkampfgeschwader 102*), August 25, 1943-October 18, 1943; Commander, 2nd Group, 102nd Ground-Attack Wing (*Schlachtgeschwader 102*), October 18, 1943-January 24, 1944; Commander, 1st Group, 102nd Ground-Attack Wing, June 20, 1944-October 15, 1944 and January 10, 1945-February 4, 1945; and Commander, 1st Group, 103rd Ground-Attack Wing (*Schlachtgeschwader 103*), March 1945-April 16, 1945. He won the *Luftwaffe* Honor Goblet on June 1, 1942 and the German Cross in Gold on September 29, 1942 as a first lieutenant in the 3rd Group, 3rd Stuka Wing (*Sturzkampfgeschwader 3*). He was promoted to Captain (*Hauptmann*) on August 1, 1942. As a squadron commander in the 1st Group, 2nd Stuka Wing, First Lieutenant Eyer took part in seriously damaging the British aircraft carrier *HMS Formidable* off Crete on May 26, 1941.[13]

Ernst Fach

Captain Ernst Fach was born July 6, 1912 in Remscheid, Westphalia. His assignments included: Commander, 9th Squadron (Train), 3rd Bomber Wing "Blitz" (*Kampfgeschwader 3 "Blitz"*). He won the German Cross in Gold on May 22, 1942 as a first lieutenant in the 6th Squadron, 3rd Bomber Wing. He was killed in action on May 15, 1943 at Poltava, Soviet Union. Ernst Fach was posthumously awarded the Knight's Cross of the Iron Cross on September 3, 1943. During his career, he destroyed 8 bridges, 216 locomotives, 2 ammunition trains and 19 tanks.[14]

Hans von Fichte

Brigadier General Hans von Fichte was born in Kassel on September 9, 1894. He entered the German Army on August 11, 1914 as an officer candidate with the Guard Foot Artillery Regiment, but soon transferred to the flying corps. He was wounded in action and later captured by the British at Ypres. Von Fichte left the Army in 1920, rejoined in 1928, and transferred to the *Luftwaffe* on May 1, 1934. His significant *Luftwaffe* assignments included: Adjutant [IIa], 7th Air Division (*7. Flieger-Division*), August 15, 1938-December 19, 1940; Adjutant [IIa], 11th Air Corps (*XI. Flieger-Korps*), December 19, 1940-December 31, 1943; and Commander, Staff Troops, German *Luftwaffe* in the North Balkans, January 1, 1944-November 14, 1944. His promotions included: Lieutenant Colonel (*Oberstleutnant*), October 1, 1937; Colonel (*Oberst*), June 1, 1940; and Brigadier General (*Generalmajor*), April 1, 1944. He was reduced to the grade of lieutenant colonel on November 30, 1944 for reasons unknown. Hans von Fichte died on November 20, 1963.[15]

Hans-Dieter Frank

Major Hans-Dieter Frank was born in Kiel, Schleswig-Holstein, on July 8, 1919. He entered the *Luftwaffe* in November 1937 as an officer candidate and was posted to the 1st Group, 1st Destroyer Wing (*Zerstörergeschwader 1*) in early 1940 as a second lieutenant – the unit later converted to be the 1st Group, 1st Night Fighter Wing (*Nachtjagdgeschwader 1*). He scored his first aerial victory on the night of April 10-11, 1941, and by the end of the year he had five. He was awarded the German Cross in Gold on November 27, 1942. Hans-Dieter Frank won the Knight's Cross of the Iron Cross on June 20, 1943 and became the 417th recipient of the Oak Leaves to the Knight's Cross on March 2, 1944 (posthumous). His significant assignments included: Commander, 2nd Squadron, 1st Night Fighter Wing, August 8, 1942-July 1, 1943; and Commander 1st Group, 1st Night Fighter Wing, July 1, 1943-September 28, 1943. On the night of September 27-28, 1943, Hans-Dieter Frank's Heinkel He 219A-0 crashed into another German night fighter northwest of Celle while attempting to land. Frank bailed out, but was killed. He was posthumously promoted to major. During his career, Hans-Dieter Frank scored 55 nighttime aerial victories.[16]

Heinz Frank

Major Heinz "Allan" Frank was born December 12, 1914 in Arnstadt, Thuringia. He joined the *Luftwaffe* in 1934 and joined the 20th Air Group (*Fliegergruppe 20*), which became the 2nd Group (Stuka), 2nd Demonstration Wing (*Lehrgeschwader 2*) on November 1, 1938. He won the Iron Cross 2nd Class on October 28, 1939, the Iron Cross 1st Class on June 27, 1940, the *Luftwaffe* Honor Goblet on December 22, 1940 and the German Cross in Gold on March 6, 1942. Frank won the Knight's Cross of the Iron Cross on September 3, 1942 as a first lieutenant for flying 500 combat missions. He received the Oak Leaves to the Knight's Cross, the 172nd recipient, on January 8, 1943 for flying his 700th combat mission. Frank's significant wartime assignments included: acting commander, 3rd Squadron, 1st Ground-Attack Wing (*Schlachtgeschwader 1*), January 1943-March 1, 1942; Commander, 3rd Squadron, 1st Ground-Attack Wing (*Schlachtgeschwader 1*), March 1, 1942-March 1943; Commander, Supplemental Ground-Attack Group (*Ergänzungs-Schlachtgruppe*), March 1943-May 31, 1943; acting commander, 2nd Group, 1st Stuka Wing (*Sturzkampfgeschwader 1*), September 24, 1943-October, 1943; Commander, 2nd Group, 2nd Ground-Attack Wing "Immelmann" (*Schlachtgeschwader 2 "Immelmann"*), October 15, 1943-July 1944; Commander, 4th Group, 152nd School Wing (*Schul-Geschwader 152*), July 1944-August 7, 1944; and Commander, 1st Group, 151st School Wing (*Schul-Geschwader 151*), August 7, 1944-October 7, 1944 – the last two assignments with training units. He was promoted to major on June 1, 1943. Frank died in a hospital in Yugoslavia on October 7, 1944 of complications following a shooting accident (his unit was involved in anti-partisan operations in Yugoslavia). Frank is buried in Arnstadt, Thuringia. During the war, Heinz Frank flew 900 combat missions and scored 8 aerial victories, flying Henschel Hs 123, Messerschmitt Me 109 and Focke-Wulf Fw 190 aircraft.[17]

Ernst Frömming

Major Ernst Frömming was born on February 4, 1911 in Rotenburg an der Wümme near Stade in Lower Saxony. He entered the German Army on May 1, 1930 and initially served in the 18th Infantry Regiment. Frömming then transferred to the engineers and was promoted through the enlisted ranks, making master sergeant on June 1, 1938. He fought in the French campaign in 1940 with the Army's 34th Engineer Battalion, winning the Iron Cross 2nd Class on June 12, 1940 and receiving the Iron Cross 1st Class on November 12, 1940. He transferred to the *Luftwaffe* on March 24, 1941 and joined the Paratroop Engineer Battalion (*Fallschirm-Pionier-Bataillon*), jumping into Crete on May 20, 1941 as part of the

German airborne invasion of the island. He was promoted to second and first lieutenant on November 1, 1941. His other promotions included: Captain (*Hauptmann*), May 21, 1943; and Major (*Major*), May 31, 1944. Ernst Frömming received the Knight's Cross of the Iron Cross on November 18, 1944. In November 1943, Frömming became the acting commander of the 1st Paratroop Engineer Battalion (*Fallschirm-Pionier-Bataillon 1*); he assumed full command of the battalion on June 13, 1944.[18]

Werner Gayko

First Lieutenant Werner Gayko was born on May 22, 1923 in Wuhlau/Königsberg, in East Prussia. Gayko joined the German Army in 1940 and transferred to the *Luftwaffe* in 1943. He shot down 13 enemy aircraft during the war, his first coming on November 25, 1943. His significant assignments included: Commander 9th Squadron, 5th Fighter Wing "Polar Sea" (*Jagdgeschwader 5 "Eismeer"*), July 1944-February 1945; and Commander, 5th Squadron, 5th Fighter Wing "Polar Sea," February 1945-May 8, 1945. He won the Iron Cross 2nd and 1st Class, and the Operational Flying Clasp for Fighters in Gold with a 200 Mission Pendant. He survived the war and joined the new German defense forces, retiring as a colonel. Werner Gayko died on October 11, 1994.[19]

Franz Götz

Major Franz Götz was born January 28, 1913 in Obertsrot/Rastatt in Baden. He transferred from the Army to the *Luftwaffe* in 1935 and became a fighter pilot, beginning the war assigned to the 9th Squadron, 53rd Fighter Wing "Ace of Spades" (*Jagdgeschwader 53 "Pikas"*). His assignments included: Commander, 9th Squadron, 53rd Fighter Wing, September 17, 1940-November 1942; Commander, 3rd Group, 53rd Fighter Wing, November 1942-January 28, 1945; and Commodore, 26th Fighter Wing "Schlageter" (*Jagdgeschwader 26 "Schlageter"*), January 28, 1945-May 7, 1945. Franz Götz won the *Luftwaffe* Honor Goblet on November 14, 1940, the German Cross in Gold on October 17, 1941 and the Knight's Cross of the Iron Cross on September 4, 1942. He was promoted to Major (*Major*) on January 1, 1944. He died on May 4, 1980 at Aschaffenburg, Bavaria. During the war, he flew 766 combat missions and scored 63 aerial victories, of which 19 were on the Eastern Front, for a sortie-to-victory ratio of 12.15 to 1.[20]

Kurt von Greiff

Colonel Kurt von Greiff's significant assignments included: Commander, 1st Squadron, 51st Bomber Wing "Edelweiss" (*Kampfgeschwader 51 "Edelweiss"*), 1940; Commander, 1st Group, 51st Bomber Wing "Edelweiss," August 12, 1940-February 14, 1941; Operations Officer [Ia Op 1], 3rd Air Fleet (*Luftflotte 3*), February 15, 1941-May 31, 1941; and Chief Operations Branch, *Luftwaffe* Operations Staff, September 4, 1944-April 28, 1945. He received the German Cross in Gold on January 6, 1943, while a major on the staff of *Luftwaffe* Command Don. He was promoted to Colonel (*Oberst*) on April 1, 1945.[21]

Kurt Gröschke

Colonel Kurt Gröschke was born July 17, 1907 in Berlin-Charlottenburg. Serving in the Police, he became a member of Land Police Group "General Göring" and transferred to the *Luftwaffe* on October 1, 1935. His significant assignments included: Commander, 2nd Battalion, 1st Paratroop Regiment (*Fallschirmjäger-Regiment 1*), February 20, 1942-January 22, 1944 and February 12, 1944-July 24, 1944; acting commander, 1st Paratroop Regiment, January 22, 1944-February 11, 1944; Commander, 15th Paratroop Regiment (*Fallschirmjäger-Regiment 15*), July 24, 1944-April 4, 1945; and acting commander, 5th Paratroop Division (*5. Fallschirmjäger-Division*), April 4, 1945-May 9, 1945. Gröschke won the Iron Cross 2nd Class on October 20, 1939, the Iron Cross 1st Class on May 22, 1940 and the German Cross in Gold on June 21, 1943. He received the Knight's Cross of the Iron Cross on June 9, 1944 and the Oak Leaves to the Knight's Cross on January 9, 1945. His promotions included: Captain (*Hauptmann*), February 1, 1940; Major (*Major*), April 1, 1942; Lieutenant Colonel (*Oberstleutnant*), June 1, 1944; and Colonel (*Oberst*), February 10, 1945. During the war he fought in Holland in 1940, and on Crete during 1941 as the commander of the 2nd Company, 1st Paratroop Regiment. Kurt Gröschke died on March 26, 1996 at Odenthal in North Rhine-Westphalia. He is buried there in the *Stadtfriedhof* (Section 18).[22]

Reinhard Günzel

Lieutenant Colonel Reinhard Günzel was born February 2, 1907 in Posen. He transferred from the Police to the *Luftwaffe* in 1935; in 1938 he served with the Condor Legion in Spain. His significant assignments included: Commander, 2nd Group, 27th Bomber Wing "Boelcke" (*Kampfgeschwader "Boelcke"*), August 1940-January 1943; and Commander,

1st Bomber Observer School (*Kampfbeobachterschule 1*), February 2, 1943-August 11, 1944. He won the Iron Cross 2nd Class on September 16, 1939 and the Iron Cross 1st Class on June 23, 1940. Reinhard Günzel received the Knight's Cross of the Iron Cross on September 17, 1941 as a captain and 2nd Group Commander. He became the 184th recipient of the Oak Leaves to the Iron Cross on January 22, 1943. He also won the German Cross in Gold on September 24, 1942. In 1940, his unit served in the 3rd Air Fleet during the Battle of Britain. In 1941, his unit transferred to Romania and flew during "Operation Barbarossa" in southern Russia. In 1942, the 2nd Group, as part of the 8th Air Corps, flew in support of German Army units at Stalingrad. He was promoted to lieutenant colonel (*Oberstleutnant*) on May 1, 1944. During the entire war, he flew 535 combat missions, mostly in the Heinkel He 111. After the war, Reinhard Günzel joined the new German air force and rose to the grade of lieutenant colonel. He died on October 29, 1970 at Plön, Schleswig-Holstein.[23]

Anton Hackl

Major Anton "Toni" Hackl was born on March 25, 1915 at Regensburg, Bavaria. He joined the Army in 1932, serving with an infantry regiment, before transferring to the *Luftwaffe* and completing pilot training in the autumn of 1936. Sergeant Toni Hackl joined the 2nd Group, 333rd Fighter Wing (*Jagdgeschwader 333*) – later to become the 2nd Group, 77th Fighter Wing "Ace of Hearts" (*Jagdgeschwader 77 "Herzas"*) – on April 1, 1938. His significant wartime assignments included: Commander, 5th Squadron, 77th Fighter Wing, October 1, 1941-February 4, 1943; Commander, 3rd Group, 11th Fighter Wing (*Jagdgeschwader 11*), October 1, 1943-April 1944; Commodore, 11th Fighter Wing, April 1944-April 15, 1944; Commodore, 76th Fighter Wing (*Jagdgeschwader 76*), July 1944-October 8, 1944; Commander, 2nd Group, 26th Fighter Wing "Schlageter" (*Jagdgeschwader 26 "Schlageter"*), October 9, 1944-January 30, 1945; acting commodore, 300th Fighter Wing (*Jagdgeschwader 300*), January 30, 1945-February 20, 1945; and Commodore, 11th Fighter Wing, February 20, 1945-May 8, 1945. He received the Iron Cross 2nd Class on March 6, 1940 and the Iron Cross 1st Class on July 2, 1940. Anton Hackl received the Knight's Cross of the Iron Cross on May 25, 1942. He received the Oak Leaves to the Knight's Cross on August 6, 1943. He won the Swords to the Oak Leaves on July 13, 1944. He was promoted to Major (*Major*) on May 1, 1944. Anton Hackl survived the war and died on July 9, 1984 in Regensburg, Bavaria. He flew about 1000 combat missions and shot down 192 enemy aircraft, for a sortie-to-victory ratio of 5.20 to 1. Some 131 of his victories were over the Eastern front, and of the 61 victories in Africa and over the Western Front, 34 were four-engine bombers. He was shot down 8 times and wounded 4 times. He is buried in Regensburg at the *Oberen Katholischen Friedhof* (Section 8 b, Grave 31.)[24]

Franz Hahn

First Lieutenant Franz Hahn's significant assignments included: Commander, 2nd Squadron, 77th Fighter Wing "Ace of Hearts" (*Jagdgeschwader 77 "Herzas"*), August 31, 1940-November 21, 1940; and Commander, 11th Squadron, 51st Fighter Wing "Mölders" (*Jagdgeschwader 51 "Mölders"*), November 21, 1940-July 31, 1942. He received the German Cross in Gold on April 3, 1944 after being killed in action on January 22, 1944, while serving with the 4th Fighter Wing (*Jagdgeschwader 4*). Hahn shot down approximately 20 enemy aircraft.[25]

Gotthardt Handrick

Colonel Gotthardt Handrick was born October 25, 1908 in Zittau, Saxony. He won the Olympic Gold Medal for Germany in 1936 for the Modern Pentathlon. His *Luftwaffe* assignments included: Commander, 88th Fighter Group [Spain] (*Jagdgruppe 88*, [J/88]), July 18, 1937-September 10, 1938; Commander, 1st Group, 26th Fighter Wing "Schlageter" (*Jagdgeschwader 26 "Schlageter"*), September 11, 1938-June 24, 1940; Commodore, 26th Fighter Wing "Schlageter," June 24, 1940-August 21, 1940; Commander, 2nd Supplemental Fighter Group (*Ergänzungs-Jagdgruppe 2*), August 26, 1940-October 7, 1940; Commander, 3rd Group, 52nd Fighter Wing (*Jagdgeschwader 52*), October 15, 1940-June 22, 1941; Commodore, 77th Fighter Wing "Ace of Hearts" (*Jagdgeschwader 77 "Herzas"*), June 23, 1941-February, 1942; Commodore, 5th Fighter Wing "Polar Sea" (*Jagdgeschwader 5 "Eismeer"*), May 1, 1942-September 11, 1943; Fighter Commander Ostmark (*Jagdfliegerführer Ostmark*), September 1943-June 15, 1944; and Commander, 8th Fighter Division (*8. Jagddivision*), June 15, 1944-May 8, 1945. He won the Spanish Cross in Gold with Swords. He also won the German Cross in Gold on October 17, 1943. He was promoted to Colonel (*Oberst*) on October 1, 1943. Handrick shot down 20 enemy aircraft, including 5 in Spain. Gotthardt Handrick died on May 30, 1978 in Gross-Hansdorf (Hamburg). He is buried in Murnau am Staffelsee, Bavaria (Section 13, Row 4, Grave 42).[26]

Martin Harlinghausen

Major General Martin Harlinghausen was born January 17, 1902 in Rheda, Westphalia. He entered the German Navy on April 1, 1923 and spent over ten years in naval positions relating to torpedoes and naval aviation. On October 1, 1933 Harlinghausen transferred to the *Luftwaffe*, where he initially continued to serve in those same areas of expertise. He also served for a year as the commander of the sea reconnaissance squadron (*Aufklärungsstaffel See* [AS/88]) in the Condor Legion fighting in the Spanish Civil War. Harlinghausen's significant assignments included: Chief of Staff, 10th Air Corps (*X. Fliegerkorps*), November 1, 1939-March 31, 1941; Air Commander Atlantic (*Fliegerführer Atlantik*), March 31, 1941-January 5, 1942; Air Commander Tunisia (*Fliegerführer Tunisien*), November 9, 1942-February 22, 1943; acting commander, 2nd Air Corps (*II. Fliegerkorps*), February 23, 1943-June 25, 1943; Commander, 14th Air District Wiesbaden (*Luftgau XIV*), September 21, 1944-April 26, 1945; and Commander, *Luftwaffe* Command West (*Luftwaffen-Kommandos West)*, April 27, 1945-May 8, 1945. Harlinghausen's promotions included: Major (*Major*), August 1, 1938); Lieutenant Colonel (*Oberstleutnant*), January 30, 1941; Colonel (*Oberst*), July 1, 1942; Brigadier General (*Generalmajor*), December 1, 1942; and Major General (*Generalleutnant*), December 1, 1944. He received the Iron Cross 2nd Class on January 30, 1940, the Iron Cross 1st Class on February 3, 1940, the Knight's Cross of the Iron Cross on May 4, 1940 and the Oak Leaves to the Knight's Cross on January 30, 1941 (the 8th recipient of the award). He also was awarded the Combined Pilot's and Observer's Badge in Gold with Diamonds, and the Spanish Cross in Gold with Diamonds. Harlinghausen joined the new German Air Force in 1957 and served as the Commanding General, *Luftwaffen* Group North, before differences of opinion with the German Defense Minister caused him to retire in 1961. Martin Harlinghausen died March 22, 1986 in Gütersloh, Westphalia. He is buried there at the *Johannesfriedhof* (Protestant area, Section 1, Grave 127/129).[27]

Richard Heidrich

Lieutenant General Richard Heidrich was born July 28, 1896 in Lawalde/Löbau, Saxony. He entered the Army on August 18, 1914, at the beginning of World War I. During that conflict, Heidrich won both the Iron Cross 2nd and 1st Class. Between the wars, Heidrich served in the infantry and was an instructor at the Infantry School in Dresden and the War Academy at Potsdam, before transferring to the *Luftwaffe* on January 1, 1939. His key *Luftwaffe* assignments included: Commander, 3rd Paratroop Regiment (*Fallschirmjäger-Regiment 3*), June 1, 1940-July 31, 1942; Commander, 7th Air Division (*7. Fliegerdivision*), August 1, 1942-April 30, 1943; Commander, 1st Paratroop Division (*1. Fallschirmjäger-Division*), May 1, 1943-November 16, 1944; and Commander, 1st Paratroop Corps (*I. Fallschirmkorps*), November 16, 1944-May 3, 1945. His promotions included: Lieutenant Colonel (*Oberstleutnant*), January 1, 1939; Colonel (*Oberst*), April 20, 1940; Brigadier General (*Generalmajor*), August 4, 1942; Major General (*Generalleutnant*), July 1, 1943; and Lieutenant General (*General der Fallschirmtruppe*), October 31, 1944. Heidrich won the 1939 Clasp to the Iron Cross 2nd Class on May 25, 1941 and the 1939 Clasp to the Iron Cross 1st Class the same day. He received the Knight's Cross of the Iron Cross on June 14, 1941 for his actions during the airborne invasion of Crete, and won the Oak Leaves to the Knight's Cross on February 5, 1944. Richard Heidrich also received the Swords to the Oak Leaves (the 55th recipient) on March 25, 1944. He died on December 22, 1947 at Hamburg-Bahrenfeld.[28]

Joachim Helbig

Colonel Joachim Helbig was born September 10, 1915 in Börln/Grimma, Saxony. He joined the German Army's 4th Artillery Regiment in 1935 and transferred to the *Luftwaffe* the following year. His key assignments included: Commander, 4th Squadron, 1st Demonstration Wing (*Lehrgeschwader 1*), June 1940-November 5, 1941; Commander, 1st Group (Bomber), 1st Demonstration Wing, November 5, 1941-January 24, 1943; and Commodore, 1st Demonstration Wing, August 14, 1943-May 1, 1945. Helbig received the Iron Cross 2nd Class on September 16, 1939 and the Iron Cross 1st Class on June 20, 1940. On October 6, 1940, he won the *Luftwaffe* Honor Goblet and followed that by receiving the Knight's Cross of the Iron Cross on November 24, 1940. Helbig received the Oak Leaves to the Knight's Cross on January 16, 1942 and the Swords – as the 20th recipient – on September 28, 1942. He was promoted to Colonel (*Oberst*) on July 1, 1944. In September 1944, he was seriously wounded, when his staff car was strafed by enemy fighters in the Eifel. An independent officer, he ran afoul of Field Marshal Wolfram von Richthofen and Albert Kesselring during the war. After the war, he became the manager of a brewery in Berlin. Joachim Helbig died on October 5, 1985 in Malente, Spain in an auto accident.[29]

Dietrich Hrabak

Colonel Dietrich Hrabak was born December 19, 1914 in Gross Deuben/Leipzig, Saxony. He entered the German Navy in April 1934 and transferred to the *Luftwaffe* in November 1935 as an officer cadet. His *Luftwaffe* assignments included: Commander, 1st Squadron, 76th Fighter Wing (*Jagdgeschwader 76*), May 1, 1939-July 6, 1940; Commander, 4th Squadron, 54th Fighter Wing "Green Hearts" (*Jagdgeschwader 54 "Grünherz"*), July 6, 1940-August 5, 1940; Commander, 2nd Group, 54th Fighter Wing, August 5, 1940-November 1, 1942; Commodore, 52nd Fighter Wing (*Jagdgeschwader 52*), November 1, 1942-October 1, 1944; and Commodore, 54th Fighter Wing, October 1, 1944-May 8, 1945. He won the Knight's Cross of the Iron Cross on October 21, 1940 and the Oak Leaves to the Knight's Cross on November 25, 1943. He also received the *Luftwaffe* Honor Goblet on September 28, 1940 and the German Cross in Gold on July 10, 1944. He was promoted to Colonel (*Oberst*) on September 1, 1944. During the war, Dietrich Hrabak flew over 1,000 combat missions and shot down 125 enemy aircraft; 16 victories occurred in the West. Dietrich Hrabak died September 15, 1995 in Pfaffenhofen, Bavaria.[30] He is buried in Fürstenfeldbruck, Bavaria, at the Fürstenfeldbruck *Waldfriedhof* (Section 4, Grave 202).[31]

Joachim-Friedrich Huth

Brigadier General Joachim-Friedrich Huth was born on July 31, 1896 in Neuhof/Salzwedel in Saxony. He entered the Army on July 13, 1914 and served as an infantry platoon leader and company commander before becoming a fighter pilot. In this role, he served in the 14th Fighter Squadron before being seriously wounded on March 23, 1918 – he would spend more than a year in a hospital and have a leg amputated. Huth left the Army in 1920 after serving in *Freikorps Küttner*.[32] He joined the *Luftwaffe* on March 1, 1934. His significant assignments included: Commander, 2nd Group, 132nd Fighter Wing "Richthofen" (*Jagdgeschwader 132 "Richthofen"*), August 1, 1938-October 31, 1938; Commander, 1st Group, 1st Destroyer Wing (*Zerstörergeschwader 1*), November 1, 1938-December 14, 1939; Commodore, 26th Destroyer Wing "Horst Wessel" (*Zerstörergeschwader 26 "Horst Wessel"*), December 14, 1939-November 1, 1940; Commander, 2nd Destroyer School, Memmingen (*Zerstörer-Schule 2*), November 2, 1940-July 31, 1941; 2nd Fighter Commander (*Jagdfliegerführer 2*), August 1, 1941-August 16, 1942; acting commander, 4th Fighter Division (*4. Jagd-Division*), August 17, 1942-August 14, 1943; Commander, 4th Fighter Division, August 14, 1943-November 10, 1943; Commander 5th Fighter Division (*5. Jagd-Division*), November 11, 1943-February 5, 1944; Commander, 7th Fighter Division (*7. Jagd-Division*), February 6, 1944-November 30, 1944; acting commander, 2nd Fighter Corps (*II. Jagd-Korps*), November 30, 1944-January 26, 1945; and Commander, 2nd Fighter Corps, January 26, 1945-May 8, 1945. He was awarded the Knight's Cross of the Iron Cross on September 11, 1940. Huth's promotions included: Lieutenant Colonel (*Oberstleutnant*), January 1, 1939; Colonel (*Oberst*), November 1, 1940; Brigadier General (*Generalmajor*), April 1, 1943; and Major General (*Generalleutnant*), July 1, 1944. After the war, Huth joined the new German air force in 1956 and rose to the grade of major general. Joachim-Friedrich Huth died at Koblenz, Rhineland-Pfalz, on March 27, 1962.[33]

Max-Josef Ibel

Brigadier General Max-Josef Ibel was born January 2, 1896 in Munich, Bavaria. Ibel entered the Army on July 5, 1915 and served in various engineer units during the war, to include a flamethrower regiment. He retired from the Army as a first lieutenant in 1928 (to train at Lipezk, Russia), but was re-activated in 1931. He joined the *Luftwaffe* on April 1, 1934. His significant *Luftwaffe* assignments included: Commander, 1st Group, 135th Fighter Wing (*Jagdgeschwader 135*), March 1, 1937-October 31, 1938; Commodore, 231st (later 3rd) Fighter Wing (*Jagdgeschwader 231/3*), November 7, 1938-September 26, 1939; Commodore, 27th Fighter Wing (*Jagdgeschwader 27*), September 27, 1939-October 12, 1940; Commander, 4th Fighter School, Fürth (*Jagdfliegerschule 4*), October 13, 1940-June 5, 1941; 3rd Fighter Commander (*Jagdfliegerführer 3*), June 6, 1941-November 30, 1942; Higher Fighter Commander West (*Höherer Jagdfliegerführer West*), December 1, 1942-September 14, 1943; and Commander, 2nd Fighter Division (*2. Jagd-Division*), October 1, 1943-December 31, 1944. His promotions included: Lieutenant Colonel (*Oberstleutnant*), June 1, 1938; Colonel (*Oberst*), July 21, 1940; and Brigadier General (*Generalmajor*), January 1, 1944. He received the Knight's Cross of the Iron Cross on August 22, 1940. Ibel was in charge of the Fighter Control Board on the battlecruiser Scharnhorst during "Operation Cerberus," the surprise dash up the English Channel by three major warships of the *Kriegsmarine* – the *Scharnhorst*, *Gneisenau* and heavy cruiser *Prinz Eugen* – February 11-13, 1942. He joined the new German air force in 1957 and rose to the grade of brigadier general. Max-Josef Ibel died on March 19, 1981 at Rheinbach, North Rhine-Westphalia. He is buried at the *Waldfriedhof* (Old Section) in Munich (Section 96, Row W, Grave 40).[34]

Eberhard Jakob

Major Eberhard Jacob was born January 18, 1917 in Taulkinnen, East Prussia. During 1939 and 1940, he served as a pilot and group adjutant in the 2nd Group, 2nd Stuka Wing "Immelmann" (*Sturzkampfgeschwader 2 "Immelmann"*) in both the Polish and French campaigns. Jacob won the *Luftwaffe* Honor Goblet on March 18, 1942 and the German Cross in Gold on April 24, 1942. Captain Eberhard Jacob received the Knight's Cross of the Iron Cross on February 29, 1944. He died February 27, 1982 at Bad Orb in Hesse. He is buried there at the *Stadtfriedhof* (Section 27, Grave 143/144).[35]

Johannes Janke

Captain Johannes Janke's significant assignments included: Commander, 7th Squadron, 134th Fighter Wing (*Jagdgeschwader 134*), March 15, 1936-March 3, 1937; Commander, 11th Squadron, 132nd Fighter Wing (*Jagdgeschwader 132*), March 3, 1937-July 1, 1938; Commander, 4th Group, 132nd Fighter Wing, July 1, 1938-October 31, 1938; Commander, 1st Group, 331st Fighter Wing (*Jagdgeschwader 331*), October 31, 1938-May 1, 1939; Commander, 1st Group, 77th Fighter Wing "Ace of Hearts" (*Jagdgeschwader 77 "Herzas"*), May 1, 1939-November 21, 1940; and Commander, 4th Group, 51st Fighter Wing (*Jagdgeschwader 51*), November 21, 1940-February 18, 1941.[36]

Karl Kennel

Major Karl Kennel was born on January 17, 1914 at Pirmasens in the Pfalz. Originally a policeman in Ludwigshaven, he joined the *Luftwaffe* on May 9, 1935. He underwent military training at Schleissheim before learning to fly at Weimar and Oldenburg. In May 1938, Kennel was assigned to the 132nd Fighter Wing "Richthofen" (*Jagdgeschwader 132 "Richthofen"*), but then transferred to a Destroyer unit. At the beginning of World War II, Corporal Kennel was serving with the 1st Group, 26th Destroyer Wing "Horst Wessel" (*Zerstörergeschwader 26 "Horst Wessel"*). He received the *Luftwaffe* Honor Goblet on September 9, 1941. On March 16, 1942, Kennel was awarded the German Cross in Gold. On September 19, 1943, Captain Karl Kennel was awarded the Knight's Cross of the Iron Cross for flying 500 combat missions and achieving 28 aerial victories. Captain Karl Kennel was awarded the Oak Leaves to the Knight's Cross (the 666th *Wehrmacht* soldier to be so honored) on November 25, 1944 for 800 combat missions. In October 1942, First Lieutenant Kennel was appointed commander of the 5th Squadron, 1st Ground-Attack Wing (*Schlachtgeschwader 1*); on November 11, 1943, he was appointed the commander of 1st Group, 152nd Ground-Attack Wing (*Schlachtgeschwader 152*). He was appointed the acting commander of 2nd Group, 2nd Ground-Attack Wing "Immelmann" (*Schlachtgeschwader 2 "Immelmann"*) on July 29, 1944. Karl Kennel died on July 1, 1999 at Pirmasens. He is buried there at the *Waldfriedhof* (Section 2a, Row 1, Grave 44).[37]

Otto Kittel

First Lieutenant Otto Kittel was born on February 21, 1917 in Kronsdorf in the Sudetenland. He entered the *Luftwaffe* in January 1939 and ten months later attended pilot training. In February 1941 he reported to the 2nd Squadron, 54th Fighter Wing "Green Hearts" (*Jagdgeschwader 54 "Grünherz"*); on May 31, Sergeant Kittel suffered technical difficulties in a Messerschmitt Me 109F-2, necessitating a bail out near Spiekeroog on the North Sea and was injured. He achieved his first aerial victory on June 23, 1941, shooting down two Russian SB-2 twin-engine bombers. He recorded his 10th victory on September 12, 1941 and his 20th one year later on September 23, 1942. On December 21, 1942, he received the *Luftwaffe* Honor Goblet. On January 12, 1943, Kittel claimed six enemy aircraft shot down; he achieved his 30th victory on January 24, 1943. On February 19, 1943, Technical Sergeant Kittel recorded his 39th victory, which was also *Jagdgeschwader 54's* 4,000th of the war. On March 15, 1943, Kittel made an emergency landing in his Fw 190A-4, 35 miles into Russian territory. He crossed the frozen Lake Ilmen and, after three days, finally reached German territory. After hospitalization, he returned to the 2nd Squadron at the end of May. On June 11, Kittel recorded his 50th victory; his 80th came on July 27 and his 100th on September 14. On October 26, 1943, Master Sergeant Otto Kittel received the Knight's Cross of the Iron Cross for 123 victories. By the end of 1943, Kittel had 127 victories to his credit. In January 1944, Kittel was transferred as an instructor to Supplemental Fighter Group East (*Ergänzungs-Jagdgruppe Ost*) based at Biarritz, France. He was promoted to second lieutenant during his tenure there and served with the unit until March, when he returned to the 54th Fighter Wing to take up the appointment as the 3rd Squadron Commander. He claimed his 140th kill on March 30; with his score at 152, Second Leutnant Kittel was awarded the Oak Leaves to the Knight's Cross on April 11, 1944. By August 26, 1944 he recorded his 200th victory, flying an Fw

190A-6. On November 25, 1944 First Lieutenant Kittel was awarded the Swords to the Knight's Cross for 239 victories. On February 16, 1945 Otto Kittel took off in his Fw 190A-8 to intercept a flight of Russian Il-2 Sturmovik ground-attack aircraft over Dzukste, Courland. Diving into a formation of eight of the ground-attack aircraft at an altitude of about 500 feet he damaged one, but was hit by return fire, probably from the rear gunners from the other Il-2s. His aircraft burst into flames, plummeted to earth, trailing a long sheet of flame and smoke and crashed, killing him instantly. Otto Kittel flew 583 combat missions and recorded 267 victories (including at least 94 Il-2 Sturmovik ground-attack aircraft), placing him the fourth highest scoring ace of all time and giving him a sortie-to-victory ratio of 2.18 to 1.[38]

Walter Koch

Lieutenant Colonel Walter Koch was born September 10, 1910 in Bonn. He served in the German Police from 1929 to 1935 when he transferred to the *Luftwaffe* as a second lieutenant and joined the "General Göring" Regiment. His significant *Luftwaffe* assignments included: Commander, 1st Company, 1st Paratroop Regiment (*Fallschirmjäger-Regiment 1*), April 1, 1938-October 30, 1939; Commander, Assault Detachment Koch (*Fallschirmjäger-Sturm-Abteilung Koch*), October 30, 1939-July 17, 1940; Commander, 1st Battalion, 1st Paratroop Regiment, July 17, 1940-May 20, 1941; and Commander 5th Paratroop Regiment (*Fallschirmjäger-Regiment 5*), April 1, 1942-April 21, 1943. His promotions included: First Lieutenant (*Oberleutnant*), September 1, 1935; Captain (*Hauptmann*), April 20, 1938; Major (*Major*), May 16, 1940; and Lieutenant Colonel (*Oberstleutnant*), April 20, 1942. On May 10, 1940, Walter Koch won the Knight's Cross of the Iron Cross for leading the successful airborne assault against the Belgian fortress of Eben-Emael. He also won the German Cross in Gold on April 20, 1942. He was shot in the head and seriously wounded on May 20, 1941 on Hill 107 – near Máleme – during the German airborne invasion of Crete and spent several months in a hospital. Lieutenant Colonel Walter Koch died in a car accident on October 23, 1943 near Berlin. He is buried in the Bonn *Nordfriedhof* in the military section (Grave 8).[39]

Paul Koester

Colonel Paul Koester's significant assignments included: Commodore, 51st Bomber Wing "Edelweiss" (*Kampfgeschwader 51 "Edelweiss"*), September 1, 1941-July 4, 1942; and Commander, 2nd Bomber Observer School (*Kampfbeobachterschule 2*), 1943.[40]

Benno Kosch

Colonel Benno Kosch was born March 12, 1895 in Rovereto/Trient in Austria-Hungary. His assignments included: Commander, 2nd Group, 1st Bomber Wing "Hindenburg" (*Kampfgeschwader 1 "Hindenburg"*), February 1, 1940-February 1, 1941; Commodore, 55th Bomber Wing "Attack" (*Kampfgeschwader 55 "Greiff"*), February 1, 1941-August 18, 1942; Commander, 2nd Bomber Observer School (*Kampfbeobachterschule 2*), August 26, 1942-September 12, 1942; and 2nd Air Commander (*Fliegerführer 2*), January 3, 1943-February 1, 1943. During the Battle of Britain, in a bombing mission over London, Kosch was wounded three times, and his Heinkel He 111 lost one of two engines, but he managed to fly his stricken aircraft safely back to France. He won the Knight's Cross of the Iron Cross on October 1, 1940. He was promoted to Colonel (*Oberst*) on April 1, 1942. Benno Kosch died on June 16, 1975 in Vienna, Austria.[41]

Robert Kowalewski

Lieutenant Colonel Robert Kowalewski was born in Berlin, Brandenburg, on March 15, 1914. He began the war flying bomber missions as part of the 10th Air Corps. Kowalewski's significant assignments included: Commander, 6th Squadron, 26th Bomber Wing (*Kampfgeschwader 26*), January 1, 1941-January 17, 1941; Commander, 2nd Group, 26th Bomber Wing, January 18, 1941-May 14, 1941; Commander, 40th Bomber Wing (*Kampfgeschwader 40*), August 1941-September 1943; Commodore, 76th Destroyer Wing (*Zerstörergeschwader 76*), January 25, 1944-July 24, 1944; Commodore, 2nd Night Fighter Wing (*Nachtjagdgeschwader 2*), August 1944-November 1944; and Commodore, 76th Bomber Wing (*Kampfgeschwader 76*), November 1944-May 1945. He received the Knight's Cross of the Iron Cross on November 24, 1940. He also won the *Luftwaffe* Honor Goblet on September 28, 1940 and the German Cross in Gold on July 2, 1942. He was promoted to lieutenant colonel (*Oberstleutnant*) on September 1, 1944. He shot down 2 enemy aircraft as a bomber pilot. Robert Kowalewski died July 5, 1996 in Herdecke in the Ruhr, North Rhine-Westphalia.[42]

Hans Kroh

Brigadier General Hans Kroh was born May 13, 1907 in Heidelberg, Baden. He entered the German Police in 1926 and later became the commander of the 2nd Company, Police Regiment "General Göring". Kroh transferred to the *Luftwaffe* on April 1, 1936 as a first lieutenant. His significant *Luftwaffe* assignments included: Operations Officer, 7th Air Division (*Ia, Flieger-Division 7*), June 1, 1939-August 1, 1940; Commander, 1st Battalion, 2nd Paratroop Regiment (*Fallschirmjäger-Regiment 2*), August 8, 1940-July 1, 1942; acting commander, Battle Group Kroh, Paratroop Brigade Ramcke (*Kampfgruppe Kroh, Fallschirmjäger-Brigade Ramcke*), July 1, 1942-November 30, 1942; acting commander, Paratroop Brigade Ramcke (*Fallschirmjäger-Brigade Ramcke*), November 30, 1942-February 18, 1943; acting commander, 2nd Paratroop Regiment, March 1, 1943-November 20, 1943; acting commander, 2nd Paratroop Division (*2. Fallschirmjäger-Division*), November 20, 1943-December 11, 1943; Commander, 2nd Paratroop Regiment, December 16, 1943-March 17, 1944; and acting commander, 2nd Paratroop Division, March 17, 1944-September 18, 1944. His promotions included: Captain (*Hauptmann*), October 1, 1937; Major (*Major*), March 1, 1941; Lieutenant Colonel (*Oberstleutnant*), January 11, 1943; Colonel (*Oberst*), April 6, 1944; and Brigadier General (*Generalmajor*), September 13, 1944. He won the Knight's Cross of the Iron Cross on August 21, 1941, the Oak Leaves to the Knight's Cross on April 6, 1944, and the Swords to the Oak Leaves on September 12, 1944. He also won the German Cross in Gold on December 24, 1942. American troops captured him at Brest, France on September 18, 1944 and held him as a prisoner of war for almost four years. Later, Kroh entered the *Bundeswehr*, retiring in 1962 as a major general. Hans Kroh died on July 8, 1967 in Braunschweig.[43]

Kurt Kuhlmey

Colonel Kurt Kuhlmey was born in Insterburg, East Prussia on November 19, 1913. He entered the *Luftwaffe* in April 1934. His assignments included: Commander, 2nd Group, 3rd Stuka Wing (*Sturzkampfgeschwader 3*), April 1, 1942-March 31, 1943; Commodore, 3rd Stuka Wing, April 1, 1943-October 18, 1943; Commodore, 3rd Ground-Attack Wing (*Schlachtgeschwader 3*), October 18, 1943-February 1945; and Commodore, 2nd Ground-Attack Wing "Immelmann" (*Schlachtgeschwader 2 "Immelmann"*), March 14, 1945-April 20, 1945. Kuhlmey received the Knight's Cross of the Iron Cross on July 15, 1942. He also won the German Cross in Gold on November 5, 1941. His promotions included: Captain (*Hauptmann*), April 1, 1941; Major (*Major*), January 1, 1943; Lieutenant Colonel (*Oberstleutnant*), November 1, 1943; and Colonel (*Oberst*), November 1, 1944. He flew 500 combat missions and was shot down twice. Kurt Kuhlmey died on April 30, 1993 in Bonn.[44]

Bruno Loerzer

Colonel General Bruno Loerzer was born January 22, 1891 in Berlin, Brandenburg. Entering the Army in 1911, he subsequently attended pilot training during World War I, later serving in the 26th Fighter Squadron (*Jagdstaffel 26*) and as the commander of the 3rd Fighter Wing (*Jagdgeschwader 3*). A close friend of fellow aviator Hermann Göring (at Verdun, Loerzer flew a reconnaissance plane, while Göring sat in the rear as the observer), Loerzer shot down 44 aircraft and received the *Pour le Mérite*. During the 1920s, he was active in civil aviation and helped form the Lithuanian Air Force. Always well-connected (his brother was a *Gauleiter* of Braunschweig), he assumed duties as the President of the German Air Sports League in 1933 and became the National Air Sport Leader in 1935. He rejoined the *Luftwaffe* in 1935, rising to be: Commodore, 53rd Fighter Wing (*Jagdgeschwader 53*), July 15, 1937-March 31, 1938; Inspector of Fighters, April 1, 1938-January 31, 1939; Commander, 2nd Air Division (*2. Flieger-Division*), February 1, 1939-October 10, 1939; Commander, 2nd Air Corps (*II. Fliegerkorps*), October 25, 1939-February 22, 1943; and the Chief of the *Luftwaffe* Personnel Department (*Chef des Luftwaffen-Personalamts*), February 23, 1943-December 20, 1944, before going on the *Führer* Reserve list. His promotions included: Brigadier General (*Generalmajor*), April 1, 1938; Major General (*Generalleutnant*), January 1, 1940; Lieutenant General (*General der Flieger*), July 19, 1940; and Colonel General (*Generaloberst*), February 16, 1943. He received the Knight's Cross of the Iron Cross on May 29, 1940. Bruno Loerzer died in Hamburg on August 22, 1960.[45]

Eric Macard

Colonel Eric Macard's assignments included: Commander, Pilot School (C) 4, (*Flugzeugführerschule* (C) 4), 1939; and Commander, Pilot School (C) 3, (*Flugzeugführerschule* (C) 3), March 4, 1939-October 9, 1941.[46]

Günther von Maltzahn

Colonel Günther "Henri" von Maltzahn was born October 20, 1910 in Wodarg/Demmin. Originally in the Army in a cavalry regiment, he transferred to the *Luftwaffe* and soon became the adjutant of the 1st Group, 234th Fighter Wing (*Jagdgeschwader 234*). His significant assignments included: Commander, 6th Squadron, 334th Fighter Wing (*Jagdgeschwader 334*), July 1, 1937-April 1, 1939; Commander, 6th Squadron, 53rd Fighter Wing "Ace of Spades" (*Jagdgeschwader 53 "Pikas"*), April 1, 1939-August 18, 1939; Commander, 2nd Group, 53rd Fighter Wing, August 19, 1939-October 8, 1940; Commodore, 53rd Fighter Wing, October 9, 1940-October 4, 1943; and Fighter Leader Upper Italy (*Jagdfliegerführer Oberitalien*), December 4, 1943-August 29, 1944. He won the Knight's Cross of the Iron Cross on December 30, 1940 and the Oak Leaves to the Knight's Cross on July 24, 1941. He also won the *Luftwaffe* Honor Goblet on March 23, 1942 and the German Cross in Gold on December 23, 1942. He was promoted to Colonel (*Oberst*) on December 1, 1943. Von Maltzahn made numerous forced landings including an emergency landing on June 26, 1941 after being hit by enemy anti-aircraft fire, a belly-landing on June 29, 1941 after damage in aerial combat, another belly-landing on July 15, 1941 after damage sustained in aerial combat, and was actually shot down on May 11, 1942 in combat with a Spitfire. Günther von Maltzahn died on June 24, 1953 in Düsseldorf, North Rhine-Westphalia. He flew 497 combat missions and scored 68 kills, a sortie-to-victory ratio of 7.3 to 1. His total included 18 aircraft in the Mediterranean theater.[47]

Eitel-Friedrich Roediger von Manteuffel

Brigadier General Eitel-Friedrich Roediger von Manteuffel was born in Rastatt, Baden on September 24, 1895. He entered the Army on March 22, 1914 and initially served in the 109th Infantry Regiment. Von Manteuffel then underwent observer and flight training and spent the remainder of World War I in numerous fighter assignments to include the 14th Fighter Squadron and the 2nd Fighter Squadron. Released from active duty on March 31, 1920, he joined the *Luftwaffe* on January 1, 1936 and resumed his flying career. Von Manteuffel's key assignments included: Commodore, 77th Fighter Wing "Ace of Hearts" (*Jagdgeschwader 77 "Herz As"*), October 1, 1939-March 31, 1941; Fighter Commander Center (*Jagdfliegerführer Mitte*), April 1, 1941-September 30, 1941; Liaison to the Hungarian Air Force, October 1, 1941-September 1943; and Chief, *Luftwaffe* Mission in Romania, March 21, 1944-August 28, 1944. His promotions included: Lieutenant Colonel (*Oberstleutnant*), January 1, 1938; Colonel (*Oberst*), September 1, 1940; and Brigadier General (*Generalmajor*), October 1, 1944. The Soviets captured von Manteuffel in Romania on August 28, 1944 and held him as a prisoner of war until January 3, 1950. Eitel-Friedrich Roediger von Manteuffel died July 31, 1984 at Wiesbaden, Hesse. He is buried in Freiburg im Breisgau.[48]

Gerd von Massow

Major General Gerd von Massow was born in Hadersleben/Nordschleswig on September 13, 1896. He entered the Army on August 10, 1914 and spent all of World War I in the 7th Jäger Battalion. After a brief stint of service in a *Freikorps*, von Massow returned to infantry duty before undergoing secret flight training in the United States in 1930 and 1931. Von Massow's key assignments included: Commander, Fighter School Schleissheim (*Jagdfliegerschule*), April 1, 1935-June 8, 1936; Commodore, 132nd Fighter Wing "Richthofen" (*Jagdgeschwader 132 "Richthofen"*), June 9, 1936-November 1, 1938; Commodore, 131st Fighter Wing (*Jagdgeschwader 131*), November 1, 1938-May 1, 1939; Commodore, 2nd Fighter Wing "Richthofen" (*Jagdgeschwader 2 "Richthofen"*), May 1, 1939-March 7, 1940; 3rd Fighter Commander (*Jagdfliegerführer 3*), March 8, 1940-June 5, 1940; Inspector of Fighters (*Inspekteur der Jagdflieger*), June 6, 1940-December 18, 1940; Higher Commander for Fighter and Destroyer Schools, December 19, 1940-July 30, 1944; and Commanding General for Flight Training, July 31, 1944-May 8, 1945. Von Massow's promotions included: Lieutenant Colonel (*Oberstleutnant*), April 1, 1937; Colonel (*Oberst*), October 1, 1939; Brigadier General (*Generalmajor*), April 1, 1943; and Major General (*Generalleutnant*), April 20, 1945. Gerd von Massow died on June 29, 1967 at Bad Pyrmont, North Rhine-Westphalia.[49]

Eugen Meindl

Lieutenant General Eugen Meindl was born on July 16, 1892 in Donaueschingen, Baden. Meindl entered the German Army in 1912 and won the Iron Cross 2nd and 1st Class during World War I as an artillery lieutenant. At the start of World War II Meindl commanded the 112th Mountain Artillery Regiment, fighting in Poland in 1939 and Narvik in 1940. He transferred to the *Luftwaffe* on November 1, 1940. His significant *Luftwaffe* assignments included: Commander, Paratroop Air Assault Regiment (*Fallschirmjäger-Luftlande-Sturm-Regiment*), August 9, 1940-May 20, 1941; Commander, *Luftwaffe* Division "Meindl" (*Luftwaffen-Division "Meindl"*), February 26, 1942-October 1, 1942; Commander, 13th Air Corps (*XIII. Fliegerkorps*), October 1, 1942-August 1, 1943;

and Commander, 2nd Paratroop Corps (*II. Fallschirmkorps*), November 5, 1943-May 25, 1945. His promotions included: Brigadier General (*Generalmajor*), January 1, 1941; Major General (*Generalleutnant*), February 1, 1943; and Lieutenant General (*General der Fallschirmtruppe*), April 1, 1944. He won the Knight's Cross of the Iron Cross on June 14, 1941, the Oak Leaves to the Knight's Cross on August 31, 1944 and the Swords to the Oak Leaves on May 8, 1945. He also won the German Cross in Gold on July 27, 1942. Meindl was shot in the chest and wrist and seriously wounded on May 20, 1941, while trying to signal German paratroopers during the German airborne invasion of Crete. Eugen Meindl died on January 24, 1951 in Munich. He is buried next to his wife – who died in 1942 – in Donaueschingen at the *Stadtfriedhof* (Section N, Row 5, Grave 49/50).[50]

Andreas Nielsen

Major General Andreas Nielsen was born in Flensburg on December 23, 1899. He entered the Army on October 16, 1917, spending the remainder of World War I at a non-commissioned officer's school at Wetzlar. Nielsen left the Army in 1919, rejoined in 1920, took part in the unsuccessful Nazi "Beer Hall *Putsch*" in 1923, for which he later won "The Blood Order," left again in 1928 (in order to participate in secret flight training in Russia) and reentered in 1929.[51] He transferred to the *Luftwaffe* on July 1, 1935. Nielsen had a wide-variety of key assignments including: *Luftwaffe* General Staff, July 1, 1937-January 31, 1939; Commander, 1st Group, 88th Bomber Wing [K/88], Condor Legion, Spain, February 1, 1939-June 25, 1939; Commander, 3rd Group, 27th Bomber Wing "Boelcke" (*Kampfgeschwader 27 "Boelcke"*), June 26, 1939-February 24, 1940; Chief of Staff, 2nd Air Corps (*II. Fliegerkorps*), February 25, 1940-June 30, 1940; Operations Officer, 4th Air Fleet (*Luftflotte 4*), June 30, 1940-October 19, 1940; Chief of Staff, 5th Air Fleet [and Air Commander Artic Front] (*Luftflotte 5/Fliegerführer Eismeerfront*), October 20, 1940-December 31, 1943; Commanding General *Luftwaffe* in Denmark, January 1, 1944-May 1, 1944; and Chief of Staff, Air Fleet *Reich* (*Luftflotte Reich*), May 12, 1944-May 23, 1945. His promotions included: Lieutenant Colonel (*Oberstleutnant*), October 1, 1939), Colonel (*Oberst*), October 1, 1941), Brigadier General (*Generalmajor*), March 1, 1943) and Major General (*Generalleutnant*), July 1, 1944. He received the German Cross in Gold on April 20, 1942. Andreas Nielsen died on April 24, 1957 in Flensburg, Schleswig-Holstein.[52]

Karl-Gottfried Nordmann

Colonel Karl-Gottfried "Karlfried" Nordmann was born November 22, 1915 in Giessen, Hesse. By 1938 he was serving on the staff of the 1st Group, 77th Fighter Wing "Ace of Hearts" (*Jagdgeschwader 77 "Herzas"*). His key assignments included: Commander, 12th Squadron, 51st Fighter Wing (*Jagdgeschwader 51*), August 8, 1940-July 19, 1941; Commander, 4th Group, 51st Fighter Wing "Mölders" (*Jagdgeschwader 51 "Mölders"*), July 20, 1941-April 10, 1942; Commodore, 51st Fighter Wing "Mölders," April 11, 1942-August 5, 1942 and September 30, 1942-March 30, 1944; Fighter Commander 6 (*Jagdfliegerführer 6*), May 1, 1944-April 4, 1944; and Commander, 1st Fighter Division (*1. Jagddivision*), April 4, 1945-May 8, 1945. He won the Knight's Cross of the Iron Cross on August 1, 1941 and the Oak Leaves to the Knight's Cross on September 16, 1941. He was promoted to Colonel (*Oberst*) on January 30, 1945. Karl-Gottfried Nordmann died on July 22, 1982 in Greenwich, Connecticut. Nordmann flew over 800 combat missions. He shot down 78 enemy aircraft, including 8 in the West. He was seriously injured at least twice, once during a belly-landing on June 26, 1942 at Mamonovo, and once in a mid-air collision over Tschernosem on January 17, 1943 from which he had to bail out to save his life.[53]

Walter Nowotny

An Austrian by birth, Walter "Nowi" Nowotny was born on December 7, 1920 at Ceske Velenice/Gmünd on the Czechoslovakian/Austrian border. He joined the *Luftwaffe* on October 1, 1939 and soon completed flight school at the 5th Fighter Pilot School at Schwechat near Vienna. Nowotny was then posted to the 54th Fighter Wing "Greenhearts" (*Jagdgeschwader 54 "Grünherz"*) on February 23, 1941, and assigned to the 9th Squadron. His significant wartime assignments included: Commander, 1st Squadron, 54th Fighter Wing "Green Hearts," October 25, 1942-August 10, 1943; Commander, 1st Group, 54th Fighter Wing "Green Hearts," August 10, 1943-October 1943; Commander, 101st Fighter Wing (*Jagdgeschwader 101*) – an operational fighter-training unit – April 1, 1944-September 1944; and Commander, "Kommando Nowotny" – a consolidation of Messerschmitt Me 262 jet test units – September 1944-November 8, 1944. Walter Nowotny won the Knight's Cross of the Iron Cross on September 4, 1942 and the Oak Leaves to the Knight's Cross on September 4, 1943. He received the Swords to the Oak Leaves on September 22, 1943 (the 37th recipient), and on

October 19, 1943 he became the 8th recipient of the Diamonds. However, his victories came at a cost. On July 19, 1941, his Messerschmitt Me 109E-7 was shot down by a Soviet I-153, flown by the future Russian ace Alexandr Avdeev (13 victories, killed in action August 12, 1942) over Riga Bay. After three days and nights at sea in a rubber dinghy, Nowotny finally reached the shore. On August 11, 1942, his Me 109G-2 was hit in an aerial engagement and caught fire, and although Nowotny was able to bring the burning aircraft back to his base for a crash-landing, he suffered some injuries, but the worst was saved for last. By November 7, 1944, Nowotny had claimed three victories in the new jet fighter. He took off in his Me 262 on November 8, 1944, flying against USAAF bombers with a fighter escort. Ground personnel reported hearing combat above the clouds, and Nowotny reported over the radio that he had downed a B-24 four-engine bomber and probably destroyed a P-51 fighter. He then reported an engine failure and made a garbled transmission referring to "burning" over the radio. Ground observers saw his Me 262A-1a dive vertically out of the clouds and crash at Epe, 1 1/2 miles east of Hesepe.[54] He is buried at the *Zentralfriedhof* in Vienna, Austria (Section 14C, Grave 12.) Walter Nowotny flew over 442 missions and achieved 258 victories, a sortie-to-victory ratio of 1.71 to 1. Some 255 of his victories were over the Eastern Front. Of his three victories in the West, two were four-engine bombers and all three were while flying the Messerschmitt Me 262. During his service in the 1st Squadron, 54th Fighter Wing, Walter Novotny was the leader of the most famous flight in the *Luftwaffe* – composed of himself, Master Sergeant Anton Döbele, Master Sergeant Karl Schnörrer and Master Sergeant Rudi Rademacher – who, while flying together, shot down 450 enemy aircraft in Russia.[55]

Walter Oesau

Colonel Walter "Gulle" Oesau was born on June 28, 1913 at Farnewinkel/Heide in Schleswig-Holstein. He joined the Army in 1933 and served in an artillery regiment. The following year Oesau became an officer candidate, began flight training and transferred to the *Luftwaffe*. He then joined Fighter Wing "Richthofen" and served with the *Luftwaffe* in Spain in the 3rd Squadron, 88th Fighter Wing (*Jagdgruppe 88* [J/88]). While in Spain, he scored 9 aerial victories, was wounded in action and was awarded the Spanish Cross in Gold with Diamonds. On March 1, 1939, Oesau joined the 1st Group, 2nd Fighter Wing "Richthofen." His significant assignments included: Commander, 1st Squadron, 20th Fighter Group (*Jagdgruppe 20*), July 15, 1939-June 25, 1940; Commander, 7th Squadron, 51st Fighter Wing (*Jagdgeschwader 51*), June 25, 1940-August 25, 1940; Commander, 3rd Group, 51st Fighter Wing, August 25, 1940-July 28, 1941; Commander, 2nd Fighter Wing "Richthofen" (*Jagdgeschwader 2 "Richthofen"*), July 28 1941-July 1, 1943; 4th Fighter Commander, Brittany (*Jagdfliegerführer 4 Brittany*), July 1, 1943-November 11, 1943; and Commander, 1st Fighter Wing (*Jagdgeschwader 1*), November 12, 1943-May 11, 1944. He won the Knight's Cross of the Iron Cross on August 20, 1940 and the Oak Leaves to the Knight's Cross on February 6, 1941. On July 16, 1941, he became the 3rd recipient of the Swords to the Oak Leaves. He also won the German Cross in Gold on October 17, 1943. His promotions included: Captain (*Hauptmann*), July 19, 1940; Major (*Major*) July 15, 1941; and Colonel (*Oberst*), May 1, 1944. He had his adverse events as well; on January 9, 1942, his Messerschmitt Me 109F-4 rammed another fighter on the airfield during poor visibility conditions at Brest-Guipavas, France. On May 11, 1944, Oesau, leading three aircraft, took off from Paderborn to intercept Allied bombers. During his attack on the bombers he was bounced by escorting P-38 Lightnings. In the ensuing combat, his Messerschmitt Me 109G-6 was shot down and he was killed near St. Vith, Belgium. Oesau flew over 300 combat missions and accumulated 127 aerial victories (of which 74 were on the Western Front, including 14 four-engine bombers).[56]

Dietrich Peltz

Brigadier General Dietrich Peltz was born June 9, 1914 in Gera, Thuringia. He entered the Army on April 4, 1934 as an officer candidate and served in a transportation battalion. Peltz transferred to the *Luftwaffe* on October 1, 1935 and attended flight school at Salzwedel, before becoming the adjutant in *Stukageschwader 162 "Immelmann"* (based at Lübeck-Blankensee) on April 1, 1936. The unit was subsequently renamed the 2nd Stuka Wing, then the 76th Stuka Wing and finally the 3rd Stuka Wing. Peltz's promotions included: Captain (*Hauptmann*), March 1, 1941; Major (*Major*), July 18, 1942; Lieutenant Colonel (*Oberstleutnant*), December 1, 1942; Colonel (*Oberst*), March 17, 1943; and Brigadier General (*Generalmajor*), November 11, 1943. His significant operational assignments included: Commander, 1st Squadron, 3rd Stuka Wing (*Sturzkampfgeschwader 3*), May 1, 1939-November 2, 1940; squadron commander, 77th Bomber Wing (*Kampfgeschwader 77*), November 2, 1940-March 12, 1941; Commander, 2nd Group, 77th Bomber Wing,

March 13, 1941-September 9, 1941; Commander, 1st Group, 66th Bomber Wing (*Kampfgeschwader 66*), October 1942-December 31, 1942; Inspector for Bombers and Stukas, January 1, 1943-September 3, 1943; acting commander, 9th Air Corps (*IX. Fliegerkorps*), September 4, 1943-October 14, 1944; Commander, 2nd Fighter Corps (*II. Jagdkorps*), October 15, 1944-January 26, 1945; and Commander, 9th Air Corps (*IX. Fliegerkorps*), January 26, 1945-May 8, 1945. Peltz received the Knight's Cross of the Iron Cross on October 14, 1940; he received the Oak Leaves to the Knight's Cross on December 31, 1941 and the Swords to the Oak Leaves on July 23, 1943. Early in his career, he was seconds away from becoming a fatality during the "Catastrophe of Neuhammer" on August 15, 1939, when – on a practice bombing maneuver – 13 Stukas plunged through thick ground fog and crashed, killing all 26 crewmen. Peltz, in a follow-on squadron, pulled out in time to avoid certain death. Peltz also served as Attack Leader England (*Angriffsführer England*) from March 24, 1943 to September 3, 1943 – the renewed German air attacks against that country. Dietrich Peltz died on August 10, 2001 in Munich, Bavaria. His cremated remains were sent to Stuttgart for burial.[57]

Kurt Pflugbeil

Lieutenant General Kurt Pflugbeil was born on May 9, 1890 in Hütten bei Königstein, Saxony. He entered the Army on April 1, 1910 and served in several flying assignments during World War I. Pflugbeil "left" the Army in 1928 to undergo secret flight training in Russia, Sweden and Italy, but return to official duty in 1931. On October 1, 1933, he transferred to the *Luftwaffe*. His significant assignments included: Commander, Air District Staff 16 (*Luftgaustab zbV 16*), October 8, 1939-June 23, 1940; Commander, 4th Air Corps (*IV. Fliegerkorps*), August 20, 1940-September 3, 1943; Commander, 1st Air Fleet (*Luftflotte 1*), September 4, 1943-April 17, 1945; and Commander, *Luftwaffe* Command Courland (*Luftwaffenkommando Kurland*), April 17, 1945-May 8, 1945. His promotions included: Brigadier General (*Generalmajor*), January 1, 1939), Major General (*Generalleutnant*), September 1, 1940), and Lieutenant General (*General der Flieger*), February 1, 1942). He won the Knight's Cross of the Iron Cross on October 5, 1940 and was the 562nd recipient of the Oak Leaves to the Knight's Cross on August 27, 1944. Captured by the Russians in 1945, he was sentenced to 25 years imprisonment, but was released on January 4, 1954. Kurt Pflugbeil died on May 31, 1955 in Weende, Göttingen, in Lower Saxony.[58]

Fritz Prager

Major Fritz Prager was born December 17, 1905 in Chemnitz, Saxony. He entered the German Army on November 26, 1923 and served in the 10th Infantry Regiment. Prager transferred to the *Luftwaffe* on January 1, 1939. He received Iron Cross 2nd Class on October 13, 1939, the Iron Cross 1st Class on May 10, 1940, and the Knight's Cross of the Iron Cross on May 24, 1940. During the invasion of Holland in 1940, Prager and his battalion seized a key railroad bridge over the Maas River at Moerdijk and held it until relieved by the advancing 9th *Panzer* Division. During the fight, he was seriously wounded. His assignments included: Commander, 2nd Battalion, 1st Paratroop Regiment (*Fallschirmjäger-Regiment 1*), January 1, 1939-July 1, 1940; and Commander, 2nd Battalion, 3rd Paratroop Regiment (*Fallschirmjäger-Regiment 3*), July 1, 1940-December 3, 1940. His promotions included: Captain, (*Hauptmann*), April 1, 1937; and Major (*Major*), June 19, 1940. Fritz Prager died of colon cancer in a hospital in Frankfurt/Main on December 3, 1940. He is buried at the German Military Cemetery at Bautzen, Saxony (Grave 5).[59]

Josef "Pips" Priller

Colonel Josef "Pips" Priller was born on July 27, 1915 at Ingolstadt in Bavaria. In 1935, Priller was serving in the 19th Infantry Regiment in the Army. Officer candidate Priller transferred to the *Luftwaffe* and began his flight training at Salzwedel in October 1936. On April 1, 1937, he was posted to the 1st Group, 135th Fighter Wing (*Jagdgeschwader 135*), which was first designated as the 1st Group, 233rd Fighter Wing (*Jagdgeschwader 233*) and later designated the 1st Group, 51st Fighter Wing (*Jagdgeschwader 51*). Priller's significant positions included: Commander, 6th Squadron, 51st Fighter Wing (*Jagdgeschwader 51*), October 1, 1939-November 20, 1940; Commander, 1st Squadron, 26th Fighter Wing "Schlageter" (*Jagdgeschwader 26 "Schlageter"*), November 20, 1940-December 6, 1941; Commander, 3rd Group, 26th Fighter Wing "Schlageter," December 6, 1941-January 11, 1943; Commodore, 26th Fighter Wing, January 11, 1943-January 28, 1945; and Inspector Fighter Pilots East (*Inspekteur der Jagdflieger Ost*), January 28, 1945-May 8, 1945. Priller received the Knight's Cross of the Iron Cross on October 19, 1940 and the Oak Leaves on July 20, 1941. On July 2, 1944 he became the 73rd recipient of the Swords to the Oak Leaves. He also received the German Cross in Gold on December 20, 1941. Priller had a few near-death experiences: on April 17, 1942, bad weather forced him to make an emergency landing, which resulted in moderate damage to his aircraft, while on December 20, 1942, return fire from enemy bombers forced him to make a belly-landing in his Focke-Wulf Fw 190A-4. During the war, he flew 307 combat missions and scored 101 aerial victories, for a sortie-to-victory ratio of 3.03 to 1. All of his victories occurred in the West and included 68 Spitfires and 11 four-engine bombers. Josef "Pips" Priller died on May 20, 1961 of a heart attack at Böbing, Bavaria. He is buried at the *Westfriedhof* in Augsburg, Bavaria.[60]

Klaus Quaet-Faslem

Lieutenant Colonel Klaus Quaet-Faslem was born September 5, 1913 at Kiel. At the beginning of World War II Quaet-Faslem was serving as a second lieutenant in the 1st Group (Fighter), 2nd Demonstration Wing (*Lehrgeschwader 2*). His wartime assignments included: Commander, 2nd Squadron, 53rd Fighter Wing "Ace of Spades" (*Jagdgeschwader 53 "Pikas"*), November 21, 1941-August 31, 1942; and Commander, 1st Group, 3rd Fighter Wing "Udet" (*Jagdgeschwader 3 "Udet"*), August 31, 1942-January 30, 1944. He died in an air accident in his Messerschmitt Me 109G-6, during bad weather, on January 30, 1944 at Langeleben/Braunschweig. He was posthumously awarded the Knight's Cross of the Iron Cross on June 9, 1944. He also won the *Luftwaffe* Honor Goblet on September 21, 1942 and the German Cross in Gold on November 16, 1942. Klaus Quaet-Faslem shot down 49 aircraft, including 41 in the East. Of his 7 aerial victories in the west, 2 were four-engine bombers.[61]

Bernhard Ramcke

Lieutenant General Bernhard Ramcke was born January 24, 1889 in Schleswig-Friedrichsberg in Schleswig-Holstein. He entered the Navy in 1905 and served as a junior officer on several heavy cruisers before joining a naval infantry regiment engaged in ground combat in Flanders. Wounded twice, Ramcke received the King of Prussia Military Merit Cross in Gold and the Iron Cross 2nd and 1st Class. Immediately after the war, he joined *Freikorps* von Brandeis, in the Baltic States, where he was wounded again, before transferring to the Army on March 10, 1919. He remained in that service for twenty years, serving mostly in various infantry assignments. During the 1939 Polish Campaign, Ramcke won the Clasp to the Iron Cross 2nd Class for his actions at an engagement at Tomaszów. On August 1, 1940, Ramcke transferred to the *Luftwaffe* after completing airborne training. His significant positions included: acting commander, 1st Paratroop Assault Regiment (*Fallschirmjäger-Luftlande-Sturm-Regiment 1*), May 21, 1941-June 18, 1941; acting commander, 1st Paratroop Brigade (*Fallschirmjäger-Brigade 1*), April 1, 1942-February 12, 1943; Commander 11th Air Corps Operational Training Units and Schools (*Kommandeur der Ergänzungs-Einheiten und Schulen des XI. Fliegerkorps*), January 1, 1941-February 12, 1943 [dual-hatted]; acting commander, 90th Light Africa Division, September 8, 1942-September 17, 1942; Commander, 2nd Paratroop Division (*2. Fallschirmjäger-Division*), February 13, 1943-August 11, 1944; and Commandant Fortress Brest (*Kommandant der Festung Brest*), August 11, 1944-September 20, 1944. He received the Knight's Cross of the Iron Cross on August 21, 1941, the Oak Leaves on November 13, 1942, the Swords on September 19, 1944 and the Diamonds on September 19, 1944. Sentenced to 5 years imprisonment for war crimes by a French military tribunal, he was released from prison in 1951. He published his memoirs later that year. Bernhard Ramcke died July 4, 1968 in Kappeln near Schlei in Schleswig-Holstein. He is buried at the Friedrichsberg cemetery.[62]

Wolfram von Richthofen

Field Marshal Wolfram von Richthofen was born on October 10, 1895 at Gut Barzdorf/Striegau. Von Richthofen, a nephew of the famous "Red Baron" Manfred von Richthofen of World War I fame, entered the Army on March 22, 1913, initially served in the 4th Hussar Regiment and, like his famous uncle, transferred to a fighter unit and became a pilot in the 1st Air Wing (*Jagdgeschwader 1 "Richthofen"*). Shortly after the war, von Richthofen left the service, but was recalled to duty in 1923. He spent the next ten years in non-flying duties, before transferring to the *Luftwaffe* on October 1, 1933. Von Richthofen's key assignments included: Chief of Staff, Condor Legion [Spain], January 1, 1937-September 30, 1937; Commander, Condor Legion [Spain], October 1938-June 1939; Commander, 8th Air Corps (*VIII. Fliegerkorps*), October 3, 1939-June 30, 1942; Commander, 4th Air Fleet and Commander Southeast (*Luftflotte 4/Befehlshaber Südost*), July 4, 1942-September 3, 1943; acting commander, 2nd Air Fleet (*Luftflotte 2*), June 26, 1943-September 3, 1943; and Commander, 2nd Air Fleet (*Luftflotte 2*), September 4, 1943-October 27, 1944. His promotions included: Lieutenant Colonel (*Oberstleutnant*), April 20, 1936; Colonel (*Oberst*), January 23, 1938; Brigadier General (*Generalmajor*), November 1, 1938; Major General (skipped this grade); Lieutenant General (*General der Flieger*), July 19, 1940; Colonel General (*Generaloberst*), February 1, 1942; and Field Marshal (*Generalfeldmarschall*), February 16, 1943. He received the Knight's Cross of the Iron Cross on May 18, 1940 and the Oak Leaves to the Knight's Cross on July 17, 1941. He also won the Spanish Cross in Gold with Diamonds. Von Richthofen died on July 12, 1945 in a U.S. prison hospital in Bad Ischl, Austria. He is buried at the Bad Ischl *Stadtfriedhof* (*Ehrengruft*).[63]

Volprecht Riedesel zu Eisenach

Colonel Volprecht Riedesel zu Eisenbach was born on December 10, 1912 in Hofgeismar. He won the Knight's Cross of the Iron Cross on October 7, 1942 and became the 696th recipient of the Oak Leaves to the Knight's Cross on January 14, 1945. He also won the German Cross in Gold on May 11, 1942. His significant assignments included: Commander, 2nd Group, 76th Bomber Wing (*Kampfgeschwader 76*), April 1941-January 31, 1943; and Commodore, 54th Bomber Wing (*Kampfgeschwader 54*), April 1, 1943-February 9, 1945. He was promoted to Colonel (*Oberst*) on April 1, 1944. He was shot down and killed, flying a Messerschmitt Me 262A-1a two miles southeast of Camberg on February 9, 1945, while attacking a formation of B-17 Flying Fortresses.[64]

Fritz Schaffer

Major Fritz Schaffer's significant assignments included: Commander, 4th Squadron, 2nd Bomber Wing (*Kampfgeschwader 2*), November 1, 1938-October 19, 1939; Commodore, 5th Night Fighter Wing (*Nachtjagdgeschwader 5*), September 30, 1942-August 1, 1943; and Commodore, 6th Night Fighter Wing (*Nachtjagdgeschwader 6*), August 10, 1943-February 8, 1944. He was promoted to Captain (*Hauptmann*) on February 1, 1939 and Major (*Major*) on April 1, 1942.[65]

Richard Schimpf

Brigadier General Richard Schimpf was born in Eggenfelden, Bavaria on May 16, 1897. Schimpf entered the Army on February 11, 1915 and served in the infantry with the 9th Bavarian Infantry Regiment "Fürst Wrede." He stayed in the infantry after the war for five years before undertaking flight training. He then left the Army on August 31, 1929 to participate in secret flight training in Russia. Schimpf joined the *Luftwaffe* on February 1, 1935. His significant assignments included: Chief of Staff, 4th Air Fleet (*Luftflotte 4*), November 4, 1940-January 15, 1941; Chief of Staff, 8th Air District (*Luftgau VIII*), February 17, 1941-November 30, 1941; Chief of Staff, *Luftwaffe* Field District Kiev (*Feldluftgau-Kommandos Kiew*), December 1, 1941-September 9, 1942; Chief of Staff, *Luftwaffe* Field District Kharkov (*Feldluftgau-Kommandos Charkov*), September 10, 1942-September 26, 1942; acting commander *Luftwaffe* Division "Meindl," September 27, 1942-November 10, 1942; Commander, 21st *Luftwaffe* Field Division (*21. Luftwaffen-Felddivision*), November 11, 1942-October 24, 1943; Commander, 3rd Paratroop Division (*3. Fallschirmjäger-Division*), February 17, 1944-August 20, 1944 and again January 6, 1945-March 8, 1945. Schimpf won the Clasp to the Iron Cross 2nd Class on August 5, 1940 and the Clasp to the Iron Cross 1st Class on February 17, 1941. He received the German Cross in Gold on August 26, 1944, and won the Knight's Cross of the Iron Cross on October 6, 1944. His promotions included: Lieutenant Colonel (*Oberstleutnant*), April 1, 1937; Colonel (*Oberst*), October 1, 1939; Brigadier General (*Generalmajor*), March 18, 1943; and Major General (*Generalleutnant*), August 1, 1943. On August 20, 1944, Schimpf was seriously wounded in the leg by a 20mm shell during the breakout from the Falaise Pocket in Normandy. After the war, he joined the *Bundeswehr* and became a brigadier general. Richard Schimpf died on December 30, 1972 in Düsseldorf, North Rhine-Westphalia. He is buried at the *Nordfriedhof* in Düsseldorf (Section 10D, Grave 1-2).[66]

Karl-Heinz Schnell

Major Karl-Heinz "Bubi" Schnell was born January 10, 1915 in Essen. At the beginning of the war Schnell was serving with the 2nd Squadron, 20th Fighter Wing (which soon after was renamed the 8th Squadron, 51st Fighter Wing). His significant assignments included: Commander, 9th Squadron, 51st Fighter Wing (*Jagdgeschwader 51*), September 30, 1940-August 20, 1941; Commander, 5th Squadron, 51st Fighter Wing "Mölders" (*Jagdgeschwader 51 "Mölders"*), May 23, 1942-September 8, 1942; Commander, 3rd Group, 51st Fighter Wing "Mölders," September 8, 1942-October 23, 1942 and January 1943-June 1943; Commander, 1st Group, 106th Fighter Wing (*Jagdgeschwader 106*), June 1943-July 10, 1943 and August 7, 1943-1944; acting commander, 2nd Group, 53rd Fighter Wing "Ace of Spades" (*Jagdgeschwader 53 "Pikas"*), July 10, 1943-August 7, 1943; Commander, 2nd Group, 102nd Fighter Wing (*Jagdgeschwader 102*), 1944; and Commodore, 102nd Fighter Wing, 1944-April 1945. On August 20, 1941, he was shot down in aerial combat northeast of Krassniki and wounded. He received the Knight's Cross of the Iron Cross on August 1, 1941. He also won the German Cross in Gold on November 2, 1942. Karl-Heinz Schnell flew over 500 combat missions, achieving 72 aerial victories. Some 63 of the confirmed kills were over the Eastern Front. His aircraft was struck by friendly anti-aircraft fire, and he was injured during an emergency landing on October 23, 1942.[67]

Karl-Lothar Schulz

Brigadier General Karl-Lothar Schulz was born in Königsberg, East Prussia on April 30, 1907. He joined the Army on June 1, 1924 as an enlisted man in the 1st Artillery Regiment, but left one year later and served ten years in the Police. He rose in this organization to be a Police first lieutenant and served as a platoon leader and company commander in the Land Police Group "General Göring." When this formation converted to the *Luftwaffe*, so did Schulz, on October 1, 1935. His significant *Luftwaffe* assignments included: Commander, 3rd Battalion, 1st Paratroop Regiment (*Fallschirmjäger-Regiment 1*), January 1, 1940-April 17, 1942; acting operations officer, 7th Air Division (*7. Flieger-Division*), April 18, 1942-June 3, 1942; Commander, 1st Paratroop Regiment, June 4, 1942-November 17, 1944; and acting commander, 1st Paratroop Division (*1. Fallschirmjäger-Division*), November 18, 1944-May 2, 1945. His promotions included: Lieutenant Colonel (*Oberstleutnant*), October 26, 1942; Colonel (*Oberst*), October 21, 1943; and Brigadier General (*Generalmajor*), January 17, 1945. Schulz won the Iron Cross 2nd Class and the Iron Cross 1st Class on the same day, May 12, 1940. He received the Knight's Cross of the Iron Cross on May 24, 1940 and the Oak Leaves to the Knight's Cross on April 20, 1944. On November 18, 1944, Schulz received the Swords to the Oak Leaves (the 112th recipient). He also won the German Cross in Gold on March 9, 1943. Karl-Lothar Schulz died on September 26, 1972 in Wiesbaden, Hesse.[68]

Hans-Bruno Schulz-Heyn

Colonel Schulz-Heyn's significant assignments included: Commander, 1st Group, 51st Bomber Wing "Edelweiss" (*Kampfgeschwader 51 "Edelweiss"*), December 19, 1939-August 12, 1940; Commodore, 51st Bomber Wing "Edelweiss," August 12, 1940-September 1, 1941; and Commander, Airfield District 7/III (*Koflug 7/III*), October 24, 1944-May 2, 1945. He was promoted to Colonel (*Oberst*) on April 1, 1942. He survived the war.[69]

Martin Schumann

Major Martin Schumann's significant assignments included: Commander, 4th Group, 30th Bomber Wing (*Kampfgeschwader 30*), February 10, 1941-June 8, 1942.

Hannes Schwarzer

Captain Hannes Schwarzer won the German Cross in Gold on October 1, 1944 in the 1st Paratroop Anti-Tank Detachment (*Fallschirm-Panzer-Jäger-Abteilung 1*). He served as the acting commander of the detachment in November 1944.[70]

Hans Seidemann

Lieutenant General Hans Seidemann was born in Garlin/Perleberg, Brandenburg on January 18, 1902. Seidemann entered the Army on January 15, 1919 and spent most of his first year in *Freikorps Maerker*, then served in the 9th Infantry Regiment in Potsdam and left the Army as a first lieutenant in 1928 to participate in secret flight training in the Soviet Union. He re-entered the Army on November 1, 1929 and served until October 1, 1934, when he transferred to the *Luftwaffe*. His significant assignments included: Commander, 3rd Group, Demonstration Wing Greifswald (*Lehrgeschwader Greifswald*), April 1, 1938-November 30, 1938; Chief of Staff, Condor Legion [Spain], December 1, 1938-June 30, 1939; Chief of Staff, 8th Air Corps (*VIII. Fliegerkorps*), December 27, 1939-August 5, 1940; Chief of Staff, 2nd Air Fleet (*Luftflotte 2*), October 10, 1940-July 31, 1942; Air Commander Africa (*Fliegerführer Afrika*), August 24, 1942-February 11, 1943; Commander Air Corps Tunis (*Fliegerkorps Tunis*), February 12, 1943-May 14, 1943; Commander, 8th Air Corps (*VIII. Fliegerkorps*), May 18, 1943-January 25, 1945; Commander, *Luftwaffe* Command Silesia (*Luftwaffen-Kommandos Schlesien*), January 25, 1945-April 28, 1945; and Commander, *Luftwaffe* Command 8 (*Luftwaffen-Kommandos 8*), April 29, 1945-May 9, 1945. His promotions included: Lieutenant Colonel (*Oberstleutnant*), June 1, 1939; Colonel (*Oberst*), October 1, 1940; Brigadier General (*Generalmajor*), August 24, 1942; Major General (*Generalleutnant*), January 1, 1944; and Lieutenant General (*General der Flieger*), March 1, 1945. Seidemann was awarded the Knight's Cross of the Iron Cross on March 20, 1942 and the Oak Leaves to the Knight's Cross on November 18, 1944. Hans Seidemann died on December 27, 1967 in Braunschweig, Lower Saxony.[71]

Heinrich Seywald

Brigadier General Heinrich Seywald was born in Regensburg, Bavaria on December 23, 1894. Seywald entered the Army on August 10, 1914 as an officer candidate, started his career in the 11th Bavarian Infantry Regiment and became a pilot in the 23rd Fighter Squadron (*Jagdstaffel 23*). After the 1918 Armistice, Seywald flew for *Freikorps Epp* during the civil strife in Bavaria. He left the Army temporarily in 1928 to conduct secret flight training in the Soviet Union, but returned to duty in 1930. He transferred to the *Luftwaffe* on September 1, 1933. Seywald's significant *Luftwaffe* assignments included: Commander, 3rd Group, 152nd Bomber Wing "Hindenburg" (*Kampfgeschwader 152 "Hindenburg"*), March 12, 1936-March 31, 1938; Commander, Pilot School Fürth (*Flugzeugführer-Schule Fürth*), April 1, 1938-July 31, 1938; Commodore, 153rd Bomber Wing (*Kampfgeschwader 153*), February 1, 1939-March 31, 1939; Commodore, 77th Bomber Wing (*Kampfgeschwader 77*), April 1, 1939-September 13, 1939; and Commander, Main Bomber Crews' School 4, Thorn (*Grossen Kampfflieger-Schule 4*), November 15, 1939-June 15, 1942. His promotions included: Lieutenant Colonel (*Oberstleutnant*), October 1, 1936; Colonel (*Oberst*), January 1, 1939; and Brigadier General (*Generalmajor*), November 1, 1941. Heinrich Seywald died on September 15, 1973 in Regensburg, Bavaria. He is buried there at the *Unteren Katholischen Friedhof* (Section 8, Row 2, Grave 63/64).[72]

Helmut Sorge

Colonel Helmut Sorge was born March 27, 1905. His key assignments included: Commander, 2nd Group, 3rd Stuka Wing (*Sturzkampfgeschwader 3*), May 31, 1941-December 1941; acting commander, 1st Group, 1st Stuka Wing (*Sturzkampfgeschwader 1*), December 1941-January 13, 1942; Chief of Staff, 8th Air Corps (*VIII. Flieger Korps*), March 24, 1945-April 1945; and Chief of Staff, 2nd Air Corps (*II. Flieger-Korps*), April 1945. He won the German Cross in Gold on December 15, 1941. He was promoted to Colonel (*Oberst*) on April 1, 1944.[73]

Wilhelm Stemmler

Lieutenant Colonel Wilhelm Stemmler was born in Hamburg on August 28, 1912. His assignments included: Commander, 4th Group 51st Bomber Wing "Edelweiss" (*Kampfgeschwader 51 "Edelweiss"*), February 25, 1942-December 13, 1942; Commodore, 77th Bomber Wing (*Kampfgeschwader 77*), February 12, 1943-July 7, 1944; and Commodore, 26th Bomber Wing "Lions" (*Kampfgeschwader 26 "Löwen"*), November 1944-January 1945. He received the Knight's Cross of the Iron Cross on October 6, 1944. Stemmler also won the German Cross in Gold on October 1, 1944. Stemmler was shot down behind Russian lines in the summer of 1941 and severely burned, but was later rescued by German mountain troops and brought to safety. He was promoted to lieutenant colonel (*Oberstleutnant*) on October 1, 1944. Wilhelm Stemmler died in Hamburg on May 12, 1967.[74]

Werner Streib

Colonel Werner Streib was born in Pforzheim, Baden on June 13, 1911. He joined the German Army in 1934 and transferred to the *Luftwaffe* the following year. In 1936, Streib was commissioned a second lieutenant and sent to a reconnaissance group, but transferred in 1938 to Fighter Wing "Richthofen" (*Jagdgeschwader "Richthofen"*). Soon, he moved again, to be the signal officer for the 1st Group, 1st Destroyer Wing (*Zerstörergeschwader 1*). On May 10, 1940, Streib shot down his first enemy aircraft, a British Blenheim. His significant assignments included: Commander, 2nd Squadron, 1st Destroyer Wing, June 6, 1940-June 26, 1940; Commander, 2nd Squadron, 1st Night Fighter Wing (*Nachtjagdgeschwader 1*), June 26, 1940-October 7, 1940; Commander, 1st Group, 1st Night Fighter Wing, October 7, 1940-July 1, 1943; Commodore, 1st Night Fighter Wing, July 1, 1943-March 1, 1944; and Inspector of Night Fighters, March 1, 1944-May 1, 1945. Werner Streib won the Knight's Cross of the Iron Cross on October 6, 1940 and the Oak Leaves to the Knight's Cross on February 26, 1943. He became the 54th recipient of the Swords to the Oak Leaves on March 11, 1944. He also won the German Cross in Gold on March 9, 1943. He was promoted to Colonel (*Oberst*) on May 1, 1944. He served in the new German air force after the war and rose to become a brigadier general. He achieved 68 aerial victories during the war, of which 67 came at night and included 30 four-engine bombers. On July 20, 1940, Streib claimed the first *Luftwaffe* night victory of the war, when he shot down a British Whitley bomber. Werner Streib died June 15, 1986 in Munich.[75]

Kurt Student

Colonel General Kurt Student was born May 12, 1890 in Birkholz near Züllichau-Schwiebus, Brandenburg. He entered the Army in 1910 and was one of the first officers to receive pilot training in 1913. During World War I he served in several flying units; he was wounded twice in aerial combat (he also crashed once due to an engine defect) and received both the Iron Cross 2nd and 1st Class, as well as the Knight's Cross of the Royal House Order of Hohenzollern with Swords (*Ritterkreuz des königlichen Hausordens von Hohenzollern mit Schwerten*). After the war, he remained in the *Reichswehr*, alternating between aviation and infantry duties, before transferring to the *Luftwaffe* on September 1, 1933. Among his significant positions were: Commander, 3rd Air Division (*3. Flieger-Division*), April 1, 1938-July 3, 1938; Commander of Airborne and Air Landing Troops (*Fallschirmjäger und Luftlandetruppen*), July 4, 1938-August

31, 1938; Commander, 7th Air Division (*7. Flieger-Division*), September 1, 1938-September 30, 1940; Commander, 11th Air Corps (*XI. Flieger-Korps*), January 1, 1941-May 31, 1941; Commanding General of Airborne Troops (*Kommandierender General der Fallschirmjäger*), June 1, 1941-February 28, 1944; Commander-in-Chief, 1st Parachute Army (*1. Fallschirm-Armee*), March 1, 1944-November 4, 1944 and April 10, 1945-April 28, 1945; Commander-in-Chief, Army Group H (*Heeresgruppe H*), November 7, 1944-January 25, 1945; and Commander, Army Group "Student" (*Armeegruppe Student*), March 31, 1945-April 10, 1945. While he was named at the end of the war to be Commander-in-Chief of Army Group Vistula, he never actually assumed the command. His promotions included: Brigadier General (*Generalmajor*), April 1, 1938; Major General (*Generalleutnant*), January 1, 1940; Lieutenant General (*General der Flieger* [later *General der Fallschirmtruppe*]), May 29, 1940; and Colonel General (*Generaloberst*), July 13, 1944. He received the Knight's Cross of the Iron Cross on May 12, 1940 and the Oak Leaves to the Knight's Cross on September 27, 1943. Student was almost killed in action on May 14, 1940 when he was shot in the head during the fighting at Rotterdam; he convalesced in hospital and was on sick leave until January 1941. After the war, Student was charged with war crimes that allegedly took place on Crete. He was sentenced to five years imprisonment, but was released after serving two. Kurt Student died on July 1, 1978 at Lemgo, North Rhine-Westphalia.[76] He is buried at the *Friedhof am Obernberg* in Bad Sulzulfen (Section 35, Grave 35).

Gerhard Ulbricht

Colonel Gerhard Ulbricht's assignments included: Operations Officer [I a] 9th Air Division (*9. Flieger-Division*), February 7, 1940-February 15, 1940; Commander, 1st Group, 27th Bomber Wing "Boelcke" (*Kampfgeschwader 27 "Boelcke"*), June 1, 1940-October 6, 1940; and Commodore, 27th Bomber Wing, October 6, 1940-1941. He won the German Cross in Gold as a lieutenant colonel on November 24, 1941. Gerhard Ulbricht was promoted to Colonel (*Oberst*) on April 1, 1943.[77]

Karl Viek

Colonel Karl Viek's assignments included: Commander, 1st Group, 132nd Fighter Wing "Richthofen" (*Jagdgeschwader 132 "Richthofen"*), April 1, 1936-November 1, 1938; Commander, 1st Group, 2nd Fighter Wing "Richthofen" (*Jagdgeschwader 2 "Richthofen"*), November 1, 1938-September 26, 1939; Commodore, 3rd Fighter Wing (*Jagdgeschwader 3*), September 26, 1939-August 21, 1940; Commander 4th Fighter School (*Jagdfliegerschule 4*), June 6, 1941-June 30, 1941; acting Fighter Leader 2 (*Jagdfliegerführer 2*), October 23, 1942-1943; Fighter Leader 2 (*Jagdfliegerführer 2*), June 19, 1943-September 29, 1943; Commander, 4th Fighter Division (*4. Jagddivision*), September 30, 1943-September 8, 1944; and Fighter District Commander Denmark (*Jagdabschnittsführer Dänemark*), September 1944-May 1945. He was promoted to Colonel (*Oberst*) on March 1, 1942. Viek won the German Cross in Gold on November 11, 1943.[78]

Otto Weiss

Colonel Otto Weiss was born in Breslau, Silesia, on September 25, 1907. He entered the Police in 1926 and transferred to the *Luftwaffe* in 1935 as a Police lieutenant. His key *Luftwaffe* assignments included: Commander, 4th Squadron, 2nd Demonstration Wing (*Lehrgeschwader 2*), November 1, 1938-September 13. 1939; acting commander, 2nd Group (S), 2nd Demonstration Wing (*Lehrgeschwader 2*), September 13, 1939-June 26, 1940; Commander, 2nd Group (S), 2nd Demonstration Wing (*Lehrgeschwader 2*), June 26, 1940-March 29, 1941; Commodore, 1st Ground-Attack Wing (*Schlachtgeschwader 1*), January 13, 1942-June 18, 1942; Inspector of Ground-Attack and Destroyers (*Inspekteur der Schlacht- und Zerstörerflieger*), July 1942-September 1943; and Air Commander, Artic Front (*Fliegerführer Eismeerfront*), April 1944-January 1945. He won the Iron Cross 2nd Class on September 15, 1939 and the Iron Cross 1st Class on October 2, 1939. He received the Knight's Cross of the Iron Cross on May 18, 1940 and the Oak Leaves to the Knight's Cross on December 31, 1941. His promotions included: Captain (*Hauptmann*), October 1, 1936; Major (*Major*), July 1, 1940; and Colonel (*Oberst*), November 1, 1943. Otto Weiss died in Kiel on August 19, 1955 after a long illness. He flew 520 combat missions during the war, including the *Luftwaffe's* first low-level ground-attack mission of World War II – on September 1, 1939, in a Henschel Hs 123 biplane, against Polish troops in the village of Panki.[79]

Helmuth Wilberg

Lieutenant General Helmuth Wilberg was born on June 1, 1880 in Berlin. He joined the German Army on April 18, 1899 as an officer candidate and began his career in the 80th Fusilier Regiment. Wilberg joined the fledgling German air troops just before World War I. After the war, he served in various infantry and General Staff positions, before retiring in 1932 as a brigadier general. Wilberg joined the *Luftwaffe* two years later, on October 1, 1934. His key *Luftwaffe* assignments included: Commander, Air District Schools II (*Luftkreis-Schule II*), October 1, 1935-March 31, 1936; Commander, Higher *Luftwaffe* Schools (*Höheren Luftwaffen-Schule*), April 1, 1936-September 30, 1937; Commander Special Staff W [Condor Legion] in Spain (*Sonderstab W*), October 1, 1937-March 31, 1938; and Higher Flying Training Commander 4 (*Höherer Flieger-Ausbildungs-Kommandeur 4*), August 26, 1939-November 20, 1941. His promotions included: Brigadier General (*Generalmajor*), October 1, 1932; Major General (*Generalleutnant*), April 1, 1936; and Lieutenant General (*General der Flieger*), September 1, 1940. Wilberg retired from the *Luftwaffe* on March 31, 1938, but was brought back to active duty on August 26, 1939. He was killed in an air crash near Dresden on November 20, 1941.[80]

Wolf-Dietrich Wilcke

Colonel Wolf-Dietrich "Fürst" Wilcke was born in Schrimm in the district of Posen on March 11, 1913. He entered the German Army in 1934 and transferred the following year as an officer candidate to the *Luftwaffe*. He later served briefly with the Condor Legion in Spain and was awarded the Spanish Cross in Bronze with Swords. Among his significant assignments were: Commander, 7th Squadron, 53rd Fighter Wing "Ace of Spades" (*Jagdgeschwader 53 "Pikas"*), September 18, 1939-August 13, 1940; Commander, 3rd Group, 53rd Fighter Wing "Ace of Spades," August 13, 1940-May 18, 1942; and Commodore, 3rd Fighter Wing "Udet" (*Jagdgeschwader 3 "Udet"*), August 12, 1942-March 23, 1944. He received the Knight's Cross of the Iron Cross on August 6, 1941 and the Oak Leaves to the Knight's Cross on September 9, 1942. On December 23, 1942, Wilcke became the 23rd recipient of the Swords to the Oak Leaves. He also won the German Cross in Gold on November 3, 1942. Wilcke was killed in action on March 23, 1944 over Schöppenstedt/Braunschweig, when – after shooting down two enemy aircraft – his Messerschmitt Me 109G-6 was shot down by U.S. fighters. Wilcke flew 732 combat missions during the war and shot down 162 enemy aircraft, a sortie-to-victory ratio of 4.51 to 1. Some 137 of his kills came on the Eastern Front.[81]

Karl-Eduard Wilke

Brigadier General Karl-Eduard Wilke was born in Kiel on January 24, 1901. He entered the Army on March 25, 1918 as an officer candidate and became a platoon leader in the 171st Infantry Regiment. At the end of the war, Wilke served in the *Freikorps Eulenburg*. He left the Army in 1920, but rejoined in 1923 and gravitated to flight training – in 1928-1929, he underwent secret flight training in the Soviet Union. Wilke joined the *Luftwaffe* on June 15, 1934 as a captain. His significant assignments in the *Luftwaffe* included: Commodore, 55th Bomber Wing "Legion Condor" (*Kampfgeschwader 55 "Legion Condor"*), November 1, 1942-April 30, 1943; Chief of Staff, *Luftwaffe* Forces in Romania, May 1, 1943-November 15, 1943; Chief of Staff, *Luftwaffe* Command Southeast, November 16, 1943-October 31, 1944; acting commander, 2nd Fighter Corps (*II. Jagdkorps*), January 12, 1945-January 26, 1945; and Commander, 15th Air Division (*15. Flieger-Division*), January 26, 1945-April 27, 1945. He won the German Cross in Gold on March 15, 1943. Karl-Eduard Wilke died on May 10, 1990 in Hagen.[82]

Bernhard Woldenga

Colonel Bernhard Woldenga was born in Hamburg on December 4, 1901. Before joining the military, Woldenga served in the German merchant marine. He then joined the *Luftwaffe*. His assignments included: Commander, 1st Group, 131st Fighter Wing "Richthofen" (*Jagdgeschwader 131 "Richthofen"*), April 1, 1937-November 1, 1938; Commander, 1st Group, 1st Fighter Wing (*Jagdgeschwader 1*), November 1, 1938-February 13, 1940; acting commodore, 27th Fighter Wing (*Jagdgeschwader 27*), October 15, 1940-November 2, 1940; Commodore, 77th Fighter Wing "Ace of Hearts" (*Jagdgeschwader 77 "Herzas"*), January 2, 1941-June 23, 1941; acting commodore, 27th Fighter Wing (*Jagdgeschwader 27*), June 23, 1941-June 10, 1942; Fighter Commander Balkans (*Jagdfliegerführer Balkan*), June 10, 1942-1944; and Commander, 10th Air War School (*Luftkriegschule 10*), October 15, 1944-1945. He received the Knight's Cross of the Iron Cross on July 5, 1941. He was promoted to Colonel (*Oberst*) on April 1, 1943. For several years, he was the postwar manager of the New York office of Schenker & Co., an import-export firm. Bernhard Woldenga died on January 19, 1999 at Timmendorfer Strand, Schleswig-Holstein. He scored 4 aerial victories during the war; his first occurred on June 25, 1941 over Grodno and his last happened on September 16, 1941 over Staraja Russa.[83]

ENDNOTES

Introduction

[1] John R. Angolia, *For Führer and Fatherland: Military Awards of the Third Reich*, San Jose, CA: Bender Publishing, 1976, 162.

[2] John R. Angolia, *For Führer and Fatherland: Military Awards of the Third Reich*, San Jose, CA: Bender Publishing, 1976, 177.

[3] John R. Angolia, *For Führer and Fatherland: Military Awards of the Third Reich*, San Jose, CA: Bender Publishing, 1976, 183.

[4] John R. Angolia, *For Führer and Fatherland: Military Awards of the Third Reich*, San Jose, CA: Bender Publishing, 1976, 188.

[5] John R. Angolia, *For Führer and Fatherland: Military Awards of the Third Reich*, San Jose, CA: Bender Publishing, 1976, 193-195.

[6] John R. Angolia, *For Führer and Fatherland: Military Awards of the Third Reich*, San Jose, CA: Bender Publishing, 1976, 259.

Rated Officers

[1] Beurteilung Walter Matoni, III./Jagdgeschwader 27, Major u. Geschwaderkommodore Woldenga, 12.7.1941.

[2] On March 6, 1944, the 8th Air Force mounted its first full-scale daylight attack on the German capital. The attackers lost 69 bombers and 11 escort fighters – the largest number of planes lost on a single mission the 8th would experience during the war.

[3] Included in his total at the time were 11 four-engine bombers, five of which were Herausschüsse (shot out of formation, which made them almost certain kills for later fighter attacks.)

[4] Sources, Walter Matoni: Jeffrey Ethell and Alfred Price, *Target Berlin*, London" Jane's, 1981, 80, 182; Roger A. Freeman, *Mighty Eighth War Diary*, London: Jane's, 1981, 101, 187, 218; Donald L. Caldwell, *JG 26: Top Guns of the Luftwaffe*, New York: Orion Books, 1991, 224-225; John Manrho and Ron Pütz, *Bodenplatte: The Luftwaffe's Last H*ope, Browborough, England: Hikoki Publication, 2004, 43; Ernst Obermaier, *Die Ritterkreuzträger der Luftwaffe, Jagdflieger 1939-1945*, Mainz, FRG: Verlag Dieter Hoffmann, 1989, 165; Jochen Prien, Gerhard Stemmer, Peter Rodeike and Winfried Bock, *Die Jagdfliegerverbände der Deutschen Luftwaffe 1934 bis 1945, Teil 4/I: Einsatz am Kanal und über England, 26.6.1940 bis 21.6.1941*, Eutin, Germany: Struve, 421; Josef Priller, *J.G. 26: Geschichte eines Jagdgeschwaders*, Stuttgart, FRG: Motorbuch Verlag, 1980, 205, 230, 231, 247, 252, 332, 352; Veit Scherzer, *Die Träger des Deutschen Kreuzes in Gold der Luftwaffe 1941-1945*, Bayreuth, FRG: Scherzer's Militair Verlag, 1992, 210.

[5] Despite the loss of Pickard, "Operation Jericho" was a success. The attacking aircraft dropped bombs that breached the wall and blew in the doors of the prison. The explosion killed 102 prisoners, but 258 escaped, including 79 French Resistance and political prisoners; two-thirds of the escapees were later recaptured.

[6] *Vorschlag zur Beförderung zum Kriegsoffizier wegen besonderer Tapferkeit vor dem Feind Wilhelm Mayer, II./Jagdgeschwader "Schlageter" Nr. 2, Major und Gruppenkommandeur m.d.F.b. Hackl, Oberstleutnant und Geschwaderkommodore Priller, Gefechtsstand, 9.10.1944.*

[7] Sources, Wilhelm Mayer: Roger A. Freeman, *Mighty Eighth War Diary*, London: Jane's, 1981, 83; Donald L. Caldwell, *JG 26: Top Guns of the Luftwaffe*, New York: Orion Books, 1991, 182, 344, 346; Ernst Obermaier, *Die Ritterkreuzträger der Luftwaffe, Jagdflieger 1939-1945*, Mainz, FRG: Verlag Dieter Hoffmann, 1989, 165; Jochen Prien, Gerhard Stemmer, Peter Rodeike and Winfried Bock, *Die Jagdfliegerverbände der Deutschen Luftwaffe 1934 bis 1945, Teil 7: Heimatsverteidigung 1. Januar bis 31. Dezember 1942, Einsatz im Westen 1. Januar bis 31. Dezember 1942*, Eutin, Germany: Struve, 2003, 373, 375, 377; Josef Priller, *J.G. 26: Geschichte eines Jagdgeschwaders*, Stuttgart, FRG: Motorbuch Verlag, 1980, 138, 260, 314, 325, 332, 353; C. Martin Sharp and Michael J. F. Bowyer, *Mosquito*, London: Faber and Faber Limited, 1967, 242.

[8] *Beurteilung für Oblt. (Kr.O.) Maximilian Mayerl, III./ Jagdgeschwader Mölders, Major und Gruppenkommandeur Schnell, Oberstleutnant u. Geschwaderkommodore Nordmann, O.U., 5. Mai 1943.*

[9] Sources, Maximilian Mayerl: Gerhard Aders and Werner Held, *Jagdgeschwader 51 "Mölders":* Eine Chronik - Berichte, Erlebnisse, Dokumente, Motorbuch Verlag, Stuttgart, 1993, 250; Ernst Obermaier, *Die Ritterkreuzträger der Luftwaffe, Jagdflieger 1939-1945*, Mainz, FRG: Verlag Dieter Hoffmann, 1989, 166; Jochen Prien, Gerhard Stemmer, Peter Rodeike and Winfried Bock, *Die Jagdfliegerverbände der Deutschen Luftwaffe 1934 bis 1945, Teil 3: Einsatz in Dänemark und Norwegen, 9.4. bis 30.11.40, Der Feldzug im Westen, 10.5. bis 25.6.1940*, Eutin, Germany: Struve, 188; Jochen Prien, Gerhard Stemmer, Peter Rodeike and Winfried Bock, *Die Jagdfliegerverbände der Deutschen Luftwaffe 1934 bis 1945, Teil 4/II: Einsatz am Kanal und über England, 26.6.1940 bis 21.6.1941*, Eutin, Germany: Struve, 83, 88; Jochen Prien, Gerhard Stemmer, Peter Rodeike and Winfried Bock, *Die Jagdfliegerverbände der Deutschen Luftwaffe 1934 bis 1945, Teil 9/I: Winterkampf im Osten 6.12.1941 bis 30.4.1942*, Eutin, Germany: Struve, 107; Jochen Prien, Gerhard Stemmer,

Peter Rodeike and Winfried Bock, *Die Jagdfliegerverbände der Deutschen Luftwaffe 1934 bis 1945, Teil 9/II: Vom Sommerfeldzug 1942 bis zur Niederlage von Stalingrad 1.5.1942 bis 3.2.1943*, Eutin, Germany: Struve, 333.

[10] *Vorschlag zur bevorzugten Beförderung für Oberleutnant (Tr. O.) Julius Meimberg, Jagdgeschwader 53, Oberstleutnant u. Geschwaderkommodore von Maltzahn, Oberst Kosch, Generalmajor Harlinghausen, Gefechtsstand, 14.1.1943.*

[11] Sources, Julius Meimberg: Julius Meimberg, *Feindberührung: Erinnerungen 1939-1945*, Moosburg, Germany, NeunundzwanzigSechs Verlag, 2002, 342, 343, 344, 345; Ernst Obermaier, *Die Ritterkreuzträger der Luftwaffe, Jagdflieger 1939-1945*, Mainz, FRG: Verlag Dieter Hoffmann, 1989, 167; Jochen Prien, *Pik-As: Geschichte des Jagdgeschwaders 53*, Hamburg, Germany: Dr. Jochen Prien, 1991, Teil 3: 1302, 1426, 1427, 1602, 1603, 1604, 1605; Jochen Prien, Gerhard Stemmer, Peter Rodeike and Winfried Bock, *Die Jagdfliegerverbände der Deutschen Luftwaffe 1934 bis 1945, Teil 3: Einsatz in Dänemark und Norwegen, 9.4. bis 30.11.40, Der Feldzug im Westen, 10.5. bis 25.6.1940*, Eutin, Germany: Struve, 115-116; Jochen Prien, Gerhard Stemmer, Peter Rodeike and Winfried Bock, *Die Jagdfliegerverbände der Deutschen Luftwaffe 1934 bis 1945, Teil 4/I: Einsatz am Kanal und über England, 26.6.1940 bis 21.6.1941*, Eutin, Germany: Struve, 121-122; Jochen Prien, Gerhard Stemmer, Peter Rodeike and Winfried Bock, *Die Jagdfliegerverbände der Deutschen Luftwaffe 1934 bis 1945, Teil8/I: Einsatz im Mittelmeerraum November 1941 bis Dezember 1942*, Eutin, Germany: Struve, 2004, 58; John Weal, *Jagdgeschwader 2 'Richthofen,'* Osprey Aviation Elite 1, Oxford, England: Osprey Publishing, 2000, 34, 71, 77, 124.

[12] *Vorschlag zur Beförderung zum Leutnant d.R. Feldwebel Joachim Meissner, Versuchsabteilung Friedrichshafen, Hauptmann u. Abt.-Führer Koch, Hildesheim, 30. Januar 1940.*

[13] Sources, Joachim Meissner: Veit Scherzer, *Die Ritterkreuzträger: Die Inhaber des Ritterkreuzes des Eisernen Kreuzes 1939-1945*, Jena, Germany: Scherzers Militairs-Verlag, 2005, 509; Franz Thomas and Günter Wegmann, *Die Ritterkreuzträger der Deutschen Wehrmacht 1939-1945, Teil II: Fallschirmjäger*, Osnabrück, FRG: Biblio-Verlag, 1986, 178-179.

[14] *Vorschlag zur Beförderung zum Leutnant Hans Hermann Merker, Grosse Kampffliegerschule 4, Oberst Seywald, Oberst Bülowius, Thorn, 9. März 1941.*

[15] Sources, Hans Hermann Merker: Georg Brütting, *Das waren die deutschen Kampfflieger-Asse 1939-1945*, Stuttgart, FRG: Motorbuch Verlag, 1983, 229; Ernst Obermaier, *Die Ritterkreuzträger der Luftwaffe, Jagdflieger 1939-1945*, Mainz, FRG: Verlag Dieter Hoffmann, 1989, 167; Veit Scherzer, *Die Träger des Deutschen Kreuzes in Gold der Luftwaffe 1941-1945*, Bayreuth, FRG: Scherzer's Militair Verlag, 1992, 216.

[16] The German invasion at Narvik was part of "Operation *Weserübung*," the campaign to seize Denmark and Norway in 1940. The operation, pushed by the German Navy and supported by Hitler, was designed to seize the two countries to protect iron ore shipping lanes from Sweden to Germany. Much of the ore was shipped from northern Sweden to the Norwegian port of Narvik and then by ship to Germany. Possession of Norway also facilitated German control of Lend-Lease sea supply lines to Russia, and also served as a potential staging base for future German air and sea operations against the United Kingdom.

[17] *Vorschlag zur bevorzugten Beförderung für Hauptmann (Kr.O.) Heinz Meyer, Fallschirmjäger-Regiment 15, Oberstleutnant und Rgt. Kommandeur Kurt Gröschke, General der Fallschirmtruppe Eugen Meindl, 9.9.44.*

[18] Sources, Heinz Meyer: Peter D. Antill, *Crete 1941: Germany's Lightning Airborne Assault*, Osprey Campaign 147, Oxford, England: Osprey Publishing, 2005, 46; Bruce Quarrie, *German Airborne Divisions: Blitzkrieg 1940-41*, Osprey Battle Orders 4, Oxford, England: Osprey Publishing, 2004, 72; Veit Scherzer, *Die Ritterkreuzträger: Die Inhaber des Ritterkreuzes des Eisernen Kreuzes 1939-1945*, Jena, Germany: Scherzers Militairs-Verlag, 2005, 514; Franz Thomas and Günter Wegmann, *Die Ritterkreuzträger der Deutschen Wehrmacht 1939-1945, Teil II: Fallschirmjäger*, Osnabrück, FRG: Biblio-Verlag, 1986, 184-187.

[19] *Abschrift, Generalmajor Ramcke an das Gen.-Kdo.XI.Flg.-Korps – Abt. IIa – Oberleutnant Werner Milch, Oberst von Fichte, Berlin, 22.12.1942.*

[20] Sources, Werner Milch: Franz Thomas and Günter Wegmann, *Die Ritterkreuzträger der Deutschen Wehrmacht 1939-1945, Teil II: Fallschirmjäger*, Osnabrück, FRG: Biblio-Verlag, 1986, 188-190, 422.

[21] *Beurteilung Helmut Missner, 3. Staffel, I. Gruppe, Jagdgeschwader 54, Befehlstelle, Leutnant und Staffelkapitän Kittel, 5. Juli 1944.*

[22] Sources, Helmut Missner: Ernst Obermaier, *Die Ritterkreuzträger der Luftwaffe, Jagdflieger 1939-1945*, Mainz, FRG: Verlag Dieter Hoffmann, 1989, 169; Hannes Trautloft, Werner Held and Ekkehard Bob, *Die Grünherzjäger*, Friedberg, FRG: Podzun-Pallas-Verlag, 1985, 155; John Weal, *Jagdgeschwader 54 "Grünherz,"* Osprey Aviation Elite 6, Oxford, England: Osprey Publishing, 2001, 112.

[23] The formal award ceremony occurred several days later when Müller, Beisswenger, Crinius and Tonne received the award from Adolf Hitler at his headquarters.

[24] *Vorschlag zur bevorzugten Beförderung für Oberleutnant (Tr. O.) Friedrich-Karl Müller, Jagdgeschwader 53, Oberstleutnant und Geschwaderkommodore von Maltzahn, Gefechtsstand, 15.10.1942.*

[25] Sources, Friedrich-Karl Müller: Roger A. Freeman, *Mighty Eighth War Diary*, London: Jane's, 1981, 224; Ernst Obermaier, *Die Ritterkreuzträger der Luftwaffe, Jagdflieger 1939-1945*, Mainz, FRG: Verlag Dieter Hoffmann, 1989, 53; Jochen Prien, *Pik-As: Geschichte des Jagdgeschwaders 53*, Hamburg, Germany: Dr. Jochen Prien, 1991, Teil 1: 194, 388, 500, Teil 2: 559, 560; Jochen Prien, Gerhard Stemmer, Peter Rodeike and Winfried Bock, *Die Jagdfliegerverbände der Deutschen Luftwaffe 1934 bis 1945, Teil 3: Einsatz in Dänemark und Norwegen, 9.4. bis 30.11.40, Der Feldzug im Westen, 10.5. bis 25.6.1940*, Eutin, Germany: Struve, 356-357; Jochen Prien, Gerhard Stemmer, Peter Rodeike and Winfried Bock, *Die Jagdfliegerverbände der Deutschen Luftwaffe 1934 bis 1945, Teil 4/II: Einsatz am Kanal und über England, 26.6.1940 bis 21.6.1941*, Eutin, Germany: Struve, 267, 272; Jochen Prien, Gerhard Stemmer, Peter Rodeike and Winfried Bock, *Die Jagdfliegerverbände der Deutschen Luftwaffe 1934 bis 1945, Teil 6/II: Unternehmen "Barbarossa" Einsatz im Osten 22.6. bis 5.12.1941*, Eutin, Germany: Struve, 2003, 164, 166; Jochen Prien, Gerhard Stemmer, Peter Rodeike and Winfried Bock, *Die Jagdfliegerverbände der Deutschen Luftwaffe 1934 bis 1945, Teil8/II: Einsatz im Mittelmeerraum November 1941 bis Dezember 1942*, Eutin, Germany: Struve, 2004, 77.

[26] *Beurteilungsnotiz über den Leutnant (Tr.O.) Horst Müller, II./ Kampfgeschwader 76, Hauptmann u.m.d.F.d.Gr.b. Riedesel zu Eisenach, Gefechtsstand, 12.2.1942.*

[27] Sources, Horst Müller: Veit Scherzer, *Die Träger des Deutschen Kreuzes in Gold der Luftwaffe 1941-1945*, Bayreuth, FRG: Scherzer's Militair Verlag, 1992, 227; Veit Scherzer, *Die Ritterkreuzträger: Die Inhaber des Ritterkreuzes des Eisernen Kreuzes 1939-1945*, Jena, Germany: Scherzers Militairs-Verlag, 2005, 529.

[28] During the air battle of Sicily from July 10 to August 17, 1943, the *Luftwaffe* lost 1,850 aircraft over the island.

[29] *Brief, Festsetzung des Rangdienstalters Oblt. Dr. Otte, Jagdgeschwader 77, von Manteuffel, Gefechtsstand, 17.7.40.*

[30] It is likely that post-war sources are incorrect as to the location where he was killed and actually mean, Koschniza, Bulgaria.

[31] Sources, Dr. Maximilian Otte: Georg Brütting, *Das waren die deutschen Stuka-Asse, 1939-1945*, Stuttgart, FRG: Motorbuch Verlag, 1976, 157-158; Ernst Obermaier, *Die Ritterkreuzträger der Luftwaffe, Stuka und Schlachtflieger 1939-1945*, Mainz, FRG: Verlag Dieter Hoffmann, 1976, 47; Veit Scherzer, *Die Träger des Deutschen Kreuzes in Gold der Luftwaffe 1941-1945*, Bayreuth, FRG: Scherzer's Militair Verlag, 1992, 243; Franz Thomas, *Die Eichenlaubträger 1940-1945, Band 2: L-Z*, Osnabrück, Germany: Biblio-Verlag, 1998, 137.

[32] *Beurteilungsnotiz über den Oberleutnant Flugzeugführer Karl August Paulsen, IV. / Kampfgeschwader 30, Major und Kommandeur Schumann, O.U., 5 März 1942.*

[33] Next to the Group Commander's signature block is the phrase translated to "Was written by the officer." This is only one of two examples of this phrase, which could mean one of two things. It is either a notation that the rater wrote the evaluation, or it could mean that the rated officer wrote his own recommendation – on himself – and submitted it to the rater for use in the report.

[34] Sources, Karl August Paulsen: Veit Scherzer, *Die Träger des Deutschen Kreuzes in Gold der Luftwaffe 1941-1945*, Bayreuth, FRG: Scherzer's Militair Verlag, 1992, 246; Veit Scherzer, *Die Ritterkreuzträger: Die Inhaber des Ritterkreuzes des Eisernen Kreuzes 1939-1945*, Jena, Germany: Scherzers Militairs-Verlag, 2005, 558.

[35] *Stellungnahme der Zwischendienststellen Viktor Petermann, Jagdgeschwader 52, Major u. stellv. Geschwaderkommodore, Im Felde, 26. 6. 1943.*

[36] Another sources states Petermann flew 374 combat missions. Sources also vary concerning kills while flying a Messerschmitt Me 262 jet. Some state he was credited with two kills in the jet; others state he had none.

[37] Sources, Viktor Petermann: Manfred Boehme, *Jagdgeschwader 7: Die Chronik eines Me 262-Geschwaders 1944/45*, Stuttgart, FRG: Motorbuch Verlag, 1984, 257; Ernst Obermaier, *Die Ritterkreuzträger der Luftwaffe, Jagdflieger 1939-1945*, Mainz, FRG: Verlag Dieter Hoffmann, 1989, 178; Jochen Prien, Gerhard Stemmer, Peter Rodeike and Winfried Bock, *Die Jagdfliegerverbände der Deutschen Luftwaffe 1934 bis 1945, Teil 9/II: Vom Sommerfeldzug 1942 bis zur Niederlage von Stalingrad 1.5.1942 bis 3.2.1943*, Eutin, Germany: Struve, 393; John Weal, *Jagdgeschwader 52: The Experten*, Aviation Elite Units 15, Oxford, England: Osprey Publishing, 2004, 103.

[38] *Kriegs-Beurteilung zum 18 Januar 1945 über den Hauptmann (Kr.) Karl Peters, Lehrgeschwader 1, Oberst und Geschwaderkommodore Helbig, 18. Januar 1945.*

[39] Sources, Karl Peters: Veit Scherzer, *Die Träger des Deutschen Kreuzes in Gold der Luftwaffe 1941-1945*, Bayreuth, FRG: Scherzer's Militair Verlag, 1992, 248; Veit Scherzer, *Die Ritterkreuzträger: Die Inhaber des Ritterkreuzes des Eisernen Kreuzes 1939-1945*, Jena, Germany: Scherzers Militairs-Verlag, 2005, 561; Christopher Shores and Brian Cull, *Air War for Yugoslavia, Greece and Crete*, Carrollton, TX: Squadron Signal Publications, 1987, 238; Peter Taghorn, *Die Geschichte des Lehrgeschwaders 1*, Band 2 (1942-1945), Zweibrucken, Germany: 2004, 487, 534.

[40] One source reports that during this combat, Pölz's radio operator, who also parachuted out of the aircraft, was machine-gunned by U.S. fighters while descending in his parachute.

[41] *Kriegs-Beurteilung zum Oblt. (Kr.O.) Hubert Pölz, III./ Schlachtgeschwader 3, Hauptmann u. Gruppenkommandeur m.d.W.d.G.b. Eyer, Oberstleutnant und Geschwaderkommodore Kuhlmey, Gefechtsstand, 3.3.1944.*

[42] Sources, Hubert Pölz: V. I. Achkasov and N. B. Pavlovich, *Soviet Naval Operations in the Great Patriotic War 1941-1945*, Annapolis, Maryland: Naval Institute Press, 1981, 276-280; Georg Brütting, *Das waren die deutschen Stuka-Asse, 1939-1945*, Stuttgart, FRG: Motorbuch Verlag, 1976, 170-172; Ernst Obermaier, *Die Ritterkreuzträger der Luftwaffe, Stuka und Schlachtflieger 1939-1945*, Mainz, FRG: Verlag Dieter Hoffmann, 1976, 53; Franz Thomas, *Die Eichenlaubträger 1940-1945, Band 2: L-Z*, Osnabrück, Germany: Biblio-Verlag, 1998, 162.

[43] *Beurteilungsnotiz über den Leutnant und Staffeloffizier Dietrich Puttfarken, I./Kampfgeschwader 51, Hauptmann und Kommandeur der I./K.G. 51, Oberstleutnant u. Geschwaderkommodore Schultz-Heyn, Oberst und Geschwaderkommodore Koester, O.U., 11. Nov. 1940.*

[44] Sources, Dietrich Puttfarken: Georg Brütting, *Das waren die deutschen Kampfflieger-Asse 1939-1945*, Stuttgart, FRG: Motorbuch Verlag, 240; Ernst Obermaier, *Die Ritterkreuzträger der Luftwaffe, Jagdflieger 1939-1945*, Mainz, FRG: Verlag Dieter Hoffmann, 1989, 181; Parry, Simon W. *Intruders Over Britain: The Story of the Luftwaffe's Night Intruder Force*, Surbiton/ Surrey, England: Air Research Publications, 1987, 106, 187, 188, 192; Veit Scherzer, *Die Träger des Deutschen Kreuzes in Gold der Luftwaffe 1941-1945*, Bayreuth, FRG: Scherzer's Militair Verlag, 1992, 258.

[45] *Antrag auf Beförderung des Ofw. Rudi Rademacher zum Kriegsoffizier wegen Tapferkeit vor dem Feinde, 1. Staffel, I./ Jagdgeschwader 54, Oberleutnant u. Staffelkapitän Nowotny, von Bonin, O.U., 16.9.1943.*

[46] Another source, Hugh Morgan and John Weal, *German Jet Aces of World War 2* (page 88), state that Rademacher shot down 8 aircraft while piloting the Me 262.

[47] Sources, Rudolf Rademacher: Ernst Obermaier, *Die Ritterkreuzträger der Luftwaffe, Jagdflieger 1939-1945*, Mainz, FRG: Verlag Dieter Hoffmann, 1989, 183, 229; Jochen Prien, Gerhard Stemmer, Peter Rodeike and Winfried Bock, *Die Jagdfliegerverbände der Deutschen Luftwaffe 1934 bis 1945, Teil 9/I: Winterkampf im Osten 6.12.1941 bis 30.4.1942*, Eutin, Germany: Struve, 200, 201.

[48] However, according to Jochen Prien's *Die Jagdfliegerverbände der Deutschen Luftwaffe 1934 bis 1945, Teil 4/I: Einsatz am Kanal und über England, 26.6.1940 bis 21.6.1941*, one of the most comprehensive sources on German fighter pilot victories of the period, there is no confirmation of these five kills.

[49] *Kriegsbeurteilung über den Oberleutnant (Tr.O) Hans Roehrig, III./Jagdgeschwader 53, Hauptmann und Gruppenkommandeur m.d.W.d.G.b. Götz.*

[50] Sources, Hans Roehrig: Ernst Obermaier, *Die Ritterkreuzträger der Luftwaffe, Jagdflieger 1939-1945*, Mainz, FRG: Verlag Dieter Hoffmann, 1989, 187; Jochen Prien, *Pik-As: Geschichte des Jagdgeschwaders 53*, Hamburg, Germany: Dr. Jochen Prien, 1991, *Teil 1*: 414, *Teil 2*: 568; Jochen Prien, Gerhard Stemmer, Peter Rodeike and Winfried Bock, *Die Jagdfliegerverbände der Deutschen Luftwaffe 1934 bis 1945, Teil 6/II: Unternehmen "Barbarossa" Einsatz im Osten 22.6. bis 5.12.1941*, Eutin, Germany: Struve, 2003, 114; Jochen Prien, Gerhard Stemmer, Peter Rodeike and Winfried Bock, *Die Jagdfliegerverbände der Deutschen Luftwaffe 1934 bis 1945, Teil8/II: Einsatz im Mittelmeerraum November 1941 bis Dezember 1942*, Eutin, Germany: Struve, 2004, 81, 213.

[51] *Beurteilung Oberfeldwebel Herbert Röwer, III./Kampfgeschwader 3, Hauptmann Fach, Gruppengefechtsstand, 27.4.1943.*

[52] Sources, Herbert Röwer: Georg Brütting, *Das waren die deutschen Kampfflieger-Asse 1939-1945*, Stuttgart, FRG: Motorbuch Verlag, 244; Veit Scherzer, *Die Träger des Deutschen Kreuzes in Gold der*

Luftwaffe 1941-1945, Bayreuth, FRG: Scherzer's Militair Verlag, 1992, 275; Veit Scherzer, *Die Ritterkreuzträger: Die Inhaber des Ritterkreuzes des Eisernen Kreuzes 1939-1945*, Jena, Germany: Scherzers Militairs-Verlag, 2005, 609.

[53] *Vorschlag zur Beförderung eines Offiziers (Kr.O.) zum nächsthöheren Dienstgrad Erich Rudorffer, II./Jagdgeschwader Richthofen Nr. 2, Oberleutnant und stellv. Gruppenkommandeur Dickfeld, General der Flieger Loerzer, Gefechtsstand, 3. Dezember 1942.*

[54] Sources, Eric Rudorffer: Ernst Obermaier, *Die Ritterkreuzträger der Luftwaffe, Jagdflieger 1939-1945*, Mainz, FRG: Verlag Dieter Hoffmann, 1989, 39; Jochen Prien, Gerhard Stemmer, Peter Rodeike and Winfried Bock, *Die Jagdfliegerverbände der Deutschen Luftwaffe 1934 bis 1945, Teil 5: Heimatverteidigung 10. Mai 1940 bis 31. Dezember 1941, Einsatz im Mittelmeerraum Oktober 1940 bis November 1941, Einsatz im Westen 22. Juni bis 31. Dezember 1941, Die Ergänzungsjagdgruppen Einsatz 1941 bis zur Auflösung Anfang 1942*, Eutin, Germany: Struve, 2003, 438-441; Jochen Prien, Gerhard Stemmer, Peter Rodeike and Winfried Bock, *Die Jagdfliegerverbände der Deutschen Luftwaffe 1934 bis 1945, Teil 7: Heimatsverteidigung 1. Januar bis 31. Dezember 1942, Einsatz im Westen 1. Januar bis 31. Dezember 1942*, Eutin, Germany: Struve, 2003, 260; Jochen Prien, Gerhard Stemmer, Peter Rodeike and Winfried Bock, *Die Jagdfliegerverbände der Deutschen Luftwaffe 1934 bis 1945, Teil8/I: Einsatz im Mittelmeerraum November 1941 bis Dezember 1942,* Eutin, Germany: Struve, 2004, 51, 53; Franz Thomas, *Die Eichenlaubträger 1940-1945, Band 2: L-Z*, Osnabrück, Germany: Biblio-Verlag, 1998, 230; John Weal, *Jagdgeschwader 2 'Richthofen,'* Osprey Aviation Elite 1, Oxford, England: Osprey Publishing, 2000, 36, 74.

[55] The unit was named for World War I Field Marshal, and later President of the Weimar Republic, Paul von Hindenburg.

[56] Assault Detachment Koch had several missions that day: first, by surprise glider landings, to capture the bridges of Vroenhoven, Veltwezelt and Canne intact; second, to destroy with explosives the artillery and works of Fort Eben Emael; and, third, to hold these positions at the bridges and the fort until the arrival of German ground forces who were to relieve them.

[57] *Vorschlag zur bevorzugten Beförderung zum Major für Hauptmann (Tr.O.) Martin Schächter, 3. Fallschirmjäger Division, Generalleutnant und Divisionskommandeur Schimpf, Generaloberst Student, Div. St. Qu., 30.10.1944.*

[58] Sources, Martin Schächter: Franz Thomas and Günter Wegmann, *Die Ritterkreuzträger der Deutschen Wehrmacht 1939-1945, Teil II: Fallschirmjäger*, Osnabrück, FRG: Biblio-Verlag, 1986, 248-249.

[59] The unit flew Heinkel He 51 biplanes and then Messerschmitt Me 109Bs.

[60] *Taran* (Russian for ram attack) was a tactic in air combat, with the goal of outright ramming the enemy aircraft or to destroy its controls using either your propeller or wing. It was sometimes used when pilot ran out of ammunition or when his plane had already been damaged. Though risky, it was believed that the pilot stood a fair chance of surviving. Three types of taran attacks were made: using the propeller and attack from the rear to destroy the controls in the tail of the enemy aircraft; using the wing to cut off the wing or tail of the enemy aircraft; *d*irect ramming (*taranyy udar*), the easiest to perform, but also the most dangerous.

[61] Sources, Wolfgang Schellmann: Ernst Obermaier, *Die Ritterkreuzträger der Luftwaffe, Jagdflieger 1939-1945*, Mainz, FRG: Verlag Dieter Hoffmann, 1989, 193; Jochen Prien, Gerhard Stemmer, Peter Rodeike and Winfried Bock, *Die Jagdfliegerverbände der Deutschen Luftwaffe 1934 bis 1945, Teil 6/I: Unternehmen "Barbarossa" Einsatz im Osten 22.6. bis 5.12.1941*, Eutin, Germany: Struve, 2003, 158; Karl Ries and Hans Ring, *Legion Condor, 1936-1939: Eine illustrierte Dokumentation*, Mainz, Germany: Verlag Dieter Hoffmann, 1980, 251, 265-266; Christopher Shores and Brian Cull, *Air War for Yugoslavia, Greece and Crete*, Carrollton, TX: Squadron Signal Publications, 1987, 266; John Weal, *Jagdgeschwader 2 'Richthofen,'* Osprey Aviation Elite 1, Oxford, England: Osprey Publishing, 2000, 28, 33, 64, 66; John Weal, *Jagdgeschwader 27 'Afrika,'* Osprey Aviation Elite 1, Oxford, England: Osprey Publishing, 2000, 40, 43, 48.

[62] *Beurteilung zum 15. November 1937 über den Oberleutnant Wolfgang Schellmann, Jagdgeschwader 135, Major und Gruppen Kdr. Ibel, Major u. Gr. Kdr. Viek, Oberstleutnant u. Kommodore des Jagdgeschwader Richthofen von Massow, Bad Aibling, 29.9.37.*

[63] *Zusatz zur Beurteilungsnotiz des Major (Tr.O.) Wolfgang Schenk, Generalkommando des II. Fliegerkorps, Generalleutnant Bülowius, Generalfeldmarschall von Richthofen, Gefechtsstand, 11.10.1943.*

[64] The test proved less than successful; the aircraft had no real bombsight and was too fast to be used as a dive-bomber – the only other way of achieving required accuracy.

[65] Sources, Wolfgang Schenck: Chris Bishop, *Luftwaffe Squadrons 1939-45*, Stapelhurst, England: Spellmont, 2006, 165; Ernst Obermaier, *Die Ritterkreuzträger der Luftwaffe, Jagdflieger 1939-1945*, Mainz, FRG: Verlag Dieter Hoffmann, 1989, 55; Ernst Obermaier, *Die Ritterkreuzträger der Luftwaffe, Stuka und Schlachtflieger 1939-1945*, Mainz, FRG: Verlag Dieter Hoffmann, 1976, 43; Franz Thomas, *Die Eichenlaubträger 1940-1945, Band 2: L-Z*, Osnabrück, Germany: Biblio-Verlag, 1998, 251.

[66] *Beurteilungsnotiz über den Oblt. Horst Schiller, I./ Sturzkampfgeschwader 1, Major und Gruppenkommandeur Sorge, Gefechtsstand, 28.9.1941.*

[67] The infraction is not listed in the report.

[68] Sources, Horst Schiller: Cajus Bekker, *The Luftwaffe War Diaries*, London: MacDonald & Co., 1967, 25; Georg Brütting, *Das waren die deutschen Stuka-Asse, 1939-1945*, Stuttgart, FRG: Motorbuch Verlag, 1976, 247; Ernst Obermaier, *Die Ritterkreuzträger der Luftwaffe, Stuka und Schlachtflieger 1939-1945*, Mainz, FRG: Verlag Dieter Hoffmann, 1976, 137; Veit Scherzer, *Die Träger des Deutschen Kreuzes in Gold der Luftwaffe 1941-1945*, Bayreuth, FRG: Scherzer's Militair Verlag, 1992, 289.

[69] *Vorschlag zur Beförderung zum Kriegsoffizier Horst Schimpke, Fallschirm-Panzerjäger Abteilung, Hauptmann und Abteilungskommandeur Brückner, Generalmajor und Divisionskommandeur Heidrich.*

[70] Sources, Horst Schimpke: Franz Thomas and Günter Wegmann, *Die Ritterkreuzträger der Deutschen Wehrmacht 1939-1945, Teil II: Fallschirmjäger*, Osnabrück, FRG: Biblio-Verlag, 1986, 256-257.

[71] *Vorschlag zur Beförderung zum Kriegsoffizier wegen Tapferkeit vor dem Feind Leonhard Schmidt, I. / Fallschirm-Jäger Rgt. 1, Major u. Btl.-Kommandeur Graf v.d. Schulenburg.*

[72] There is no record in the German Archives (*Bundesarchiv*) of official approval for the Knight's Cross. It is likely that it was approved through the Commander, 1st Paratroop Corps, but the request never made it to Berlin.

[73] Sources, Leonhard Schmidt: Chris Ellis, *7th Flieger Division: Student's Fallschirmjäger Elite*, Surrey, England: Ian Allan Publishing, 2002, 22, 23; Veit Scherzer, *Die Träger des Deutschen Kreuzes in Gold der Luftwaffe 1941-1945*, Bayreuth, FRG: Scherzer's Militair Verlag, 1992, 294; Veit Scherzer, *Die Ritterkreuzträger: Die Inhaber des Ritterkreuzes des Eisernen Kreuzes 1939-1945*, Jena, Germany: Scherzers Militairs-Verlag, 2005, 148; Franz Thomas and Günter Wegmann, *Die Ritterkreuzträger der Deutschen Wehrmacht 1939-1945, Teil II: Fallschirmjäger*, Osnabrück, FRG: Biblio-Verlag, 1986, 268-269.

[74] *Beurteilungs-Notizen für Oblt. Otto Schmidt, I./Sturzkampfgeschwader 77, Oblt. Bruck, 10.2.41.*

[75] Sources, Otto Schmidt: Georg Brütting, *Das waren die deutschen Stuka-Asse, 1939-1945*, Stuttgart, FRG: Motorbuch Verlag, 1976, 247-248; Ernst Obermaier, *Die Ritterkreuzträger der Luftwaffe, Stuka und Schlachtflieger 1939-1945*, Mainz, FRG: Verlag Dieter Hoffmann, 1976, 138-139; Veit Scherzer, *Die Träger des Deutschen Kreuzes in Gold der Luftwaffe 1941-1945*, Bayreuth, FRG: Scherzer's Militair Verlag, 1992, 294.

[76] *Vorschlag zur Beförderung zum Leutnant, Heinz Schnaufer, Flugzeugführerschule (C) 3, Oberst und Kommandeur Macard, General der Flieger und Höh.Fl.Ausb.Kdr.4 General der Flieger Wilberg, Alt-Lönnewitz, 18.3.1941.*

[77] Peenemünde, on the Baltic coast, was the site of experimental and development work by German rocket designers. The RAF dispatched 596 four-engine aircraft; 560 reached the objective and these planes dropped 1,795 tons of high explosive and incendiary bombs on the target. Forty bombers were lost on the mission (a loss rate of 6.7%). The raid killed 178 German scientists and technical personnel (the stated goal of the attack was to kill as many as possible), but also killed about 500 foreign workers forced into the research program. The British Official History estimated the German rocket program, including the V-1 and V-2, was delayed two months due to the attack, while German sources placed the setback at 4-6 weeks.

[78] Sources, Heinz Schnaufer: Dieter Hölsken, *V-Missiles of the Third Reich, the V-1 and V-2*, Sturbridge, Massachusetts, Monogram Aviation Publications, 1994, 90; Franz Kurowski, *Luftwaffe Aces: German Combat Pilots of WWII*, translated by David Johnston, Mechanicsburg, PA: Stackpole, 2004, 326; Martin Middlebrook, *The Peenemünde Raid; The Night of 17-18 August 1943*, London: Allen Lane, 1982, 97-98; Ernst Obermaier, *Die Ritterkreuzträger der Luftwaffe, Jagdflieger 1939-1945*, Mainz, FRG: Verlag Dieter Hoffmann, 1989, 25; Veit Scherzer, *Die Ritterkreuzträger: Die Inhaber des Ritterkreuzes des Eisernen Kreuzes 1939-1945*, Jena, Germany: Scherzers Militairs-Verlag, 2005, 647; Franz Thomas, *Die Eichenlaubträger 1940-1945, Band 2: L-Z*, Osnabrück, Germany: Biblio-Verlag, 1998, 273.

[79] *Beurteilung, Herbert Schob, Z.G. 76, Major und Geschwaderkommodore m.d.W.d.G.b. Kowalewski, Oberst Handrick, 10.5.44.*

[80] Sources, Herbert Schob: Jeffrey Ethell and Alfred Price, *Target Berlin*, London" Jane's, 1981, 80; Ernst Obermaier, *Die Ritterkreuzträger der Luftwaffe, Jagdflieger 1939-1945*, Mainz, FRG: Verlag Dieter Hoffmann, 1989, 200.

[81] *Kriegsbeurteilung zum 1. Juni 1943 über den Hauptmann (d.R.), Gruppenkommandeur II./N.J.G.5 m.d.W.d.G.b. Rudolf Schoenert, Nachtjagdgeschwader 5, Major u. Geschwaderkommodore m.d.W.d.G.b. X, Generalmajor beauftragt mit der Wahrnehmung der Geschäfte des Kommandeurs der 4. Jagddivision Hüth, O.U., 30.4. 1943.*

[82] Between July 24 and August 3, 1943, RAF Bomber Command flew six major nighttime missions against the city, while the USAAF 8th Air Force flew two major daylight missions. The raids destroyed a large part of the city; on one night alone, Hamburg lost 40,000 people.

[83] RAF Bomber Command lost 96 of 799 bombers (12%) deployed on this "maximum effort" against the city. Due to these losses, and poor weather conditions over the target, Nuremburg was only lightly damaged.

[84] Sources, Rudolf Schoenert: Peter Hinchliffe, *The Lent Papers: Helmut Lent*, Bristol, England: Cerberus Publishing, 2003, 208, 209, 210, Martin Middlebrook and Chris Everitt, *The Bomber Command War Diaries*, New York: Viking Penguin, 1987, 177; Middlebrook, Martin, *The Battle of Hamburg: Allied Bomber Forces Against a German City*, New York: Charles Scribner's Sons, 1980, 264; Middlebrook, Martin. *The Nuremberg Raid: The Worst Night of the War, March 30-31, 1944*, New York: William Morrow & Company, 1974, 230; Ernst Obermaier, *Die Ritterkreuzträger der Luftwaffe, Jagdflieger 1939-1945*, Mainz, FRG: Verlag Dieter Hoffmann, 1989, 64; Franz Thomas, *Die Eichenlaubträger 1940-1945, Band 2: L-Z*, Osnabrück, Germany: Biblio-Verlag, 1998, 278.

[85] *Vorschlag zur Beförderung zum Truppen bzw. Kriegsoffizier, Fj.-Ofw. Walter Schuck, 9./Jagdgeschwader 5, Leutnant Gayko, Oberst und Vertreter im Kommando d. Fl.Fhr.3 Weiss, Gefechtsstand, 5. 6. 1944.*

[86] Sources, Walter Schuck: Hugh Morgan and John Weal, *German Jet Aces of World War 2*, Osprey Aircraft of the Aces 17, Oxford, England: Osprey Publishing, 1998, 56; Ernst Obermaier, *Die Ritterkreuzträger der Luftwaffe, Jagdflieger 1939-1945*, Mainz, FRG: Verlag Dieter Hoffmann, 1989, 69.

[87] *Vorschlag zur bevorzugten Beförderung für Major (z.V.) Wolf-Werner Graf von der Schulenburg, Fallschirm-Jäger Rgt. 1, Oberst und Regimentskommandeur Schulz, Generalleutnant und Div. Kommandeur Heidrich, 4. April 1944.*

[88] Sources, Wolf Werner Graf von der Schulenburg: Erich Busch, *Die Fallschirmjäger-Chronik 1935-1945*, Friedberg, FRG: Podzun-Palls-Verlag, 1983, 122; Stephen Thomas Previtera, *The Iron Time: A History of the Knight's Cross*, Richmond, VA: Winidore Press, 1999, 311; Franz Thomas and Günter Wegmann, *Die Ritterkreuzträger der Deutschen Wehrmacht 1939-1945, Teil II: Fallschirmjäger*, Osnabrück, FRG: Biblio-Verlag, 1986, 274-275.

[89] Sources, Franz Schwaiger: Ernst Obermaier, *Die Ritterkreuzträger der Luftwaffe, Jagdflieger 1939-1945*, Mainz, FRG: Verlag Dieter Hoffmann, 1989, 204; Jochen Prien, Gerhard Stemmer, Peter Rodeike and Winfried Bock, *Die Jagdfliegerverbände der Deutschen Luftwaffe 1934 bis 1945, Teil8/I: Einsatz im Mittelmeerraum November 1941 bis Dezember 1942,* Eutin, Germany: Struve, 2004, 89; Jochen Prien, Gerhard Stemmer, Peter Rodeike and Winfried Bock, *Die Jagdfliegerverbände der Deutschen Luftwaffe 1934 bis 1945, Teil 9/II: Vom Sommerfeldzug 1942 bis zur Niederlage von Stalingrad 1.5.1942 bis 3.2.1943*, Eutin, Germany: Struve, 150.

[90] *Vorschlag zur Beförderung zum Leutnant (d.B.) Georg Seelmann, I./Jagdgeschwader 77, Oberleutnant u. Staffelkapitän Hahn, Hauptmann u. Gruppenkommandeur Janke, Gefechtsstand, 4.Okt.1940.*

[91] Sources, Georg Seelmann: Ernst Obermaier, *Die Ritterkreuzträger der Luftwaffe, Jagdflieger 1939-1945*, Mainz, FRG: Verlag Dieter Hoffmann, 1989, 204; Jochen Prien, Gerhard Stemmer, Peter Rodeike and Winfried Bock, *Die Jagdfliegerverbände der Deutschen Luftwaffe 1934 bis 1945, Teil 6/I: Unternehmen "Barbarossa" Einsatz im Osten 22.6. bis 5.12.1941*, Eutin, Germany: Struve, 2003, 334-351; Jochen Prien, Gerhard Stemmer, Peter Rodeike and Winfried Bock, *Die Jagdfliegerverbände der Deutschen Luftwaffe 1934 bis 1945, Teil8/II: Einsatz im Mittelmeerraum November 1941 bis Dezember 1942,* Eutin, Germany: Struve, 2004, 8; Jochen Prien, Gerhard Stemmer, Peter Rodeike and Winfried Bock, *Die Jagdfliegerverbände der Deutschen Luftwaffe 1934 bis 1945, Teil 9/II: Vom Sommerfeldzug 1942 bis zur Niederlage von Stalingrad 1.5.1942 bis 3.2.1943*, Eutin, Germany: Struve, 361.

[92] *Vorschlag zur bevorzugten Beförderung für Hauptmann (Tr.O.) Günther Sempert, Fallschirm-Panzerjäger-Abteilung 1, Hauptmann Schwarzer, Generalleutnant und Divisionskommandeur Heidrich, 4.11.44.*

[93] In 1943, with the war going badly, Italy changed sides and Mussolini was arrested. Hitler launched "Operation Oak" to free the Duce

from a mountaintop resort, in which he was held, in order to install him as the leader of a new Fascist government in northern Italy.

94 Sources, Günther Sempert: Franz Thomas and Günter Wegmann, *Die Ritterkreuzträger der Deutschen Wehrmacht 1939-1945, Teil II: Fallschirmjäger*, Osnabrück, FRG: Biblio-Verlag, 1986, 286-287.

95 *Kriegs-Beurteilung zum 14. Juni 1944 über den Oblt. Friedrich Seyffardt, II./Schlachtgeschwader 2 Immelmann, Major Frank, 14.6.1944.*

96 Sources, Friedrich Seyffardt: Ernst Obermaier, *Die Ritterkreuzträger der Luftwaffe, Stuka und Schlachtflieger 1939-1945*, Mainz, FRG: Verlag Dieter Hoffmann, 1976, 143.

97 *Beurteilungs-Notizen für Major Walter Sigel, Sturzkampfgeschwader Immelmann 2, Oberstlt u. Geschw. K'dore, Im Felde, 20.6.41.*

98 Sources, Walter Sigel: Chris Bishop, *Luftwaffe Squadrons 1939-45*, Stapelhurst, England: Spellmont, 2006, 61; Ernst Obermaier, *Die Ritterkreuzträger der Luftwaffe, Stuka und Schlachtflieger 1939-1945*, Mainz, FRG: Verlag Dieter Hoffmann, 1976, 42; Franz Thomas, *Die Eichenlaubträger 1940-1945, Band 2: L-Z*, Osnabrück, Germany: Biblio-Verlag, 1998, 323.

99 *Beurteilung Leutnant der Reserve Eduard Peter Skrzipek, II./Kampfgeschwader "Boelcke" Nr. 27, Hauptmann und Gruppenkommandeur Günzel, Oberstleutnant Ulbricht, Generalleutnant Pflugbeil, Bourges, 31,12,1940.*

100 Sources, Eduard Skrzipek: Georg Brütting, *Das waren die deutschen Kampfflieger-Asse 1939-1945*, Stuttgart, FRG: Motorbuch Verlag, 1983, 172; Veit Scherzer, *Die Ritterkreuzträger: Die Inhaber des Ritterkreuzes des Eisernen Kreuzes 1939-1945*, Jena, Germany: Scherzers Militairs-Verlag, 2005, 680; Franz Thomas, *Die Eichenlaubträger 1940-1945, Band 1: A-K, Band 2: L-Z*, Osnabrück, Germany: Biblio-Verlag, 1998, 330.

101 *Kriegs-Beurteilung zum 1. Oktober 1944 über den Oblt. (Tr.O.) Rudolf Smola, II./Schlachtgeschwader 2 Immelmann, Hauptmann und Gruppenkommandeur Kennel, 1.10.1944.*

102 Sources, Rudolf Smola: Ernst Obermaier, *Die Ritterkreuzträger der Luftwaffe, Stuka und Schlachtflieger 1939-1945*, Mainz, FRG: Verlag Dieter Hoffmann, 1976, 143-144.

103 *Bevorzugte Beförderung von Offizieren, Hauptmann Willi Sölter, Kampfgeschwader 77, Major und Kommodore m.d.W.d.G.b. Stemmler, Gefechtsstand, 22.5.1944.*

104 Sources, Willi Sölter: Veit Scherzer, *Die Ritterkreuzträger: Die Inhaber des Ritterkreuzes des Eisernen Kreuzes 1939-1945*, Jena, Germany: Scherzers Militairs-Verlag, 2005, 681; Rudi Schmidt, *Achtung – Torpedos Los!* Koblenz, Germany: Bernhard & Graefe Verlag, 1991, 249.

105 *Vorschlag zur Überführung des Lt. Stadermann (Kriegsoffizier) zu den aktiven Friedensoffizieren, II./ Kampfgeschwader 77, Hauptmann und Gruppenkommandeur Peltz, Gefechtsstand, 14.4.1941.*

106 Sources, Waldemar Stadermann: Georg Brütting, *Das waren die deutschen Kampfflieger-Asse 1939-1945*, Stuttgart, FRG: Motorbuch Verlag, 1983, 257.

107 *Beurteilung über den Oberfeldwebel Heinz Sterr, II. / Jagdgeschwader 54, Hauptmann und Führer der Jagdgruppe Rudorffer, von Bonin, Gefechtsstand, 12.9. 1943.*

108 *Beurteilung Heinz Sterr, IV. / Jagdgeschwader 54, Major u. Gruppenkommandeur Späte, Der Kommandeur 3. Jagddivision Grabmann, Der Kommandierende General des I. Jagdkorps Schmid, 29.9. 1944.*

109 Sources, Heinrich Sterr: Ernst Obermaier, *Die Ritterkreuzträger der Luftwaffe, Jagdflieger 1939-1945*, Mainz, FRG: Verlag Dieter Hoffmann, 1989, 210; John Weal, *Focke-Wulf Fw 190 Aces of the Russian Front*, Osprey Aircraft of the Aces 6, Oxford, England: Osprey Publishing, 1995, 27, 58, 93;

110 *Kriegs-Beurteilung zum 1. April 1945 über den Major i.G. Walter Stimpel, Luftwaffenführungsstab Ia, Oberstlt.i.G. u. Abt. Chef von Greiff, Generalmajor Christian, H.Qu., 28.3.1945.*

111 Sources, Walter Stimpel: Ernst Obermaier, *Die Ritterkreuzträger der Luftwaffe, Stuka und Schlachtflieger 1939-1945*, Mainz, FRG: Verlag Dieter Hoffmann, 1976, 147.

112 The attack killed 1,800 and injured 2,400. It destroyed 171 industrial buildings and 3,000 houses. Bomber Command lost 5.4% of the attacking force.

113 *Kriegs-Beurteilung für Leutnant Heinz Strüning, I./Nachtjagdgeschwader 1, Hauptmann m.d.W.d.G.b. Frank, Major m.d.W.d.G.b. Streib, O.U., 7. Juli 1943.*

114 The RAF Bomber Command attack killed 380 and injured 2,152. It destroyed 2,331 buildings. Bomber Command lost 3.8% of the attacking force.

115 *Luftwaffe* night fighters hammered the Wesseling attackers, shooting down 37 of the 133 bombers, a loss rate of 27.8%.

116 Sources, Heinz Strüning: Martin Middlebrook and Chris Everitt, *The Bomber Command War Diaries*, New York: Viking Penguin, 1987, 125, 194, 385, 401, 427, 532; Ernst Obermaier, *Die Ritterkreuzträger der Luftwaffe, Jagdflieger 1939-1945*, Mainz, FRG: Verlag Dieter Hoffmann, 1989, 67; Franz Thomas, *Die Eichenlaubträger 1940-1945, Band 2: L-Z*, Osnabrück, Germany: Biblio-Verlag, 1998, 365.

117 *Vorschlag zur Bevorzugten Beförderung für Hauptmann (Tr.O.) Karl Stefan Tannert, Fallschirmjäger-Regiment 2, Oberst u. Rgt.-Kdr. Hans Kroh, Generalleutnant u. Div. Kdr. Bernhard Ramcke, O.U., 9.6. 1944.*

118 Sources, Karl Tannert: Franz Thomas and Günter Wegmann, *Die Ritterkreuzträger der Deutschen Wehrmacht 1939-1945, Teil II: Fallschirmjäger*, Osnabrück, FRG: Biblio-Verlag, 1986, 310-312.

119 *Beurteilung Gerhard Thyben, II./Jagdgeschwader Udet, Major u. selbst. Gruppenkommandeur Brändle, Gefechtsstand, 1. Aug. 1943.*

120 Sources, Gerhard Thyben: Chris Bishop, *Luftwaffe Squadrons 1939-45*, Stapelhurst, England: Spellmont, 2006, 184; Ernst Obermaier, *Die Ritterkreuzträger der Luftwaffe, Jagdflieger 1939-1945*, Mainz, FRG: Verlag Dieter Hoffmann, 1989, 75; Franz Thomas, *Die Eichenlaubträger 1940-1945, Band 2: L-Z*, Osnabrück, Germany: Biblio-Verlag, 1998, 381.

121 *Beurteilung über den Leutnant d.R. Cord Tietjen, II. / Fallschirm-Jäger Rgt. 1, Hauptmann und Bataillonsführer Prager, Oberstleutnant und Rgt.-Kommandeur Bräuer, Stendal, 27.6.1939.*

122 Sources, Cord Tietjen: Veit Scherzer, *Die Ritterkreuzträger: Die Inhaber des Ritterkreuzes des Eisernen Kreuzes 1939-1945*, Jena, Germany: Scherzers Militairs-Verlag, 2005, 717; Franz Thomas and Günter Wegmann, *Die Ritterkreuzträger der Deutschen Wehrmacht 1939-1945, Teil II: Fallschirmjäger*, Osnabrück, FRG: Biblio-Verlag, 1986, 316-318.

123 Sources, Erich Timm: Martin Blumenson, *Anzio: The Gambit That Failed*, Philadelphia: J.B. Lippincott, 1963, 124; Erich Busch, *Die Fallschirmjäger-Chronik 1935-1945*, Friedberg, FRG: Podzun-Palls-Verlag, 1983, 110-119; Bruce Quarrie, *German Airborne Divisions: Blitzkrieg 1940-41*, Osprey Battle Orders 4, Oxford, England: Osprey Publishing, 2004, 53; Veit Scherzer, *Die Ritterkreuzträger: Die Inhaber des Ritterkreuzes des Eisernen Kreuzes 1939-1945*, Jena, Germany: Scherzers Militairs-Verlag, 2005, 717; Franz Thomas and Günter Wegmann, *Die Ritterkreuzträger der Deutschen Wehrmacht 1939-1945, Teil II: Fallschirmjäger*, Osnabrück, FRG: Biblio-Verlag, 1986, 320-321.

124 *Bevorzugte Beförderung des Oblt. Ubben (Kurt), III./J.G. 77, Generalkommando des IV. Flieger-Korps, Generalleutnant Pflugbeil, 14 Dezember 1941.*

[125] Sources, Kurt Ubben: Ernst Obermaier, *Die Ritterkreuzträger der Luftwaffe, Jagdflieger 1939-1945*, Mainz, FRG: Verlag Dieter Hoffmann, 1989, 48; Jochen Prien, Gerhard Stemmer, Peter Rodeike and Winfried Bock, *Die Jagdfliegerverbände der Deutschen Luftwaffe 1934 bis 1945, Teil 6/II: Unternehmen "Barbarossa" Einsatz im Osten 22.6. bis 5.12.1941*, Eutin, Germany: Struve, 2003, 368, 372, 378; Jochen Prien, Gerhard Stemmer, Peter Rodeike and Winfried Bock, *Die Jagdfliegerverbände der Deutschen Luftwaffe 1934 bis 1945, Teil8/II: Einsatz im Mittelmeerraum November 1941 bis Dezember 1942,* Eutin, Germany: Struve, 2004, 327; Christopher Shores and Brian Cull, *Air War for Yugoslavia, Greece and Crete*, Carrollton, TX: Squadron Signal Publications, 1987, 357; Franz Thomas, *Die Eichenlaubträger 1940-1945, Band 2: L-Z*, Osnabrück, Germany: Biblio-Verlag, 1998, 395.

[126] *Beurteilungsnotiz über den Oberleutnant Rudolf Weigel, III./Sturzkampfgeschwader 77, Hauptmann m.d.W.d.G.d. Kommandeurs b. Jakob, Major mit der Führung des Geschwaders beauftragt Bruck, Gefechtsstand,.1.3.1943.*

[127] Sources, Rudolf Weigel: Georg Brütting, *Das waren die deutschen Stuka-Asse, 1939-1945*, Stuttgart, FRG: Motorbuch Verlag, 1976, 257; Ernst Obermaier, *Die Ritterkreuzträger der Luftwaffe, Stuka und Schlachtflieger 1939-1945*, Mainz, FRG: Verlag Dieter Hoffmann, 1976, 153-154; Peter C. Smith, *Stuka Squadron*, Wellingborough, England: Patrick Stephens, 1990, 184.

[128] *Vorschlag zur Beförderung zum Leutnant, Ernst Weismann, IV. / Jagdgeschwader 51, Leutnant u. Staffelführer Seelmann, 14. Oktober 1941.*

[129] Sources, Ernst Weismann: Ernst Obermaier, *Die Ritterkreuzträger der Luftwaffe, Jagdflieger 1939-1945*, Mainz, FRG: Verlag Dieter Hoffmann, 1989, 221; Jochen Prien, Gerhard Stemmer, Peter Rodeike and Winfried Bock, *Die Jagdfliegerverbände der Deutschen Luftwaffe 1934 bis 1945, Teil 6/I: Unternehmen "Barbarossa" Einsatz im Osten 22.6. bis 5.12.1941*, Eutin, Germany: Struve, 2003, 334, 343, 344, 345, 347; Jochen Prien, Gerhard Stemmer, Peter Rodeike and Winfried Bock, *Die Jagdfliegerverbände der Deutschen Luftwaffe 1934 bis 1945, Teil 9/I: Winterkampf im Osten 6.12.1941 bis 30.4.1942*, Eutin, Germany: Struve, 120, 121; Jochen Prien, Gerhard Stemmer, Peter Rodeike and Winfried Bock, *Die Jagdfliegerverbände der Deutschen Luftwaffe 1934 bis 1945, Teil 9/II: Vom Sommerfeldzug 1942 bis zur Niederlage von Stalingrad 1.5.1942 bis 3.2.1943*, Eutin, Germany: Struve, 353, 354.

[130] *Brief, Oberleutnant Weissenberger, Luftflottenkommando Reich, Der Chef des Generalstabes Nielsen, 12.7.44.*

[131] Sources, Theodor Weissenberger: Ernst Obermaier, *Die Ritterkreuzträger der Luftwaffe, Jagdflieger 1939-1945*, Mainz, FRG: Verlag Dieter Hoffmann, 1989, 58; Franz Thomas, *Die Eichenlaubträger 1940-1945, Band 2: L-Z*, Osnabrück, Germany: Biblio-Verlag, 1998, 430.

[132] *Vorschlag zur Beförderung zum Kriegsoffizier wegen Tapferkeit vor dem Feinde Feldwebel Walter Werner, Fallschirmpionierbataillon 1, Major und Btl.-Kommandeur Frömming, O.U., 22.7.1944.*

[133] Sources, Walter Werner: Veit Scherzer, *Die Ritterkreuzträger: Die Inhaber des Ritterkreuzes des Eisernen Kreuzes 1939-1945*, Jena, Germany: Scherzers Militairs-Verlag, 2005, 751; Franz Thomas and Günter Wegmann, *Die Ritterkreuzträger der Deutschen Wehrmacht 1939-1945, Teil II: Fallschirmjäger*, Osnabrück, FRG: Biblio-Verlag, 1986, 361-362.

[134] *Beurteilung des Feldwebel Heinz Wernicke (K.O.A.), II./ Jagdgeschwader 54, Leutnant und Staffelführer Ademeit, Befehlstelle, 4.7.1943.*

[135] Sources, Heinz Wernicke: Ernst Obermaier, *Die Ritterkreuzträger der Luftwaffe, Jagdflieger 1939-1945*, Mainz, FRG: Verlag Dieter Hoffmann, 1989, 222; John Weal, *Jagdgeschwader 54 "Grünherz,"* Osprey Aviation Elite 6, Oxford, England: Osprey Publishing, 2001, 73, 112, 113.

[136] *Beurteilung des Feldwebel Otto Wessling, III./J.G.3, Hauptmann und Gruppenkommandeur Oesau, Gefechtsstand, 15.5.1941.*

[137] Sources, Otto Wessling: Roger A. Freeman, *Mighty Eighth War Diary*, London: Jane's, 1981, 222; Ernst Obermaier, *Die Ritterkreuzträger der Luftwaffe, Jagdflieger 1939-1945*, Mainz, FRG: Verlag Dieter Hoffmann, 1989, 68; Erwin Lenfeld and Franz Thomas, *Die Eichenlaubträger 1940-1945*, Wiener-Neustedt, Austria: Weilburg Verlag, 1983, 555; Jochen Prien, Gerhard Stemmer, Peter Rodeike and Winfried Bock, *Die Jagdfliegerverbände der Deutschen Luftwaffe 1934 bis 1945, Teil 9/I: Winterkampf im Osten 6.12.1941 bis 30.4.1942*, Eutin, Germany: Struve, 35, 36; Jochen Prien, Gerhard Stemmer, Peter Rodeike and Winfried Bock, *Die Jagdfliegerverbände der Deutschen Luftwaffe 1934 bis 1945, Teil 9/II: Vom Sommerfeldzug 1942 bis zur Niederlage von Stalingrad 1.5.1942 bis 3.2.1943*, Eutin, Germany: Struve, 98, 100, 103; Franz Thomas, *Die Eichenlaubträger 1940-1945, Band 2: L-Z*, Osnabrück, Germany: Biblio-Verlag, 1998, 440.

[138] *Bevorzugte Beförderung des Lt. (Tr.O.) Walter Wolfrum zum Oberleutnant (Tr.O.), Jagdgeschwader 52, Hrabak, Generalleutnant Seidemann, Im Felde, 31.8.1944.*

[139] Sources, Walter Wolfrum: Ernst Obermaier, *Die Ritterkreuzträger der Luftwaffe, Jagdflieger 1939-1945*, Mainz, FRG: Verlag Dieter Hoffmann, 1989, 227; Hans Schreier, *JG 52: Das erfolgreichste Jagdgeschwader des II. Weltkrieges*, Berg am See, FRG: Kurt Vowinckel Verlag, 2002, 187.

[140] *Beurteilung Oberfeldwebel Otto Würfel, III./J.G. Mölders, Oberstleutnant u. Geschwaderkommodore Nordmann, 28.11. 1943.*

[141] Sources, Otto Würfel: Ernst Obermaier, *Die Ritterkreuzträger der Luftwaffe, Jagdflieger 1939-1945*, Mainz, FRG: Verlag Dieter Hoffmann, 1989, 227; Jochen Prien, Gerhard Stemmer, Peter Rodeike and Winfried Bock, *Die Jagdfliegerverbände der Deutschen Luftwaffe 1934 bis 1945, Teil 9/II: Vom Sommerfeldzug 1942 bis zur Niederlage von Stalingrad 1.5.1942 bis 3.2.1943*, Eutin, Germany: Struve, 332.

[142] *Vorschlag zur Überführung des Kriegsoffiziers Lt. Zahn zu den aktiven Friedensoffizieren, II./Fallschirmjäger Rgt. 1, Major und Btl.-Kommandeur Kurt Gröschke, Paris, 2.6.43.*

[143] Sources, Hilmar Zahn: Franz Thomas and Günter Wegmann, *Die Ritterkreuzträger der Deutschen Wehrmacht 1939-1945, Teil II: Fallschirmjäger*, Osnabrück, FRG: Biblio-Verlag, 1986, 372-373.

[144] In 2004, Zweigart's Messerschmitt 109G-6 was recovered in the Netherlands. The Messerschmitt came down in a large marsh, losing its wings on impact, but the rest of the machine plunged deep into the soft mud. A Dutch aviation archaeology group called DARE received permission to excavate the crash site, and soon discovered the engine and the rest of the wreckage. The tail section, still showing its markings, was soon recovered and after weeks of work, the entire machine was raised. Since early July 2004, the project has been on public display in the recently opened "Atlantic Wall Museum" at Noordwijk aan Zee, a holiday resort on the Dutch north coast.

[145] *Vorschlag zur Beförderung zum Kriegsoffizier Eugen Zweigart, III./Jagdgeschwader 54, Hauptmann und Staffelkapitän Bob, 29.7.1943.*

[146] Sources, Eugen-Ludwig Zweigart: Ernst Obermaier, *Die Ritterkreuzträger der Luftwaffe, Jagdflieger 1939-1945*, Mainz, FRG: Verlag Dieter Hoffmann, 1989, 228; Jochen Prien, Gerhard Stemmer, Peter Rodeike and Winfried Bock, *Die Jagdfliegerverbände der Deutschen Luftwaffe 1934 bis 1945, Teil 6/II: Unternehmen "Barbarossa" Einsatz im Osten 22.6. bis*

5.12.1941, Eutin, Germany: Struve, 2003, 262, 268, 272; John Weal, *Jagdgeschwader 54 "Grünherz,"* Osprey Aviation Elite 6, Oxford, England: Osprey Publishing, 2001, 62, 88, 92.

Rater Biographies

[1] Sources, Horst Ademeit: Ernst Obermaier, *Die Ritterkreuzträger der Luftwaffe, Jagdflieger 1939-1945*, Mainz, FRG: Verlag Dieter Hoffmann, 1989, 60.

[2] Sources, Hans-Ekkehard Bob: Ernst Obermaier, *Die Ritterkreuzträger der Luftwaffe, Jagdflieger 1939-1945*, Mainz, FRG: Verlag Dieter Hoffmann, 1989, 90; John Weal, *Jagdgeschwader 54 "Grünherz,"* Osprey Aviation Elite 6, Oxford, England: Osprey Publishing, 2001, 31-32.

[3] Sources, Hubertus von Bonin: Franz Kurowski, *Luftwaffe Aces: German Combat Pilots of WWII*, translated by David Johnston, Mechanicsburg, PA: Stackpole, 2004, 317; Ernst Obermaier, *Die Ritterkreuzträger der Luftwaffe, Jagdflieger 1939-1945*, Mainz, FRG: Verlag Dieter Hoffmann, 1989, 91; Jochen Prien, Gerhard Stemmer, Peter Rodeike and Winfried Bock, *Die Jagdfliegerverbände der Deutschen Luftwaffe 1934 bis 1945, Teil 6/I: Unternehmen "Barbarossa" Einsatz im Osten 22.6. bis 5.12.1941*, Eutin, Germany: Struve, 2003, 277; Karl Ries and Hans Ring, *Legion Condor, 1936-1939: Eine illustrierte Dokumentation*, Mainz, Germany: Verlag Dieter Hoffmann, 1980, 251, 265-266.

[4] Sources, Kurt Brändle: Ernst Obermaier, *Die Ritterkreuzträger der Luftwaffe, Jagdflieger 1939-1945*, Mainz, FRG: Verlag Dieter Hoffmann, 1989, 52; Jochen Prien, Gerhard Stemmer, Peter Rodeike and Winfried Bock, *Die Jagdfliegerverbände der Deutschen Luftwaffe 1934 bis 1945, Teil8/I: Einsatz im Mittelmeerraum November 1941 bis Dezember 1942*, Eutin, Germany: Struve, 2004, 83.

[5] Sources, Bruno Bräuer: Karl Friedrich Hildebrand, *Die Generale der deutschen Luftwaffe 1935-1945, Band 1 Abernetty-v. Gyldenfeldt*, Osnabrück, FRG, 1990, 108-109; Franz Thomas and Günter Wegmann, *Die Ritterkreuzträger der Deutschen Wehrmacht 1939-1945, Teil II: Fallschirmjäger*, Osnabrück, FRG: Biblio-Verlag, 1986, 32-34.

[6] Sources, Helmut Bruck: Ernst Obermaier, *Die Ritterkreuzträger der Luftwaffe, Stuka und Schlachtflieger 1939-1945*, Mainz, FRG: Verlag Dieter Hoffmann, 1976, 45.

[7] Sources, Gerhard Brückner: Veit Scherzer, *Die Träger des Deutschen Kreuzes in Gold der Luftwaffe 1941-1945*, Bayreuth, FRG: Scherzer's Militair Verlag, 1992, 42; Franz Thomas and Günter Wegmann, *Die Ritterkreuzträger der Deutschen Wehrmacht 1939-1945, Teil II: Fallschirmjäger*, Osnabrück, FRG: Biblio-Verlag, 1986, 419, 419;

[8] Sources, Alfred Bülowius: Karl Friedrich Hildebrand, *Die Generale der deutschen Luftwaffe 1935-1945, Band 1 Abernetty-v. Gyldenfeldt*, Osnabrück, FRG, 1990, 129-130: Peter Taghon, *Die Geschichte des Lehrgeschwaders 1*, Band 1 1936-1942, Zweibrücken, Germany: VDM, 2004, 101.

[9] Sources, Eckhard Christian: Karl Friedrich Hildebrand, *Die Generale der deutschen Luftwaffe 1935-1945, Band 1 Abernetty-v. Gyldenfeldt*, Osnabrück, FRG, 1990, 155-156; James P. O'Donnell, *The Bunker: The History of the Reich Chancellery Group*, Boston: Houghton Mifflin Company, 1978, 120-121.

[10] Sources, Adolf Dickfeld: Ernst Obermaier, *Die Ritterkreuzträger der Luftwaffe, Jagdflieger 1939-1945*, Mainz, FRG: Verlag Dieter Hoffmann, 1989, 50; Jochen Prien, Gerhard Stemmer, Peter Rodeike and Winfried Bock, *Die Jagdfliegerverbände der Deutschen Luftwaffe 1934 bis 1945, Teil 6/II: Unternehmen "Barbarossa" Einsatz im Osten 22.6. bis 5.12.1941*, Eutin, Germany: Struve, 2003, 68, 70, 74, 75; Jochen Prien, Gerhard Stemmer, Peter Rodeike and Winfried Bock, *Die Jagdfliegerverbände der Deutschen Luftwaffe 1934 bis 1945, Teil8/I: Einsatz im Mittelmeerraum November 1941 bis Dezember 1942*, Eutin, Germany: Struve, 2004, 51; Jochen Prien, Gerhard Stemmer, Peter Rodeike and Winfried Bock, *Die Jagdfliegerverbände der Deutschen Luftwaffe 1934 bis 1945, Teil 9/II: Vom Sommerfeldzug 1942 bis zur Niederlage von Stalingrad 1.5.1942 bis 3.2.1943*, Eutin, Germany: Struve, 537.

[11] The *Fliegerzielgeschwader* towed targets for air gunnery practice and for anti-aircraft artillery training.

[12] Sources, Oskar Dinort: Karl Friedrich Hildebrand, *Die Generale der deutschen Luftwaffe 1935-1945, Band 1 Abernetty-v. Gyldenfeldt*, Osnabrück, FRG, 1990, 198-199.

[13] Sources, Fritz Eyer: Cajus Bekker, *The Luftwaffe War Diaries*, London: MacDonald & Co., 1967, 200; Veit Scherzer, *Die Träger des Deutschen Kreuzes in Gold Der Luftwaffe 1941-1945*, Bayreuth, FRG: Scherzer's Militair Verlag, 1992, 73; Christopher Shores and Brian Cull, *Air War for Yugoslavia, Greece and Crete*, Carrollton, TX: Squadron Signal Publications, 1987, 378.

[14] Sources, Ernst Fach: Georg Brütting, *Das waren die deutschen Kampfflieger-Asse 1939-1945*, Stuttgart, FRG: Motorbuch Verlag, 1983, 194.

[15] Sources, Hans von Fichte: Karl Friedrich Hildebrand, *Die Generale der deutschen Luftwaffe 1935-1945, Band 1 Abernetty-v. Gyldenfeldt*, Osnabrück, FRG, 1990, 278-279; Kurt Mehner and Reinhard Teuber, *Die Deutsche Luftwaffe 1939-1945 Führung und Truppe*, Norderstedt, Germany; Militair-Verlag Klaus D. Patzwall, 1993, 67.

[16] Sources, Hans-Dieter Frank: Ernst Obermaier, *Die Ritterkreuzträger der Luftwaffe, Jagdflieger 1939-1945*, Mainz, FRG: Verlag Dieter Hoffmann, 1989, 61.

[17] Sources, Heinz Frank: Ernst Obermaier, *Die Ritterkreuzträger der Luftwaffe, Stuka und Schlachtflieger 1939-1945*, Mainz, FRG: Verlag Dieter Hoffmann, 1976, 43.

[18] Sources, Ernst Frömming: Peter D. Antill, *Crete 1941: Germany's Lightning Airborne Assault*, Osprey Campaign 147, Oxford, England: Osprey Publishing, 2005, 46; Ken Ford, *Cassino 1944: Breaking the Gustav Line*, Osprey Campaign 134, Oxford, England: Osprey Publishing, 2004, 62-63; Bruce Quarrie, *German Airborne Divisions: Mediterranean Theater 1942-45*, Osprey Battle Orders 15, Oxford, England: Osprey Publishing, 2005, 79-80; Franz Thomas and Günter Wegmann, *Die Ritterkreuzträger der Deutschen Wehrmacht 1939-1945, Teil II: Fallschirmjäger*, Osnabrück, FRG: Biblio-Verlag, 1986, 63-64.

[19] Sources, Werner Gayko: Werner Girbig, *Jagdgeschwader 5 "Eismeerjäger": Eine Chronik aus Dokumenten und Berichten 1941-1945*, Stuttgart, FRG: Motorbuch Verlag, 1976, 345, 346, 352.

[20] Sources, Franz Götz: Ernst Obermaier, *Die Ritterkreuzträger der Luftwaffe, Jagdflieger 1939-1945*, Mainz, FRG: Verlag Dieter Hoffmann, 1989, 119; Jochen Prien, Gerhard Stemmer, Peter Rodeike and Winfried Bock, *Die Jagdfliegerverbände der Deutschen Luftwaffe 1934 bis 1945, Teil8/II: Einsatz im Mittelmeerraum November 1941 bis Dezember 1942*, Eutin, Germany: Struve, 2004, 213.

[21] Sources, Kurt von Greiff: Wolfgang Dierich, *Kampfgeschwader 51 "Edelweiss" Eine Chronik aus Dokumenten and Berichten 1937-1945*, Stuttgart, FRG: Motorbuch Verlag, 1973, 296; Kurt Mehner and Reinhard Teuber, *Die Deutsche Luftwaffe 1939-1945 Führung und Truppe*, Norderstedt, Germany; Militair-Verlag Klaus D. Patzwall, 1993, 9; Veit Scherzer, *Die Träger des Deutschen Kreuzes in Gold der Luftwaffe 1941-1945*, Bayreuth, FRG: Scherzer's Militair Verlag, 1992, 100; Christian Zweng, *Die Dienststellen, Kommandobehörden und Truppenteile der Luftwaffe 1935-1945, Band 1 Nr. 1-10*, Osnabrück, Germany; Biblio Verlag, 1999, 168.

[22] Sources, Kurt Gröschke: Franz Thomas and Günter Wegmann, *Die Ritterkreuzträger der Deutschen Wehrmacht 1939-1945, Teil II: Fallschirmjäger*, Osnabrück, FRG: Biblio-Verlag, 1986, 89-91.

[23] Sources, Reinhard Günzel: Georg Brütting, *Das waren die deutschen Kampfflieger-Asse 1939-1945*, Stuttgart, FRG: Motorbuch Verlag, 1983, 169; Veit Scherzer, *Die Träger des Deutschen Kreuzes in Gold der Luftwaffe 1941-1945*, Bayreuth, FRG: Scherzer's Militair Verlag, 1992, 104; Christian Zweng, *Die Dienststellen, Kommandobehörden und Truppenteile der Luftwaffe 1935-1945*, Band 1 Nr. 1-10, Osnabrück, Germany, Biblio Verlag, 1999, 90. Other sources state he died on December 5, 1970 in Berlin.

[24] Sources, Anton Hackl: Ernst Obermaier, *Die Ritterkreuzträger der Luftwaffe, Jagdflieger 1939-1945*, Mainz, FRG: Verlag Dieter Hoffmann, 1989, 37; Jochen Prien, Gerhard Stemmer, Peter Rodeike and Winfried Bock, *Die Jagdfliegerverbände der Deutschen Luftwaffe 1934 bis 1945, Teil 6/II: Unternehmen "Barbarossa" Einsatz im Osten 22.6. bis 5.12.1941*, Eutin, Germany: Struve, 2003, 322.

[25] Sources, Franz Hahn: Gerhard Aders and Werner Held, *Jagdgeschwader 51 "Mölders":* Eine Chronik - Berichte, Erlebnisse, Dokumente, Motorbuch Verlag, Stuttgart, 1993, 251, 258; Jochen Prien, Gerhard Stemmer, Peter Rodeike and Winfried Bock, *Die Jagdfliegerverbände der Deutschen Luftwaffe 1934 bis 1945, Teil4/II: Einsatz am Kanal und über England, 26.6.1940 bis 21.6.1942*, Eutin, Germany: Struve, 101.

[26] Sources, Gotthard Handrick: Erwin Feuerstein, *Mit und ohne Ritterkreuz*, Stuttgart, FRG: Motorbuch Verlag, 1974, 48; Jochen Prien, Gerhard Stemmer, Peter Rodeike and Winfried Bock, *Die Jagdfliegerverbände der Deutschen Luftwaffe 1934 bis 1945, Teil 5: Heimatverteidigung 10. Mai 1940 bis 31. Dezember 1941, Einsatz im Mittelmeerraum Oktober 1940 bis November 1941, Einsatz im Westen 22. Juni bis 31. Dezember 1941, Die Ergänzungsjagdgruppen Einsatz 1941 bis zur Auflösung Anfang 1942*, Eutin, Germany: Struve, 2003, 229; Jochen Prien, Gerhard Stemmer, Peter Rodeike and Winfried Bock, *Die Jagdfliegerverbände der Deutschen Luftwaffe 1934 bis 1945, Teil 9/I: Winterkampf im Osten 6.12.1941 bis 30.4.1942*, Eutin, Germany: Struve, 267; Karl Ries and Hans Ring, *Legion Condor, 1936-1939: Eine illustrierte Dokumentation*, Mainz, Germany: Verlag Dieter Hoffmann, 1980, 251, 265-266; Veit Scherzer, *Die Träger des Deutschen Kreuzes in Gold der Luftwaffe 1941-1945*, Bayreuth, FRG: Scherzer's Militair Verlag, 1992, 111; Christian Zweng, *Die Dienststellen, Kommandobehörden und Truppenteile der Luftwaffe 1935-1945, Band 1 Nr. 1-10*, Osnabrück, Germany; Biblio Verlag, 1999, 447.

[27] Sources, Martin Harlinghausen: Karl Friedrich Hildebrand, *Die Generale der deutschen Luftwaffe 1935-1945, Band 2 Habermehl-Nuber*, Osnabrück, FRG, 1991, 32-33; Karl Ries and Hans Ring, *Legion Condor, 1936-1939: Eine illustrierte Dokumentation*, Mainz, Germany: Verlag Dieter Hoffmann, 1980, 251, 265-266.

[28] Sources, Richard Heidrich: Karl Friedrich Hildebrand, *Die Generale der deutschen Luftwaffe 1935-1945, Band 2 Habermehl-Nuber*, Osnabrück, FRG, 1991, 47-48; Franz Thomas and Günter Wegmann, *Die Ritterkreuzträger der Deutschen Wehrmacht 1939-1945, Teil II: Fallschirmjäger*, Osnabrück, FRG: Biblio-Verlag, 1986, 99-102.

[29] Sources, Joachim Helbig: Georg Brütting, *Das waren die deutschen Kampfflieger-Asse 1939-1945*, Stuttgart, FRG: Motorbuch Verlag, 1983, 81-100; Franz Kurowski, *Luftwaffe Aces: German Combat Pilots of WWII*, translated by David Johnston, Mechanicsburg, PA: Stackpole, 2004, 24, 33, 39, 41.

[30] Sources, Dietrich Hrabak: Ernst Obermaier, *Die Ritterkreuzträger der Luftwaffe, Jagdflieger 1939-1945*, Mainz, FRG: Verlag Dieter Hoffmann, 1989, 59; Jochen Prien, Gerhard Stemmer, Peter Rodeike and Winfried Bock, *Die Jagdfliegerverbände der Deutschen Luftwaffe 1934 bis 1945, Teil 9/I: Winterkampf im Osten 6.12.1941 bis 30.4.1942*, Eutin, Germany: Struve, 216; Jochen Prien, Gerhard Stemmer, Peter Rodeike and Winfried Bock, *Die Jagdfliegerverbände der Deutschen Luftwaffe 1934 bis 1945, Teil 9/II: Vom Sommerfeldzug 1942 bis zur Niederlage von Stalingrad 1.5.1942 bis 3.2.1943*, Eutin, Germany: Struve, 387.

[31] Fürstenfeldbruck is about 30 minutes west of Munich.

[32] The term *Freikorps* was used to name several far-right paramilitary organizations that arose in Germany as soldiers returned in defeat from World War I. During the period, many German veterans felt disconnected from civilian life and joined the *Freikorps* in search of stability within a military structure, or joined in an effort to put down numerous Communist uprisings throughout Germany. In addition to fighting in the Ruhr, Bavaria, Berlin and central Germany, several *Freikorps* fought in the Baltic, Silesia and Prussia, sometimes with significant success even against regular troops, before they were officially disbanded in 1920.

[33] Sources, Joachim-Friedrich Huth: Karl Friedrich Hildebrand, *Die Generale der deutschen Luftwaffe 1935-1945, Band 2 Habermehl-Nuber*, Osnabrück, FRG, 1991, 129-130.

[34] Sources, Max-Josef Ibel: Karl Friedrich Hildebrand, *Die Generale der deutschen Luftwaffe 1935-1945, Band 2 Habermehl-Nuber*, Osnabrück, FRG, 1991, 131-132; Ernst Obermaier, *Die Ritterkreuzträger der Luftwaffe, Jagdflieger 1939-1945*, Mainz, FRG: Verlag Dieter Hoffmann, 1989, 138.

[35] Sources, Eberhard Jacob: Cajus Bekker, *The Luftwaffe War Diaries*, London: MacDonald & Co., 1967, 200; Ernst Obermaier, *Die Ritterkreuzträger der Luftwaffe, Stuka und Schlachtflieger 1939-1945*, Mainz, FRG: Verlag Dieter Hoffmann, 1976, 98; Veit Scherzer, *Die Träger des Deutschen Kreuzes in Gold der Luftwaffe 1941-1945*, Bayreuth, FRG: Scherzer's Militair Verlag, 1992, 143.

[36] Sources, Johannes Janke: Jochen Prien, Gerhard Stemmer, Peter Rodeike and Winfried Bock, *Die Jagdfliegerverbände der Deutschen Luftwaffe 1934 bis 1945, Teil 1: Vorkriegszeit und Einsatz über Polen – 1934 bis 1939*, Eutin, Germany: Struve, 2000, 150, 269, 368; Jochen Prien, Gerhard Stemmer, Peter Rodeike and Winfried Bock, *Die Jagdfliegerverbände der Deutschen Luftwaffe 1934 bis 1945, Teil 2: Der "Sitzkrieg", 1.9.39 bis 9.5.1940*, Eutin, Germany: Struve, 454; Jochen Prien, Gerhard Stemmer, Peter Rodeike and Winfried Bock, *Die Jagdfliegerverbände der Deutschen Luftwaffe 1934 bis 1945, Teil4/II: Einsatz am Kanal und über England, 26.6.1940 bis 21.6.1942*, Eutin, Germany: Struve, 101.

[37] Sources, Karl Kennel: Ernst Obermaier, *Die Ritterkreuzträger der Luftwaffe, Jagdflieger 1939-1945*, Mainz, FRG: Verlag Dieter Hoffmann, 1989, 70; Ernst Obermaier, *Die Ritterkreuzträger der Luftwaffe, Stuka und Schlachtflieger 1939-1945*, Mainz, FRG: Verlag Dieter Hoffmann, 1976, 54; Franz Thomas, *Die Eichenlaubträger 1940-1945, Band 1: A-K*, Osnabrück, Germany: Biblio-Verlag, 1998, 357.

[38] Sources, Otto Kittel: Ernst Obermaier, *Die Ritterkreuzträger der Luftwaffe, Jagdflieger 1939-1945*, Mainz, FRG: Verlag Dieter Hoffmann, 1989, 39; Jochen Prien, Gerhard Stemmer, Peter Rodeike and Winfried Bock, *Die Jagdfliegerverbände der Deutschen Luftwaffe 1934 bis 1945, Teil 5: Heimatverteidigung 10. Mai 1940 bis 31. Dezember 1941, Einsatz im Mittelmeerraum Oktober 1940 bis November 1941, Einsatz im Westen 22. Juni bis 31. Dezember 1941, Die Ergänzungsjagdgruppen Einsatz 1941 bis zur Auflösung Anfang 1942*, Eutin, Germany: Struve, 2003, 121; Hannes Trautloft, Werner Held and Ekkehard Bob, *Die Grünherzjäger*, Friedberg, FRG: Podzun-Pallas-Verlag, 1985; John Weal, *Focke-Wulf Fw 190 Aces of the Russian Front*, Osprey

Aircraft of the Aces 6, Oxford, England: Osprey Publishing, 1995, 16, 55, 84; John Weal, *Jagdgeschwader 54 "Grünherz,"* Osprey Aviation Elite 6, Oxford, England: Osprey Publishing, 2001, 115-116.

[39] Sources, Walter Koch: Franz Thomas and Günter Wegmann, *Die Ritterkreuzträger der Deutschen Wehrmacht 1939-1945, Teil II: Fallschirmjäger*, Osnabrück, FRG: Biblio-Verlag, 1986, 138-140.

[40] Sources, Paul Koester: Wolfgang Dierich, *Kampfgeschwader 51 "Edelweiss" Eine Chronik aus Dokumenten and Berichten 1937-1945*, Stuttgart, FRG: Motorbuch Verlag, 1973, 295; Christian Zweng, *Die Dienststellen, Kommandobehörden und Truppenteile der Luftwaffe 1935-1945, Band 1 Nr. 1-10*, Osnabrück, Germany; Biblio Verlag, 1999, 52, 227.

[41] Sources, Benno Kosch: Georg Brütting, *Das waren die deutschen Kampfflieger-Asse 1939-1945*, Stuttgart, FRG: Motorbuch Verlag, 1983, 218; Christian Zweng, *Die Dienststellen, Kommandobehörden und Truppenteile der Luftwaffe 1935-1945, Band 1 Nr. 1-10*, Osnabrück, Germany; Biblio Verlag, 1999, 160.

[42] Sources, Robert Kowalewski: Georg Brütting, *Das waren die deutschen Kampfflieger-Asse 1939-1945*, Stuttgart, FRG: Motorbuch Verlag, 1983, 221; Ernst Obermaier, *Die Ritterkreuzträger der Luftwaffe, Jagdflieger 1939-1945*, Mainz, FRG: Verlag Dieter Hoffmann, 1989, 150.

[43] Sources, Hans Kroh: Karl Friedrich Hildebrand, *Die Generale der deutschen Luftwaffe 1935-1945, Band 2 Habermehl-Nuber*, Osnabrück, FRG, 1991, 250-251; Franz Thomas and Günter Wegmann, *Die Ritterkreuzträger der Deutschen Wehrmacht 1939-1945, Teil II: Fallschirmjäger*, Osnabrück, FRG: Biblio-Verlag, 1986, 148-151.

[44] Sources, Kurt Kuhlmey: Georg Brütting, *Das waren die deutschen Stuka-Asse, 1939-1945*, Stuttgart, FRG: Motorbuch Verlag, 1976, 219-220; Ernst Obermaier, *Die Ritterkreuzträger der Luftwaffe, Stuka und Schlachtflieger 1939-1945*, Mainz, FRG: Verlag Dieter Hoffmann, 1976, 107-108;

[45] Sources, Bruno Loerzer: Matthew Cooper, *The German Air Force 1933-1945: An Anatomy of Failure*, London: Jane's, 1981, 27; Karl Friedrich Hildebrand, *Die Generale der deutschen Luftwaffe 1935-1945, Band 2 Habermehl-Nuber*, Osnabrück, FRG, 1991, 309-310; Samuel Mitcham, Jr., *Men of the Luftwaffe*, Novato, CA: Presidio, 1988, 2-3.

[46] Sources, Eric Macard: Kurt Mehner and Reinhard Teuber, *Die Deutsche Luftwaffe 1939-1945 Führung und Truppe*, Norderstedt, Germany; Militair-Verlag Klaus D. Patzwall, 1993, 222.

[47] Sources, Günther von Maltzahn: Ernst Obermaier, *Die Ritterkreuzträger der Luftwaffe, Jagdflieger 1939-1945*, Mainz, FRG: Verlag Dieter Hoffmann, 1989, 46; Jochen Prien, Gerhard Stemmer, Peter Rodeike and Winfried Bock, *Die Jagdfliegerverbände der Deutschen Luftwaffe 1934 bis 1945, Teil 6/II: Unternehmen "Barbarossa" Einsatz im Osten 22.6. bis 5.12.1941*, Eutin, Germany: Struve, 2003, 95; Jochen Prien, Gerhard Stemmer, Peter Rodeike and Winfried Bock, *Die Jagdfliegerverbände der Deutschen Luftwaffe 1934 bis 1945, Teil8/II: Einsatz im Mittelmeerraum November 1941 bis Dezember 1942,* Eutin, Germany: Struve, 2004, 43.

[48] Sources, Eitel-Friedrich Roediger von Manteuffel: Karl Friedrich Hildebrand, *Die Generale der deutschen Luftwaffe 1935-1945, Band 2 Habermehl-Nuber*, Osnabrück, FRG, 1991, 352-353; Christian Zweng, *Die Dienststellen, Kommandobehörden und Truppenteile der Luftwaffe 1935-1945*, Band 1 Nr. 1-10, Osnabrück, Germany, Biblio Verlag, 1999, 90.

[49] Sources, Gerd von Massow: Karl Friedrich Hildebrand, *Die Generale der deutschen Luftwaffe 1935-1945, Band 2 Habermehl-Nuber*, Osnabrück, FRG, 1991, 364-365; Jochen Prien, Gerhard Stemmer, Peter Rodeike and Winfried Bock, *Die Jagdfliegerverbände der Deutschen Luftwaffe 1934 bis 1945, Teil 1: Vorkriegszeit und Einsatz über Polen – 1934 bis 1939,* Eutin, Germany: Struve, 2000, 107, 108.

[50] Sources, Eugen Meindl: Karl Friedrich Hildebrand, *Die Generale der deutschen Luftwaffe 1935-1945, Band 2 Habermehl-Nuber*, Osnabrück, FRG, 1991, 372-373; G.C. Kiriakopoulos, *Ten Days to Destiny: The Battle for Crete 1941*, New York: Franklin Watts, 1985, 195; Franz Thomas and Günter Wegmann, *Die Ritterkreuzträger der Deutschen Wehrmacht 1939-1945, Teil II: Fallschirmjäger*, Osnabrück, FRG: Biblio-Verlag, 1986, 173-177.

[51] "The Blood Order," or the Decoration of November 9, 1923, (*Ehrenzeichen vom 9. November 1923*) was one of the most prestigious decorations in the Nazi Party. Instituted in 1934, this decoration was awarded to participants in the *putsch* who had joined the party or one of its formations by January 1932 (continuous service).

[52] Sources, Andreas Nielsen: Karl Friedrich Hildebrand, *Die Generale der deutschen Luftwaffe 1935-1945, Band 2 Habermehl-Nuber*, Osnabrück, FRG, 1991, 448-449; Samuel Mitcham, Jr., *Men of the Luftwaffe*, Novato, CA: Presidio, 1988, 133.

[53] Sources, Karl-Gottfried Nordmann: Ernst Obermaier, *Die Ritterkreuzträger der Luftwaffe, Jagdflieger 1939-1945*, Mainz, FRG: Verlag Dieter Hoffmann, 1989, 47; Jochen Prien, Gerhard Stemmer, Peter Rodeike and Winfried Bock, *Die Jagdfliegerverbände der Deutschen Luftwaffe 1934 bis 1945, Teil 6/I: Unternehmen "Barbarossa" Einsatz im Osten 22.6. bis 5.12.1941*, Eutin, Germany: Struve, 2003, 329; Jochen Prien, Gerhard Stemmer, Peter Rodeike and Winfried Bock, *Die Jagdfliegerverbände der Deutschen Luftwaffe 1934 bis 1945, Teil 9/I: Winterkampf im Osten 6.12.1941 bis 30.4.1942*, Eutin, Germany: Struve, 44, 116; Jochen Prien, Gerhard Stemmer, Peter Rodeike and Winfried Bock, *Die Jagdfliegerverbände der Deutschen Luftwaffe 1934 bis 1945, Teil 9/II: Vom Sommerfeldzug 1942 bis zur Niederlage von Stalingrad 1.5.1942 bis 3.2.1943*, Eutin, Germany: Struve, 242, 245, 246.

[54] Several sources postulate that he was shot down by First Lieutenant Edward "Buddy" Haydon of the 357th Fighter Group and Captain Ernest "Feeb" Fiebelkorn of the 20th Fighter Group, USAAF who was credited with a shared Me 262 victory at 12:45 that day over Achmer.

[55] Sources, Walter Nowotny: Ernst Obermaier, *Die Ritterkreuzträger der Luftwaffe, Jagdflieger 1939-1945*, Mainz, FRG: Verlag Dieter Hoffmann, 1989, 22.

[56] Sources, Walter Oesau: Ernst Obermaier, *Die Ritterkreuzträger der Luftwaffe, Jagdflieger 1939-1945*, Mainz, FRG: Verlag Dieter Hoffmann, 1989, 29; Jochen Prien, Gerhard Stemmer, Peter Rodeike and Winfried Bock, *Die Jagdfliegerverbände der Deutschen Luftwaffe 1934 bis 1945, Teil 5: Heimatverteidigung 10. Mai 1940 bis 31. Dezember 1941, Einsatz im Mittelmeerraum Oktober 1940 bis November 1941, Einsatz im Westen 22. Juni bis 31. Dezember 1941, Die Ergänzungsjagdgruppen Einsatz 1941 bis zur Auflösung Anfang 1942*, Eutin, Germany: Struve, 2003, 405; Jochen Prien, Gerhard Stemmer, Peter Rodeike and Winfried Bock, *Die Jagdfliegerverbände der Deutschen Luftwaffe 1934 bis 1945, Teil 6/I: Unternehmen "Barbarossa" Einsatz im Osten 22.6. bis 5.12.1941*, Eutin, Germany: Struve, 2003, 135; Jochen Prien, Gerhard Stemmer, Peter Rodeike and Winfried Bock, *Die Jagdfliegerverbände der Deutschen Luftwaffe 1934 bis 1945, Teil 7: Heimatsverteidigung 1. Januar bis 31. Dezember 1942, Einsatz im Westen 1. Januar bis 31. Dezember 1942*, Eutin, Germany: Struve, 2003, 213; Karl Ries and Hans Ring, *Legion Condor, 1936-1939: Eine illustrierte Dokumentation*, Mainz, Germany: Verlag Dieter Hoffmann, 1980, 265-266.

[57] Sources, Dietrich Peltz: Cajus Bekker, *The Luftwaffe War Diaries*, London: MacDonald & Co., 1967, 42-43; Georg Brütting, *Das waren die deutschen Kampfflieger-Asse 1939-1945*, Stuttgart, FRG: Motorbuch Verlag, 1983, 67-80; Karl Friedrich Hildebrand, *Die Generale der deutschen Luftwaffe 1935-1945, Band 3, Odebrecht-Zoch*, Osnabrück, FRG, 1992, 21-22.

[58] Sources, Kurt Pflugbeil: Karl Friedrich Hildebrand, *Die Generale der deutschen Luftwaffe 1935-1945, Band 3, Odebrecht-Zoch*, Osnabrück, FRG, 1992, 31-33.

[59] Sources, Fritz Prager: Franz Thomas and Günter Wegmann, *Die Ritterkreuzträger der Deutschen Wehrmacht 1939-1945, Teil II: Fallschirmjäger*, Osnabrück, FRG: Biblio-Verlag, 1986, 211-212.

[60] Sources, Josef Priller: Ernst Obermaier, *Die Ritterkreuzträger der Luftwaffe, Jagdflieger 1939-1945*, Mainz, FRG: Verlag Dieter Hoffmann, 1989, 36; Jochen Prien, Gerhard Stemmer, Peter Rodeike and Winfried Bock, *Die Jagdfliegerverbände der Deutschen Luftwaffe 1934 bis 1945, Teil 7: Heimatsverteidigung 1. Januar bis 31. Dezember 1942, Einsatz im Westen 1. Januar bis 31. Dezember 1942*, Eutin, Germany: Struve, 2003, 400, 402.

[61] Sources, Klaus Quaet-Faslem: Ernst Obermaier, *Die Ritterkreuzträger der Luftwaffe, Jagdflieger 1939-1945*, Mainz, FRG: Verlag Dieter Hoffmann, 1989, 182.

[62] Sources, Bernhard Ramcke: Karl Friedrich Hildebrand, *Die Generale der deutschen Luftwaffe 1935-1945, Band 3, Odebrecht-Zoch*, Osnabrück, FRG, 1992, 76-78.

[63] Sources, Wolfram von Richthofen: Karl Friedrich Hildebrand, *Die Generale der deutschen Luftwaffe 1935-1945, Band 3, Odebrecht-Zoch*, Osnabrück, FRG, 1992, 107-108; Carlos Caballero Jurado, *The Condor Legion: German Troops in the Spanish Civil War*, Osprey Elite 131, Oxford, England: Osprey Publishing, 2006, 15; Samuel Mitcham, Jr., *Men of the Luftwaffe*, Novato, CA: Presidio, 1988, 40; Karl Ries and Hans Ring, *Legion Condor, 1936-1939: Eine illustrierte Dokumentation*, Mainz, Germany: Verlag Dieter Hoffmann, 1980, 251, 265-266.

[64] Sources, Volprecht Riedesel zu Eisenbach: Georg Brütting, *Das waren die deutschen Kampfflieger-Asse 1939-1945*, Stuttgart, FRG: Motorbuch Verlag, 1983, 177; Hugh Morgan and John Weal, *German Jet Aces of World War 2*, Osprey Aircraft of the Aces 17, Oxford, England: Osprey Publishing, 1998, 37;

Siegfried Radtke, *Kampfgeschwader 54, von der Ju 52 zur Me 262*, Munich, Germany: Schild Verlag, 1990, 258, 371.

[65] Sources, Fritz Schaffer: Gebhard Aders, *History of the German Night Fighter Force 1917-1945*, London: Jane's, 1979, 229-230; Ulf Balke, *Der Luft-Krieg in Europa, Die operativen Einsätze des Kampf-Geschwaders 2 im Zweiten Weltkrieg*, Teil 2, Koblenz, FRG: Bernhard & Graefe Verlag, 1990, 409.

[66] Sources, Richard Schimpf: Karl Friedrich Hildebrand, *Die Generale der deutschen Luftwaffe 1935-1945, Band 3, Odebrecht-Zoch*, Osnabrück, FRG, 1992, 185-186; Franz Thomas and Günter Wegmann, *Die Ritterkreuzträger der Deutschen Wehrmacht 1939-1945, Teil II: Fallschirmjäger*, Osnabrück, FRG: Biblio-Verlag, 1986, 253-254.

[67] Sources, Karl-Heinz Schnell: Ernst Obermaier, *Die Ritterkreuzträger der Luftwaffe, Jagdflieger 1939-1945*, Mainz, FRG: Verlag Dieter Hoffmann, 1989, 199; Jochen Prien, Gerhard Stemmer, Peter Rodeike and Winfried Bock, *Die Jagdfliegerverbände der Deutschen Luftwaffe 1934 bis 1945, Teil 6/I: Unternehmen "Barbarossa" Einsatz im Osten 22.6. bis 5.12.1941*, Eutin, Germany: Struve, 2003, 300, 313; Jochen Prien, Gerhard Stemmer, Peter Rodeike and Winfried Bock, *Die Jagdfliegerverbände der Deutschen Luftwaffe 1934 bis 1945, Teil 9/II: Vom Sommerfeldzug 1942 bis zur Niederlage von Stalingrad 1.5.1942 bis 3.2.1943*, Eutin, Germany: Struve, 338.

[68] Sources, Karl-Lothar Schulz: Karl Friedrich Hildebrand, *Die Generale der deutschen Luftwaffe 1935-1945, Band 3, Odebrecht-Zoch*, Osnabrück, FRG, 1992, 263-264; Franz Thomas and Günter Wegmann, *Die Ritterkreuzträger der Deutschen Wehrmacht 1939-1945, Teil II: Fallschirmjäger*, Osnabrück, FRG: Biblio-Verlag, 1986, 277-278.

[69] Sources, Hans-Bruno Schultz-Heyn: Wolfgang Dierich, *Kampfgeschwader 51 "Edelweiss" Eine Chronik aus Dokumenten und Berichten 1937-1945*, Stuttgart, FRG: Motorbuch Verlag, 1973, 295-296.

[70] Sources, Hannes Schwarzer: Veit Scherzer, *Die Träger des Deutschen Kreuzes in Gold der Luftwaffe 1941-1945*, Bayreuth, FRG: Scherzer's Militair Verlag, 1992, 311.

[71] Sources, Hans Seidemann: Karl Friedrich Hildebrand, *Die Generale der deutschen Luftwaffe 1935-1945, Band 3, Odebrecht-Zoch*, Osnabrück, FRG, 1992, 289-290; Samuel Mitcham, Jr., *Men of the Luftwaffe*, Novato, CA: Presidio, 1988, 209; Karl Ries and Hans Ring, *Legion Condor, 1936-1939: Eine illustrierte Dokumentation*, Mainz, Germany: Verlag Dieter Hoffmann, 1980, 251.

[72] Sources, Heinrich Seywald: Karl Friedrich Hildebrand, *Die Generale der deutschen Luftwaffe 1935-1945, Band 3, Odebrecht-Zoch*, Osnabrück, FRG, 1992, 297-299.

[73] Sources, Helmut Sorge: Christian Zweng, *Die Dienststellen, Kommandobehörden und Truppenteile der Luftwaffe 1935-1945, Band 1 Nr. 1-10*, Osnabrück, Germany; Biblio Verlag, 1999, 38, 105, 188, 441.

[74] Sources, Wilhelm Stemmler: Georg Brütting, *Das waren die deutschen Kampfflieger-Asse 1939-1945*, Stuttgart, FRG: Motorbuch Verlag, 1983, 260; Wolfgang Dierich, *Kampfgeschwader 51 "Edelweiss" Eine Chronik aus Dokumenten and Berichten 1937-1945*, Stuttgart, FRG: Motorbuch Verlag, 1973, 163-164; Veit Scherzer, *Die Träger des Deutschen Kreuzes in Gold der Luftwaffe 1941-1945*, Bayreuth, FRG: Scherzer's Militair Verlag, 1992, 694.

[75] Sources, Werner Streib: Cajus Bekker, *The Luftwaffe War Diaries*, London: MacDonald & Co., 1967, 204; Ernst Obermaier, *Die Ritterkreuzträger der Luftwaffe, Jagdflieger 1939-1945*, Mainz, FRG: Verlag Dieter Hoffmann, 1989, 36.

[76] Sources, Kurt Student: Karl Friedrich Hildebrand, *Die Generale der deutschen Luftwaffe 1935-1945, Band 3, Odebrecht-Zoch*, Osnabrück, FRG, 1992, 363-365; Franz Thomas and Günter Wegmann, *Die Ritterkreuzträger der Deutschen Wehrmacht 1939-1945, Teil II: Fallschirmjäger*, Osnabrück, FRG: Biblio-Verlag, 1986, 301-304.

[77] Sources, Gerhard Ulbricht: Veit Scherzer, *Die Träger des Deutschen Kreuzes in Gold der Luftwaffe 1941-1945*, Bayreuth, FRG: Scherzer's Militair Verlag, 1992, 345; Christian Zweng, *Die Dienststellen, Kommandobehörden und Truppenteile der Luftwaffe 1935-1945, Band 1 Nr. 1-10*, Osnabrück, Germany; Biblio Verlag, 1999, 474.

[78] Sources, Karl Viek: Veit Scherzer, *Die Träger des Deutschen Kreuzes in Gold der Luftwaffe 1941-1945*, Bayreuth, FRG: Scherzer's Militair Verlag, 1992, 349; Christian Zweng, *Die Dienststellen, Kommandobehörden und Truppenteile der Luftwaffe 1935-1945*, Band 1 Nr. 1-10, Osnabrück, Germany, Biblio Verlag, 1999, 120.

[79] Sources, Otto Weiss: Cajus Bekker, *The Luftwaffe War Diaries*, London: MacDonald & Co., 1967, 28; Georg Brütting, *Das waren die deutschen Stuka-Asse, 1939-1945*, Stuttgart, FRG: Motorbuch Verlag, 1976, 139-140; Franz Kurowski, *Luftwaffe Aces: German Combat Pilots of WWII*, translated by David Johnston, Mechanicsburg, PA: Stackpole, 2004, 112; Ernst Obermaier, *Die Ritterkreuzträger der Luftwaffe, Stuka und Schlachtflieger 1939-1945*, Mainz, FRG: Verlag Dieter Hoffmann, 1976, 40.

[80] Sources, Helmuth Wilberg: Karl Friedrich Hildebrand, *Die Generale der deutschen Luftwaffe 1935-1945, Band 3, Odebrecht-Zoch*, Osnabrück, FRG, 1992, 513-514.

[81] Sources, Wolf-Dietrich Wilcke: Ernst Obermaier, *Die Ritterkreuzträger der Luftwaffe, Jagdflieger 1939-1945*, Mainz, FRG: Verlag Dieter Hoffmann, 1989, 33; Jochen Prien, Gerhard Stemmer, Peter Rodeike and Winfried Bock, *Die Jagdfliegerverbände der Deutschen Luftwaffe 1934 bis 1945, Teil 8/II: Einsatz im Mittelmeerraum November 1941 bis Dezember 1942,* Eutin, Germany: Struve, 2004, 213.

[82] Sources, Karl-Eduard Wilke: Karl Friedrich Hildebrand, *Die Generale der deutschen Luftwaffe 1935-1945, Band 3, Odebrecht-Zoch*, Osnabrück, FRG, 1992, 522-523.

[83] Sources, Bernhard Woldenga: Ernst Obermaier, *Die Ritterkreuzträger der Luftwaffe, Jagdflieger 1939-1945*, Mainz, FRG: Verlag Dieter Hoffmann, 1989, 226; Jochen Prien, Gerhard Stemmer, Peter Rodeike and Winfried Bock, *Die Jagdfliegerverbände der Deutschen Luftwaffe 1934 bis 1945, Teil 6/I: Unternehmen "Barbarossa" Einsatz im Osten 22.6. bis 5.12.1941*, Eutin, Germany: Struve, 2003, 157-158; Jochen Prien, Gerhard Stemmer, Peter Rodeike and Winfried Bock, *Die Jagdfliegerverbände der Deutschen Luftwaffe 1934 bis 1945, Teil8/I: Einsatz im Mittelmeerraum November 1941 bis Dezember 1942,* Eutin, Germany: Struve, 2004, 107; Christian Zweng, *Die Dienststellen, Kommandobehörden und Truppenteile der Luftwaffe 1935-1945, Band 1 Nr. 1-10*, Osnabrück, Germany; Biblio Verlag, 1999, 513.

GLOSSARY

Abitur – qualification examination to enter a university
A Schule – primary flying training school
A/B Schule – primary/advanced flying training school
Ab – from
Abschuss – aerial victory
Abteilung – detachment (roughly equivalent to a battalion)
Abteilungsführer – acting detachment commander
Abteilungskommandeur – detachment commander
Abwehrkämpfe – defensive battles
Adjutant – adjutant (often with executive officer authority)
Ärmelband "Kreta" – Crete cufftitle
Aktiver Wehrdienst – active duty
Angriff – attack
Anlage – enclosure
April – April
Armee – army
Artillerie – artillery
Aufklärer – reconnaissance pilot
Aufklärungsabteilung – ground reconnaissance detachment/ battalion
August – August
Ausbildung – training
ausgefüllt – fulfilled
Auszeichnungen – awards

Bataillon – battalion
Bataillonsführer – acting battalion commander
Bataillons-Kommandeur – battalion commander
Batterie – artillery battery
Batteriechef – battery commander
Batterieführer – acting battery commander
Bauchlanden – belly-landing
Beförderung – promotion
befürwortet – seconded (in agreement with)
Begründung – reason for consideration
Beobachter – observer
Beobachterabzeichen – observer's badge
Beruf – profession (normally associated with civilian profession before entering the service)
Bestrafung -- punishment
Beurteilung – judgment, estimation, evaluation
bevorzugten Beförderung – preferred, preferential (accelerated) promotion
Bordfunker – radio operator
Bordmechaniker – flight engineer

Chef des Generalstab(e)s – chief of staff

Deutsches Kreuz in Gold – German Cross in Gold
Dezember – December
Dienstantritt – date entered military service
Dienstgrad – grade/rank
Dienstellung – duty position
Division – division
Divisionskommandeur – division commander
Divisions Stabsquartier (Div.St.Qu.) – division headquarters
Draufgänger – daredevil
dunkle Nachtjagd (Dunaja) – dark night fighting (radar directed, not using searchlights)
Durchschnitt – average

Ehrenpokal für besondere Leistungen – Honor Goblet for Outstanding Achievement
Ehrenschale für hervorragende Kampfleistung – Honor Salver for Distinguished Achievement
Eichenlaub – oak leaves
Einheit – unit
einverstanden – in agreement
Eisernes Kreuz I. Klasse (E.K. I) – Iron Cross 1st Class
Eisernes Kreuz II. Klasse (E.K. II) – Iron Cross 2nd Class
Entlassung – discharge
Ergänzungs – Supplemental
Ergänzungsgeschwader – supplemental wing (an operational training unit)
Ergänzungsgruppe – supplemental group (an operational training unit)
Erprobungsgruppe – operational test group
Erprobungsstaffel – operational test squadron
erweiterter Luftwaffen-Flugzeugführerschein (ELF) – *Luftwaffe* Advanced Pilot's Certificate

Fallschirm – parachute
Fallschirmabsprung – parachute jump
Fallschirm-Fla-MG-Bataillon – anti-aircraft machine-gun battalion
Fallschirmjäger – paratrooper
Fallschirmschützenabzeichen – paratrooper's badge

Familienname – family, or last, name
Februar – February
Feind – enemy
Feindflug – flight against the enemy
Feldwebel – technical sergeant
Fernaufklärung – long-distance reconnaissance
Fernaufklärungsgruppe – long-distance reconnaissance group
Fernnachtjagd – long-range night fighting (usually over Britain)
Flak – anti-aircraft
Fliegerdivision – flying division (first associated with airborne, later with flying elements)
Fliegerführer – aircraft command/control headquarters, or its commander
Fliegerkorps – air corps
Fliegerschütze – aerial gunner
Fliegerschützenabzeichen – air gunner's badge
Fliegertruppe – flying troops
Fluglehrer – flight instructor
Flugzeug – aircraft
Flugzeugführer – pilot
Flugzeugführer-Abzeichen – pilot's badge
Frieden – peacetime
Friedhof – cemetery
Frontflugspange – operational flying clasp
Führungs- oder Bedienungsfehler – pilot or crew error (often associated with a fatal crash)

Geburtsdatum/Geburtstag – birth date
Geburtsort – place of birth
gefallen – killed in action
Gefangener – prisoner
Gefecht – battle, action, combat
Gefechtsstand – field headquarters, command post
geheim – secret
geeignet – suitable
Gemeinsames Flugzeugführer und Beobachterabzeichen – combined pilot's and observer's badge
General der Fallschirmtruupe (General of Parachute Troops) – lieutenant general (3-stars)
General der Flieger (General of Flying Troops) – lieutenant general (3-stars)
Generalfeldmarschall – field marshal (5-stars)
Generalleutnant – major general (2-stars)
Generalmajor – brigadier general (1-star)
Generaloberst – colonel general (4-stars)
geschieden – divorced
Geschwader – wing; air force operational unit of between 3 to 5 groups
Geschwaderkommodore – wing commodore/commander
Gruppe – air force operational flying unit of about 27 aircraft
Gruppenführer – acting commander
Gruppenkommandeur – group commander
gut ausgefüllt – well fulfilled

Hauptfeldwebel – first sergeant
Hauptmann – captain
Hauptquartier – headquarters
Heimatanschrift – home mailing address
helle Nachtjagd – bright night fighting; in conjunction with searchlights
Heer – the Army
Herausschuss – damaging an enemy aircraft so that it is forced to fall out of formation
heute – today

im Felde – in the field
Improvisationstalent – talent for improvisation
in Vertretung (i.V.) – acting as, representing
Infanterie – infantry
Inspekteur – inspector

Jagdbomber (Jabo) – fighter-bomber
Jäger – rifleman
Jagdabschnittsführer – fighter district commander
Jagdflieger – fighter pilot
Jagdfliegerführer – fighter command/control headquarters, or its commander
Jagdflugzeug – fighter aircraft
Jagdgeschwader (JG) – fighter wing
Jagdgruppe – fighter group
Jagdkorps – fighter corps
Jagdstaffel – fighter squadron
Jagdverband – fighter formation
Jahrgang – year group (Jahrgang 1922 equates to all military personnel born that year)
Januar – January
Juli – July
Juni – June

Kamerad – comrade
Kampfflieger – bomber pilot
Kampffliegergruppe – bomb group
Kampfgeschwader (KG) – bomb wing
Kampfgeschwader z.b.V. – special purpose transport wing
Kampfgruppe – bomb group (also battle group)
Katschmarek – slang term for wingman
Kette – 3 aircraft element
Kettenführer – leader of a 3-aircraft element
Kinder – children
Kompanie – company
Kompaniechef – company commander
Kompanieführer – temporary company commander
Konfession – religious affiliation
Korps – corps
krank – sick, ill
Krieg – war
Kriegsakademie – war college
Kriegsmarine – the Navy
Kriegsoffizier-Anwärter (KOA) – candidate for wartime commission
Kriegsoffizier-Bewerber (KOB) – applicant for wartime commission
Kriegsverdienstkreuz – War Service Cross
Küstenflieger – unit operating in cooperation with the Navy

Landung – landing
ledig – single/bachelor
Lehrgang – course of instruction
Lehrgeschwader – demonstration wing (which was also a combat unit)
leichtverwundet – slightly wounded
Leistung – achievement
Leutnant – second lieutenant
Lichtbild – photo
Luftflotte – air fleet (corresponded to a US Army Air Corps numbered air force)
Luftflottenchef – air fleet commander
Luftgau – air force administrative command
Lufthansa – the German national airline

Luftkampf – air battle
Luftkreis – air force service area
Luftlandgeschwader – air transport glider wing
Luftsieg – aerial victory
Luftwaffe – the Air Force
Luftwaffenkommando – a small Luftfflotte
Luftwaffenpersonalamt – air force personnel office

März – March
Mai – May
Major – major
mit der Führung beauftragt (m.d.F.b.) – in temporary command
mit Wahrnehmung der Geschäfte beauftragt (m.W.d.G.b.) – tasked with attending to the duties of; acting commander, subject to confirmation

Nachrichten – signal
Nachtabschüssen – nighttime shootdowns
Nachtjagd – night fighting
Nachtjagdgeschwader – night fighter wing
Nachtjagdgruppen – night fighter group
Nachwuchs – new pilot, rookie
nächsthöheren – next higher
Nahaufklärung – close/local reconnaissance
Nahaufklärungsgruppe – close reconnaissance group
Nationalsozialist – National Socialist
Neuaufstellung – reorganization, new organization
nicht ausgefüllt – not fulfilled
nichts hinzufügen – nothing to be added
notlanden – emergency landing, forced landing
November – November

Oberbefehlshaber – commander of an army or higher formation
Oberfähnrich – master sergeant officer candidate
Oberfeldwebel – master sergeant
Oberleutnant – first lieutenant
Oberst – colonel
Oberstleutnant – lieutenant colonel
Offizier – officer
Offiziersanwärter – officer candidate
Offizierbewerber – officer applicant
Oktober – October
Ordonnanzoffizier – special missions staff officer
Ortsunterkunft (O.U.) – billets

Pak – anti-tank gun
Panzerabteilung – tank detachment/battalion
Panzerabwehrabteilung – anti-tank detachment/battalion
Panzerjägerabteilung – anti-tank detachment/battalion
Panzerjägerkompanie – anti-tank company
Pionier – engineer
Pionierbataillon – engineer battalion

Quartiermeister (Ib) – supply officer of a division or corps

Rangliste – rank list
Rangdienstalter – official date of rank
Regiment – regiment
Reichsarbeitsdienst – Reich Labor Service
Reichsluftfahrtministerium – German Air Ministry
Reserveoffizier – reserve officer
Reservelazerette – general hospital
Ritterkreuz des Eisernen Kreuz – Knight's Cross of the Iron Cross
Ritterkreuzträger – Knight's Cross winner
Rotte – two aircraft element
Rottenflieger – wingman in a two-aircraft formation
Rottenführer – leader of a two-aircraft formation

Sacharbeiter – technical staff officer with a special skill such as architect
Schlacht – battle
Schlachtflieger – ground-attack pilot
Schlachtgeschwader (SG) – ground-attack wing
Schlachtgruppe – ground-attack group
Schnellkampfgeschwader – fast bomber wing
Schule – school
schwache Seiten – weak traits
Schwarm – flight; flying formation of 4 aircraft (two *Rotten*)
Schwarmführer – leader of a formation of 4 aircraft
Schwerter – swords
schwerverwundet – seriously wounded
Seeaufklärungs – sea reconnaissance
Seeflieger – naval aviator
Seenotdienst – Air-sea rescue
Segelflugzeug – glider
sehr gut ausgefüllt – very well fulfilled
September – September
Sonder – special
Spähtrupp – patrol, reconnaissance patrol
Spange – clasp
Spanienkreuz – Spanish Cross
Spitzenzug – advance platoon
Splitter – fragment, shrapnel
sportlich – athletic
Stab – staff
Stabschwarm – staff flight
Stabsquartier – headquarters
Staffel – squadron
Staffelführer – acting, temporary squadron commander
Staffelkapitän – squadron commander
Standort – post, garrison
starke Seiten – strong traits
Start – take-off
Stellungswechsel – change of position
stellvertretend – acting, deputy
stellvertretender Führer – second-in-command
Stellvertreter – deputy, substitute
Sturzkampfflugzeug (Stuka) – dive bomber
Sturzkampfgeschwader (StG) – Stuka wing

Tapferkeit – bravery
Technischer Offizier – technical officer
Tiefflugangriff – low-level aerial attack
Torpedo – torpedo
Transportflugzeug – transport aircraft
Transportgeschwader – transport wing
Transportgruppe – transport group
Truppenteil – troop organization

über Durchschnitt – above average
Umgangformen – manners
unbesiegt vom Feind – unconquered by the foe; pilot who died in an accident, not by enemy action
unermüdlich – untiring
unter Durchschnitt – below average
Unternehmen – operation, undertaking
Unteroffizier – sergeant

Verbindungsoffizier – liaison officer
verheiratet – married

Verwaltung – administration
verwitwet – widowed
verwundet – wounded
Verwundetenabzeichen in Gold – wound badge in gold (5 wounds)
Verwundetenabzeichen in Schwarz – wound badge in black (1-2 wounds)
Verwundetenabzeichen in Silber – wound badge in silver (3 wounds)
vorbildlicher – exemplary
Vorschlag – proposal, nomination
Verwaltung – administration

Waffengattung – branch within a service: such as paratroops, flying troops, etc.
Wehrkreis – military service area
Wehrmacht – Armed Forces
Wehrmachtbericht – Armed Forces Bulletin (similar to Mentioned in Dispatches)
Wehrmachtteil – Service: Army, Navy, Air Force
Wilde Sau – wild boar; freelance night fighting over the bombers' target

Zahme Sau – tame boar; freelance night fighting within the bomber approach stream
Zerstörer – twin-engine long-range fighter (also navy destroyer)
Zerstörer-Ergänzungsgruppe – Destroyer Supplemental Group
Zerstörerflugzeug – twin-engine long-range aircraft
Zerstörergeschwader (ZG) – twin-engine long-range wing
Zerstörergruppe – twin-engine long-range group
zivil – civilian
Zug – platoon

German presentation of calendar dates

For all German military documents from World War II, dates are presented in the following order: day, month, and year. Thus, 12. 10. 1943 represents October 12, 1943, not December 10, 1943. Some additional examples follow:

1. 9. 1939 = September 1, 1939
8. 7. 1940 = July 8, 1940
7. 8. 1941 = August 7, 1941
10. 4. 1942 = April 10, 1942
11. 12. 1943 = December 11, 1943
1. 5. 1944 = May 1, 1944
8. 3. 1945 = March 8, 1945

BIBLIOGRAPHY

Books

Achkasov, V.I. and N.B. Pavlovich, *Soviet Naval Operations in the Great Patriotic War 1941-1945*, Annapolis, Maryland: Naval Institute Press, 1981.

Aders, Gebhard. *History of the German Night Fighter Force 1917-1945*, London: Jane's, 1979.

Aders, Gebhard and Werner Held. *Jagdgeschwader 51 "Mölders,"* Stuttgart, FRG: Motorbuch Verlag, 1985.

Amadio, Jill. *Günther Rall: A Memoir – Luftwaffe Ace and NATO General*, Santa Ana, CA: Tangmere Productions, 2002.

Angolia, John R. *For Führer and Fatherland: Military Awards of the Third Reich*, San Jose, CA: Bender Publishing, 1976.

Angolia, John R. *On The Field Of Honor: A History of the Knight's Cross Bearers*, Volume 2, San Jose, CA: Bender Publishing, 1980.

Antill, Peter D. *Crete 1941: Germany's Lightning Airborne Assault*, Osprey Campaign 147, Oxford, England: Osprey Publishing, 2005.

Balke, Ulf. *Der Luft-Krieg in Europa, Die Operativen Einsätze des Kampf-Geschwaders 2 im Zweiten Weltkrieg*, Teil 2, Koblenz, FRG: Bernhard & Graefe Verlag, 1990.

Baumbach, Werner. *The Life and Death of the Luftwaffe*, translated by Frederick Holt, New York: Coward-McCann, Inc., 1960.

Bekker, Cajus. *The Luftwaffe War Diaries*, London: MacDonald & Co., 1967.

Bishop, Chris. *Luftwaffe Squadrons 1939-45*, Stapelhurst, England: Spellmont, 2006.

Blumenson, Martin. *Anzio: The Gambit That Failed*, Philadelphia: J.B. Lippincott, 1963.

Blumenson, Martin. *Breakout and Pursuit*, U.S. Army in World War II, The European Theater of Operations, Washington, D.C: Department of the Army, Office of the Chief of Military History, 1961.

Boehme, Manfred. *Jagdgeschwader 7: Die Chronik eines Me 262-Geschwaders 1944/45*, Stuttgart, FRG: Motorbuch Verlag, 1984.

Brehde, Dietrich. *Der Blaue Komet: Geschichte des IV. Bataillons des Luftlande-Sturmregiments 1940-1945*, Munich, FRG: Schild Verlag, 1988.

Brütting, Georg. *Das waren die deutschen Kampfflieger-Asse, 1939-1945*, Stuttgart, FRG: Motorbuch Verlag, 1983.

Brütting, Georg. *Das waren die deutschen Stuka-Asse, 1939-1945*, Stuttgart, FRG: Motorbuch Verlag, 1976.

Busch, Erich. *Die Fallschirmjäger-Chronik 1935-1945*, Friedberg, FRG: Podzun-Palls-Verlag, 1983.

Caldwell, Donald L. *JG 26: Top Guns of the Luftwaffe*, New York: Orion Books, 1991.

Cooper, Matthew. *The German Air Force 1933-1945: An Anatomy of Failure*, London: Jane's, 1981.

Dierach, Wolfgang. *Kampfgeschwader 51 "Edelweiss": Eine Chronik aus Dokumenten und Berichten 1937-1945*, Stuttgart, FRG: Motorbuch Verlag, 1973.

Edwards, Roger. *German Airborne Troops 1936-1945*, Garden City, NJ: Doubleday & Company, 1974.

Ellis, Chris. *7th Flieger Division: Student's Fallschirmjäger Elite*, Surrey, England: Ian Allan Publishing, 2002.

Ellis, John. *Cassino: The Hollow Victory*, London: André Deutsch Limited, 1984.

Ethell, Jeffrey, and Alfred Price. *Target Berlin*, London: Jane's, 1981.

Feuerstein, Erwin. *Mit und ohne Ritterkreuz*, Stuttgart, FRG: Motorbuch Verlag, 1974.

Ford, Ken. *Cassino 1944: Breaking the Gustav Line*, Osprey Campaign 134, Oxford, England: Osprey Publishing, 2004.

Freeman, Roger A. *Mighty Eighth War Diary*, London: Jane's, 1981.

Galland, Adolf. *The First And The Last: The Rise and Fall of the German Fighter Forces, 1938-1945*, translated by Mervyn Savill, New York: Henry Holt and Company, 1954.

Girbig, Werner. *Jagdgeschwader 5 "Eismeerjäger": Eine Chronik aus Dokumenten und Berichten 1941-1945*, Stuttgart, FRG: Motorbuch Verlag, 1976.

Hildebrand, Karl Friedrich. *Die Generale der deutschen Luftwaffe 1935-1945, Band 1 Abernetty-v. Gyldenfeldt*, Osnabrück, FRG, 1990.

Hildebrand, Karl Friedrich. *Die Generale der deutschen Luftwaffe 1935-1945, Band 2 Habermehl-Nuber*, Osnabrück, FRG, 1991.

Hildebrand, Karl Friedrich. *Die Generale der deutschen Luftwaffe 1935-1945, Band 3, Odebrecht-Zoch*, Osnabrück, FRG, 1992.

Hinchliffe, Peter. *The Lent Papers: Helmut Lent*, Bristol, England: Cerberus Publishing, 2003.

Jurado, Carlos Caballero. *The Condor Legion: German Troops in the Spanish Civil War*, Osprey Elite 131, Oxford, England: Osprey Publishing, 2006.

Kiriakopoulos, G.C. *Ten Days to Destiny: The Battle for Crete 1941*, New York: Franklin Watts, 1985.

Kurowski, Franz. *Luftwaffe Aces: German Combat Pilots of WWII*, translated by David Johnston, Mechanicsburg, PA: Stackpole, 2004.

Lenfeld, Erwin and Franz Thomas. *Die Eichenlaubträger 1940-1945*, Wiener-Neustedt, Austria: Weilburg Verlag, 1983.

Lucas, James. *Storming Eagles: German Airborne Forces in World War Two*, London: Arms and Armour Press, 1988.

MacLean, French. *The Cruel Hunters: SS-Sonderkommando Dirlewanger, Hitler's Most Notorious Anti-partisan Unit*. Atglen, PA: Schiffer Publishing Co., 1998.

MacLean, French L. *Quiet Flows the Rhine: German General Officer Casualties of World War II*, Winnipeg, Canada: J.J. Fedorowicz, 1996.

Manrho, John, and Ron Pütz. *Bodenplatte: The Luftwaffe's Last Hope*, Browborough, England: Hikoki Publication, 2004.

Mehner, Kurt and Reinhard Teuber. *Die Deutsche Luftwaffe 1939-1945 Führung und Truppe*, Norderstedt, Germany; Militair-Verlag Klaus D. Patzwall, 1993.

Meimberg, Julius. *Feindberührung: Erinnerungen 1939-1945*, Moosburg, Germany, NeunundzwanzigSechs Verlag, 2002.

Middlebrook, Martin. *The Battle of Hamburg: Allied Bomber Forces Against a German City*, New York: Charles Scribner's Sons, 1980.

Middlebrook, Martin. The *Nuremberg Raid: The Worst Night of the War, March 30-31, 1944*, New York: William Morrow & Company, 1974.

Middlebrook, Martin and Chris Everitt. *The Bomber Command War Diaries*, New York: Viking Penguin, 1987.

Mitcham, Samuel Jr. *Men of the Luftwaffe*, Novato, CA: Presidio, 1988.

Mombeek, Eric. *Defending the Reich: The History of Jagdgeschwader 1 "Oesau,"* Norwich, England: JAC Publications, 1992.

Morgan, Hugh and John Weal. *German Jet Aces of World War 2*, Osprey Aircraft of the Aces 17, Oxford, England: Osprey Publishing, 1998.

Obermaier, Ernst. *Die Ritterkreuzträger der Luftwaffe, Jagdflieger 1939-1945*, Mainz, FRG: Verlag Dieter Hoffmann, 1989.

Obermaier, Ernst. *Die Ritterkreuzträger der Luftwaffe, Stuka und Schlachtflieger 1939-1945*, Mainz, FRG: Verlag Dieter Hoffmann, 1976.

O'Donnell, James P. *The Bunker: The History of the Reich Chancellery Group*, Boston: Houghton Mifflin Company, 1978.

Parry, Simon W. *Intruders Over Britain: The Story of the Luftwaffe's Night Intruder Force*, Surbiton/Surrey, England: Air Research Publications, 1987.

Potter, John Deane. *Fiasco: The Break-out of the German Battleships*, New York: Stein & Day, 1970.

Previtera, Stephen Thomas. *The Iron Time: A History of the Knight's Cross*, Richmond, VA: Winidore Press, 1999.

Prien, Jochen. *Pik-As: Geschichte des Jagdgeschwaders 53*, Hamburg, Germany: Self-published, 1991.

Prien, Jochen. *Geschichte des Jagdgeschwaders 77*, Teil 1, Hamburg, Germany: Self-published, 1992.

Prien, Jochen, Gerhard Stemmer, Peter Rodeike and Winfried Bock. *Die Jagdfliegerverbände der Deutschen Luftwaffe 1934 bis 1945, Teil 1: Vorkriegszeit und Einsatz über Polen - 1934 bis 1939*, Eutin, Germany: Struve, 2000.

Prien, Jochen, Gerhard Stemmer, Peter Rodeike and Winfried Bock. *Die Jagdfliegerverbände der Deutschen Luftwaffe 1934 bis 1945, Teil 2: Der "Sitzkrieg", 1.9.39 bis 9.5.1940*, Eutin, Germany: Struve.

Prien, Jochen, Gerhard Stemmer, Peter Rodeike and Winfried Bock. *Die Jagdfliegerverbände der Deutschen Luftwaffe 1934 bis 1945, Teil 3: Einsatz in Dänemark und Norwegen, 9.4. bis 30.11.40, Der Feldzug im Westen, 10.5. bis 25.6.1940*, Eutin, Germany: Struve.

Prien, Jochen, Gerhard Stemmer, Peter Rodeike and Winfried Bock. *Die Jagdfliegerverbände der Deutschen Luftwaffe 1934 bis 1945, Teil 4/I: Einsatz am Kanal und über England, 26.6.1940 bis 21.6.1941*, Eutin, Germany: Struve.

Prien, Jochen, Gerhard Stemmer, Peter Rodeike and Winfried Bock. *Die Jagdfliegerverbände der Deutschen Luftwaffe 1934 bis 1945, Teil 4/II: Einsatz am Kanal und über England, 26.6.1940 bis 21.6.1941*, Eutin, Germany: Struve.

Prien, Jochen, Gerhard Stemmer, Peter Rodeike and Winfried Bock. *Die Jagdfliegerverbände der Deutschen Luftwaffe 1934 bis 1945, Teil 5: Heimatverteidigung 10. Mai 1940 bis 31. Dezember 1941, Einsatz im Mittelmeerraum Oktober 1940 bis November 1941, Einsatz im Westen 22. Juni bis 31. Dezember 1941, Die Ergänzungsjagdgruppen Einsatz 1941 bis zur Auflösung Anfang 1942*, Eutin, Germany: Struve, 2003.

Prien, Jochen, Gerhard Stemmer, Peter Rodeike and Winfried Bock. *Die Jagdfliegerverbände der Deutschen Luftwaffe 1934 bis 1945, Teil 6/I: Unternehmen "Barbarossa" Einsatz im Osten 22.6. bis 5.12.1941*, Eutin, Germany: Struve, 2003.

Prien, Jochen, Gerhard Stemmer, Peter Rodeike and Winfried Bock. *Die Jagdfliegerverbände der Deutschen Luftwaffe 1934 bis 1945, Teil 6/II: Unternehmen "Barbarossa" Einsatz im Osten 22.6. bis 5.12.1941*, Eutin, Germany: Struve, 2003.

Prien, Jochen, Gerhard Stemmer, Peter Rodeike and Winfried Bock. *Die Jagdfliegerverbände der Deutschen Luftwaffe 1934 bis 1945, Teil 7: Heimatsverteidigung 1. Januar bis 31. Dezember 1942, Einsatz im Westen 1. Januar bis 31. Dezember 1942*, Eutin, Germany: Struve, 2003.

Prien, Jochen, Gerhard Stemmer, Peter Rodeike and Winfried Bock. *Die Jagdfliegerverbände der Deutschen Luftwaffe 1934 bis 1945, Teil8/I: Einsatz im Mittelmeerraum November 1941 bis Dezember 1942*, Eutin, Germany: Struve, 2004.

Prien, Jochen, Gerhard Stemmer, Peter Rodeike and Winfried Bock. *Die Jagdfliegerverbände der Deutschen Luftwaffe 1934 bis 1945, Teil8/II: Einsatz im Mittelmeerraum November 1941 bis Dezember 1942*, Eutin, Germany: Struve, 2004.

Prien, Jochen, Gerhard Stemmer, Peter Rodeike and Winfried Bock. *Die Jagdfliegerverbände der Deutschen Luftwaffe 1934 bis 1945, Teil 9/I: Winterkampf im Osten 6.12.1941 bis 30.4.1942*, Eutin, Germany: Struve.

Prien, Jochen, Gerhard Stemmer, Peter Rodeike and Winfried Bock. *Die Jagdfliegerverbände der Deutschen Luftwaffe 1934 bis 1945, Teil 9/II: Vom Sommerfeldzug 1942 bis zur Niederlage von Stalingrad 1.5.1942 bis 3.2.1943*, Eutin, Germany: Struve.

Priller, Josef. *J.G. 26: Geschichte eines Jagdgeschwaders*, Stuttgart, FRG: Motorbuch Verlag, 1980.

Quarrie, Bruce. *German Airborne Divisions: Blitzkrieg 1940-41*, Osprey Battle Orders 4, Oxford, England: Osprey Publishing, 2004.

Quarrie, Bruce. *German Airborne Divisions: Mediterranean Theater 1942-45*, Osprey Battle Orders 15, Oxford, England: Osprey Publishing, 2005.

Radtke, Siegfried. *Kampfgeschwader 54, von der Ju 52 zur Me 262*, Munich, Germany: Schild Verlag, 1990.

Reschke, Willi. *Jagdgeschwader 301/302 "Wilde Sau,"* Stuttgart, Germany: Motorbuch Verlag, 1998.

Ries, Karl and Hans Ring. *Legion Condor, 1936-1939: Eine illustrierte Dokumentation*, Mainz, Germany: Verlag Dieter Hoffmann, 1980.

Rosch, Barry C. *Luftwaffe Codes, Markings and Units, 1939-1945*, Atglen, PA: Schiffer Publishing, 1995.

Scheibert, Horst. *Die Träger der Ehrenblattspange des Heeres und der Waffen-SS, Die Träger der Ehrentafelspange der Kriegsmarine, Die Inhaber des Ehrenpokals für besondere Leistung im Luftkrieg*, Friedberg, FRG: Podzun-Pallas-Verlag, 1986.

Scherzer, Veit. *Die Träger des Deutschen Kreuzes in Gold der Luftwaffe 1941-1945*, Bayreuth, FRG: Scherzer's Militair Verlag, 1992.

Scherzer, Veit. *Die Ritterkreuzträger: Die Inhaber des Ritterkreuzes des Eisernen Kreuzes 1939-1945*, Jena, Germany: Scherzers Militairs-Verlag, 2005.

Schlang, Georg. *Die deutschen Lastensegler-Verbände 1937-1945*, Stuttgart, FRG: Motorbuch Verlag, 1985.

Schliephake, Hanfried. *The Birth of the Luftwaffe*, Chicago: Henry Regnery Company, 1971.

Schmidt, Rudi. *Achtung – Torpedos Los!* Koblenz, Germany: Bernhard & Graefe Verlag, 1991.

Schreier, Hans. *JG 52: Das erfolgreichste Jagdgeschwader des II. Weltkrieges*, Berg am See, FRG: Kurt Vowinckel Verlag, 2002.

Sharp, C. Martin and Michael J. F. Bowyer. *Mosquito*, London: Faber and Faber Limited, 1967.

Shores, Christopher and Brian Cull. *Air War for Yugoslavia, Greece and Crete*, Carrollton, TX: Squadron Signal Publications, 1987.

Shores, Christopher, Hans Ring and William Hess. *Fighters Over Tunisia*, London: Neville Spearman, 1975.

Smith, Peter C. *Stuka Squadron*, Wellingborough, England: Patrick Stephens, 1990.

Spick, Mike. *Luftwaffe Fighter Aces: The Jagdflieger and Their Combat Tactics and Techniques*, Mechanicsburg, PA: Stackpole Books, 2003.

Taghorn, Peter. *Die Geschichte des Lehrgeschwaders 1*, Band 1 (1936-1942), Zweibrücken, Germany: 2004.

Taghorn, Peter. *Die Geschichte des Lehrgeschwaders 1*, Band 2 (1942-1945), Zweibrücken, Germany: 2004.

Tessin, Georg. *Verbände und Truppen der deutschen Wehrmacht und Waffen-SS im Zweiten Weltkrieg 1939-1945, Vierzehnter Band: Die Landstreitkräfte: Namensverbände/Die Luftstreitkräfte (Fliegende Verbände)/Flakeinsatz im Reich 1943-1945*, Osnabrück, FRG: Biblio Verlag, 1980.

Thomas, Franz. *Die Eichenlaubträger 1940-1945, Band 1: A-K, Band 2: L-Z*, Osnabrück, Germany: Biblio-Verlag, 1998.

Thomas, Franz and Günter Wegmann. *Die Ritterkreuzträger der Deutschen Wehrmacht 1939-1945, Teil II: Fallschirmjäger*, Osnabrück, FRG: Biblio-Verlag, 1986.

Toliver, Raymond F. and Trevor J. Constable. *Das waren die Deutschen Jagdflieger-Asse 1939-1945*, Stuttgart, FRG: Motorbuch Verlag, 1981.

Trautloft, Hannes, Werner Held and Ekkehard Bob. *Die Grünherzjäger*, Friedberg, FRG: Podzun-Pallas-Verlag, 1985.

Trevor-Roper, H.R., *Blitzkrieg to Defeat: Hitler's War Directives, 1939-1945*, New York: Holt, Rinehart and Winston, 1964.

Weal, John. *Focke-Wulf Fw 190 Aces of the Russian Front*, Osprey Aircraft of the Aces 6, Oxford, England: Osprey Publishing, 1995.

Weal, John. *Jagdgeschwader 2 'Richthofen,'* Osprey Aviation Elite 1, Oxford, England: Osprey Publishing, 2000.

Weal, John. *Jagdgeschwader 27 'Afrika,'* Osprey Aviation Elite 12, Oxford, England: Osprey Publishing, 2000.

Weal, John. *Jagdgeschwader 52: The Experten*, Aviation Elite Units 15, Oxford, England: Osprey Publishing, 2004.

Weal, John. *Jagdgeschwader 54 "Grünherz,"* Osprey Aviation Elite 6, Oxford, England: Osprey Publishing, 2001.

Weal, John. *Luftwaffe Schlachtgruppen*, Aviation Elite Units 13, Oxford, England: Osprey Publishing, 2003.

Zweng, Christian. *Die Dienststellen, Kommandobehörden und Truppenteile der Luftwaffe 1935-1945, Band I Nr. 1-10*, Osnabrück, Germany; Biblio Verlag, 1999.

Government Publications

Hofmann, Rudolf. *German Efficiency Report System*, MS# P-134, Königstein, Germany: U.S. Army Europe Historical Division, 1952.

Unpublished Manuscripts

In addition to the actual promotion, recommendation and other personnel reports, generously made available by private sources (mostly in Germany), other unpublished manuscripts appear in this work.

Spires, David Nelson. "The Career of the *Reichswehr* Officer," PhD Dissertation, University of Washington, 1979.

Internet Sites

Tomasz Gronczewski, "Camouflage & Markings: Early Focke-Wulf Fw 190s," http://www.ipmsstockholm.org/magazine/2004/08/stuff_eng_profile_fw190a4.htm.

Volksbund Deutsche Kriegsgräberfürsorge Website, http://www.volksbund.de.

Interviews

Interview with former Private First Class Myron MacLean, who was assigned to the U.S. 1st Battalion, 39th Infantry Regiment, 9th Infantry Division, Decatur, Illinois, April 28, 2006.